Philosophical Problems
of Causation

edited by
TOM L. BEAUCHAMP
Georgetown University

DICKENSON PUBLISHING COMPANY, INC.

Encino, California and Belmont, California

ISBN-0-8221-0121-1
Library of Congress Catalog Card Number: 73-92476

Printed in the United States of America
Printing (last digit): 9 8 7 6 5 4 3 2 1

CONTENTS

DICKENSON SERIES IN PHILOSOPHY *v*
PREFACE *vii*

PART ONE: *HISTORICAL BACKGROUND IN HUME AND KANT 1*

Introduction *1*
1. C. J. Ducasse   Critique of Hume's Conception of Causality *6*
2. W. A. Suchting   Kant's Second Analogy of Experience *12*
3. L. W. Beck   Once More Unto the Breach: Kant's Answer to Hume, Again *24*
4. Jeffrie G. Murphy   Kant's Second Analogy as an Answer to Hume *28*
5. L. W. Beck   Rejoinder to Professor Murphy *31*
Suggested Readings for Part One *34*

PART TWO: *MODERN NECESSITY THEORIES 36*

Introduction *36*
6. Karl Popper   Causality, Explanation, and the Deduction of Predictions *39*
7. Karl Popper   A Note on Natural Laws and So-called "Contrary-to-fact Conditionals" *42*
8. William Kneale   Natural Laws and Contrary-to-fact Conditionals *46*
9. Karl Popper   Kneale and Natural Laws *50*
10. William Kneale   Universality and Necessity *53*
11. G. C. Nerlich and W. A. Suchting   Popper on Law and Natural Necessity *63*
12. Karl Popper   A Revised Definition of Natural Necessity *66*
13. Karl Popper   Addendum, 1968 *72*
Suggested Readings for Part Two *73*

PART THREE: *MODERN REGULARITY THEORIES 74*

Introduction *74*
14. A. J. Ayer   What Is a Law of Nature? *77*
15. Ernest Nagel   Contrary-to-fact Universals *91*
16. J. L. Mackie   Counterfactuals and Causal Laws *95*
17. George Molnar   Kneale's Argument Revisited *106*
Suggested Readings for Part Three *114*

PART FOUR: THE MANIPULABILITY THEORY 115

Introduction   *115*
18. R. G. Collingwood   Three Senses of the Word "Cause"   *118*
19. Douglas Gasking   Causation and Recipes   *126*
20. G. H. von Wright   Causality and Causal Explanation   *133*
Suggested Readings for Part Four   *137*

PART FIVE: THE SINGULARIST THEORY 138

Introduction   *138*
21. C. J. Ducasse   Analysis of the Causal Relation   *142*
22. Bernard Berofsky   Causality and General Laws   *153*
23. Arthur Pap   A Note on Causation and the Meaning of
    "Event"   *160*
24. Edward H. Madden and James Humber   Nonlogical Necessity and
    C. J. Ducasse   *163*
25. Edward H. Madden   A Third View of Causality   *178*
26. Donald Davidson   Causal Relations   *190*
Suggested Readings for Part Five   *200*

PART SIX: CAUSAL EXPLANATION AND CAUSAL CONTEXT 201

Introduction   *201*
27. Norwood Russell Hanson   Causality   *204*
28. David Braybrooke and Alexander Rosenberg   Vincula Revindi-
    cata   *217*
29. H. L. A. Hart and A. M. Honoré   The Analysis of Causal Con-
    cepts   *222*
30. Samuel Gorovitz   Causal Judgments and Causal Explana-
    tions   *235*
Suggested Readings for Part Six   *248*

THE DICKENSON SERIES IN PHILOSOPHY

Philosophy, said Aristotle, begins in wonder—wonder at the phenomenon of self-awareness, wonder at the infinitude of time, wonder that there should be anything at all. Wonder in turn gives rise to a kind of natural puzzlement: How can mind and body interact? How is it possible that there can be free will in a world governed by natural laws? How can moral judgments be shown to be true?

Philosophical perplexity about such things is a familiar and unavoidable phenomenon. College students who have experienced it and taken it seriously are, in a way, philosophers already, well before they come in contact with the theories and arguments of specialists. The good philosophy teacher, therefore, will not present his subject as some esoteric discipline unrelated to ordinary interests. Instead he will appeal directly to the concerns that already agitate the student, the same concerns that agitated Socrates and his companions and serious thinkers ever since.

It is impossible to be a good teacher of philosophy, however, without being a genuine philosopher oneself. Authors in the Dickenson Series in Philosophy are no exceptions to this rule. In many cases their textbooks are original studies of problems and systems of philosophy, with their own views boldly expressed and defended with argument. Their books are at once contributions to philosophy itself and models of original thinking to emulate and criticize.

That equally competent philosophers often disagree with one another is a fact to be exploited, not concealed. Dickenson anthologies bring together essays by authors of widely differing outlook. This diversity is compounded by juxtaposition, wherever possible, of classical essays with leading contemporary materials. The student who is shopping for a world outlook of his own has a large and representative selection to choose among, and the chronological arrangements, as well as the editor's introduction, can often give him a sense of historical development. Some Dickenson anthologies treat a single group of interconnected problems. Others are broader, dealing with a whole branch of philosophy, or representative problems from various branches of philosophy. In both types of collections, essays with opposed views on precisely the same questions are included to illustrate the argumentative give and take which is the lifeblood of philosophy.

Joel Feinberg
Series Editor

PREFACE

The selections reprinted here are concerned with several central problems in the philosophy of causation. They have been selected to reflect the dominant historical and analytical concerns of recent English-speaking philosophers. Since Hume and Kant have special relevance and have recently received extended treatment, Part One is devoted exclusively to their theories. Modern systematic work has settled on the surprisingly complex task of providing a correct analysis of the concept of causation, and the remaining parts of this text all center on this task. Of course analysis of causation directly pertains to many other important contemporary problems such as the structure of historical and scientific explanations, the problem of induction, and the nature of human action. But these problems have been given a secondary position here. The choice was between a thin survey of all the diverse problems of causation and a concentrated, reasonably complete treatment of recent interests in causal analysis. I chose the second alternative.

In compiling this anthology, I decided not to include selections from the writings of Hume and Kant for three reasons. First, their inclusion would have forced the omission of several other selections. Second, the relevant works of Hume and Kant are easily accessible in existing paperbound editions. Third, so much of Hume's work should be read by all students of causation that I hesitated to make an editorial decision of exclusion and inclusion. Despite the fact that Hume is the most widely read author ever to write on causation, it is my view that too little of his work is read. Had I selected, say, Chapter IV and VII from his *Enquiry Concerning the Human Understanding* and some similar snippets from his *Treatise of Human Nature*, I would have been guilty of perpetuating this mistake. (Minimally students should read Hume's *Treatise*, Book I, Part III, Sections I-VIII, XI-XII, XIV-XV, and his *Enquiry*, Sections IV-VIII.)

The actual part headings and the order of articles might have been differently arranged. Indeed, I hope some enterprising teacher will attempt several different arrangements and inform me of the result. My main intention has been to provide readers with the most significant available work on causation—not to provide a definitive arrangement of schools of thought. However, I have specifically arranged the articles, insofar as possible, in an order which reflects a controversy among authors. In most parts the later articles build upon or criticize the earlier articles. This same sense of mounting controversy is present to a lesser extent in the order of the parts themselves. The bibliographies also reflect divergent views on the major issues. Some of the entries overlap controversies and might have been suggested for more than one part. I hope my sometimes arbitrary bibliographical listings will not offend those authors who find their articles suggested under a heading which in their judgment is alien to their intentions. I must also explain a noticeable bibliographical omission. At my final press deadline I was able to peruse, through the kindness of the author, the uncorrected proofs of J. L. Mackie's book, *The Cement of the Universe: A Study of Causation* (Oxford: Clarendon Press, 1973). This splendid book will be welcomed by all students of causation. It is directly relevant to every section of this anthology.

I also wish to thank a number of friends and advisers who have helped with the production of this book. For largely internal matters of structure, content, and novel ways of conceiving issues of causaion, I am indebted to Stephen F. Barker, Max Deutscher, and Harry Silverstein. For largely external matters of editing and revising the manuscript, I am indebted to John Hospers, Samuel Gorovitz, Henry Byerly, Joel Feinberg, Richard Trudgen, Tom Mappes, and my wife, Martha. I also wish to express appreciation to my friends at Dalhousie University, Canada, where a good measure of the work on this book was done when I was there as Visiting Professor. Finally, I have learned a great deal about exotic causal circumstances from Hegel, A-Plus, and Lee Roy—still man's greatest source of encouragement.

Tom L. Beauchamp

PART ONE

HISTORICAL BACKGROUND IN HUME AND KANT

INTRODUCTION

David Hume's celebrated analysis of the idea of causation spawned most of the controversies discussed in this book. To begin with any theory other than his would be inappropriate.

Hume's account of causation was significantly influenced by his epistemological views, especially his general empiricist thesis that meaningful ideas are analyzable in terms of the sensory impressions from which they are derived. According to this latter theory, the meaning of a term is exhausted by those features of experience with which the term is in every case associated; that is, meaning is constituted by a set of essential core features which lead us to say that an item is an *X* instead of a *Y* or a *Z*. Armed with this method of proceeding, Hume isolated three empirical relations—*contiguity, succession,* and *constant conjunction*—and proclaimed them the essential elements of the idea of causation. Additionally, and somewhat surprisingly, he cited an apparently non-empirical element, *necessary connection.* Hume's theory of causation largely consists of a close analysis of these four relations. Special attention was given to constant conjunction and necessary connection, the latter of which Hume thought to be subjective in origin. There is no better summary of his basic doctrine than that which he provided in his *Abstract of a Treatise of Human Nature:*

> Here is a billiard-ball lying on the table, and another ball moving towards it with rapidity. They strike; and the ball, which was formerly at rest, now acquires a motion. . . . There was no interval betwixt the shock and the motion. *Contiguity* in time and place is therefore a requisite circumstance to the operation of all causes. 'Tis evident likewise, that the motion, which was the cause, is prior to the motion, which was the effect. *Priority* in time, is therefore another requisite circumstance in every cause. But this is not all. Let us try any other balls of the same kind in a like situation, and we shall always find, that the impulse of the one produces motion in the other. Here, therefore is a *third* circumstance, *viz.* that of a constant conjunction betwixt the cause and effect. Every object like the cause, produces always some object like the effect. Beyond these three circumstances of contiguity, priority, and constant conjunction, I can discover nothing in this cause. . . .

> In the considering of motion communicated from one ball to another, we could find nothing but contiguity, priority in the cause, and constant conjunction. But, besides these circumstances, 'tis commonly

suppos'd, that there is a necessary connexion betwixt the cause and effect, and that the cause possesses something, which we call a *power*, or *force*, or *energy*. The question is, what idea is annex'd to these terms? If all our ideas or thoughts be derived from our impressions, this power must either discover itself to our senses, or to our internal feeling. But so little does any power discover itself to the senses in the operations of matter . . . [and] our own minds afford us no more notion of energy than matter does. . . . Upon the whole, then, either we have no idea at all of force and energy, and these words are altogether insignificant, or they can mean nothing but that determination of the thought, acquired by habit, to pass from the cause to its usual effect.*

Rationalist philosophers before Hume maintained that an effect *must* follow its cause. They tended to assimilate causal connection to logical necessitation. Hume set out to show both that the rationalists and all other previous philosophers were mistaken in thinking that there is a relation of necessity or power in causation and that causes in no sense logically entail effects. He maintained negatively that we are never able in any instance whatsoever to discover any quality which binds the cause to the effect and positively that it is constant conjunction which leads us to believe that objects are necessarily connected. Necessary connection, then, is not something objective in nature, according to Hume, but rather is a subjective feeling of connection that arises in linking one object to another.

Despite the psychological context in which Hume stated his arguments, his polemic against objective causal necessitation is perhaps best understood as an extension of his scepticism concerning inductive conclusions drawn by human reason. He saw no conclusive justification for inferences drawn from statements of the form

1. "All *examined* X's are followed by Y's" to
2. "*All* X's are followed by Y's."

He regarded such inferences as logically tenuous, because the conclusion is always uncertain when some portion of the possible evidence is not available. But he had far more scruples concerning inferences from 2 to

3. "All X's are *necessarily* followed by Y's."

Hume could find no conceivable justification for this movement of thought. He believed the only relevant explanation to be in terms of a psychological association of ideas; but this psychological explanation does not constitute a philosophical justification. Hume apparently thought that no justification could be given precisely because the explanation showed the true, psychological grounds of the inference.

Nonetheless, Hume did not jettison the notion of causal relatedness. He conceived it afresh. He provided two definitions of causation, one of which emphasizes constancy of conjunction and the other emphasizes necessary connection in the form of a "determination of thought":

---

*Reprinted by permission of Cambridge University Press from the 1938 edition, edited by J. M. Keynes and P. Sraffa.

[D$_1$] We may define a cause to be "an object precedent and contiguous to another, and where all the objects resembling the former are plac'd in like relations of precedency and contiguity to those objects, that resemble the latter."

[D$_2$] We may define a cause to be "an object precedent and contiguous to another, and so united with it, that the idea of the one determines the mind to form the idea of the other, and the impression of the one to form a more lively idea of the other."*

Several connected problems are submerged in these two definitions of causation. In the first article in Part One *C. J. Ducasse* points to some of them. He maintains that only the first of Hume's two definitions is tenable, because the second harbors causal language which requires analysis in terms of the first. If correct, Ducasse's proposal shows that causation is correctly definable in Hume's system only as empirical regularity of sequence. Whether necessity is so easily eliminated from the definition of cause is a controversial matter in contemporary Hume scholarship. But on either interpretation, uniformity of sequence is a necessary condition of causation for Hume. Ducasse also finds this conclusion unsatisfactory. He argues that many examples of perfectly uniform sequence seem noncausal, while many examples normally judged to be causal do not involve observation of regularity. In Ducasse's view constancy of conjunction merely raises the question of whether there is a causal relation; it neither defines it nor forms a necessary condition of it. Ducasse also finds numerous other faults both with the premises of Hume's arguments and with the conclusions. Most importantly, Ducasse claims to uncover deficiencies in Hume's contentions that individual causal relatedness cannot be perceived and that causal relatedness cannot be detected by a single case of change. Ducasse even argues that Hume himself is committed by some passages to a singularist analysis of causation. (The tension between Ducasse's singularity analysis and Hume's regularity theory is further explored in Part Five.)

The remaining articles in this first part are concerned with the character and adequacy of Immanuel Kant's reply to Hume. Kant's reply seems to include both a criticism of Hume and a constructive alternative account, but it is difficult to understand exactly how it is either. Quite frequently Kant appears to be augmenting rather than criticizing Hume's theory. He describes the schema of cause, for example, in the following way: The schema of cause is "the real upon which, whenever posited, something else always follows. It consists therefore in the succession of the manifold in so far as that succession is subject to a rule" (First *Critique*, B 183). The phrase "subject to a rule" is not easy to interpret, but certainly in some interpretations this account does not appear significantly different from the Humean analysis in terms of constancy of sequence. In other passages Kant suggests that the notion of cause contains a strong empirical component: "Sequence in time is the sole empirical criterion of an effect in its relation to the causality of the cause that precedes it" (B 249). Nonetheless, Kant clearly indicates a belief that the synthesis of cause and effect cannot be empirically expressed. Claims that one sort of event causes another are universal, he maintains, in a way which could not apply to mere empirical generalizations (a thesis amplified by W. Kneale in Part Two into

---

*Hume, *Treatise*, Oxford edition, p. 170.

a major criticism of Hume). Kant contends that causal connections involve a form of nonlogical, nonempirical necessity and that this necessity is a prerational pattern imposed by the mind. But again it is difficult to see how this argument constitutes a reply to Hume, since the latter recognizes causal necessity of a similar sort. A relation of necessity between cause and effect which is imposed by the mind is recognized fully as much by Hume as by Kant. And both of them recognize that the locus of the necessity is a mental activity which builds unity into conjoined perceptions. How, then, are we to understand the difference between Hume and Kant?

The usual approach to this question is to dissect carefully the main arguments throughout Kant's "Second Analogy of Experience," the section of his work which is generally regarded as containing his reply to Hume. In this section Kant asks how it is possible to distinguish a merely subjective from an objective succession of perceptions. His task is to distinguish a mere change in perceptions (a succession in perception) from the perception of a change in objects (succession in that which is perceived) and to show that the former is not sufficient for the latter. He argues that the manifestation of causality in experience is the occurrence of an irreversible or determinate time-order among perceptions for which an empiricism such as Hume's cannot account.

W. A. Suchting's article is a careful attempt to set forth and to appraise the structure of Kant's arguments. Some of the more important conclusions Suchting reaches are the following: (1) "It is quite unclear whether Kant thought that 'Necessarily, every event has a cause' entails 'If A is a cause of B, then A and B are necessarily connected.' If he did, then he was wrong, for the two are logically independent of one another." (2) Contra many commentators, it is plausible to construe Kant's Second Analogy as one continuous argument rather than as several separate arguments. (3) "Kant may be taken to be arguing the required connection between objective temporal succession and causality in the following way:

a. Necessarily, if A and B are the constituents of an event-perception, then A and B occupy successive places in objective, pure time.

b. Necessarily, the relation between A and B reproduces, empirically, the relation between the successive places in pure time that they occupy.

c. Necessarily, successive parts of pure time are necessarily connected.

d. Therefore, necessarily, the relation between A and B is the relation of necessary succession in time. But the latter is just the causal relation. Therefore, necessarily, if A and B are the constituents of an event-perception, then A and B are causally connected."

The status of an "event-perception," as it appears in this argument, becomes of major significance in the final readings in this section. *L. W. Beck* and *J. G. Murphy* are basically concerned with the philosophical adequacy of Kant's reply to Hume, though Beck also is concerned to answer the question "*What* was Kant's answer to Hume?" Beck finds in Kant the argument that the apprehension of objective events, as distinguished from merely enduring states of affairs, requires a recognition that event-perceptions must stand in a fixed, irreversible position in the order of representations. Otherwise their seriality could not be distinguished from the seriality of representations of an objective sequence of states of affairs. He finds in Kant the thesis that "the order in which I apprehend the representations of events is fixed by the events, whereas the order in which I apprehend representations of enduring states of affairs is fixed by me or by accident." The notion of an event-sequence is held to be the crucial ingredient in Kant's theory of causation because the condition under which one event A cannot occur before another B is that A is the *cause* of B. A *must* uniformly occur before B as its conditioning event because the order of *events* is fixed. This is the essential feature of Kant's critique of Hume, according to Beck: Hume has no philosophical means for distinguishing between impressions of objective events and impressions of states of affairs. To just this extent his philosophy of causation is declared by Beck to be deficient.

Murphy finds Beck's assessment unconvincing. He maintains that both Beck and Kant are unsuccessful because they presuppose rather than demonstrate their theses. As Murphy sees it, the question is whether our ability to identify an impression as an event-impression is intuitive or discursive, i.e., given or conceptual. Kant tries to show that such identification requires the application of a rule or criterion and that this rule is the schematized category of causation. Unfortunately, says Murphy, Kant himself has to rely on our having just that ability, the existence of which is incompatible with his own answer to Hume; namely, an ability to recognize immediately that an impression is an event-impression. Kant presupposes this ability by assuming that one cannot reverse the order of perceptions without intuitively seeing that a different order of events would result. Thus, according to Murphy, the crucial conceptual criterion of an irreversible time-order presupposes rather than explains the distinction between event order and non-event order: "if you reverse in imagination the order of perceptions of an event you will just see that you have thereby imagined a different event!"

Beck replies that Murphy inaccurately interprets Kant by applying the irreversibility criterion to imagination rather than to *apprehension,* as Kant does. Of course you can *imagine* a different sequence of events, Beck insists, but can you *see* one? You can imagine a boat going downstream when you in fact see it going upstream, but can you apprehend it going downstream when in fact it is going upstream? Beck answers in the negative and charges that Hume cannot account for the presupposed objective event-order. But Murphy contends that Beck's distinction between apprehension and imagination is still not sufficient to save the Kantian position from collapse. Perhaps the most difficult remaining questions, assuming Beck's *interpretation* of Kant is correct, are whether Hume's system of thought can adequately account for the difference between events and non-events and whether there is a philosophical need to do so.

C. J. DUCASSE

1. Critique of Hume's Conception of Causality

The ubiquity and consequent vast importance of the causality relation both for practical and for theoretical purposes is made evident by the very large number of verbs of causation in the language; e.g., to push, to bend, to corrode, to cut, to make, to ignite, to transport, to convince, to compel, to remind, to irritate, to influence, to create, to motivate, to stimulate, to incite, to mislead, to induce, to offend, to effect, to prevent, to facilitate, to produce, etc.

Such verbs are employed not only by every person on innumerable ordinary occasions, but also by scientists in their technical works and by philosophers in formulating various of their hypotheses, reasonings, and conclusions.

The importance of the causality relation was emphasized by David Hume, who, in his *Enquiry concerning Human Understanding,* declared that "if there be any relation among objects which it imports us to know perfectly, it is that of cause and effect. On this are founded all our reasonings concerning matter of fact or existence. By means of it alone we attain any assurance concerning objects which are removed from the present testimony of our memory and senses. The only immediate utility of all sciences, is to teach us, how to control and regulate future events by their causes. Our thoughts and enquiries are, therefore, every moment, employed about this relation."[1]

In modern philosophy, the conception of causality that has proved most challenging has undoubtedly been that of Hume. Kant, in the Introduction to his *Prolegomena to Any Future Metaphysics,* wrote: "I confess freely: the admonition of David Hume [concerning causality] was the very thing which many years ago first interrupted my dogmatic slumber, and gave to my researches in the field of speculative philosophy a wholly different direction."[2]

Even today, Hume's conception of causality is still influential and, therefore, must now be examined with care.

1. HUME'S CONCEPTION OF CAUSALITY

Hume sets forth his conception of causality both in his *Treatise of Human Nature,*[3] and in his *Enquiry concerning Human Understanding* (E 79). At both

---

Reprinted by permission of the publisher from C. J. Ducasse, "Critique of Hume's Conception of Causality," *The Journal of Philosophy* vol. 63, no. 6 (March 17, 1966): 141-48. Footnotes included.

[1] Open Court edition, La Salle, Ill., 1904, hereafter referred to as E; pp. 78-79.

[2] Sämmtliche Werke; ed. Rosenkrantz, Leipzig 1838. Part III, *Prolegomena zu einer jeden künftigen Metaphysik.* Introduction, p. 9: "Ich gestehe frei: die Erinnerung des David Hume war eben dasjenige, was mir vor vielen Jahren zuerst den dogmatischen Schlummer unterbrach, und meinen Untersuchungen im Felde der spekulativen Philosophie eine ganz andere Richtung gab."

[3] Selby-Bigge edition, Oxford, 1896, hereafter T; p. 170.

places he gives two definitions of Cause, one in purely objective terms, the other employing in addition a subjective feature. The definitions are in essence the same in the *Treatise* and in the *Enquiry*, but in the *Treatise* the requirement of contiguity of cause and effect in time and place is explicit; whereas it is left tacit in the somewhat pithier wording of the *Enquiry*, where Necessary Connection is the central topic of the section where Causality is defined.

The objective definition reads there: "we may define a cause to be *an object, followed by another, and where all the objects similar to the first are followed by objects similar to the second.*" The other definition, which introduces a subjective factor, defines a cause as "*an object followed by another, and whose appearance always conveys the thought to that other.*"

The first of these two is the basic definition, since the regularity of sequence it specifies is not only implied in the second definition by the word 'always' but is in addition tacitly *used* there by employment of the verb 'conveys'—which makes that second definition circular, since 'conveys' means "*causes* to pass . . . to . . . ," and no meaning of 'causes' has yet been provided by Hume other than "is regularly followed by"; so that "always conveys the thought to that other" means only "is always followed by thought of that other." Indeed, strict adherence to the empiricism Hume professes requires that his words "is always followed" be replaced by 'has always been followed'.

Hence, when what is left tacit in Hume's second definition of a cause is made fully explicit, the definition reads: *a cause is an object which has always been followed by a certain other, and whose appearance has always been followed by thought of the other.*

2. HUME'S DEFINITION OF PSYCHOLOGICAL NECESSITY

Hume asserts that no *connection* is ever perceived between a cause and its effect and, hence, as his empiricism entails, that there is none. For the following of the effect is not necessitated by the preceding occurrence of the cause, in the sense that 'necessitated' has in logic and mathematics where what Hume calls "relations of ideas" (as distinguished from "matters of fact"; E 25) are concerned, and where truth of a *conclusion* is necessitated by truth of given *premises* in the sense that their being true and its being false would imply a contradiction.

When on the other hand, as in causation, "matters of fact" are concerned instead, then 'necessity' designates not a relation among "objects" themselves but, Hume says, only the "propensity," which custom produces, to pass from an object to the idea of its usual attendant. ". . . necessity is something, that exists in the mind, not in Objects" (T 165).

This definition of psychological as distinguished from logical necessity, however, contains three terms of causation, namely, 'custom', 'produces', and 'propensity'; and since no account of what constitutes causation, other than that it consists in empirical regularity of sequence, has yet been provided by Hume, it is in terms of such empirical regularity that those three terms of causation have to be themselves explicated, as follows:

'Produces', as Hume himself stresses on page 77 of the *Treatise*, is but a synonym of 'causes'. Hence that custom produces in a person *P* the propensity to pass from perception of an object *O* to the idea of its usual attendant *A* can only mean that the *custom*—that is, *P*'s having repeatedly observed occurrence of *O* being followed by occurrence of *A*—has *itself* been regularly followed by occurrence in *P* of "propensity" to pass from perception of *O* to the idea *I* of *O*'s usual attendant *A*.

But, 'propensity' being itself a term of causality, propensity in *P* to pass from perception of *O* to idea *I* can, for Hume, only mean that perception of *O* by *P* has been regularly followed in *P* by occurrence of idea *I*. It cannot, for Hume, mean—as commonly it does in addition and essentially—that *P*'s *now* perceiving *O is going to be* followed in *P* by occurrence of idea *I*; for Hume is emphatic that we have no proof "*that those instances, of which we have had no experience, resemble those, of which we have had experience* [T, p. 89; the italics are Hume's] . Hence, even if occurrence of the idea *I* in *P* has in the past regularly followed perception of *O* by *P* (after *P* had repeatedly observed occurrence of *A* after occurrence of *O*), even then it remains perfectly possible that, *this time*, perception of *O* by *P* will not be followed in him by occurrence of the idea *I* of *A*; for no contradiction is involved in supposing "a change in the course of nature" (89).

The upshot, then, is that, because Hume's definition of psychological necessitation is worded in terms that are inherently terms of causation—to wit, 'conveys', 'produces', and 'propensity'—and because he has offered as yet no definition of causation other than as sequence that has in fact been regular in our experience, his definition of psychological 'necessity', when explicated in terms of that definition of causation, turns out to tell us that *in the mind just as among objects,* there is *no necessity,* i.e., *no connection*; but only so much regularity of sequence as there happens to be. Indeed, Hume explicitly acknowledges that *he does not even know what he is denying* when he denies that a "connection" obtains between a cause and its effect; for he declares that "we have no idea of this connection, nor even any distinct notion what it is we desire to know, when we endeavor at a conception of it" (E 79).

3. HUME'S CONTENTION THAT CAUSATION MAY BE DETECTED BY A SINGLE EXPERIMENT

At some places in the *Treatise,* however, Hume's common sense almost gets the better of his indefensible official contention that causation ultimately consists in nothing but empirical regularity of sequence. For example (T 104), he asserts that "we may attain the knowledge of a particular cause merely by one experiment, provided it be made with judgment, and after a careful removal of all foreign and superfluous circumstances."

But of course it is paradoxical to suppose that a *single* experiment—unless it reveals a genuine *connection* between events of the kinds that figure in it—can inform us that in all past and all future cases of an event similar to the first, an event similar to the second *did,* or *will,* follow. Hume is aware of this difficulty and attempts to deal with it by saying that "tho' we are suppos'd to have had only one experiment of a particular effect, yet we have had many millions to convince us of this principle; that like objects, plac'd in like circumstances, will always produce like effects" (p. 105).

But to "convince" is only to *cause* belief; i.e., on Hume's definition of 'cause', it is *to have been regularly followed* by belief—here, belief that like objects placed in like circumstances will always "produce," i.e., be followed by, like effects. And, on an empiricism that denies that any *connection* is ever perceived between a cause and its effect, the belief mentioned is made illegitimate by the reference in it of the words 'will always' to cases not actually experienced, to wit, cases as yet future. For, as I have pointed out already in section 2, Hume stresses that we have no proof "that those instances, of which we have had no experience, resemble those, of which we have had experience" (89). The "principle" to which Hume appeals in order to meet the difficulty he recognized is, therefore, on his own premises, only an unwarranted belief, and leaves the difficulty standing.

Indeed, that "principle," taken by itself, would justify us in generalizing from *any* case of sequence we had observed—whether it was in fact an accidental or a causal sequence. The "principle" therefore has valid applicability only *after* we have somehow managed to identify the cause by one experiment. But, according to Hume, we can do this only after we have performed the prescribed preliminary "careful removal of all foreign and superfluous circumstances"; and unfortunately we cannot know which these are unless we *already* know what identifies a particular one of the circumstances as being *the cause*. But the "principle" does not inform us of this and is, therefore, useful only for *generalizing* a causal connection if, somehow, a *single* experiment has already revealed it to us. If, however, a single experiment can reveal it to us, then causation does not consist in empirical constancy of sequence, even if such constancy is entailed by causal connection.

Hume appears to be aware in the end that he has not succeeded in providing a tenable analysis of the causality relation, for he writes that "it is impossible to give any just definition of cause, except"—and this is paradoxical—"what is drawn from something extraneous and foreign to it"; and he adds that both the definitions of cause he has given are "drawn from circumstances foreign to the cause" (E 79). Moreover, in the section of the *Treatise* where Hume gives the "Rules by which to judge of causes and effects," he at first refers to causation as "that constant conjunction on which the relation of cause and effect *totally* depends" (T 173); but, lower down on the same page, what he says is not "totally" but "*chiefly*"; and, at the top of page 174, he refers to constant repetition only as that "from which the *first idea* of this relation [to wit, the causal relation] is derived" (italics mine).

4. HUME'S "RULES BY WHICH TO JUDGE OF CAUSES AND EFFECTS"

Hume, however, does in section xv of part III of the *Treatise* offer a set of "rules by which to judge of causes and effects." The fifth, sixth, and seventh of these are the clearest formulations given, not only up to his time but up to the publication in 1830 of J. F. W. Herschel's *Preliminary Discourse on the Study of Natural Philosophy* (secs. 146-162), of what John Stuart Mill later denominated the Methods of Agreement, of Difference, and of Concomitant Variations—William Minto still later rightly contending that the first two should be called the methods of *Single* Agreement, and of *Single* Difference.[4] And it might be thought that in the

---

[4] *Logic, Inductive and Deductive* (New York: Scribner's, 1904), p. 332.

fifth and sixth of them Hume gives us what we need in order to distinguish, in a single experiment, between the circumstance that *is* the cause of an occurrence and the circumstances that are "foreign and superfluous."

This, however, is not the case; but in order to see that it is not, we must view the fifth and sixth rules in the light of the fourth. The three read as follows:

> Rule 4.   The same cause always produces the same effect, and the same effect never arises but from the same cause. This principle we derive from experience, and is the source of most of our philosophical reasonings. For when by any clear experiment we have discovered the causes or effects of any phenomenon, we immediately extend our observation to every phenomenon of the same kind, without waiting for that constant repetition, from which the first idea of this relation is derived.

The fifth rule, which formulates Hume's conception of the principle of Agreement, is as follows:

> Rule 5.   There is another principle, which hangs upon this, viz., that where several different objects produce the same effect, it must be by means of some quality, which we discover to be common amongst them. For as like effects imply like causes, we must always ascribe the causation to the circumstances, wherein we discover the resemblance.

And the sixth rule, which is Hume's formulation of the principle of Difference, reads:

> Rule 6.   The following principle is founded on the same reason. The difference in the effects of two resembling objects must proceed from that particular in which they differ. For as like causes always produce like effects, when in any instance we find our expectation to be disappointed, we must conclude that this irregularity proceeds from some difference in the causes.

In commenting now on these rules, attention must be drawn first to the fact that the principle stated in the fourth rule, to wit, that "the same cause always produces the same effect, and the same effect never arises but from the same cause" is presented there explicitly as a principle for *generalizing* particular relations of cause and effect after we have discovered them by some "clear experiment." Do, then, the fifth and sixth rules tell us how to distinguish *experimentally* that circumstance which is the cause from those which are "foreign and superfluous"?

Clearly, they do not; for those two rules are presented by Hume as *corollaries* of the principle stated in the fourth, and—contrary to what he asserts in Rule 4 and for the reasons he himself gives on page 89 of the *Treatise*, which were cited in sec. 2 of the present paper—that principle *cannot* be derived from experience. For the word 'always', which Hume employs in the statement of it, makes that principle include innumerable cases that we have *not* experienced—not only all cases as yet future, but also many past and present cases that happened to go unobserved.

A much more modest principle, which experience, in Hume's sense of the term, might conceivably have yielded if we had already known how to identify causes and effects experimentally, would be that the same observed cause has been observed always to have had the same effect, and the same observed effect always to have had the same cause. But *this* principle would not entail Hume's fifth and sixth rules. Indeed, *every observation of the two kinds respectively described in these two rules would constitute a patent exception to and invalidation of that principle.* For "where several different objects produce the same effect (Rule 5), what this shows is that the same effect sometimes does result from different causes—a plain fact illustrated by the many different causes from which death can result. And where what we observe is a "difference in the effects of two resembling objects" (Rule 6), what is thereby shown is that the same cause does not always have the same effect—a fact which, as Josiah Royce once pointed out to one of his classes, one can make patent if, having stepped on a man's foot, apologized, and noted his response, one then immediately repeats accurately the stepping and the apology. For the man's response is pretty certain then to be different!

5. FACTS THAT CLASH WITH HUME'S DEFINITION OF CAUSALITY

The examination made in this paper of Hume's various statements concerning causality has shown that the only definition of causality he really offers is his first: "We may define a cause to be an object, followed by another, and where all the objects similar to the first are followed by objects similar to the second." For this is the only one of his definitions of causality which, as not itself employing any term of causality—such as 'conveys', 'produces', 'propensity',—is free from circularity.

But the conception of causality simply thus as observed regularity of occurrence of an event of kind *B* after occurrence of an event of kind *A* is untenable, as obviously clashing with certain of our most confident judgments, positive and negative, about cases of causation or of noncausation. For on the one hand a single experiment, if performed with the great care normally exercised in laboratories, unquestionably makes manifest the causation of one particular occurrence by a particular other. On the other hand, some instances of regularity of sequence are admittedly *not* instances of the cause-effect relation; for example, as Thomas Reid pointedly remarked, if the cause of an occurrence is defined as its invariable antecedent, then night must be the cause of day and day the cause of night. And, one may add, growth of hair on babies would be the cause of their growth of teeth!

John Stuart Mill, when he considers Reid's objection, states that "invariable sequence, therefore, is not synonymous with causation, unless the sequence, besides being invariable, is unconditional."[5] This, he writes, "is what writers mean when they say that the notion of cause involves the idea of necessity. If there be any meaning which confessedly belongs to the term necessity, it is *unconditionalness.* That which is necessary, that which *must* be, means that which will be, whatever supposition we may make in regard to all other things."

As Dr. Charles Mercier has pointed out, however, this definition of necessity is unfortunately worded, since such necessity as an event possesses is always *conditional* on occurrence of its cause.[6]

Nothing more need be said here concerning Mill's discussion of causality, which, on attentive examination, is seen to be a mass of confusions at most of the essential points.[7]

---

[5] *System of Logic* (8th ed.; New York: Harper, 1874), book III, ch. v, sec. 6, p. 245.

[6] *Causation and Belief* (London: Longmans Green, 1916), pp. 75-76.

[7] The grounds on which this severe judgment is based have been set forth in detail in ch. II of the writer's *Causation and the Types of Necessity* (Seattle: Univ. of Washington Press, 1924).

W. A. SUCHTING

2. Kant's Second Analogy of Experience

I

That part of the *Critique of Pure Reason* entitled "Second Analogy (of Experience)," which contains Kant's main treatment of causality, is of central importance in his system. After all, according to Kant, it was Hume's handling of causality which stimulated the "Critical" philosophy,[1] and it is the "transcendental deduction" of the principle of causality which Kant almost invariably cites as an example of that method.[2] Kant authorities as different as Adickes and Paton agree on its importance. The former calls it "truly the focus" of the whole work.[3] Paton writes that "it should be difficult to exaggerate the importance which Kant's proof" in the Second Analogy "has in the system of the Critical Philosophy"—"for Kant the real crux of his doctrine is to be found there."[4] Even some writers who consider that Kant's argumentation fails—like Jonathan Bennett in one of the most recent books on Kant—think that this section of the *Critique* is of major significance. Thus Bennett writes that the text of the first and second Analogies is "one of the great passages in modern philosophy."[5]

But despite this, and the immense literature on Kant, there is next to no measure of agreement about the correct appraisal of the argument in the Second Analogy, or even about what the argument is.[6] The main aim of the following paper is to answer both these questions. I shall not make any attempt to develop arguments which might be suggested by what Kant says, but which are more or less clearly not what he actually does say, though this is an important use to which the study of Kant may be put. I shall try as far as possible to take the Second Analogy as a self-contained piece of philosophical writing, and treat it in a way which presupposes as little as possible any detailed acquaintance with Kant.

Reprinted by permission of the author and the publisher from W. A. Suchting, "Kant's Second Analogy of Experience," *Kant-Studien* vol. 58, no. 3 (1967): 355-69. Footnotes included.

[1] *Prolegomena,* translated by P. G. Lucas, Manchester 1953, p. 9.

[2] *Critique of Pure Reason,* B 162–63, A 221/B 268, A 542/B 570, A 766/B 794 (Kemp Smith's translation, pp. 172, 240, 469f., 610f.).—Quotations from the *Critique of Pure Reason* will be in N. Kemp Smith's translation (2nd edition, 1933), page references to which are preceded by "p." As is customary, the first edition of the *Critique* is referred to as "A" and the second edition as "B."

[3] *Immanuel Kants Kritik der reinen Vernunft,* edited by E. Adickes, Berlin 1889, p. 211 n.

[4] H. J. Paton, *Kant's Metaphysic of Experience,* London 1936, Vol. II, p. 222 and n. (All further reference to Paton will be to this work.)

[5] J. Bennett, *Kant's Analytic,* Cambridge 1966, p. 181.

[6] Cf. L. W. Beck: "Once More Unto the Breach: Kant's Answer to Hume, Again," *Ratio,* June 1967 [Reprinted in this text] : "It is a continuing scandal of philosophical scholarship that after nearly two centuries the question must still be debated: *What* was Kant's answer to Hume? Until there is agreement about this, there is little reason to hope that the philosophical problem of the adequacy of a theory like Kant's to answer questions raised by a theory like Hume's can be solved." (I quote from a pre-publication copy kindly furnished me by Professor

II

To begin with, I shall say something about the aim of the argumentation in the Second Analogy. Without much doubt the goal is to prove that the principle of causality is a synthetic necessary statement.

What just has been called the principle of causality is referred to in A as the "Principle of Production (Erzeugung)" and formulated as: "Everything that happens, that begins to be, presupposes something upon which it follows according to a rule," This way of putting it is replaced in B by what is called the "Principle of Succession in Time, in accordance with the Law of Causality," which is formulated thus: "All alterations take place in conformity with the law of the connection of cause and effect." By way of gloss on this it may be remarked that Kant uses as synonyms "alteration (Veränderung)," "Geschehen," "Begebenheit" (and cognates), which may be variously translated "occurrence," "happening," "event." They all signify the coming to be or passing away of some "determination" of a substance. Thus, the freezing of water is an event, for it is the coming to be of a state of the water, namely, solidity, which did not previously exist (the water having been in the liquid state) (B 162, p. 172); again, the movement of a ship drifting down stream, from one position to another relative to the banks, is an event (A 192/B 237, p. 221).[7]

The principle of causality (as we may continue to call the above for short) is said to be synthetic, because the concept of cause is logically independent of the concept of an event.[8] This is comparatively uncontroversial. The real task is to show that the principle is also necessary, which amounts for Kant to its being knowable *a priori* as true.[9]

Besides this there seems to be a second strand running through the Second Analogy, namely the thesis that the causal relation is characterised by some non-empirical necessity, of the sort that Hume is generally taken[10] to have rejected. (That Kant held no other view of the modal status of causal laws is not absolutely definite.[11] But it is reasonably certain that it was his main view.) The typing

Beck. I am also indebted to Professor Beck for some critical comments on an earlier draft of this paper.) Beck's paper is, in part, a criticism of some recent contributions to this controversy, viz. E. W. Schipper, "Kant's Answer to Hume's Problem," *Kant-Studien*, 53 (1961), 68-74, M. E. Williams, "Kant's Reply to Hume," *Kant-Studien*, 55 (1965), 71-78, and R. P. Wolff, *Kant's Theory of Mental Activity*, Cambridge, Mass. 1963.

[7] Kant sometimes speaks of an event as a change of state of a substance (so, e.g., *a propos* the freezing of the water). But this is not appropriate for the description of his ship example, since, assuming that the motion of the ship is uniform and rectilinear, such a motion from one position to another is not, strictly, a change of the ship's state. Cf. Kant, A 207/B 252, note a, p. 230.

[8] A 9/B 13, A 301/B 357, A 737/B 765 (pp. 50f., 302, 592).

[9] E.g. B 4f., p. 44. See L. W. Beck, "The Second Analogy and the Principle of Indeterminancy," *Kant-Studien* 57 (1966), 199-205, for argument to the effect that the question of the viability of the Second Analogy is independent of any results, as regards indeterminism, of quantum physics.

[10] For queries regarding this standard view see W. A. Suchting, "Hume and Necessary Truth," *Dialogue*, 5 (1966), 47-60.

[11] On the question of Kant's views regarding the logical status of scientific laws, and the relation of the latter to the general principle of causality see G. Buchdahl, "Causality, Causal Laws and Scientific Theory in the Philosophy of Kant," *British Journal for the Philosophy of Science*, 16 (1965), 187-208.

together of the two theses comes out clearly enough, to cite just one example, where Kant contrasts the view that he is espousing with "all that has hitherto been taught in regard to the procedure of our understanding" (A 195-6/B 240-1, pp. 223f. It also emerges elsewhere, e.g., B 4-5, p. 44.) It is quite unclear whether Kant thought that "Necessarily, every event has a cause" entails "If A is a cause of B, then A and B are necessarily connected." If he did, then he was wrong, for the two are logically independent of one another. It might be that necessarily every event has a cause, but that all particular causal relations are contingent; it might be that a cause is necessarily connected with its effect, but that not all events have causes, or, if they do, that this is only contingently the case. So that whether or not Kant succeeded in proving that the principle of causality is necessary in some sense, this has no direct bearing on the question of the modality of particular causal laws followed from this overarching thesis that the mind somehow stamps laws on the intrinsically formless given (whatever this may mean).[12] But whatever may be the case about this the thesis in question does not follow from the specific argumentation of the Second Analogy, with which we are concerned here. For these reasons I shall henceforth simply ignore this view about the modal character of laws as a thesis to be proved by the argument of the Second Analogy.

III

With regard to the actual argumentation of the Second Analogy, one of the only things that practically all writers on Kant agree on is that the presentation is unclear. However, very many of the commentators on this part of the *Critique* also agree that it contains more than one argument. Divergences arise rather about just how many different arguments there are, their interrelations, and so on.

But any account of the Second Analogy which finds more than one distinct argument must surely reckon with Kant's own assertion, almost at the end of the *Critique* (A 787-8/B 815-6, p. 624), that "only *one* proof can be found for each transcendental proposition," and his citing precisely the deduction of the principle of causality as an instance of this. Of course, Kant may simply have been in error about the character of his own argument. Again, what he says here may be compatible with the existence of several distinct arguments; perhaps he meant just that there was only one general line of argument. Nevertheless Kant's own words make it reasonable to say that an interpretation which makes just one basic argument out of what is said in the Second Analogy, and which is not subject to difficulties any worse than beset any interpretation, is to be preferred on that ground alone.

In what follows I want to argue for such a univocal interpretation. Main attention will be focussed on three parts of the text. One is the second of two paragraphs which Kant added in B at the beginning of the original A text. (The first of these two paragraphs simply recapitulates the first Analogy.) This may be taken to be Kant's final, summarising word on the argument, and, insofar, its importance for the interpretation of the argument is obvious. The second part of the text to be concentrated on is the first four paragraphs of A, or counting from the beginning of the B text, as is most convenient, paragraphs 3 to 6 (A 189-94/B 234-9, pp. 219-22). A good many commentators take subsequent paragraphs in A to be, with

---

[12] Cf. on this J. Bennett, *Kant's Analytic*, pp. 156-9.

one major exception, broadly speaking different re-statements of the line of argument enunciated here and the drawing of consequences from it. The exception is the argument of paragraph 13-15 (of the B text—A 199-201/B 244-6, pp. 225f.), which has been generally taken to contain an argument quite different from anything else in this Analogy.[13] It is obvious that any attempt to find a single argument in the Second Analogy must pay special attention to this part of what Kant says, and so this will be the third of the main passages to be specially considered.

IV

A. To begin with, the following steps in Kant's argumentation may be distinguished, based on the first two of the above three passages.

(1) At least some of our perceptions of states of the same object are successive. (Kant himself asserts that all are; but this is both problematic and unnecessary for the purposes of the argument.)

(2) Of such series of successive perceptions we take some to be simply successive perceptions of coexisting states, as when we stand fairly close to a large building and look at various portions one after another. Others we take to correspond to an objective succession of states, as when we watch a boat drifting downstream.

That we are conscious of an objective order in time is assumed as a result of the general "transcendental deduction of the categories." Put otherwise, this premise asserts that succession in perception is not a sufficient condition for succession in what is perceived.

(3) Pure time, time in itself, cannot be perceived.

Therefore, which series correspond to objective successions (events) and which do not cannot be determined by reference to time itself.

(4) We have no access to things, in the sense of entities statements about which cannot be translated into statements about actual and possible perceptions.

Therefore, which series correspond to objective successions and which do not cannot be determined by reference to things. (We do not even know whether "things" are temporal in nature. "How things may be in themselves, apart from the representations through which they may affect us, is entirely outside our sphere of knowledge." A 190/B 235, p. 220.)

The phenomenalistic character of Kant's whole orientation, or at least, the fact that "things," insofar as they exist, are not objects of knowledge, is worth remarking upon here, because it is very natural to read the Second Analogy from the point of view of a realistic framework. This is even strongly apparent in the locutions by which it is not unnatural to frame Kant's premises. Thus one speaks of perceptions of states, perceptions *corresponding to* events, and so on, its being thereby almost inevitably suggested that Kant thinks of the perception of the state (for example) as being different from the state. But such a reaching is responsible for much puzzlement about Kant's meaning. For Kant the "material" content of

---

[13] See here N. Kemp Smith's *Commentary on Kant's Critique of Pure Reason*, London 1918, pp. 363, 375; A. C. Ewing, *Kant's Treatment of Causality*, London 1924, p. 74, and his *Short Commentary on Kant's Critique of Pure Reason*, London 1950[2], p. 158. Paton notes this general opinion, p. 253.

apprehension is always one and the same, namely, sense-impressions as they may be called. The different sorts of content are distinguished by the different relations of these sense-impressions to one another. Thus it would be less misleading, though intolerably awkward and prolix to speak not, for example, of perceptions of successive states, but rather of, say, successive-state-perception-series. But as long as this orientation is kept firmly in mind no great harm is done by using locutions with realistic overtones.

Assuming that there is no other avenue by which the requisite distinction might be sought, it is concluded that

(5) Which series of perceptions correspond to events must be determined by reference to characteristics of the series themselves.

B. What then is the (relational) difference between series of perceptions which correspond to events, and those which correspond to coexisting states? I shall begin consideration of this point by citing what may be taken to be the relevant passages from each of the two parts of the argumentation of the Analogy to which attention has thus far been devoted.

Suppose the series of perceptions consists of just two perceptions, A and B; and suppose the first is the preceding. Then, Kant says,

> in an appearance which contains a happening . . . B can be appre-
> hended only as following upon A. . . . The order in which the perceptions
> succeeded one another in apprehension is . . . determined (bestimmt). . . .
> In the series of . . . perceptions [of, for example, a house, there is] no
> determinate (bestimmte) order specifying at what point I must begin in
> order to connect the manifold empirically. But in the perceptions of an
> event there is always a rule that makes the order in which the perceptions
> (in the apprehension of this appearance) follow upon one another a *neces-
> sary* order. . . . The objective succession will therefore consist in that order
> of the manifold of appearance according to which *in conformity with a
> rule,* the apprehension of that which happens follows upon the apprehen-
> sion of that which precedes. . . . In conformity with such a rule there must
> lie in that which precedes an event the condition of a rule according to
> which this event invariably and necessarily follows. I cannot reverse this
> order, proceeding back from the event to determine (bestimmen) through
> apprehension that which precedes. For appearance never goes back from
> the succeeding to the preceding point of time, though it does indeed stand
> in relation to *some* preceding point of time. The advance, on the other
> hand, from a given time to the determinate (bestimmte) time that follows
> is a necessary advance. Therefore, since there certainly is something that
> follows, I must refer it necessarily to something else which precedes it and
> upon which it follows in conformity with a rule, that is, of necessity. The
> event, as the conditioned, thus affords reliable evidence of some condition,
> and this condition is what determines (bestimmt) the event. (A 192/B
> 237—A 194/B 239, pp. 221f.)

The corresponding passage in the introductory part of B runs:

> In order that . . . the *objective relation* of appearances that follow
> upon one another . . . be known as determined (bestimmt) the relation
> between the two states must be so thought that it is thereby determined
> (bestimmt) as necessary which of them must be placed before, and which
> of them after, and that they cannot be placed in the reverse relation. But
> the concept which carries with it a necessity of synthetic unity can only be
> a pure concept that lies in the understanding, not in perception; and in this

case it is the concept of the *relation of cause and effect,* the former of which determines (bestimmt) the latter in time, as its consequence. . . . (B 234, p. 219)

C. These passages may be interpreted as containing the following premises:

(6) Necessarily, if A and B are the constituents of a certain event-perception, then the temporal order of perceptibility of A and B is what may be variously described as "determined," "determinate," "in conformity with a rule," "necessary."

This is contrasted with the case of the temporal order of perceptibility of the constituents of a perception of coexistent states. In the latter case we can, in principle, go through the series in any order in time. In the stock example, we can begin with the top of the wall and move our eyes downward, or do the opposite, or undertake a number of other eye-movements. But if we choose to witness the event of a boat's floating downstream, then, given some standard physical circumstances, we can have a series of perceptions in only one order.

(7) Necessarily, if the temporal order of perceptibility of A and B is "determined" (etc.), then A and B are causally related (directly or indirectly).

The conclusion is that, necessarily, if A and B are constituents of a certain event-perception, then A and B are causally related (directly or indirectly)—which was to be demonstrated.

D. In his recent book, *Kant's Analytic* (Cambridge 1966) Jonathan Bennett has concentrated his criticism of what he takes to be Kant's explicit argument in the Second Analogy on what is essentially premise (6) in the above formulation of the argument. A consideration of what I take to be the main point of Bennett's criticism may serve at least to illuminate Kant's argument here.

In brief, Bennett takes Kant to be saying that in the case of a given series of perceptions of coexisting states of an object—what Bennett usefully calls a "survey"—I could have re-arranged my visual states, so that their order would have been different if I had behaved differently; but if, for example, I see a ship leave a harbour "no action of mine could have altered the order in which my visual states occurred."[14] Bennett objects that this cannot be a generally adequate basis for the distinction, because it is possible to construct examples in which the perception of what may be taken to be an event satisfies, not the condition described above, but rather the condition for a survey. For example, "(a) I saw a long-boat being rowed out of the harbour; which, if Kant's analysis is right, entails not just that my visual states *did* occur in a certain order but that (b) *I could not have* had them in any other order. But since the coxswain of the boat was under orders from me, I *could have* secured for myself the spectacle of the boat being back-paddled, stern foremost into the harbour. So (a) is true and (b) false, and Kant's analysis of (a) is therefore wrong."[15]

But this ignores a crucial distinction between the two cases. Consider the event of the boat's moving from one part of the harbour outwards to another part. Kant may be taken to be saying that, given the situation as it was, I could not have

---

[14] J. Bennett, *Kant's Analytic,* p. 222.
[15] J. Bennett, loc. cit.

had the perceptions making up *this* event in any order other than that which I had them. He could hardly have claimed that I could not have had similar perceptions in any other order, for clearly similar perceptions in the reverse order would have corresponded to the event of the boat's being paddled into the harbour sternwards. But this would have been a different event. And the difference between my bringing this about by orders to the coxswain and my bringing about a different order of perceptions of the parts of the wall is that in the former case I can bring about a different order of perceptions only by causally influencing the state of affairs itself, whilst in the case of the wall I can bring about the difference by causally influencing myself alone. The difference may be also brought out in the following way. If we suppose two people looking at the wall, then each can, at the same time, have a different series of perceptions of the wall. If we suppose two relevantly similar people looking at the boat leaving the harbour, then, given the same external causal conditions, each cannot but have the same series of perceptions . If we suppose that they look at the boat again, my having this time ordered the coxswain to row in backwards, then they will certainly now have a differently ordered set of perceptions; but each will still have the same series as the other.

My conclusion is that Bennett's criticism does not invalidate Kant's argument at this point.

E. Let us now turn to an independent consideration of (6) and (7). A matter of primary importance here is clearly the sense in which "determined," "necessary" (etc.) is to be taken in (6). Graham Bird in his generally very illuminating book *Kant's Theory of Knowledge* (London 1962), takes it that the necessity which Kant speaks of in the passages quoted, and which is embodied in (6), is the logical necessity that to apprehend a certain event E is just to apprehend a certain fixed, determinate sequence of states, so that to apprehend any other sequence of these states would be, by definition, to apprehend an event other than E.

If this is the sense in which "necessary" is to be taken in (6), then the latter is at the very least, very plausible indeed. But is the sense given (6) one which will also allow us to affirm (7), and so arrive at the desired conclusion? How is necessity in this sense linked with causality? Mr. Bird goes on to say, expounding Kant, and presumably, in the absence of any dissenting comment, agreeing with him:

> the idea of a determinate order between two states presupposes that of something which determines it; and this idea of a determinant or reason for such an order is that of a cause.[16]

But if this faithfully reproduces Kant's train of thought, then the argument at this crucial point rests simply on a pun. For without an equivocation how could one get from the proposition that events are *logically determinate,* in the sense that they are constituted by a determinately (i.e., definitely, specifically) ordered sequence of states, to the conclusion that this sequence is *causally determined,* i.e., such that the determinate order in question is due to some causal relation?[17] Not even the notion of "presupposing," which has been asked to carry such a diversity and weight of philosophical burdens, is capable of sustaining this transition.

---

[16] G. Bird, *Kant's Theory f Knowledge,* p. 155.

[17] A confusion of this sort is pointed to by R. E. Hobart in his undeservedly forgotten paper "Hume Without Scepticism," *Mind,* 39 (1930), pp. 287-9. Cf. also P. F. Strawson,

If such an error occurs, then it may be that Kant was misled by the very word "bestimmt" which he used, the latter being a common expression both for logically determinate as well as for causally determined. Or it could have been a fallacy of the following sort: to have inferred from (i) "Necessarily, if A and B are the constituents of a certain event-perception, then the temporal order of A and B is necessary" that (ii) "If A and B are the constituents of a certain event-perception, then necessarily, if A, then B," the latter conclusion's then being detached.

F. However, I do not think that Kant's argument is faithfully reproduced in this way, for I think that he has a specific argument in mind for the linking of that objective order of states in time, which constitutes an event, with causality, even though it involves a fallacy parallel to that just pointed out. This argument is only briefly indicated in that part of the passage already cited from A, which begins "I cannot reverse this order" and ends with the quotation. In this part Kant may be interpreted as putting forward a certain argument about the relation between the state-perceptions constituting an event, and the parts of pure time in which they occur. I suggest that just this argument is spelled out in detail in the latter paragraphs 11-15, i.e. just those paragraphs which have been widely taken to be anomalous with respect to the other parts of the text of the Second Analogy and to contain a quite different argument from the rest.[18] The main parts of this later passage are as follows:

> If . . . it is a . . . *formal condition* of all perceptions, that the preceding time necessarily determines (bestimmt) the succeeding (since I cannot advance to the succeeding time save through the preceding), it is also an indispensable law of *empirical representation* of the time-series that the appearances of past time determine all existences in the succeeding time, and that these latter, as events, can take place only in so far as the appearances of past time determine their existence in time, that is, determine them according to a rule. . . . Understanding . . . (makes) the representation of an object possible at all . . . by carrying the time-order over into the appearances and their existence. For to each of them, [viewed] as [a] consequent, it assigns, through relation to the preceding experiences, a position determined *a priori* in time . . . absolute time is not an object of perception. . . . On the contrary, the appearances must determine for one another this position in time, and make their time-order a necessary order. In other words, that which follows or happens must follow in conformity with a universal rule upon that which was contained in the preceding state. . . . (A 199-200/B 244-245, pp. 225f.)

If we adopt the interpretation suggested above, then Kant may be taken to be arguing the required connection between objective temporal succession and causality in the following way:

The Bounds of Sense. An Essay on Kant's 'Critique of Pure Reason,' London 1966, pp. 28, 137f.

[18] Paton says in a note that the passage at A 194/B 239 "bears a certain external resemblance to" the arguments at paragraphs 13-15 (p. 244 n.), and in another note (p. 253, n. 2) that "it seems . . . just possible that Kant may have regarded" the later passage "as an elaboration of what is obscurely hinted at" in the earlier. This caution is rather puzzling in view of Paton's tendency to stress the unity of Kantian arguments, and in particular his emphasis on the argument from the continuity of time to the necessity of causal connection (e.g. pp. 225, 256 n. 1., 274, 292f.). The only other writer I have come across who emphasises this strand of argument is Kuno Fischer in his *Immanuel Kant und seine Lehre,* Heidelberg 1905[5] especially pp. 464f.

(a) Necessarily, if A and B are the constituents of an event-perception, then A and B occupy successive places in objective, pure time.

(b) Necessarily, the relation between A and B reproduces, empirically, the relation between the successive places in pure time that they occupy.

(c) Necessarily, successive parts of pure time are necessarily connected.

(d) Therefore, necessarily, the relation between A and B is the relation of necessary succession in time. But the latter is just the causal relation. Therefore, necessarily, if A and B are the constituents of an event-perception, then A and B are causally connected.

Before looking critically at this version of the argument, a couple of comments may be made about the grounds for taking this to be actually Kant's argument. It has already been suggested that a part of the first statement in A may be taken to be a highly compressed version of the later paragraphs 13-15. Nor is it impossible to find a connection with the passage already quoted from B. Such a connection may be discerned in the statement, right at the beginning of the part cited earlier to the effect that if the objective relation of states in time is to be "known as determined" it must be thought in accordance with the principle of causality. This may be taken to be suggesting that causal relations between states make possible the knowledge of the objective temporal relations which obtain between them and which obtain by virtue of their occupying successive parts of pure time. Again, the very closing sentences of the Second Analogy recapitulate this very argument:

> In the same manner . . . in which time contains the sensible *a priori* condition of the possibility of a continuous advance of the existing to what follows, the understanding, by virtue of the unity of apperception, is the *a priori* condition of the possibility of a continuous determination of all positions for the appearances in this time, through the series of causes and effects, the former of which inevitably lead to the existence of the latter, and so render the empirical knowledge of the time-relation valid universally for all time, and therefore objectively valid. (A 210-11/B 256, pp. 232f. Compare also A 411/B 438, p. 388.)

Finally, the conjecture that the above is the essential line of the proof in the Second Analogy is supported by the central importance of this mode of argument in the First Analogy ("In all change of appearances substance is permanent"). In the A proof Kant writes, for example:

> the permanent is the *substratum* of the empirical representation of time itself. . . . Permanence . . . expresses time in general. . . .

In B he says:

> time . . . is that in which . . . succession or coexistence can alone be represented. Now time cannot by itself be perceived. Consequently there must be found in the objects of perception . . . the substratum which represents time in general; and all change or coexistence must, in being apprehended, be perceived in this substratum, and through relation of the appearances to it. (B 225, p. 212)

G. At any rate, in what sense or senses, if any, do preceding parts of time "in itself," "pure" time (time considered in abstraction from changes in observable states of affairs) determine, necessarily, succeeding parts? And what is the relevance of this to the way in which one observable state of affairs may be said (causally) to determine another?

Kant says that "I cannot advance to the succeeding time save through the preceding." This may be construed as meaning that the past can be experienced only as before the future. But since, given some point of reference for the past, the past is, analytically, what comes before the future, this gets us no further. Suppose it be understood rather as saying that successive periods of time for a series in which no term can bear the same relation to that which precedes as to that which follows. But the only condition that this places on temporally qualified phenomena is that what is past with respect to something else cannot also be present or future with respect to it. But this is not equivalent to, nor does it entail that the same future must follow on the same past, i.e., that if a particular sequence has occurred once it must occur again whenever the relevant conditions are the same. Again, it might be understood as meaning that the limit of any period of time is fixed, on one side, by the time prior to it. Being a relation only, a period of pure time is wholly determined by external time-relations, for it is nothing but these. But when this period is considered concretely, as a qualitatively characterised series, its external time-relations constitute only one feature of it.

Therefore, all that the argument would establish is that one aspect of the nature of time is determined by one of the relations it bears to other phenomena, i.e. the relation it bears to them as preceding or succeeding them in time. Furthermore, since the aspect thus determined is just its temporal relations to them as preceding or succeeding them in time, this is just a tautology. (This is also seen by considering the fact that a certain moment of time is determined not only by the preceding moment but also by the succeeding one.) The distinction between *events in* time and *moments of time* is just that an event is a particular which has characteristics other than its determinate temporal position, whereas a moment has only the latter (and any entailed relations). That t occurs before t+t' entails that it is logically impossible that the latter should occur before the former, i.e., it is logically impossible that two moments of pure time should thus reverse their positions. Therefore it is simply analytic that two moments of time necessarily stand in the relative positions in which they do in fact stand.[19]

H. Finally, I want to consider a possible interpretation of the Kantian argument, the basis of which is not at all clear in the text of the Second Analogy itself, but might be read out of the argument of the Third Analogy.

The Third Analogy is concerned with judgements of objective coexistence, as the Second is concerned with judgements of objective succession. Kant repeats the point, already made in the Second Analogy, that if A and B are two coexistent states of a substance, then they can be perceived in either order. But he goes on to argue that the fact that they can be perceived in either order (as found by actual trial, for example) is not sufficient for objective coexistence. For suppose that whenever A is perceived, B temporarily vanishes, but reappears when attention is directed to where it was; and suppose A behaves similarly. Then, though A and B are perceivable in either order, they are not coexistent. In sum, the actual perceivability of A and B in either order is a necessary, but not sufficient condition for judging truly that A and B are objectively coexistent. Kant goes on to say that

---

[19] The criticisms advanced here have been made already by Ewing in his *Kant's Treatment of Causality*, London 1924, pp. 74-6, and by C. D. Broad, "Kant's First and Second Analogies of Experience," *Proceedings of the Aristotelian Society*, 26 (1925-26) pp. 208-10. For a defence of Kant here see Paton, especially pp. 254 n. 8, 255 n. 5, 256.

actual perceivability of A and B in either order is necessary and sufficient for judging truly that A and B are objectively coexistent, only relatively to the conditions that they are necessary conditions for the existence of each other (A 211/B 257, p. 234). That A and B are necessary conditions for the existence of the other guarantees that whilst one is perceived the other is coexistent with it.

This line of argument may be applied to the case of judgements of objective succession. If A and B are two successive states of a substance, then they can be perceived in only one order. But that they can be perceived thus is not sufficient for objective successiveness. For suppose that whenever the first member is perceived it immediately passes out of sight (hearing, etc.) though it continues to exist. Then though A and B are perceivable in only one order they would be objectively coexistent and not successive. Thus, actual perceivability of A and B in only one order is a necessary, but not sufficient condition for judging truly that A and B are objectively successive. Kant might be taken to be arguing further that this is only necessary and sufficient relatively to the satisfaction of some condition that one does not exist until the other does. The requisite condition is, in the simplest case, that one state should be a causally necessary condition (in the circumstances) for the existence of the other. (In more complex cases it might be that one is simultaneous with a causal condition of the other, or that each is simultaneous with one of the two causally related states, and so on.) For, if in the simplest case, one is not a causally necessary condition for the existence of the other, it would always be possible that A and B should coexist.

I. But this argument would not show that there could not be an objective sequence that was not a causal sequence. It could be taken as suggesting an argument according to which the assumption of a causal relation between A and B is a necessary and sufficient condition for *reliably* judging them to stand in a relation of objective succession. (Further filling in of the argument would be necessary here however in view of Kant's belief that "the great majority of efficient natural causes are simultaneous with their effects," A 203/B 248, p. 228.) It might be that an independent argument can be worked out along these lines. But such an argument would have a conclusion a great deal weaker than the official conclusion of the Second Analogy. Kant does indeed speak in the course of the latter of one's being "justified in asserting" that such and such a manifold is successive as dependent on that manifold's being subject to a rule (A 193/B 238, p. 222, and also A 195/B 240, p. 223). But this can only be a manner of speaking, for the central thesis of the Second Analogy relates to the impossibility of uncaused events, and not merely to the condition, if there are any, under which certain sequences of perceptions may be justifiably or reliably judged to be event-perceptions.

In fact, it is very difficult to see how it would be possible validly to get from (6) to the conclusion in question. It is plausible to say, with regard to (6), that if A B constitute an event, then the order of apprehension is, given certain standard circumstances, independent of us. This is as much as to say that any similar person in just these circumstances would have the perceptions in this order. But it still does not follow from this that A and B must be causally related (even in contingent fashion). For it seems possible that, for example, A should have occurred in a causally determined way, but that the later B should have been causally undetermined. Then since B had not occurred when A occurred, the order of perceptibility is subject to the universal in question, but A and B are not causally related. (There may well be epistemic difficulties as to how it could be *known* that B *was* later, and not merely *noticed* later, but this does not affect the point being made.)

V

A final point concerning the interpretation of Kant's argument may be made. Kant has frequently been regarded as offering, in the tradition initiated by Leibniz, a causal theory of the nature of time, as suggesting that temporal relations are constituted by, or explicitly definable in terms of causal relations.[20] But, as has been seen, this is not the intent of Kant's argument at all. That Kant does not attempt to define temporal notions in terms of causal ones is clear both from the general lines of his system and from specific passages in the *Critique of Pure Reason*. He uses the notion of something's following something else in time quite freely as a primitive notion, as is indeed proper, constitutive questions regarding time having already been dealt with in the *Aesthetic*. Again, Kant says very explicitly that the ordinary notion of cause makes essential reference to the notion of time. Thus:

> If I omit from the concept of cause the time in which something follows upon something else in conformity with a rule, I should find in the pure category nothing further than that there is something from which we can conclude to the existence of something else. In that case ... ly would we be unable to distinguish cause and effect from one and ... it since the power to draw such inferences requires conditions of ... I know nothing, the concept would yield no indication how it applies ... any object. (A 243/B 301, p. 262)

With regard to the distinction of cause and effect mentioned in this passage, Kant earlier noted in the Second Analogy that

> sequence in time is ... the sole empirical criterion of an effect in its relation to the causality of the cause which precedes it. (A 203/B 249, p. 228)

Hence, as Schopenhauer for one pointed out long ago,[21] Kant could not, non-circularly, say that A's being earlier than B is constituted by its being the cause of B (or simultaneous with a cause of B, etc.). Finally, any such project would have been thoroughly unKantian, since it involves the attempt to derive a form of sensibility (time) from a form of the understanding (causality). And Kant criticised precisely

---

[20] For a linking of Leibniz and Kant in this way, see, for example, H. Mehlberg, "Essai sur la théorie causae du temps," *Studia Philosophica*, 1 (1935), pp. 135f., 158, etc. H. Scholz, "Eine Topologie der Zeit im Kantischen Sinne, *Dialectica*, 9 (1955), p. 73, G. J. Whitrow, *The Natural Philosophy of Time*, London 1961, p. 273 (but cf. p. 177), A. Grünbaum, *Philosophical Problems of Space and Time*, London 1963, p. 179.—Leibniz's path-breaking ideas in this direction are contained in his *Initia rerum mathematicarum metaphysica*, written in 1716, but not published till 1863 in C. I. Gerhardt's edition of Leibniz's *Mathematische Schriften*, Vol. VII. See especially the passage on p. 18 (translated on p. 1083 of Vol. II of L. E. Loemker's edition of *Leibniz's Philosophical Papers and Letters*, Chicago 1956).

[21] *Über die vierfache Wurzel des Prinzips des zureichenden Grundes*, Section 23, *Sämtliche Werke*, edited by J. Frauenstädt and A. Hübscher, Wiesbaden 1948, Vol. I, p. 91.

Leibniz's theory of space and time just on the ground that he had "intellectualised these forms of sensibility":[22]

> If I attempted, by the mere understanding, to represent to myself outer relations of things, this can only be done by means of a concept of their reciprocal action; and if I seek to connect two states of one and the same thing, this can only be in the order of grounds and consequences. Accordingly, Leibniz conceived space as a certain order in the community of substances, and time as the dynamical sequence of their states. That which space and time seem to possess as proper to themselves, in independence of things, he ascribed to the *confusion* in their concepts, which has led us to regard what is mere form of dynamical relations as being a special intuition, self-subsistent and antecedent to the things themselves. (A 275-6/B 331-2, pp. 285f.)

---

[22] E. Cassirer has argued that Kant's account of Leibniz's views in the following quotation is inaccurate (*Leibniz's System in seinen wissenschaftlichen Grundlagen*, Marburg 1902, pp. 264ff.). But whether this is so is clearly irrelevant to the point being made by means of this citation of Kant's view.

L. W. BECK

3. Once More Unto the Breach: Kant's Answer to Hume, Again

It is a continuing scandal of philosophical scholarship that after nearly two centuries the question must still be debated: *What* was Kant's answer to Hume? Until there is agreement about this, there is little reason to hope that the philosophical problem of the adequacy of a theory like Kant's to answer questions raised by a theory like Hume's can be solved.

Two recent contributions[1] ascribe to Kant much the same answer. Mrs. Schipper (p. 73) holds that the existence of objectively valid physical science is a fundamental hypothesis of Kant and that this science presupposes the law of causality; hence, she concludes by a magnificent *non sequitur*, "We can have knowledge of such a necessary sequence, since we presuppose it in our laws or 'legislate it to nature'" (p. 74). One is reminded of Lord Russell's acute remark that presupposing has all the advantages over demonstrating that theft has over honest labor.

The second author criticizes Mrs. Schipper's paper for giving neither "an answer to Hume's problem nor . . . Kant's definitive solution" (p. 71); but seven pages later concludes that "Kant has shown that the human mind, *if it is to have certain knowledge*, must employ the categories as the a priori presuppositions of Experience" (pp. 77-8, italics added). Of course if we are to say we have certain

---

Reprinted by permission of the author and the publisher, Basil Blackwell, from L. W. Beck, "Once More Unto the Breach: Kant's Answer to Hume, Again," *Ratio* vol. 9, no. 1 (June 1967): 33-37. Footnotes included.

[1] E. W. Schipper, "Kant's Answer to Hume's Problem," *Kant-Studien*, LIII (1961), 68-74; M. E. Williams, "Kant's Reply to Hume," Ibid., LV (1965), 71-8.

knowledge, then we must reject the arguments or premises of the skeptic who has striven to show that we do not. There is nothing in the logic of those two papers that Kant would have embraced more gladly than he would have espoused those "who took for granted that which [Hume] doubted, and demonstrated with zeal and often with impudence that which he never thought of doubting" (*Prol.*, Ak. ed., 258).

Professor Wolff's recent book[2] has dealt with the problem of Kant's answer to Hume at great length and with admirable subtlety. Inasmuch as Professor Wolff has paid me the compliment of taking one of my footnotes very seriously and has written an extended criticism of the argument it contained in concentrated, indeed inspissated, form, I should like to comment upon his argument and, at more length and with thanks to his critical analysis, try to make my argument somewhat stronger. Wolff summarizes my argument in the following words:

> A regressive analysis beginning from mathematics and science will not refute Hume, for mathematics and science is [sic] precisely what Hume professes to doubt. But if the very same principles (premises) which produce (imply) science and mathematics also imply the distinction between even apparently objective and subjective, etc., etc., then Hume will have been convincingly answered, for not even he can deny them (p. 49).

Now Wolff's criticism of me is like mine of Schipper and Williams: the regressive method does not prove the truth of the premises even if the truth of the conclusion is assumed. Such an argument merely affirms a consequent. Since I was fully alert to the danger of this fallacy, I argued, perhaps too briefly, that conditions *sufficient* to establish the truth of propositions Hume doubted are *necessary* to propositions he accepted. Professor Wolff apparently interpreted me as saying merely that Kant's premises are also Hume's premises, whereas in fact I said:

> The justification of the principles is not merely that they produce the kind of knowledge Hume doubted; rather, they are, Kant argued, the *necessary* conditions also for *any* connected experience in time . . . which any sane man, including Hume, would have to grant.[3]

There is an important logical difference here, for affirming a consequent is valid if the antecedent is a necessary condition.

Let K represent a set of propositions accepted by Kant and doubted or denied by Hume; let H represent a set of propositions Hume (and, incidentally, Kant) accepted; let P stand for propositions sufficient to support K (thus P implies K). Kant's answer to Hume is to show that P is necessary to H (thus H implies P).

In my footnote, I mentioned propositions necessary for the distinction between erroneous and veridical perception as the crucial assumption Hume had to make in order to support the inductive arguments he needed even for his truncated causal explanations. Now, however, I wish to direct attention to a passage which discusses causation in a way which conforms to the logical pattern just proffered; and though Hume is not mentioned, this passage constitutes, in my opinion, Kant's "answer to Hume." The passage, A 195-6 = B 240-241, occurs in the discussions of

---

[2] Robert Paul Wolff, *Kant's Theory of Mental Activity* (Cambridge, Harvard University Press), 1963.

[3] From my Introduction to *Kant's Prolegomena* (New York, Liberal Arts Press, 1951), p. xix note. The word "necessary" was not italicized in the original text; but it was there.

the third proof of the Second Analogy, and in order to understand it we must see it in the context of this Analogy.

Kant has been arguing that the apprehension of an objective event, in contradiction to that of an enduring state of affairs, requires a recognition that the representation we call a representation of an event must occur in a fixed position in the order of our representations, for otherwise we would not be able to distinguish the seriality of our representations of enduring states of affairs from the seriality of our representations of an objective sequence of states of affairs, the transition from one to another of which constitutes an event. The order in which I apprehend the representations of events is fixed by the events, whereas the order in which I apprehend representations of enduring states of affairs is fixed by me or by accident. But an order in appearances (objects and events) is one in which one appearance occurs before another or along with it, and this order has a different status from the order of representations, since always one representation occurs before another even when we are representing to ourselves a state of affairs in which one ingredient does not 'take place' before another. We are able to decide that a sequence of representations is evidence of a sequence of events only if the order of the representations is such that we believe (rightly or wrongly) that one of the representations must occur before the other. For in that case, we interpret the first representation, call it R_a, as evidence for the event A, and if R_a cannot (we believe) occur after R_b, we think (rightly or wrongly) that B cannot occur before A. Now the condition under which an event B cannot occur before A is that A is a cause of B. Hence the decision that a given representation R_n is a representation of an event is dependent upon the belief (which may be right or wrong) that what R_n represents occurs after what is represented by R_m and could not occur before it. Hence Kant concludes: The experience of something happening is possible only on the assumption that appearances in their succession, that is, that appearances as they happen (= events), are determined by the preceding state.[4]

We now come to the application of this analysis to the views of Kant's predecessors, presumably Hume. It is generally assumed, Kant says, (i) that we discover that A is the cause of B by induction from observations of A's regularly preceding B's; and (ii) "that this is the way we are first led to construct for ourselves the concept of cause." Hume argued for both these propositions, and we may call (i) the "*Enquiry*-thesis" and (ii) the "*Treatise*-thesis," after the works in which they are most fully and characteristically elaborated.

Kant fully accepts (i). He is in complete agreement with Hume that our knowledge of causal connections between specific events is a posteriori not a priori, synthetic not analytic, inductive not logical, probable not certain. His methods for finding the cause of B are exactly those which Hume prescribed, and the chances of success in this venture, as estimated by Kant and Hume, are very much the same. Kant's first answer to Hume, then, is to agree with him, and to disagree with the rationalists who thought that logical insight into causal connections was possible.

But Kant denies (ii). While we can make "logically clear" the conception of the relation of cause to effect only after we have "employed in experience," (as in [i]), the general rule, to wit, that for B to be an event there must have been *some*

---

[4] A paraphrase of part of the last sentence in the paragraph beginning on A 195 = B 240.

other event as the condition for its position in a serial, temporal order, "the recognition of the rule, as a condition of the synthetic unity of appearances in time, has been the ground of the experience [of the sequence of A to B] itself."

What does Hume need in order to find that A is the cause of B? For though he challenges the common and the metaphysical interpretation of 'cause', he certainly knows how to use it in experience, and he tells us how we do and should use it in order to avoid mistakes that would damage us in practical life.

He needs (a) to know that some impression I is an impression of (or evidence for) an event and not of a state of affairs (like the side of a house); and (b) to find some other impression I' which regularly precedes I and is likewise the impression of an event.[5] Task (b) is the inductive task, and Kant accedes to Hume's arguments in respect to how it is carried out and what the limitations upon it are. But to accomplish (a), Hume has to be able to decide which of the various impressions are impressions of objective events. He never discussed this problem; no one before Kant even saw that it was a problem. Kant's thesis is that (a) can be accomplished only if we accept the rule that representations are to be taken as representations of events only if the representations are already thought to have an order fixed by events which are themselves in a fixed temporal order—even if our thought about the specific order be in fact incorrect. (For the Analogies are regulative principles, not constitutive; they tell us where and when to look for causes and substances, and do not guarantee that we will discover them in specific cases.) To return now to our logical pattern:

K. "Everything that happens, that is, begins to be, presupposes something upon which it follows by rule." (Kant's Second Analogy).

P. Events can be distinguished from objective enduring states of affairs, even though our apprehension of each is serial (the accomplishment of Hume's task [a]).

H. Among events, we find empirically some pairs of similar ones which tend to be repeated, and we then make the inductive judgment: events like the first members of the pairs are causes of events like the second (the accomplishment of Hume's task [b]).

P implies K. by the arguments of the Second Analogy, which give a sufficient reason for K. H implies P, since if events cannot be distinguished, pairs of events cannot be found, and thus P is a necessary condition of H. Hence: H implies P and P implies K, therefore H implies K. That is Kant's answer to Hume.

---

[5] It is one of the merits of Mrs. Schipper's article that she argues that Hume and Kant are not using "experience" in the same sense; but she carries this point, in my opinion, too far, in arguing that Kant's analysis applies only to scientific, not to "familiar experience." It would have been better for her to argue that Hume has not yet reached "familiar experience" in which he could distinguish events from enduring states of affairs solely on the basis of the (subjective) association of ideas.

JEFFRIE G. MURPHY

4. Kant's Second Analogy as an Answer to Hume

In a recent article (*Ratio*, June 1967; reprinted above), Professor Lewis White Beck has argued that Kant's long-sought "answer to Hume" on causality is to be found in that section of the *Critique of Pure Reason* entitled "The Second Analogy," specifically at A 195-6 = B 240-1.[1] Beck makes a persuasive case for reading the Second Analogy as an argument addressed to Hume's problem but is, I think, quite wrong in suggesting that its argument provides a non question-begging answer to Hume. Indeed, the view ascribed by Beck to Kant has the very fault that Beck finds in other interpretations: it presupposes rather than demonstrates.

The issue between Kant and Hume may be viewed in the following terms: is our knowledge of causality susceptible to a wholly empirical analysis? Hume argues that it is. Causation is a concept analysable in terms of event-impressions. When event-impressions stand in certain associated relationships with each other (contiguity, priority, etc.) we say that they are causally connected. This, according to Hume, exhausts the meaning of 'cause.' Kant disagrees and, in the manner suggested by Beck, he attempts a very subtle sabotage of Hume's empiricist analysis. For the question never raised by Hume (though he presupposed an answer to it) is the following: How do we identify an impression as an event-impression? Not all impressions are event-impressions (an impression of a house or any other *thing* is not, for example), so how is the distinction drawn? Hume must suppose that the distinction is simply given. Thus if Kant can show that the distinction is not given, but rather can be drawn only through the application of conceptual criteria, then he has shown that no wholly empirical analysis of causation is possible or, in his own idiom, that empirical association has a transcendental ground. As Beck remarks:

> What does Hume need in order to find that A is the cause of B? . . . He needs (a) to know that some impression I is an impression of (or evidence for) an event and not a state of affairs (like the side of a house); and (b) to find some impression I' which regularly precedes I and is likewise the impression of an event. . . . But to accomplish (a), Hume has to be able to decide which of the various impressions are impressions of objective events. He never discussed this problem; no one before Kant even saw that it was a problem. Kant's thesis is that (a) can be accomplished only if we accept the rule that representations are already thought to have an order fixed by events which are themselves in a fixed temporal order.

Reprinted by permission of the author and the publisher, Basil Blackwell, from Jeffrie G. Murphy, "Kant's Second Analogy as an Answer to Hume," *Ratio* vol. 11, no. 1 (June 1969): 75-78. Footnotes included.

[1] Beck develops a similar argument in his article "The Second Analogy and the Principle of Indeterminancy," *Kant-Studien*, Band 57, Heft 1-3, 1966, pp. 199-205.

The question, then, is simply this: Is our ability to identify an impression as an event-impression intuitive or discursive?[2] Can we immediately recognize an impression as an event-impression, or do we have to apply some conceptual criteria for such identification? Hume supposes the former and Kant argues for the latter. Kant's answer to Hume then consists in an attempt to demonstrate that the identification of an impression as an event-impression involves the application of a rule or criterion and that this rule just is the schematized category of causation.

This is a remarkably subtle attempt to avoid question-begging against Hume. But it is, alas, only an attempt—not a success. For Kant, in providing his own explication of what it is like for the category of causality to apply in experience, has to rely upon our having just that ability the existence of which is incompatible with his attempted answer to Hume—namely, an ability to immediately recognize an impression as an event-impression. Indeed, the very possibility of schematizing the category tacitly rests upon our having this intuitive ability.[3]

For what, according to Kant, is the manifestation of causality in experience? It is, he argues, the occurrence of an irreversible or determinate time order among perceptions. And to elaborate on this he tells, in the Second Analogy, his famous story about the difference between perceiving a ship sailing down a river (an event) and perceiving the side of a house (a thing). The former, though not the latter, manifests a determinate or irreversible time order.

But what does this less than transparent claim mean? I am inclined to think that, as Kant develops it, it means no more than the following: There is something characteristic of events that is not characteristic of non-events—namely, that if you reverse in imagination the order of perceptions of an event you will *just see* that you have thereby imagined a different event! Thus our ability to understand the schematism of causality, our ability to understand what Kant means by an irreversible time order, presupposes our ability to recognize immediately the difference between one event and another. If we lacked this ability, we would be in

---

[2] In drawing an intuitive-discursive or given-conceptual contrast, I have in mind something like the following: Some terms we are able to apply to the world on the basis of immediate perceptual inspection. Other terms require, for their application, a procedure or criterion which has to be *gone through*. 'White' is an example of a term of the first sort 'guilty' an example of a term of the latter sort. The issue between Kant and Hume can then be put in this way: Hume believes that 'event' is a term of the first sort, Kant that it is a term of the second sort. Both Kant and Hume probably believed that distinctions of this kind are less variable than they indeed are.

[3] Kant believes, for certain systematic reasons, that we are unable to apply a category to experience without knowing those 'marks' manifested in experience which render the application of the category appropriate. A principle which states necessary and sufficient 'marks' for the application of a category is the *schema* of that category. A somewhat crude way of putting this is to say that Kant feels that any complex relational concept, though not itself ostensibly teachable (you cannot point to a cause, for example), is teachable only by relating it to concepts which are ostensibly teachable. Kant, if he is to answer Hume, must deny that 'event' is ostensibly teachable. But, if he is to explain the application of causality to experience, he must suppose that 'event' is ostensibly teachable. For an elaboration of the view that the Schematism section functions as an attempt to argue that two sorts of rules are necessary for teaching and applying concepts ('referential' and 'nonreferential' rules), see Stephan Körner's *Kant*, Chapter Four (Pelican Books, 1955).

no position even to appreciate the difference between the house example and the ship example. But this is just the ability which the empiricist, must deny we have. He seems caught in the very kind of trap he set for Hume.

Indeed Kant's argument in the Second Analogy, at least if viewed as an attempt to provide a criterion for the identification of events, is astonishingly and uncharacteristically feeble. He says again and again[4] that, when our perceptions are of an event, we *cannot* reverse the order of these perceptions in imagination. But he never tells his reader exactly what he takes the force of this modal operator to be. Presumably such imaginative reversal is something that we are psychologically *capable* of doing, and thus the "cannot" must simply mean "cannot without thereby imagining a different event." Irreversible time sequence, as a criterion for the identification of events, is thus hopeless circular.[5]

I do not mean to deny, of course, that events do have a determinate or irreversible time order. All I want to deny is that this order functions as a criterion for the *identification* of events as events, that provides us with a technique enabling us to do something we would be unable to do without it. It fails in this function simply because we cannot understand what Kant means by an irreversible time order unless we already are able to identify events, unless we already are quite at home with the application of event language to the world. In pointing out that all events have a determinate or irreversible temporal order, Kant makes a valuable point in the conceptual analysis of 'event'. But this does not allow him to make the genetic supposition that one would have to *know* this analysis *before* one would be in a position to identify events as events.[6] One might as well make the claim that no one is in a position to make any true statements about material objects until an adequate philosophical analysis of material object statements is developed. But since Hume's analysis of causality does not commit him to an *analysis* of 'event', but only to the claim that we are able to immediately *recognize* certain impressions as event-impressions, Kant's own analysis (however useful on other grounds) is beside this point.[7]

---

[4] For example: "In an appearance which contains a happening (the preceding state of the perception we may call A, and the succeeding B) B *can* be apprehended only as following upon A; the perception of A *cannot* follow upon B but only precede it" (A 192 = B 237). And immediately following: "It is *impossible* that in the apprehension of this appearance the ship should first be perceived lower down the stream and afterwards higher up."

[5] Beck's own formulation of the principle of the Second Analogy preserves this circularity: "Everything that *happens*, that is, begins to be, presupposes something upon which it follows by rule." The principle contains the very locution for which it is supposed to provide the criterion of application.

[6] If Kant has one characteristic fault, it is his tendency to fail to see a difference between a logical analysis and a genetic psychological claim—i.e. a claim that we have to know a certain principle *before* we can make a certain discrimination. This tendency is preserved in Beck's genetic formulation of what is wrong with Hume's analysis: 'What does Hume *need* in order to *find* that A is the cause of B? . . . Kant's thesis is that (this) can be accomplished. . . .' Or, even more obviously, in his *Kant-Studien* paper: 'Hence in supposing that we observe sequences of events and *then* [Beck's emphasis] come to know by generalization that the earlier event is the cause of the latter, Hume put the cart before the horse' (p. 201).

[7] In commenting on this paper, Professor Beck has pointed out that Kant speaks of reversal in *apprehension* whereas I speak of reversal in *imagination*. But this correction will not save Kant's argument. If I am apprehending a ship sailing down a river, could I apprehend it

moving upstream? If I am apprehending a house from basement to roof, could I apprehend it from roof to basement? I still do not see an interesting difference. Could I *at the same time?*: the answer to both is *no*. Could I *at some different time?*: the answer to both is *yes*. Of course if I *describe* what I am apprehending as "a ship sailing down a river," then it is obviously false (because *analytically* false) that I could at any other time see *just this* in reverse order. But this is so for uninteresting tautological reasons—namely, that if P has a determinate order built into its very description, then it is analytically true that my apprehension of P is irreversible. But Kant wants the necessity of the causal principle to be *synthetic*.

L. W. BECK

5. Rejoinder to Professor Murphy

Professor Jeffrey Murphy has mounted a strong counterattack on my formulation of Kant's "answer to Hume." But inasmuch as he confesses, in his second paragraph, that Hume 'presupposed an answer' to a question he never explicitly raised, Mr. Murphy cannot claim more than a draw, since his accusation at the beginning of his paper is that Kant presupposed and did not demonstrate an answer to the same question. If Murphy is correct, we are back where Mrs. Schipper and Miss Williams left the problem, viz., with a Hume-presupposition vs. a Kant-presupposition.

But Murphy is actually intent upon making a more damaging attack on Kant than this. His accusation that Kant begs the question does not, in fact, accurately give voice to his real complaint. For his paper as a whole does not accuse Kant of begging the question, but of using an exclusively Humean concept in the construction of his own anti-Humean argument. A *petitio principii* has the logical merit of self-consistency. Murphy is actually saying that Kant's argument is inconsistent because it has a Humean premise. He thus tries to turn my argument that Hume was using a Kantian premise.

Murphy says there are two concepts of events: an intuitive and a discursive one. Hume uses the former, having never thought of the alternative. Kant denies the former, having nevertheless used it. Here is Kant's alleged inconsistency. Murphy finds evidence of it in three places: in the schematism (end of his third paragraph), in the formulation of the Analogy in A (his footnote 5, the wording of which he erroneously attributed to me); and in the 'irreversibility criterion'. I think the first two are incorrect, but they are of little importance compared to the third, to which I shall confine myself here.

Murphy's argument may be put succinctly as follows. Any sequence of impressions may be imagined to occur in reverse order. If the original sequence was one of impressions of events, the reversed sequence is one of imagined impressions of another event which did not take place. If the original sequence was not one of

Reprinted by permission of the author and the publisher, Basil Blackwell, from L. W. Beck, "Rejoinder to Professors Murphy and Williams," *Ratio* vol. 11, no. 1 (June 1969): 82-86. Footnotes included.

I am grateful to my colleague Professor Robert L. Holmes for criticizing an earlier draft of this paper, but I do not wish him to be held accountable for any errors, weaknesses, or discourtesies which remain.

impressions of events, the reversed sequence is one of imagined impressions of a static state of affairs. There is nothing to guide us in the decision as to whether the reversed sequence is to be interpreted as a sequence of imagined impressions of an event which did not take place or of a static state of affairs, *except* a prior decision as to whether the original sequence was evidence of an event. That decision was made independently of the reversibility of the sequence. Hence reversibility-irreversibility is not a criterion for the distinction between state of affairs and event. The Humean concept of event (naive, intuitive) must have been used by Kant, therefore, in setting up his house-ship paradigm.

This is a beautifully ingenious argument. There are, in my opinion, only two things wrong with it: (a) it mislocates the problem; (b) in carrying it out, Murphy commits an *ignoratio elenchi.*

(a) At crucial stages in his argument Murphy speaks of "reverse . . . in imagination," whereas Kant *contrasts* the sequence of perceptions (apprehensions) with "the sequence that may occur solely in imagination" (B 234, lines 18-20 in Kemp Smith). Murphy writes that Kant "says again and again that, when our perceptions are of an event, we *cannot* reverse the order of these perceptions in imagination," but the two sentences he quotes in support of this statement do not even allude to imagination, and I recall none which supports his reading.

Kant's irreversibility criterion is applied to apprehension, not to imagination. I can *imagine* anything; the question is, what can I *see?* I can *imagine* the boat going downstream when I see it going upstream. I *cannot see* it going downstream when it is in fact going upstream. I can *imagine* seeing the roof before the basement and the basement before the roof; and—here is the difference—I can *see* the basement before the roof and the roof before the basement without saying that there are two houses. If I can see the boat first here and then there, and then there and subsequently here, I do say that there are two things, viz., two events.

It is hard to talk about irreversibility if we do not bring in the imagination. Every sequence is fixed, even the house-sequence, because any sequence whatsoever is unique. But, on the other hand, *every* sequence (and not merely the house-sequence) is reversible in imagination. Murphy is right, then, in arguing that reversibility in imagination is not criterial. But he is wrong in thinking that reversibility in imagination is Kant's criterion.

We have to ask which sequences are reversible *in apprehension.* We must do so by a counterfactual which is difficult to analyse, and neither Kant nor Hume contributed anything to its analysis. The interpolation of imagination does not materially lessen the difficulties. If it is difficult to analyse:

(1) Could I see y and then x when in fact I see x and then y?

it is no less difficult to analyse

(2) Could I imagine seeing y and then x, when in fact I imagine seeing x and then y?

whereas it is not difficult at all to analyse

(3) Could I imagine seeing y and then x when in fact I see x and then y?

Since (3) is not germane (as I have argued against Murphy), and since (1) and (2) are equally resistant to analysis (but equally easy to use if we do not demand utter logical transparency), the use of "imagine" in (2) does not significantly clarify the issue and gives us no reason to think (2) is clear and (1) is obscure. But whereas (2) and (3) can, I suppose, always be answered affirmatively even if, as Murphy acutely notices, the significance of an affirmative answer is not always the same (sometimes indicating a state of affairs, sometimes another event), (1) cannot be answered affirmatively when there is an event occurring. Hence only the first question is criterial.

We have to ask: Could I *see* this ship now here, now there? If the ship is moving downstream, no. Can I imagine it? Surely; I would be imagining another event which I cannot see, because it is not taking place. Could I *see* the roof and then the basement even if in fact I see the basement and then the roof? Yes, because nothing is happening except a change in me, moving my eyes. There is nothing happening in the house.

(b) It is at this stage of his argument that Murphy commits his *ignoratio elenchi.* He concludes that one must be able immediately to recognize the differ-ence (let us call it difference$_1$) between one event and another (the ship going upstream and the ship going downstream, regardless of whether one or both are imagined). But the question he is attempting to answer in the affirmative is stated as follows: Does one have the ability to recognize immediately (intuitively) one impression as an event-impression and another as a state-impression? Let us call the difference between these two impressions difference$_2$. From Murphy's conclusions that difference$_1$ is immediately recognized there follows nothing as to whether difference$_2$ is immediately recognized.

Moreover, I see no reason why Kant should not (and I think there is evidence that he does) think that difference$_1$ is immediately recognizable. Whatever categorial concepts and schematic apparatus and rules might be required to recog-nize difference$_2$, the recognition of difference$_1$ could be as immediate as (though perhaps requiring a longer time-span than) recognition of the difference between a battleship and a cruiser. The only difference between the sequence of impressions of the boat moving upstream and of the boat moving downstream is an empirical difference in the order in which specific impressions (actual or imaginary) do or can occur, and the difference$_1$ is surely given 'intuitively' and 'immediately'. But dif-ference$_2$ between either of these orders fixed in the apprehension or in the imagina-tion of an event and the order of state-impressions fixed in neither apprehension nor imagination is not found by inspection of the actual or imagined orders of the impression. In fact, one of the orders involved in difference$_1$ may be empirically identical with the order which has a difference$_2$ from it. Hence the immediacy of our recognition of difference$_2$.

At the end of his paper Professor Murphy issues a useful warning against confusing knowing how to use categorial concepts (such as 'event' and state') and knowing the analysis of such concepts. He charges Kant (and me) with ignoring the difference between them, and hence with confusing genetic and categorial consid-erations. The warning is well given. One would not accept any argument, such as Kant's allegedly is, which would keep us from saying that we *just see* the ship moving, if refusal to say we *just see* it move meant that one would have to infer, using a category and following a rule, that it is moving. I do not think, however, that Kant would refuse to say we *just see* it move (see A 195 = B 240, line 5 in

Kemp Smith). But *just see* does not mean *just apprehend,* any more than *just see* means *just have a sense datum. Just apprehend* means to receive passively a sequence of impressions and to hold them in consciousness. What must be added to the passive reception of a sequence of impressions in order to interpret some of them as event-impressions and others as state-impressions is what Kant was trying to determine. It is something for which Murphy and Hume see no need. In common, ordinary seeing of ships and houses, that there is an addendum to apprehension of sense-data, as if two events were taking place in the mind of the seer, is hard to discern and may be even hard to believe, and insistence that it be before consciousness of objects and events invites the confusion against which Murphy rightly warns us. It is precisely because it is hard to discern in ordinary cases of seeing that the analysis in my *Kant-Studien* paper to which Murphy alludes seemed to me to have some merit. For I was there concerned to show that in the uncommon observations of microphysics, knowledge of the rules and criteria does have a place in the very *genesis* of the difference between just seeing a cloud chamber and observing a microphysical event which cannot be *just seen* at all.

Suggested Readings for Part One

Aronson, Jerrold. "The Legacy of Hume's Analysis of Causation." *Studies in History and Philosophy of Science* 2 (1971): 135-56.

Beauchamp, Tom L.. "Hume's Two Theories of Causation." *Archiv für Geschichte der Philosophie* (1973-74).

Beauchamp, Tom L. and Mappes, Thomas. "Is Hume Really a Sceptic about Induction?" *American Philosophical Quarterly* 11 (1974).

Beck, L. W. "The Second Analogy and the Principle of Indeterminacy." *Kant-Studien* Band 57 (1966): 199-205.

Ducasse, C. J. *Causation and the Types of Necessity.* New York: Dover Publications, 1969, chapters 1, 3, 7.

Feigl, Herbert. "What Hume Might Have Said to Kant." In *The Critical Approach to Science and Philosophy,* edited by Mario Bunge. New York: Free Press of Glencoe, 1964, pp. 45-51.

Gotterbarn, Donald. "Hume's Two Lights on Cause." *Philosophical Quarterly* 21 (1971): 168-71.

Hausman, Alan, "Hume's Theory on Relations." *Nous* 1 (1967): 255-82.

Lesher, James H. "Hume's Analysis of 'Cause' and the 'Two Definitions' Dispute." *Journal of the History of Philosophy* 11 (1973): 387-92.

Livingston, D. "Hume on Ultimate Causation." *American Philosophical Quarterly* 8 (1971): 63-70.

Madden, Edward H. "Hume and the Fiery Furnace." *Philosophy of Science* 38 (1971): 64-78.

Robinson, J. A. "Hume's Two Definitions of 'Cause.' " *Philosophical Quarterly* 12 (1962). Reprinted in V. C. Chappell, *Hume.* Garden City, N.Y.: Doubleday & Company, 1966, pp. 129-47 with a "Reconsideration," pp. 162-68. The latter is a reply to Thomas J. Richards, "Hume's Two Definitions of 'Cause,' " pp. 148-61.

Schipper, E. W. "Kant's Answer to Hume's Problem." *Kant-Studien* Band 53
    (1961): 68-74.
Smith, Norman Kemp. *The Philosophy of David Hume.* New York: Macmillan
    Company, 1941, chapters 4, 12, 16-18.
Strawson, P. F. *The Bounds of Sense: An Essay on Kant's Critique of Pure Reason.*
    London, Eng.: Methuen and Company, 1966, Part 2, chapter 3, sections
    4-5.
Williams, M. E. "Kant's Reply to Hume." *Kant-Studien* Band 56 (1965): 71-78.

PART TWO

MODERN NECESSITY THEORIES

INTRODUCTION

Since Hume and Kant, philosophers have increasingly resisted analysis of causation in terms of objective necessity. Hume's attempted reduction of the objective content of causal relations to constant conjunctions has received wide acceptance and has been labeled the Regularity Theory. According to the Regularity Theory one never empirically observes a third thing (necessity) connecting a cause with its effect, and therefore each causal statement about an individual causal circumstance is logically tied to at least one general causal statement. For this reason singular causal statements are held to be analyzable in terms of the causal regularities or laws of nature of which they are instances. In this view, to regard an individual sequence as causal is to regard it as an instance of a general law, and to confirm that a sequence is causal is to confirm a causal law.

Since this theory requires that a logical connection be present between individual and general causal statements, it is easily identifiable as a *conceptual* version of Hume's *psychological* thesis that causal inference depends on a constant conjunction and mental association between ideas. The modern claim is that universality and not objective necessity is that which is central to the concept of cause and also that which is implicit in any use of causal terminology. The philosophical problem of causation has thus largely come to be interpreted in this regularity tradition as the problem of a proper analysis of causal laws. Regularity exponents analyze laws as true, contingent, universal generalizations which are omnispatially and omnitemporally unrestricted in scope. Purported necessary connections between the antecedent and consequent events described in the law are regarded as gratuitous.

William Kneale has provided the foremost recent challenge to this regularity account, as indicated in this part by his controversy with Karl Popper. Kneale argues that the only appropriate way to distinguish lawlike generalizations from mere universal generalizations of fact is by resorting to the notion of natural necessity. Kneale does not confine his attention to any one species of laws of nature, but his thesis is quite clearly intended to cover both causal laws in general and the Regularity Theory in particular. Nomological generalizations are properly expressed as modal statements, Kneale contends, while de facto universals are properly expressed as categorical statements. Defenders of the Regularity Theory have attempted to distinguish laws from non-laws by arguing that the former are expressed through universals of fact which are spatio-temporally unrestricted in scope, while the latter are merely universals of fact restricted to a limited range of instances. Kneale regards this device as insufficient. He agrees that laws are not established a priori and are not experientially certain, but he also contends that one of the essential functions of laws is to express a boundary on empirical possibility. If "All X's are followed by Y's" is a genuine nomological satement, then anyone who asserts the law thereby rules out as empirically impossible a situation where an X is not followed by a Y. For this reason Kneale concludes that generalizations of law express the factually necessary relation, "Whenever X, Y *must* ensue."

It is sometimes presumed that Kneale regards laws as "logical necessities somehow embodied in the structure of things," as Antony Flew once put it.* Kneale's view seems to be, however, that nomological necessity is *sui generis* and not to be confused with logical necessity. He does say that the *notion* of necessity used in both logic and natural science is the same—viz. "the notion of a situation without alternatives"—but causal laws are not said to be comparable to logical necessities in any other way. Laws assert connections that are weaker than logically necessary connections but stronger than mere contingent conjunctions. Kneale does not appear to challenge the Humean view that universal statements are either logically necessary or logically contingent. But he does contend that a distinction is to be drawn between two types of logically contingent universal statements, namely, (1) factual statements which express constant conjunctions and (2) nomological generalizations which express empirically necessary connections. Kneale regards this modal component as irreducible and as not further explicable, but he at least conceives it as the same type of necessary connection which Hume attempted to discredit and hence as an embarrassment to regularity analyses of causation.

Kneale's central argument for the non-Humean conception of laws exploits the notion of counterfactual conditional statements. The concept of lawlikeness, he alleges, is incompletely captured by reduction to universal statements of antecedent-consequent form, because this analysis fails to account satisfactorily for the way in which laws sustain counterfactuals. According to Kneale, Hume's analysis asserts that the unrestricted universal statement "All X's are followed by Y's" is translatable as "There is not an X which is not followed by a Y." This statement is exhaustively analyzable into a conjunction of three temporally distinct statements:

1. All past X's were followed by Y's.
2. All present X's are followed by Y's.
3. All future X's will be followed by Y's.

But, according to Kneale, the conjunction of these statements will not support the counterfactual "If an X were to occur, it would be followed by a Y." Yet this is precisely the sort of statement laws support. Kneale suggests that the nomological status accorded certain statements is not entirely dependent upon categorical statements of fact; indeed, the question whether true universal generalizations are nomological, as distinguished from merely accidental, is quite independent of the question of whether they categorically assert facts. For this purpose a modal terminology is needed to express the strong connection. Kneale concludes that the entailment of counterfactuals is a necessary condition of lawlikeness. Since Hume's analysis does not satisfy this condition, it is deficient at least in the ways the program set out by necessitarians is not. (A vigorous defense of Kneale against recent counterreplies is provided by George Molnar at the end of Part Three.)

Hume's Philosophy of Belief (London: Routledge & Kegan Paul, 1961), p. 135.

Sir Karl Popper largely agrees with some aspects of Kneale's polemic against the Regularity Theory but remains sympathetic to the latter and also unconvinced that philosophical concern over a correct definition of "natural necessity" is significant. A brief history of their discussion through 1961 is contained in section three of Kneale's second article, "Universality and Necessity." Prior to 1959 Popper was inclined to a basically Humean type of Regularity Theory. This position is represented in the first two articles by Popper. But, as Kneale points out, Popper seemed to concede in 1959 (in an Appendix to his *Logic of Scientific Discovery*— here entitled "Kneale and Natural Laws") that some stronger ingredient is needed to distinguish causal laws from accidental generalizations. The evolution of Popper's views, which have constantly been under Kneale's scrutiny, is especially instructive as an illustration of the difficulties involved in explaining the nature of scientific law while remaining sympathetic to the Regularity Theory. Popper never fully departs from this theory, and it is an urgent question in modern philosophy of causation whether his mediating position is a tenable one.

The substantial agreement between Kneale and Popper can perhaps best be understood by considering Tarski's account of *logical* necessity. A statement is logically necessary, according to Tarski, if and only if it is deducible from a statement function which is satisfied by every model. Such universally valid statement functions are true in all possible worlds. Popper formally defines the notion of natural necessity in a parallel fashion: a statement is naturally necessary if and only if it is deducible from a statement function which is satisfied by the class of worlds which differ from ours only by having different initial conditions. Such "universally valid" statements are true in all worlds which are members of this limited class. The "possible worlds" formula is a device used to exclude accidental universals. The latter statements are not naturally necessary because they are false in at least one of the possible worlds. The truth of a genuine law does not vary with changes in initial conditions, but the truth of an accidental generalization does. Kneale finds Popper's interpretation of natural necessity "acceptable," because "it connects the notion of natural law with that of validity for states of affairs other than the actual; . . . what holds for all possible worlds is obviously necessary."

Graham Nerlich and *W. A. Suchting* direct their arguments against Popper's formal definition of natural necessity. They argue that since Popper holds that laws are contingent and not logically necessary, he is committed to a position contrary to Kneale's; and they further contend that his definition is deficient in these two respects:

1. "It is at least verbally defective, . . . imposing no distinction on the class of universal propositions true of our world."

2. Either a revised version would be equivalent to a view which Popper wishes to reject or a revised version would involve circularity.

Popper accepts much of their argument but claims that he had largely anticipated such criticisms in the very work they use to criticize him. He also expresses some doubt—as does my interpretation—that they have correctly represented Kneale. He then attempts to provide a revised definition of natural necessity which is "less circular" than his original account. The final note by Popper indicates that he still is not satisfied with his efforts and that he is generally dissatisfied with attempts to define natural necessity despite his firm conviction that the idea is neither meaningless nor gratuitous.

In the end the issue between Kneale and Popper does not involve the propriety of employing the concept of "natural necessity" but only concerns how this notion is to be interpreted. Popper seems to draw the line at making laws logically stronger than mere universal generalizations (Hume effectively made them *psychologically* stronger), whereas Kneale seems to want the increased strength to reflect in addition the view that laws report necessities in nature. "Natural necessity" is thus for Kneale a primitive concept, one which cannot be illuminatingly reduced to other concepts or defined in terms of the notation of extensional logic. He also thinks we understand the nature of natural necessity, despite our inability to analyze it in terms of other concepts. (Perhaps one could say that for Kneale natural necessity is an irreducible, but causal category in our conceptual framework.) Popper, on the other hand, regards natural necessity as a notion that needs "rehabilitation" by logical analysis, and he continues to nourish the hope that some analysis may succeed. Until this analysis has been carried out, Popper seems to think we adequately understand that to which we refer when we "use the concept intuitively." [*Note:* A discussion of C. J. Ducasse's version of the Necessity Theory, and an alternative proposed by Edward Madden, are presented in Part Five.]

KARL POPPER

6. Causality, Explanation, and the Deduction of Predictions

To give a *causal explanation* of an event means to deduce a statement which describes it, using as premises of the deduction one or more *universal laws,* together with certain singular statements, the *initial conditions.* For example, we can say that we have given a causal explanation of the breaking of a certain piece of thread if we have found that the thread has a tensile strength of 1 *lb.* and that a weight of 2 *lbs.* was put on it. If we analyse this causal explanation we shall find several constituent parts. On the one hand there is the hypothesis: "Whenever a thread is loaded with a weight exceeding that which characterizes the tensile strength of the thread, then it will break"; a statement which has the character of a universal law of nature. On the other hand we have singular statements (in this case

Reprinted by permission of the author and the publisher from Karl Popper, *The Logic of Scientific Discovery* (London: Hutchinson & Co., sixth impression, 1972), Section 12. Footnotes included. (*The Logic of Scientific Discovery* was first published in 1934 as the German edition *Logik der Forschung.*) (The author suggests that reference should also be made to his *The Poverty of Historicism,* Sections 28 and 31.)

Note: Footnotes have been renumbered for the purposes of this text.

two) which apply only to the specific event in question: "The weight characteristic for this thread is 1 *lb.*," and "The weight put on this thread was 2 *lbs.*"[1]

We have thus two different kinds of statement, both of which are necessary ingredients of a complete causal explanation. They are (1) *universal statements, i.e.,* hypotheses of the character of natural laws, and (2) *singular statements,* which apply to the specific event in question and which I shall call "initial conditions." It is from universal statements in conjunction with initial conditions that we *deduce* the singular statement, "This thread will break." We call this statement a specific or singular *prediction.*[2]

The initial conditions describe what is usually called the *cause* of the event in question. (The fact that a load of 2 *lbs.* was put on a thread with a tensile strength of 1 *lb.* was the "cause" of its breaking.) And the prediction describes what is usually called the *effect.* Both these terms I shall avoid. In physics the use of the expression *causal explanation* is restricted as a rule to the special case in which the universal laws have the form of laws of "action by contact"; or more precisely, of *action at a vanishing distance,* expressed by differential equations. This restriction will not be assumed here. Furthermore, I shall not make any general assertion as to the universal applicability of this deductive method of theoretical explanation. Thus I shall not assert any *principle of causality* (or "principle of universal causation").

The "principle of causality" is the assertion that any event whatsoever *can* be causally explained—that it *can* be deductively predicted. According to the way in which one interprets the word "can" in this assertion, it will be either tautological (analytic), or else an assertion about reality (synthetic). For if "can" means that it is always logically possible to construct a causal explanation, then the assertion is tautological, since for any prediction whatsoever we can always find universal statements and initial conditions from which the prediction is derivable. (Whether these universal statements have been tested and corroborated in other cases is of course quite a different question.) If, however, "can" is meant to signify that the world is governed by strict laws, that it is so constructed that every specific event is an instance of a universal regularity or law, then the assertion is admittedly synthetic. But in this case it is *not falsifiable,* as will be seen later, in section 78. I shall, therefore, neither adopt nor reject the "principle of causality"; I shall be content simply to exclude it, as "metaphysical," from the sphere of science.

I shall, however, propose a methodological rule which corresponds so closely to the "principle of causality" that the latter might be regarded as its metaphysical version. It is the simple rule that we are not to abandon the search for universal laws and for a coherent theoretical system, nor ever give up our attempts

---

[1] A clearer analysis of this example—and one which distinguishes *two* laws as well as two initial conditions—would be the following: "For every thread of a given structure S (determined by its material, thickness, etc.) there is a characteristic weight w, such that the thread will break if any weight exceeding w is suspended from it."—"For every thread of the structure S_1, the characteristic weight w_1 equals 1 *lb.*" These are the two universal laws. The two initial conditions are, "This is a thread of structure S_1," and, "The weight to be put on this thread is equal to 2 *lbs.*"

[2] The term "prediction," as used here, comprises statements about the past ("retrodictions"), or even "given" statements which we wish to explain (*explicanda*); *cf.* my *Poverty of Historicism,* 1945, p. 133 of the edition of 1957, and the *Postscript,* section *15.

to explain causally any kind of event we can describe.[3] This rule guides the scientific investigator in his work. The view that the latest developments in physics demand the renunciation of this rule, or that physics has now established that within one field at least it is pointless to seek any longer for laws, is not accepted here.[4]

---

[3] The idea of regarding the principle of causality as the expression of a rule or of a decision is due to H. Gomperz, *Das Problem der Willensfreiheit*, 1907. *Cf.* Schlick, *Die Kausalität in der gegenwartigen Physik, Naturwissenschaften* 19, 1931, p. 154.

*I feel that I should say here more explicitly that the decision to search for causal explanation is that by which the theoretician adopts his aim—or the aim of theoretical science. His aim is to find *explanatory theories* (if possible, *true* explanatory theories); that is to say, theories which describe certain structural properties of the world, and which permit us to deduce, with the help of initial conditions, the effects to be explained. It was the purpose of the present section to explain, if only very briefly, what we mean by causal explanation. A somewhat fuller statement will be found in appendix *x, and in my *Postscript*, section *15. My explanation of explanation has been adopted by certain positivists or "instrumentalists" who saw in it an attempt to explain it away—as the assertion that explanatory theories are *nothing but* premises for deducing predictions. I therefore wish to make it quite clear that I consider the theorist's interest in *explanation*—that is, in discovering explanatory theories—as irreducible to the practical technological interest in the deduction of predictions. The theorist's interest in *predictions*, on the other hand, is explicable as due to his interest in the problem whether his theories are true; or in other words, as due to his interest in testing his theories—in trying to find out whether they cannot be shown to be false. See also appendix *x, note 4 and text.

[4] The view here opposed is held for example by Schlick; he writes, *op. cit.* p. 155: "... this impossibility ..." (he is referring to the impossibility of exact prediction maintained by Heisenberg) "... means that it is impossible to *search for* that formula." (*Cf.* also note 1 to section 78.)

KARL POPPER

7. A Note on Natural Laws and So-called "Contrary-to-fact Conditionals"

I

In this note I wish to show that a certain argument concerning natural laws and their logical import is invalid. The argument in question can be summarised as follows.

Natural laws may be written simply as universal statements, such as "All planets move in ellipses." But if we formulate them in this form, then we do not give full expression to what is meant—we do not fully cover our *use* of natural laws. If we wish to give some expression to their logical peculiarities, we should rather write something like "All planets must move in ellipses" or "Planets can move only in ellipses" or "Planets necessarily move in ellipses"; in any case, we should indicate that natural laws are *logically stronger* than ordinary universal statements; an ordinary universal statement always follows from the natural law, and it can replace the natural law for many purposes, but it is not equal in logical strength to the law and should be distinguished from it.

This contention is supported by pointing out that, if we admit *subjunctive conditionals* into the language in which a natural law is formulated, we can see intuitively that a certain type of subjunctive conditionals follows from natural laws, while we can also see that the corresponding subjunctive conditionals do not follow from such universal statements which do not express natural laws. Accordingly, so runs the argument, natural laws are logically stronger than mere universal statements, and their superior logical strength should somehow be expressed in their linguistic formulation.

An example of a subjunctive conditional which follows intuitively from the natural law expressed by "All planets move in ellipses" is "If the moon were a planet, she would move in an ellipse."

An example of a universal statement from which the corresponding conditional does not follow is: "All my friends know French." For we cannot deduce from this the statement: "If Confucius were a friend of mine, then he would speak French."

In order to bring out the difference between the two types of universal statements, we might feel inclined to change the formulation of the second type rather than the first, and write "All my friends happen to speak French." But even this way of writing would indicate that the difference between the two types is a

Reprinted by permission of the author and the publisher from Karl Popper, "A Note on Natural Laws and So-called 'Contrary-to-Fact Conditionals,' " *Mind* vol. 58, no. 229 (January 1949): 62-66. Footnotes included.

Note: Footnotes have been renumbered for the purposes of this text.

modal one, the first type being more necessary than the second (even though perhaps not logically necessary), the second less necessary and more "accidental."[1]

The whole argument may be summed up by saying that a non-modal or extensional language is incapable of doing justice to the logical peculiarity of natural laws as distinct from those other universal statements which, in spite of their universal form, state a more or less "accidental" fact.

II

Before criticising the above arguments, I shall try to strengthen it. Take the following statement:

> (2.0) "All planets in our planetary system move round the sun in the same direction."

This statement can be interpreted (1) as a law of nature, expressing, say, that planets in a planetary system *can only* move in one direction, or (2) as stating an accidental fact. If we interpret it in the first way, we obtain from it

> (2.1) "If the moon (or any other body you may choose) were a planet in our own planetary system, then it would move round the sun in the same direction as the others."

If, however, we interpret (2.0) in the second way, then we cannot deduce (2.1); for we would have to say, on the contrary, that the following statement (2.2) is compatible with (2.0), if (2.0) is so interpreted:

> (2.2) "It is possible that a body (the moon, for example) may become a planet in our planetary system, and yet not move in the same direction as the others."

This shows that (2.0) can be interpreted in two different ways, or that it means two different things, according to whether we intend it as a formulation, either of a natural law, or of a merely accidental fact. But since to these two meaning of (2.0) correspond two different logical forces—one stronger, one weaker—we should choose formulations which make this difference apparent; and for this, we need a modal or non-extensional language which contains such words as "necessarily" or "accidentally."

III

I now proceed to my criticism. It is very simple. I assert that the difference in logical force is only apparent.

From a statement like

"All men are mortal"

or

> (3.0) "All *A*'s are *B*'s"

---

[1] *Cp.* F. L. Will; "The Contrary-to-Fact-Conditional," *Mind*, N.S., vol. lvi, pp. 236ff.

we can always deduce the indicative conditional

"If x is one of the A's then x is one of the B's."

We can also deduce the subjunctive conditional

(3.1) "If x were one of the A's then x would be one of the B's."

But we can never deduce

(3.2) "If x were added to the A's, then it would be one of the B's."
("Added to" is here intended to express some operation corresponding to the class-addition $\left\{x\right\}$ + A.")

Nor can we deduce the indicative correlate of (3.2).

The argument developed in (I) looks convincing; but it is not, because it merely shows that statements of the type (3.1) follow from natural laws, while statements of the type (3.2) do not follow from the more "accidental" type of universal propositions. But this is trivial.

That it is indeed this mistake which we made can be easily seen. From "All my friends speak French" we cannot deduce "If Confucius were a friend of mine, then he would speak French," because this latter statement means: "If Confucius were to join, or to be added to, the people whom I call my friends, then . . ."; that is to say, it is of the type (3.2). But the following statement, of the type (3.1), could of course be deduced "If Confucius were identical with one of (those here referred to as) my friends, then he would speak French."

Similarly, we can now see that, from "All planets move in ellipses," we can of course deduce "If the moon were a planet, it would move in an ellipse." (For this means: "If the moon were one of the planets, or belonging to the class of planets, then. . . .") But we cannot deduce "If we extend the class of things covered by the name "planet" so as to include the moon, then she would move in an ellipse."

We thus find that we made a mistake because we neglected the extensional or class-aspect of our terms; we did not see that, in the cases of type (3.1), we kept our terms extensionally constant, while in the case of type (3.2) we assumed that the extension of our terms may vary (which is, of course, impermissible in extensional logic).

This explains also our examples in (II). The two interpretations of the statement (2.0) turn out to be merely two interpretations of the term "planets of our planetary system." In the first case, we interpret this to cover all physical bodies satisfying a certain condition—say, that they move in ellipses round the sun. In the second interpretation, we interpret the same term to cover a certain limited collection of particular physical bodies (also moving in ellipses). No wonder that our second statement turns out to be logically weaker. The two interpretations can be given in an extensional language as follows:

(2.01) All solar systems constituted similar to our own (including those with more planets in them) are such that all planets move in the same direction.

(2.02) In our own solar system, all those bodies which we now call "planets" move in the same direction.

Clearly, (2.01) is stronger than (2.02); and clearly, from (2.01) we can deduce what would happen if we would introduce a new planet, while from (2.02) we cannot deduce what would happen in such a case.

IV

One can also explain the position as follows.

The terms ("A"; "B"; etc.) which enter into (1) a universal law are never defined by enumeration of the elements which belong to them; this is what makes the law "*strictly universal.*" On the other hand, the corresponding terms of (2) an "accidental" universal statement are either defined by enumeration of their elements, or can be so defined; statements of this kind are only "*numerically universal.*" Accordingly, the phrase

"If x were an A . . ."

can be interpreted (1) if "A" is a term in a strictly universal law, to mean "If x has the property A . . ." (but it *can* also be interpreted in the way described under (2)); and (2), if "A" is a term in an "accidental" or numerically universal statement, it *must* be interpreted "If x is identical with one of the elements of A." If the phrase is thus interpreted, we may deduce in both cases subjunctive conditionals from the universal statements. If, however, we interpret the phrase in the second case qualitatively, as we are permitted to do in the first, then we simply change the extension, and therefore the meaning of our term (committing what classical logic called a fallacy of ambiguity). No wonder that we find that the resulting inference is invalid, and that we can establish this fact by counterexamples.

Thus it seems that a reference to a fallacy described by Aristotle can solve this modern riddle.

We can also say: there is no need to admit that the two types of statements are different in import or in logical form, except in the structure of their *terms* which, in the case of natural laws, may be called "strictly universal (or qualitative or perhaps intensional) terms," and, in the case of numerically universal statements, "numerically universal (or enumerative or individual or singular or particular or perhaps extensional) terms." The ambiguity in question arises from using the same expression as a name for terms of both kinds.

All this leads up to the suggestion that the following is a valid rule of inference for a language L_1 containing ordinary universal statements as well as subjunctive conditionals (which, we assume, do not imply that the antecedent is false, but leave this question open).

A statement like

"All A's are B's"

or the equivalent statement

"For all x: if x is an A then x is a B"

is logically equivalent with, or mutually deducible from,

"For all x: if x were an A, then x would be a B."

Accordingly, we can deduce from each of these for any y (whether variable or constant)

"If y were an A, then y would be a B."

(In all these cases, "x is an A" is to be taken, of course, as equivalent to "x is identical with one of the elements of A.")

If our analysis is correct, then there is no need to operate with subjunctive conditionals, since a universalised subjunctive conditional is equivalent to an ordinary universal statement.

V

In a previous publication,[2] I have expressed the view that natural laws are statements which may be characterised as (a) introduced by the often suppressed phrase "For all (finite) regions of space and periods of time," (b) not containing any reference to any singular or particular thing or event or space-time region, and (c) stating that things or events of a certain kind (e.g. two planets moving in different directions round a central body) do not occur. This characterisation is intended to insure the "qualitative" or non-numerical character of strictly universal statements.

I do not think that the discussion of the so-called "contrary to fact conditional" has so far brought to light reasons for modifying this view. But it may be useful and, for some purposes, necessary to assume a general principle stating that every kind of event that is compatible with the accepted natural laws does in fact occur in some (finite) space-time region.

[2] Cp. my Logik der Forschung, sections 13 to 16; see also my Poverty of Historicism II, p. 121 (Economica, N.S., vol. xi.)

WILLIAM KNEALE

8. *Natural Laws and Contrary-to-fact Conditionals*

In *Analysis* 10.3 (January 1950) Mr. Pears argues against the view that the possibility of deriving contrary-to-fact conditionals from statements of natural law shows the latter to be something different from universal material implications of the form:

$$(x) \cdot \phi(x) \supset \psi(x)$$

It is true, he says, that a singular contrary-to-fact conditional cannot be deduced from a universal material implication, but that is only because the former implies that its antecedent is false, whereas the latter says nothing either way about that antecedent considered in itself: on the contrary, "the impossibility of deducing its purely hypothetical element (interpreted truth-functionally) from its parent general hypothetical ... is in fact an illusion ... produced by concealing the universal

Reprinted by permission of the author and the publisher, Basil Blackwell, from William Kneale, "Natural Laws and Contrary-to-Fact Conditionals," *Analysis* vol. 10, no. 6 (June 1950): pp. 121-25.

reference of the parent general hypothetical." In support of this assertion he cites a note by Professor Popper in *Mind* LVIII (January 1949) [reprinted immediately above].

If contrary-to-fact conditionals were of the form:

$$\sim \phi(a) \cdot \phi(a) \supset \psi(a)$$

what Mr. Pears says would obviously be correct. But one of the concerns of those who have recently raised the problem of contrary-to-fact conditionals is precisely to deny the sufficiency of the analysis which Mr. Pears seems to accept in his parenthetical remark. And in order to see the queerness of that analysis we need only reflect that the formula given above follows from '$\sim \phi(a)$' as sole premiss. Surely a man who says "If this bird were a raven, it would be black" thinks, and thinks rightly, that he is saying more than "This bird is not a raven." If we want to use the notion of material implication in explaining what he means, we must suppose that his remark contains an implicit reference to a *universal* material implication. That is to say, we must offer some such analysis as:

$$\sim \phi(a) \cdot (x) \cdot \phi(x) \supset \psi(x)$$

If this interpretation were correct, a contrary-to-fact conditional would indeed follow from the negation of its antecedent taken together with a universal material implication of the appropriate kind; for it would be just a conjunction of those two premisses. But the second interpretation seems to me no better than the first. I do not want to dwell here on the falsity of the suggestion that a precisely formulated universal material implication can be derived from every contrary-to-fact conditional; for this difficulty might perhaps be removed by putting the reference in a vaguer form. My main reason for dissatisfaction is that I cannot see the relevance of any material implication to the proposition we are trying to analyse. In order to explain my point I shall consider Professor Popper's account of the matter.

In the note mentioned by Mr. Pears Professor Popper says that the difficulties of persons like myself arise from failure to notice the difference between terms which can be defined extensionally and those which cannot be so defined. It is true, he says, that "All my friends speak French" does not entail "If Confucius were one of my friends he would speak French," but that is because anyone who utters the first statement is thinking of the class of his friends as closed, whereas anyone who utters the second statement is thinking of the class of his friends as open. In other words, the expression "my friends" is not used in quite the same way in the two sentences. When, however, it is said that sentences which purport to state natural laws are equivalent to universal material implications, it is to be understood that the terms involved are not mere substitutes for lists of proper names but unrestricted descriptions. And once this distinction has been made clear, there cannot, he maintains, be any serious objection to saying that statements of natural law are equivalent to universal material implications. For a universal material implication in which the terms are unrestricted descriptions does indeed allow inference to contrary-to-fact conditionals.

In this argument Professor Popper seems to assume, like Mr. Pears, that a contrary-to-fact conditional is of the form:

$$\sim \phi(a) \cdot \phi(a) \supset \psi(a)$$

But I am not concerned now with that difficulty. My present purpose is to point out that universal material implications have no relevance to contrary-to-fact conditionals. In order to make this clear it is important to consider a suitable example phrased in ordinary speech.

When we see the formula:

$$(x) \cdot \text{raven}\ (x) \supset \text{black}\ (x)$$

we commonly read it to ourselves as though it were an abbreviation of the statement:

Anything, if it is raven, is black.

Now the second expression has indeed the logical form of a suggestion of law; for the word 'if' and the timeless present are well-known devices for the formulation of laws. But to get an accurate rendering of the original formula into ordinary English we should first transform it into the equivalent formula:

$$\sim (\exists\ x) \cdot \text{raven}\ (x) \cdot \sim \text{black}\ (x)$$

and then read this as an abbreviation for:

There has never been a raven that was not black, and there will never be a raven that is not black.

This rendering, with its explicit distinction of times, has the merit of not containing any expressions which beg the question at issue, and I think it will be agreed that it does not look very like a statement of law. But let us examine it in more detail.

Clearly the second part, which refers to the future, has no special interest for a man who wonders whether in certain conditions which did not in fact obtain there would have been ravens that were not black. Is the first part any more useful to him? Surely not. For there is no incompatibility between this and the suggestion that if ravens had been tempted to live in a very snowy region they would have produced descendants that were white although still recognizably ravens. The fact, if it is a fact, that no ravens have lived in very snowy regions may be only an accident of history, and so too the fact, if it is a fact, that there has never been a raven that was not black. But to say this is just to say that, even if (*per impossibile*) we could know the second fact, we should still not be entitled to assert such a contrary-to-fact conditional as "If some inhabitants of snowy regions were ravens, they would be black."

Philosophers who treat suggestions of law as universal material implications say in effect that there is no sense in talking of historical accidents on the cosmic scale. According to their account of the matter there are only two possibilities to be considered: either (i) it is a law of nature that all ravens are black, or (ii) there has been or will be somewhere at some time a raven that was not or is not black. For if they are right, the first of these is just the contradictory of the second, and any one who tries to deny both at once abandons the principle of the excluded middle. Perhaps Professor Popper has this in mind when he says at the end of his note: "It may be useful and, for some purposes, necessary to assume a general principle stating that every kind of event that is compatible with the accepted natural laws does in fact occur in some (finite) space-time region." But if so, he does not go far enough. The principle to which he refers cannot be for him a mere assumption which we may find it useful or necessary to adopt for certain purposes. It is a direct consequence of his thesis that statements of law are universal material implications; and if it is unplausible, so too is that thesis. I shall offer two examples from different fields to show that the principle is inconsistent with our ordinary view of natural laws.

It is at least conceivable that there has never been a chain reaction of plutonium within a strong steel shell containing heavy hydrogen, and it is also conceivable that there never will be. But in order to accept these two suggestions we need not suppose that there is a law of nature excluding such events. The fact, if it is a fact, that none has occurred in the past may be explained satisfactorily by the extreme improbability of the occurrence of suitable conditions without human planning; and the fact, if it is fact, that none will occur in the future may be explained by the prevalence of a belief that such an event would have disastrous consequences.

Again, let us suppose that a musician composes an intricate tune in his imagination while he is lying on his death bed too feeble to speak or write, and that he says to himself in his last moments "No human being has ever heard or will ever hear this tune," meaning by "this tune" a certain complex pattern of sounds which could be described in general terms. Obviously he does not think of his remark as a suggestion of natural law. It is, of course, irrelevant to my argument whether any musician has ever made or will ever make such a remark correctly. For my purpose it is sufficient that we can conceive an unrestrictedly universal material implication without regarding it as a statement of law. In short, we do not ordinarily believe that every natural possibility must be realized somewhere at some time.

What I have said about universal material implications of the kind Professor Popper considers has an obvious bearing on the problem of confirmation. Let us return once more to the formula:

$$(x) \cdot \text{raven} (x) \supset \text{black} (x)$$

Clearly this is equivalent to a conjunction of the three sentences:

(1) There has never been an observed raven that was not black.

(2) There has never been an unobserved raven that was not black.

(3) There will never be a raven that is not black.

For to obtain these three sentences we need only subdivide the first of the two assertions discussed in an earlier paragraph. Now statement (1) above is very well confirmed by the evidence at our disposal. And so this evidence may perhaps be said to provide confirmation for the conjunction of (1), (2) and (3), but only in the sense in which the fact that it is raining provides some confirmation for the conjunctive statement that it is raining and the moon is made of green cheese. When we wish to make inferences to the unobserved, (2) and (3) are the only parts of our triple assertion that can be of any use to us as premisses. But neither of these is more reliable merely because it belongs to a conjunction which has been confirmed in the Pickwickian sense just mentioned. We do, of course, think that suggestions of law may be confirmed in a useful way by observed facts, but that is only because our notion of confirmation is bound up with a policy of trying to find laws which are not merely universal material implications.

KARL POPPER

9. Kneale and Natural Laws

My present treatment of [Kneale's] problem differs, intuitively, from a version previously published.[1] I think that it is a considerable improvement, and I gladly acknowledge that I owe this improvement, in a considerable measure, to Kneale's criticism. Nevertheless, from a more technical (rather than an intuitive) point of view the changes are slight. For in that paper, I operate (a) with the idea of natural laws, (b) with the idea of conditionals which *follow* from natural laws; but (a) and (b) together have the same extension as N [a name of the class of statements which are necessarily true, in the sense of natural or physical necessity; that is to say, true whatever the initial conditions may be]. . . . (c) I suggest that "subjunctive conditionals" are those that follow from (a), i.e., are just those of the class (b). And (d) I suggest (in the last paragraph) that we may have to introduce the supposition that all logically possible initial conditions (and therefore all events and processes which are compatible with the laws) are somewhere, at some time, realized in the world; which is a somewhat clumsy way of saying more or less what I am saying now with the help of the idea of all worlds that differ (if at all) from our world only with respect to the initial conditions.[2]

My position of 1949 might indeed be formulated with the help of the following statement. Although our world may not comprise all logically possible worlds, since worlds of another structure—with different laws—may be logically possible, it comprises all physically possible worlds, in the sense that all physically possible initial conditions are realized in it—somewhere, at some time. My present view is that it is only too obvious that this metaphysical assumption may possibly be true—in both senses of "possible"—but that we are much better off without it.

Yet once this metaphysical assumption is adopted, my older and my present views become (except for purely terminological differences) equivalent, as far as *the status of laws* is concerned. Thus my older view is, if anything, more "metaphysical" (or less "positivistic") than my present view, even though it does not make use of the *word* "necessary" in describing the status of laws.

Reprinted by permission of the author and publisher from Karl Popper, *The Logic of Scientific Discovery* (London: Hutchinson & Co., sixth impression, 1972), Sections 14-16 of Appendix X, pp. 436-39. Footnotes included.

Note: Footnotes have been renumbered for the purposes of this text.

[1] *Cf.* "A Note on Natural Laws and So-Called Contrary-to-Fact Conditionals," *Mind* 58, N.S., 1949, pp. 62-66 [Reprinted in this text]. See also my *Poverty of Historicism*, 1957 (first published 1945) the footnote on p. 123.

[2] I call my older formulation "clumsy" because it amounts to introducing the assumption that somewhere moas have once lived, or will one day live, under ideal conditions; which seems to me a bit far-fetched. I prefer now to replace this supposition by another—that among the "models" of our world—which are not supposed to be real, but logical constructions as it were—there will be at least one in which moas live under ideal conditions. And this, indeed, seems to me not only admissible, but obvious. Apart from terminological changes, this seems to be the only change in my position, as compared with my note in *Mind* of 1949. But I think that it is an important change.

To a student of method who opposes the doctrine of induction and ad-heres to the theory of falsification, there is not much difference between the view that universal laws are nothing but strictly universal statements and the view that they are "necessary": in both cases, we can only test our conjecture by attempted refutations.

To the inductivist, there is a crucial difference here: he ought to reject the idea of "necessary" laws, since these, being logically stronger, must be even less accessible to induction than mere universal statements.

Yet inductivists do not in fact always reason in this way. On the contrary, some seem to think that a statement asserting that laws of nature are necessary may somehow be used to justify induction—perhaps somewhat on the lines of a "prin-ciple of the uniformity of nature."

But it is obvious that no principle of this kind could ever justify induction. None could make inductive conclusions valid or even probable.

It is quite true, of course, that a statement like "there exist laws of nature" might be appealed to if we wished to justify our search for laws of nature.[3] But in the context of this remark of mine, "justify" has a sense very different from the one it has in the context of the question whether we can justify induction. In the latter case, we wish to establish certain statements—the induced generalizations. In the former case, we merely wish to justify an activity, the search for laws. Moreover, even though this activity may, in some sense, be justified by the knowl-edge that true laws exist—that there are structural regularities in the world—it could be so justified even without that knowledge: the hope that there may be some food somewhere certainly "justifies" the search for it—especially if we are starving—even if this hope is far removed from knowledge. Thus we can say that, although the knowledge that true laws exist would add something to the justification of our search for laws, this search is justified, even if we lack knowledge, by our curiosity, and by the mere hope that we may succeed.

Moreover, the distinction between "necessary" laws and strictly universal statements does not seem to be relevant to this problem: whether necessary or not, the knowledge that laws exist would add something to the "justification" of our search, without being needed for this kind of "justification."

I believe, however, that the idea that there are necessary laws of nature, in the sense of natural or physical necessity explained under point (12), is meta-physically or ontologically important, and of great intuitive significance in connec-tion with our attempts to understand the world. And although it is impossible to establish this metaphysical idea either on empirical grounds (because it is not falsi-fiable) or on other grounds, I believe that it is true, as I indicated in sections 79, and 83 to 85. Yet I am now trying to go beyond what I said in these sections by

---

[3] *Cf.* Wittgenstein's *Tractatus,* 6.36: "If there were a law of causality, it might run: 'There are natural laws.' But that can clearly not be said; it shows itself." In my opinion, what shows itself, if anything, is that this clearly *can* be said: it *has* been said by Wittgenstein, for example. What can clearly not be done is to *verify* the statement that there are natural laws (or even to falsify it). But the fact that a statement is not verifiable (or even that it is not falsifiable) does not mean that it is meaningless, or that it cannot be understood, or that it "can clearly not be said," as Wittgenstein believed.

emphasizing the peculiar ontological status of universal laws (for example, by speaking of their "necessity," of their "structural character"), and also by emphasizing the fact that the metaphysical character or the irrefutability of the assertion that laws of nature exist need not prevent us from discussing this assertion rationally—that is to say, critically. (See my *Postscript,* especially sections *6, *7, *15, and *120.)

Nevertheless, I regard, unlike Kneale, "necessary" as a mere word—as a label useful for distinguishing *the universality of laws* from "accidental" universality. Of course, any other label would do just as well, for there is not much connection here with logical necessity. I largely agree with the spirit of Wittgenstein's paraphrase of Hume: "A necessity for one thing to happen because another has happened does not exist. There is only logical necessity."[4] Only in one way is $a \underset{N}{\to} b$ connected with logical necessity: the necessary link between a and b is neither to be found in a nor in b, but in the fact that the corresponding ordinary conditional (or "material implication," $a \to b$ without 'N') follows *with logical necessity* from a law of nature—that it is necessary, relative to a law of nature.[5] And it may be said that a law of nature is necessary in its turn because it is logically derivable from, or explicable by, a law of a still higher degree of universality, or of greater "depth." (See my *Postscript,* section *15.) One might suppose that it is this logically necessary dependence upon true statments of higher universality, conjectured to exist, which suggested in the first instance the idea of "necessary connection" between cause and effect.[6]

---

[4] *Cf. Tractatus,* 6.3637.

[5] I pointed this out in *Aristotelian Society Supplementary Volume 22,* 1948, pp. 141 to 154, section 3; see especially p. 148. In this paper I briefly sketched a programme which I have largely carried out since.

[6] *Cf.* my paper quoted in the foregoing footnote.

WILLIAM KNEALE

10. Universality and Necessity*

In this paper I wish to consider some attempts which philosophers have made to define the notion of necessity by reference to universality. I think these attempts are mistaken, and I shall put forward some arguments in justification of my view; but my main purpose is not so much to argue a case against the suggested definitions as to bring them together and to point out some similarities and differences which have not been sufficiently noticed. I think that by so doing I may perhaps arouse doubts in the minds of some who have not felt doubts on the subject before. But apart from that I shall be glad to hear a discussion of the subject, and that is my main reason for choosing it.

1

The first reductionist attempt to which I wish to draw attention is that of Hume. In his analysis of the notion of causation he remarks that this relation is supposed to involve necessary connection and asks whence the idea of such connection can be derived. The question seems puzzling to him because he has committed himself to the principle that every simple idea is derived from a simple impression and yet finds himself driven to say that no necessary connection can ever be discovered by perception between events we call causes and events we call effects. After a lot of beating about the neighbouring fields he comes in the end to the conclusion that the necessity of which we speak in this connection is merely a projection upon the world of a feeling of inevitability which we have when we pass in thought from a cause to its effect, and that this feeling of inevitability is the result of an association established by constant conjunction of instances of the first with instances of the second.

Now this is not strictly speaking a definition of causal necessity in terms of universality, but it is certainly an attempt to explain away the necessity of which many philosophers have spoken in this connection. Hume does not for a moment deny that in ordinary life and in science we talk of necessary connection in nature, but he tries to explain how this can be so without admitting that there are in truth any necessary connections in nature, and he thinks that the key to an understanding of the situation is recognition of the importance of the constant conjunction of the events we call cause and effect. As though to mark the crucial importance of this notion, he prints the words "constant conjunction" in small capitals at their first appearance.

Probably no modern philosopher would wish to defend Hume's doctrine of causation just as it stands. It is now obvious that he made a mistake in talking of antecedent causation as the only relation between events by reliance on which we

Reprinted by permission of the author and the publisher, Cambridge University Press, from William Kneale, "Universality and Necessity," *The British Journal for the Philosophy of Science* vol. 12, no. 46 (August 1961): 89-102. Footnotes included.

*Read to the Annual Conference of the British Society for the Philosophy of Science held at Bristol, September 1960.

can make inferences from the observed to the unobserved. It is obvious also that what he says about causation does not suffice to distinguish a cause from a sure sign of something to come. And his psychological account of the origin of our talk of causal necessity is not likely to find much favour with anyone now. But there are a great many modern philosophers who think that Hume was right in principle; and if asked to say just what it was he contributed here to philosophy, they reply that he freed the notion of natural law from a confusion with logical necessity in which it had been involved by previous philosophers. These modern followers of Hume do not, of course, wish to deny that we often talk of an event's being made necessary by another, but they think they can explain this by an adaptation of Hume's argument. Instead of saying that talk of necessity is projection of our feelings on the world, they say that it arises in connection with the use of natural laws as premises for inference and is quite correct so long as it is understood in that connection. When I find something which is A, I may properly say that it must be B, if I am speaking to people who are already convinced that every A thing is B. For in this context the word "must" serves only to indicate that my assertion is an inference from the premises "Every A thing is B, and this is an A thing." But, they say, philosophers have sometimes mistakenly supposed that the word "must" indicates a necessity in the law itself. Frege seems to have held this view of natural necessity when he excused himself in his *Begriffsschrift* for not dealing with modal notions. There is a very clear presentation of this view in Professor Popper's contribution to a symposium on the question, "What can Logic do for Philosophy?" in the *Aristotelian Society Proceedings, Supplementary Volume for* 1948. I do not think it is unfair to describe it as a modern version of Hume's theory and to say that it is an attempt to explain physical or natural necessity by reference to universality.

Historically the doctrine that there is no necessity in nature itself has often been associated with a conventionalist account of such necessities as men claim to know *a priori,* but I do not think it is quite correct to father the conventionalist thesis on Hume. When he spoke of relations between ideas and contrasted them with matters of fact, he may sometimes have meant relations of inclusion such as would be revealed by definitions; but I think that he sometimes had in mind relations of positive opposition, for example between colours, and that his philosophy contained in fact a remnant of Locke's doctrine of *a priori* knowledge as knowledge of relations between ideas. So far as I know, the first clear statement of the conventionalist thesis in conjunction with a denial of necessity in nature is to be found in Berkeley's *Philosophical Commentaries,* §§ 732-5, where he writes:

> The reason why we can demonstrate so well about signs is that they are perfectly arbitrary and in our power,—made at pleasure. The obscure ambiguous term *relation,* which is said to be the largest field of knowledge, confounds us, deceives us. Let any man show me a demonstration, not verbal, that does not depend either on some false principle or at best on some principle of nature which is the effect of God's will and we know not how soon it may be changed. *Qu:* What becomes of the *aeternae veritates? Ans:* They vanish.

In recent years the thesis has been popularised by Wittgenstein, Whether or not he intended to preach a conventionalist theory of *a priori* knowledge when he published his *Tractatus,* I do not know: there are some indications that he did not.

But that was the interpretation which his disciples put on his work, and he certainly held the doctrine in his later years. Because he said that all necessity was logical necessity, what we claim to know *a priori* is often now said to be all logical, even though some of it is not obviously connected with the subject studied by Aristotle and Frege. I think this usage has misled a lot of philosophers, but there is no need to discuss it here.

2

So far what I have said is common knowledge. But I come now to views that are not so well known—those of Bolzano and Tarski about logical necessity. In his *Wissenschaftslehre* of 1837 Bolzano produced an account of logic as the science of sciences, which is very different from the psychologising empiricism of Hume. Because he was a Roman Catholic priest and a professor of the philosophy of religion in Prague until deposed for expressing liberal opinions on politics, it has sometimes been supposed that he derived his characteristic views from medieval sources. He may no doubt have been influenced by reading of medieval authors, but he does not often quote them in his *Wissenschaftslehre*. In fact I have found there only three references to medieval philosophers, and those not very important. On the other hand there are many references to "the great Leibniz," and it seems to me reasonable to think of Bolzano as working in the Leibnizian tradition, though, at the time he wrote, most of Leibniz's important work on logic was still unpublished. In various places Leibniz had pointed out that conventionalism was an unsatisfactory theory of logical necessity, since even conventions such as definitions must be shown to be consistent, and in his *Dialogue on the Connexion between Words and Things* he had ridiculed the suggestion that truth could be said to belong to sentences considered as patterns of ink. In his view, if we talk of the truth of sentences (i.e. *propositiones* in his Latin), we must consider not only actual sentences but also possible sentences, since there may well be undiscovered truths, and this introduction of talk about possible sentences shows that we are not really concerned with the speech habits of human beings but with something deeper which is presupposed in any attempt to regulate speech habits. Bolzano talks in this context of *Sätze an sich* (or propositions in the modern sense of that word). The phrase is difficult, if not impossible, to translate into English, because we have no word with precisely the same range of uses as the German *Satz*. Like our "statement" it can mean either a form of words or what a form of words expresses, but unlike "statement" it need not be confined to the context of assertion. Sometimes it has the sense of our "clause" as in the grammatical term *Nebensatz*. Sometimes, on the other hand, it has the sense of "thesis" or "principle" as in the phrase *der sweite Satz der Wärmelehre* for "the second law of thermodynamics." I mention all this for two reasons, first in order to show that Bolzano did not belong to the Berkeley-Hume-Mill tradition but rather to what one might call the tradition of logical realism of which Leibniz and Frege are the greatest representatives, and secondly in order to explain his terminology.

According to Bolzano a proposition (i.e., a *Satz an sich*) is analytic with respect to a certain constituent if the class of propositions that we can obtain by substitution for that constituent (including here under "substitution" replacement of the original constituent) consists entirely of true propositions or entirely of false propositions. Bolzano himself admits that the notion of analytic proposition which he has defined in this way is much wider than that of Kant; and he says that, if the part of an analytic proposition which is considered invariant (i.e. not open to substitution) contains only logical notions, it may perhaps be useful to describe the whole proposition as logically analytic, or analytic in the stricter sense (*Wissenschaftslehre*, §§ 147-148). Apparently he thinks that this is something like the sense intended by Kant; but he does not attach much importance to it, because he does not think it possible to draw a clear line between logical and non-logical notions.

There are a number of curious features in this passage of Bolzano's work. The first is a purely verbal point. Bolzano has so defined the word "analytic" that it can be applied to false propositions. This is contrary to Kant's usage, but it is easy to see why Bolzano thought it reasonable. He wanted to use the words "analytic" and "synthetic" as exhaustive of the realm of propositions, and he noticed that according to Kantian usage self-contradictory propositions would be neither analytic nor synthetic. The practice of later philosophers has followed Kant's lead rather than Bolzano's and it seems that we must either reconcile ourselves to saying that "analytic" and "synthetic" are not contradictory opposites or try to secure the exhaustiveness of the division by applying it only to truths. Secondly, Bolzano's account of analytic propositions seems to be based on the very naive assumption that a proposition must contain distinguishable constituents corresponding to all the distinguishable constituents of a sentence that express it, and *vice versa*. I shall say no more about this. Thirdly, Bolzano has given a definition of "analytic" such that a proposition can be analytic by virtue of natural laws or even by virtue of mere accidents. Consider for example the sentence "Kant was not an eighteenth-century philosopher who died on the anniversary of his birth." If it so happens that no eighteenth-century philosopher died on the anniversary of his birth, all the sentences that can be made from this by substitution of other names for "Kant" express true propositions, and so the proposition expressed by the original sentence is analytic with respect to the constituent Kant according to Bolzano's discussion.

The most interesting and valuable element in Bolzano's discussion of the distinction between analytic and synthetic propositions is his recognition of the fact that there are certain characters which belong to propositions in virtue of their structure. According to his way of talking a proposition may be universally valid (*allgemeingültig*) and so analytic with regard to substitution for certain constituents though not with respect to substitution for certain others. This is intelligible, but rather confusing, and it seems preferable to say (as later logicians have done) that universal validity (or validity for short) belongs primarily to certain propositional patterns and only secondarily to the propositions which exemplify them. Similar paraphrases can be applied also to what Bolzano says of compatibility and derivability.

According to Bolzano's own way of describing the matter, the propositions M, N, O, . . . follow or are derivable (*ableitbar*) from the propositions A, B, C, D, . . . with regard to the constituents i, j. . . . if any set of ideas which yield a set of true propositions when substituted for i, j, . . . in A, B, C, D . . . do the same when substituted for i, j . . . in M, N, O, . . . (*Wissenschaftslehre*, § 154). In other words this means that a proposition called a conclusion is entailed by a set of propositions called premises if the argument constituted by the association of the premises and the conclusion exemplifies a pattern of argument for which every exemplification with true premises also has a true conclusion. For a reason which I shall notice later, it is not now considered correct to identify following-from with being-derivable-from, as Bolzano does, but without going into details of modern discoveries we can see that there is something wrong in the use of the word "derivability" for the relation defined by Bolzano. For a proposition cannot properly be said to be derivable from a set of premises unless it is possible to establish that if the premises are true the proposition is also true without first establishing whether or not the premises and the proposition are true. But the relation defined by Bolzano might hold when this condition was not fulfilled. Just as according to his definitions a proposition can be analytically true by accident, so too one proposition may follow from another by accident, that is to say in such a way that the truth of the universal proposition about the results of substitution can be known only by an examination of the individual results. This can be seen most easily from consideration of the limiting case where the proposition called a consequence has no constituents in common with any of the premises. For then, according to Bolzano's definition, its being a consequence of the premises depends solely on its being true. He does not make this point explicitly in his section on the relation of being a consequence, but in his previous section on compatibility he says that a false proposition which contains none of the constituents for which substitution may be made in a certain set of propositions is incompatible with those propositions (*Wissenschaftslehre*, § 154), and according to his own account of the connection between the two sections this is just another way of saying what I have just said about being a consequence. Perhaps Bolzano overlooks it because he wants to think of the relation of being a consequence as holding always in virtue of a general rule. For he says in a note at the end of this section that when Aristotle uses the phrase συμβαίνει ἐξ ἀνάγκης ("it follows of necessity") to describe the relation of the conclusion to the premises in a valid syllogism, even though premises and conclusion may be alike false, he must surely mean that every argument of the form exemplified leads to a true conclusion if only the premises are true.

All this might be dismissed as of no more than antiquarian interest were it not for the fact that Bolzano's theory has been restated independently in our time by Tarski. In his article "On the Concept of Logical Consequence" (first published in Polish in 1936 and republished in English in *Logic, Semantics, Metamathematics*, p. 409) he rejected the Wittgensteinian account of logical necessity as unclear and said that Gödel's discoveries had shown the need for a new account of the relation of consequence:

> In order to obtain the proper concept of consequence, which is close in essentials to the common concept, we must resort to quite different methods and apply quite different conceptual apparatus in defining it.

The method which he then proposed was in essentials that of Bolzano, though at the time of his first publication on the subject he knew nothing of this part of Bolzano's work.

Tarski himself has summarised his account of the consequence relation as follows:

> Let L be any class of sentences. We replace all extra-logical constants which occur in the sentences belonging to L by corresponding variables, like constants being replaced by like variables, and unlike by unlike. In this way we obtain a class L' of sentential functions. An arbitrary sequence of objects which satisfies every sentential function of the class L' will be called a *model* or *realization of the class L of sentences*. . . . If in particular the class L consists of a single sentence X, we shall also call the model of the class L *the model of the sentence X*. In terms of these concepts we can define the concept of logical consequence as follows:
> *The sentence X follows logically from the sentences of the class K if, and only if, every model of the class K is also a model of the sentence X.*

Later he adds:

> We can agree to call a class of sentences *contradictory* if it possesses no model. Analogously a class of sentences can be called *analytical* if every sequence of objects is a model of it. Both of these concepts can be related not only to classes of sentences but also to single sentences.

Tarski himself insists that his essay is an attempt to work out clearly the implications of the old doctrine that the relation of logical consequence holds between statements in virtue of their forms. But his development of the doctrine has some curious features. I wish to draw attention to one only, and for this purpose I shall quote again from his own work. At the end he writes:

> Underlying our whole construction is the division of the terms of the language discussed into logical and extra-logical. This division is certainly not arbitrary. . . . If, for example, we were to include among the extra-logical signs the implication sign, or the universal quantifier, then our definition of the concept of consequence would lead to results which obviously contradict ordinary usage. On the other hand, no objective grounds are known to me which permit us to draw a sharp boundary between the two groups of terms. It seems to be possible to include among logical terms some which are usually regarded by logicians as extra-logical without running into consequences which stand in sharp contrast to ordinary usage. In the extreme case we could regard all terms of the language as logical. The concept of *formal* consequence would then coincide with that of *material* consequence.

By "material consequence" he evidently means here the converse of what logicians call material implication. We may add that in this extreme case the concept of the analytic would coincide with that of the true.

In effect Tarski expresses the same doubts as Bolzano about the possibility of drawing a clear line between the logical and the extra-logical; and having made this point he rightly goes on to show that by placing the boundary between formal and material in different places we can pass from the ordinary notion of logical consequence to much weaker notions. For just as many philosophers who profess to follow Hume have said that the necessity with which an effect follows its cause is no more than the inclusion of this particular sequence in a constant natural association, so he says that the necessity with which a consequence follows in the logical sense of "follows" from premises is no more than the inclusion of this particular sequence in a universal fact about the satisfaction of certain sentential functions. If, following his own suggestion, we enlarge the range of sentential functions under consideration by including among the constant factors of our sentences not only the traditional logical constants but all unrestricted general terms such as "man," "iron," "fire," etc., we find that his definition of consequence covers not only logical consequence but also all consequences in virtue of natural laws. In short, his account of necessity amounts to a generalisation of the constancy theory of natural necessity. But the result can give no pleasure to followers of Hume, since it involves rejection of their view that there is a fundamental difference of kind between logical and natural necessity.

In defence of Tarski's definition it may perhaps be argued that for a sentential function such as "If p then not-not-p" we can know a priori that it is satisfied by every sequence of objects, whereas for a sentential function such as "If x has taken arsenic x will die" we can only conjecture universal satisfaction on empirical grounds. This is true, but there is nothing in Tarski's account of the matter to explain the difference, and he does not allude to it himself. Nor is it appropriate that a distinction of kinds of consequence should be made to depend on a distinction between cases in which we can and cases in which we cannot gain knowledge a priori. On the contrary, the epistemological distinction should be explained by an account of the difference of the cases; and it is just this which is lacking so far.

3

For my own part I do not agree with the project of trying to define necessity by reference to universality, and I have argued against even the more popular part of the project, namely that of accounting for natural necessity by a modernised version of Hume's analysis. In my *Probability and Induction* of 1949 I pointed out that when we enunciate a natural law, or what we suppose to be such, in the form "Every F thing is G," we do not think of it as a merely *de facto* generalisation of the kind logicians express by writing "(x) $[Fx \supset Gx.]$." Although we may not use any modal word such as "must" or "necessarily," we assume that our pronouncement commits us not only to asserting that everything which actually has been or will be F has been or will be G but also to asserting that if anything which is not as a matter of fact F were F it would also be G. This, I thought, was sufficient to show the inadequacy of a Humean account of natural law. The same point has been made by a number of other philosophers, but the conclusion which I have drawn has not been accepted by all, or indeed by many. Although it seems to be generally agreed that subjunctive conditional statements can be inferred from statements of natural law, and that statements of natural law must for this reason be distinguished from statements of accidental universality such as we find in works of history and geography, for example "All mountains in the United Kingdom are of less than 5,000 feet in height," it is sometimes thought that this feature of statements of law can be explained without supposing that they involve any more than Hume allowed.

Already in 1948 Professor Popper argued for this view in the symposium "What can Logic do for Philosophy?" and he defended it again in 1949 in "A Note on Natural Laws and so-called 'Contrary-to-fact' Conditionals" which he contributed to *Mind.* His thesis was that the difficulties of persons like myself arose from failure to notice the difference between terms which can be defined extensionally and those which cannot be so defined. It is true, he said, that "All my friends speak French" does not entail "If Confucius were one of my friends he would speak French," but that is because anyone who utters the first statement is thinking of the class of his friends as closed, whereas anyone who utters the second statement is thinking of the class of his friends as open. In other words, the expression "my friends" is not used in quite the same way in the two statements. When, however, it is maintained that sentences which purport to state natural laws are equivalent to universal material implications, it is to be understood that the terms involved are not mere substitutes for lists of proper names but unrestricted general descriptions. And once this is conceded, there should in his opinion be no difficulty about the derivation of contrary-to-fact conditionals.

Against this I argued in a paper contributed to *Analysis* in 1950 (later reprinted in Miss Margaret Macdonald's collection *Philosophy and Analysis*) that Popper's theory would not do what he wanted of it because it still allowed for no distinction between laws and merely accidental generalities. Philosophers who treat suggestions of law as universal material implications say in effect that there is no sense in talking of historical accidents on the cosmic scale. According to their account of the matter, when we consider the hypothesis of a connection between any two characters expressed by unrestricted general descriptions, there are only two possibilities with which we have to reckon. Either it is a law of nature that every A thing is B, or there has been or will be somewhere at some time an A thing that was not or is not B. In short, they are committed to the view that every natural possibility (i.e., every state of affairs not excluded by a law of nature) must be realised somewhere at some time. But this is certainly not what we ordinarily think, and any philosophical theory which leads to this conclusion should be regarded with great suspicion.

In an appendix to his *Logic of Scientific Discovery* of 1959, Popper concedes that something more must be done to distinguish laws from accidental generalities and produces the following definition of natural necessity:

> A statement may be said to be naturally or physically necessary if, and only if, it is deducible from a statement function which is satisfied in all worlds that differ from our world, if at all, only with respect to initial conditions (p. 433).

As he goes on to remark, this proposed definition makes all laws of nature, together with all their logical consequences, naturally or physically necessary, but excludes from that status generalisations which hold merely because of the *de facto* arrangements of things in the world we know. Personally I find it acceptable. For to say that a statement function is satisfied in all worlds that differ from the actual world, if at all, only with respect to initial conditions is to say in effect that it holds for all *possible* worlds that contain instances of the same attributes and relations as are exemplified in the actual world and of these only; and what holds for all possible worlds is obviously necessary. I agree, of course, with Popper that we cannot know for certain whether a generalisation which we put forward is in truth a law of nature with natural necessity as he defined it; but to say this is only to admit that we cannot establish laws of nature *a priori.* Obviously experience, which is always of the actual world, cannot guarantee a generalisation which is supposed to hold for worlds other than the actual world, and those who speak, as I have done, for natural necessity do not wish to say that it can. The important thing in Popper's new definition, and what makes it acceptable to me, is just that it connects the notion of natural law with that of validity for states of affairs other than the actual. Unfortunately, however, Popper himself seems to be in some confusion about the effect of his concession. Perhaps I have misunderstood him. If so, I hope to be enlightened. But some passages which I am going to quote seem to me very puzzling indeed.

Just before his new definition of natural necessity Popper writes:

> As Tarski has shown, it is possible to explain *logical necessity* in terms of universality: a statement may be said to be logically necessary if and only if it is deducible (for example by particularisation) from a "universally valid" statement function, that is to say, from a statement function that is *satisfied by every model* (this means true in all possible worlds). I think we may explain by the same method what we mean by *natural necessity*; for we may adopt the following definition (*L.S.D.* p. 432).

But a few pages later he says:

> I regard, unlike Kneale, "necessary" as a mere word, as a label for distinguishing the universality of laws from "accidental universality." Of course any other label would do as well, for there is not much connection here with logical necessity. I largely agree with the spirit of Wittgenstein's paraphrase of Hume: "A necessity for one thing to happen because another has happened does not exist. There is only logical necessity" (*L.S.D.* p. 438).

As they stand, these two passages are inconsistent. For the first recommends a new account of natural necessity by saying that it is framed after the pattern of Tarski's account of logical necessity, whereas the second says there is no important connection between natural necessity and logical necessity. And the first implies acceptance of Tarski's account of logical necessity, whereas the second implies acceptance of Wittgenstein's account of logical necessity, which Tarski himself, as we have seen, found unsatisfactory. I do not wish, however, to dwell on the second passage, and I quote it here only in order to indicate that there seems to be some uncertainty in Popper's own mind about his commitments. It is the first passage which interests me, and it is this I wish to examine.

At the beginning Popper says that Tarski has shown that it is possible to explain logical necessity in terms of universality. I think this is at any rate a correct report of Tarski's intention. But, as I have already remarked, neither Bolzano nor Tarski ever produced a delimitation of the logical realm which satisfied him, and there is something unsatisfactory in a theory of logical necessity which does not even explain why logic is an *a priori* science. It is obvious, of course, that truths of logic are either themselves universal in the way explained by Bolzano and Tarski or cases falling under generalisations of the kind those authors discuss. That has been taken for granted by all the great logicians, Aristotle, Chrysippus, Leibniz, Boole, Frege, and Russell. But it is not so obvious that there is nothing more to be said about logical necessity.

Towards the end of the passage I have quoted, Popper tries to make the theory more acceptable by adding in brackets "this means true in all possible worlds." This phrase is supposed to explain the immediately preceding phrase "satisfied by every model," but according to Tarski's own explanation a model is an arbitrary sequence of objects which satisfies a statement function or class of statement functions, and an analytic statement is one for which every sequence of objects is a model, i.e. one satisfied by every sequence of objects, or as we may say in another terminology, one which turns out true for every interpretation of its extra-logical signs. There is nothing here about possible worlds, and it seems clear to me that, so far as Tarski is concerned, the truth of a formula under all interpretations is just a fact about the actual world, though this actual world may be taken to include not only physical objects but an infinity of sets belonging to various levels. Indeed, if Tarski's programme is what Popper says at the beginning of the paragraph, namely to explain logical necessity in terms of universality, he has no right to speak of possible worlds at all. It was no doubt correct for Leibniz to say that necessary truths are true in all possible worlds, and even to offer this as a definition of necessity; but he did not think that he was explaining necessity in terms of universality and so showing the superfluity of modal expressions. For him the definition was merely an explanation of one modal notion in terms of another which some people find easier to grasp. If Tarski were willing to work with the notion of possibility as Popper supposes, he could define the notion of consequence much more easily than he has done, by saying simply that a statement is a consequence of a class of premises if the conjunction of the premises with the negation of the statement does not represent any possible state of affairs. But I feel sure that he would think this a less satisfactory definition than that he has given, precisely because it contains a modal word.

Immediately after the sentence about possible worlds Popper goes on to say "I think we may explain by the same method what we mean by natural necessity," and the explanation that he gives is indeed an explanation of the Leibnizian type. For it involves generalisation over all worlds that differ from our world, if at all, only in initial conditions, and these must clearly be naturally possible worlds with instances of the same attributes and relations as we find exemplified in our actual world. I hold therefore that Popper is mistaken if he thinks, as apparently he does, that he has succeeded in improving on the Humean account of natural laws while remaining true to the principle that necessity can be explained without remainder in terms of universality. In fact he has only defined one modal notion in terms of another; but he has hidden this from himself for the moment by talking of all worlds which differ from our world, if at all, only in initial conditions.

In my opinion, it is a mistake to try to explain away the modal notions. Instead of trying to reduce necessity to universality we should, I think, take the notion of necessitation as fundamental and say that the logical constants, about whose recognition Bolzano and Tarski were both puzzled, are just those signs which can be defined without remainder by formulation of principles of necessitation. Popper himself has taken this line in a number of papers written about 1947-8 (in particular two papers "On the Theory of Deduction" which he contributed to the *Proceedings of the Royal Netherlands Academy of Sciences* in 1948), and I have tried to follow him in a paper called "The Province of Logic" which I contributed to *Contemporary British Philosophy, Third Series*. What I suggest is simply that we should regard formal logic as the pure theory of necessitation, that is as the study of what can be said about necessitation in general without regard to those special principles of necessitation which hold for various subject matters. Although he has come very near to saying this, Popper has in the end drawn back and professed himself a follower of Hume and Wittgenstein, that is, an upholder of the anti-scientific doctrine of conventionalism which was first promulgated in modern times by Berkeley. His reason for taking the line which he does is apparently that he cannot understand what a non-formal principle of necessitation would be and suspects that admission of any such would commit him to a terrible evil called essentialism. To this I reply that a non-formal principle of necessitation would be exactly what he has allowed a law of nature to be, namely a generalisation which holds for all possible worlds of some kind, and that it is highly paradoxical to suggest, as he does in a passage which I quoted, that there is none but an arbitrary linguistic connection between natural and logical necessity.

G. C. NERLICH
W. A. SUCHTING

11. *Popper on Law and Natural Necessity*

1. In Appendix *10 of *The Logic of Scientific Discovery*,[1] Professor Sir Karl Popper, following upon an earlier treatment,[2] has sought to define the notion of a law of nature, which is characterised by "natural or physical necessity" (p. 428). Such a law is said to be (1) "logically stronger" than just a true, strictly universal statement (pp. 426, 431, 432). For example, suppose that every member of the (now extinct) New Zealand moas died before the age of fifty; that "moa" is taken to be a "universal name"; and finally that omnitemporally there are no other moas. Then it is a true, strictly universal statement (call it "*M*") that "All moas die before the age of fifty." But, supposing, for example, that the deaths before fifty of all moas were due to the presence of certain viruses, *M* would not be called a law of nature, but rather a merely accidental universal (pp. 427f.). This concedes (for example) William Kneale's argument that the characterisation of a law, from a common Humean standpoint, as just a true, strictly universal statement is neither logically sufficient nor intuitively adequate (p. 427). Nevertheless, as against

Reprinted by permission of the authors and the publisher, Cambridge University Press, from G. C. Nerlich and W. A. Suchting, "Popper on Law and Natural Necessity," *The British Journal for the Philosophy of Science* vol. 18 (1967): 233-35. Footnotes included.

Note: Footnotes have been renumbered for the purposes of this text.

[1] This is one of the additions to the original *Logik der Forschung* included in the English translation (London, 1959), to which all page numbers in the text refer.

[2] "A Note on Natural Laws and so-called 'Contrary-to-Fact Conditionals,' " *Mind*, 58 (1949), 62-66 [reprinted in this text].

Kneale, Popper holds that (2) laws of nature are not logically necessary; "compared with logical tautologies" they are contingent, accidental (pp. 429, 432, 438). On Professor Popper's positive account, "a statement may be said to be naturally or physically necessary if, and only if, it is deducible from a statement function which is satisfied in all worlds that differ from our world, if at all, only with respect to initial conditions" (p. 433—original italicised).

2. But this definition cannot be taken quite literally, for as it stands it does not afford a basis for any differentiation at all among the universal propositions true of our world. The device of a range of worlds is to eliminate some of these universal propositions, viz., certain empirical strictly universal ones, as not physically necessary, because false in at least one among the range of worlds. Yet the limits of the range are specified as those which "differ from our world, if at all, *only* with respect to initial conditions" (our italics). But a world which differs from ours in respect of any empirical strictly universal proposition such as M does not differ only with respect to initial conditions. M is not a statement of initial conditions. Hence, a world in which M can be false is one outside the range of worlds which the definition provides. Therefore, despite Popper's claim for his example, the proposition M, not being a statement of initial conditions, is true in all the worlds thus specified, and *a fortiori* it is deducible from a statement function which is satisfied in all such worlds; therefore it is not excluded from physical necessity by the definition in question.

3. However, what would seem to be the import of the definition may be brought out in the following way. Consider M again. Call a statement about the presence of certain viruses, which formulates relevant initial conditions, "C." Then we may assume that M follows from the conjunction of C and some set of general statements about the structure, functioning, evolution, etc., of organisms, which we may call "L." Then M is said not to be a law of nature, because its truth is not invariant with respect to change in initial conditions (presence versus absence of viruses). But L is, presumably, a genuine law, because its truth is so invariant: whatever the special conditions of life organisms are subject to the conditions stated there. We suggest then that the intent of the definition may be expressed as follows: a statement may be said to be naturally or physically necessary if, and only if, it is deducible from a statement function which is satisfied in all worlds which instantiate the properties and relations of our world but which may differ from our world with respect to initial conditions.

4. Now what, more exactly, is the possible range of variation of the initial conditions? *A priori* there would seem to be two and only two alternatives. One is that the freedom to vary initial conditions stops short only at those embodying recognisably self-contradictory forms. But a consequence of this would be that laws of nature are logically necessary; in so generously provided a range of worlds we should be able to find singular propositions which are contraries of every logically contingent universal proposition. Put otherwise, if "p is a law" entails that p is deducible from a statement function which is satisfied in all worlds which instantiate the properties and relations of our world whatever the (logically possible) initial conditions, then if q formulates certain initial conditions, and p and q together entail r, r must of necessity hold in the "world" so described. But if p is genuinely contingent, it must be possible that, though p and q together entail r,

nevertheless in fact q and not-r. In brief, this interpretation yields a position indistinguishable from Kneale's.[3] On this ground alone it may be concluded that this cannot be the intent of Professor Popper's definition.

5. In addition Popper says that "natural laws . . . I restrict the (logically) possible choice of singular facts" (p. 430). This brings us to the second of the two possible alternatives regarding the range of permitted variation of initial conditions, viz., that the class of possible initial conditions is the class of physically (rather than logically) possible ones. Now it is generally agreed that a physically possible condition is one which is not inconsistent with a physically necessary statement, or law of nature. But this restriction on the class of possible initial conditions makes the definition (both original and revised) clearly circular. For it would now read: a statement may be said to be naturally or physically necessary if, and only if, it is deducible from a statement function which is satisfied in all worlds which instantiate the properties and relations of our world but which may differ from our world with respect to physically possible initial conditions, i.e., initial conditions which are not inconsistent with a naturally or physically necessary statement.

6. In sum, we have argued three points with regard to Professor Popper's definition of a law of nature, or of natural or physical necessity: (1) that it is at least verbally defective, as imposing, as it stands, no distinctions on the class of universal propositions true of our world; (2) that a version verbally revised in this respect may be interpreted, at a crucial point, in only two possible ways, one of which renders it equivalent to a view which Professor Popper wishes to reject; and (3) the other renders the definition circular.

---

[3] Kneale has in fact claimed that Popper has committed himself to just this position which he intends to reject. See "Universality and Necessity" this *Journal*, 12 (1962), 99, 101 [reprinted in this text] and (with M. Kneale) *The Development of Logic* (Oxford, 1962), pp. 630f.

KARL POPPER

12. A Revised Definition of Natural Necessity

I

I agree in the main with the opinions expressed in the note by G. C. Nerlich and W. A. Suchting. I disagree with their presentation of some of these opinions as a criticism of doctrines which I am supposed to have published. They overlook, or at any rate they do not mention, the fact that some of the things they point out in their criticism were explicitly pointed out (and discussed) by myself in the very appendix (*The Logic of Scientific Discovery* = *L.Sc.D.*, appendix *x) which they criticise.

Though I am largely in agreement with Messrs Nerlich and Suchting, this does not mean that I do not find much to criticise in their note. But I shall confine myself to one point of criticism, and to a revised treatment of the problem of natural necessity.

Nerlich and Suchting's note is in its entirety directed against my italicised definition of natural necessity, printed in *L.Sc.D.* at the top of page 433, and quoted by Nerlich and Suchting at the end of their paragraph 1. Unfortunately this definition has no special name in *L.Sc.D.* and this has led to some (minor) muddles in my text. I will therefore call this definition in what follows "definition (N°)."

In their summary (paragraph 6) Nerlich and Suchting state three criticisms of my definition (N°):

(1) "that it is at least verbally defective, . . . imposing no distinction on the class of universal propositions true of our world" (this point is argued in their second paragraph),

(2) that either a revised version would be "equivalent to a view which Professor Popper wishes to reject" (that is, to what they call "Kneale's position": see their fourth paragraph), or

(3) that a revised version would be a circular definition (see their fifth paragraph).

As far as (2) goes, I can only say that "Kneale's position," as Nerlich and Suchting call it (I doubt whether this is indeed Kneale's position) was at any rate ruled out at some length in my text; and I disagree with Nerlich and Suchting that a revised version of (N°) would, if not circular, be equivalent to either "Kneale's position" or else to what I believe to be Kneale's actual position.

On the other hand, Nerlich and Suchting indicate in their point (3) that if I reject "Kneale's position" then my definition (N°) becomes circular. What they fail to indicate is that I not only reject Kneale's position but *that I have also*

Reprinted by permission of the author and the publisher, Cambridge University Press, from Karl Popper, "A Revised Definition of Natural Necessity," *The British Journal for the Philosophy of Science* vol. 18 (1967): pp. 316-21. Footnotes included.

pointed out the circularity myself. For although they quote from *L.Sc.D.* my definition (N°) (Nerlich and Suchting, end of paragraph 1), they fail to quote from the same appendix the following critical comments of mine on the *definiens* of definition (N°) (*L.Sc.D.*, p. 435):

> Nevertheless, the phrase [from the *definiens* of (N°)] "all worlds which differ (if at all) from our world only with respect to the initial conditions" undoubtedly contains the ideas of laws of nature. What we mean is "all worlds which have the same structure—or the same natural laws—as our own world." In so far as our *definiens* [the *definiens* of (N°)] contains implicitly the idea of laws of nature [(N°), and therefore the later definition (D) which depends on (N°)] . . . , may be said to be circular.

Having stated this I continue: "But all definitions must be circular *in this sense* . . ."; and I go on to say: "Our definition is not, however, circular in a more technical sense."

I should like to explain here this technical sense more fully.

We may, in some formal system, choose the term "*P*" as one of our undefined symbols; and we may, for example, decide to interpret the formula

$$a \epsilon P$$

to mean "*a* is possible." We may then continue (assuming negation is part of our system) to interpret "$\sim((\sim a)\epsilon P)$," or "$\sim q \notin P$," as "not-*a* is not possible." This allows us to *define logical necessity with the help of logical possibility* (as is customary)

(K) $a \epsilon N \longleftrightarrow \sim a \notin P$

This definition of necessity or of "*a* is necessary" is, like all definitions (except those which involve an infinite regress), circular *in a sense*, because "possible" may be said to mean "*compatible with what is necessary.*" ("Possible" also means, clearly, "not impossible," and "impossible" means, just as clearly, "necessarily wrong" or "necessarily excluded," or something similar.) Nevertheless, the definition (K) is *technically not circular*, because we have chosen *P* as our undefined term, and because we define *N* with its help.

Accordingly, anybody who adopts the position described by Nerlich and Suchting in their fifth (penultimate) paragraph, defining *N* (in the sense of naturally or physically necessary) with the help of the class of physically possible initial conditions (this class being used as an undefined term), would obtain a definition of *N* which like (K) would be circular *in a sense*, but which might be technically even less circular then (K).

Thus far my *criticism* of Nerlich and Suchting.

On the other hand, what I have quoted from point (1) of their summary seems to me to be a valid criticism of my definition (N°), which indeed is "at least verbally defective." In the rest of this note I shall attempt to improve it. I shall call my revised definition '(N)', and an interpretation or translation of it "(N')." From an intuitive point of view (N') turns out to be very similar to (N°). Nevertheless there will be a considerable improvement; (N) or (N') will turn out to be not only less circular than (N°) or (K) but a good deal less circular than I previously thought possible. For this reason I am very grateful to Nerlich and Suchting for their helpful criticism.

II

I shall make use of Tarski's theory of deductive systems. (See A. Tarski, *Logic, Semantics, Metamathematics,* chapters v, xii, and xvi).

If A is any set of statements, then $Cn(A)$ is the class of all logical consequences of A, or the smallest deductive system containing A as a subset: we have $A \subset Cn(A)$, and $Cn(Cn(A)) = Cn(A)$.

(Tarski, op. cit. p. 343, calls the system $Cn(O)$ "the set of all logically valid" statements, or "L" while I shall use "L" for the set of all statements of our object language.)

The sets of statements with which we operate can be interpreted in a "realistic" way: we can speak (and I will do so later) of sets of possible, or of actual, facts, instead of sets of (logically) possible, or of true, statements.

I shall use the following metamathematical term T first introduced and defined by Alfred Tarski, and more recently defined by others. T is the set of all those statements (of some language L) which are true in our own world. It is easily seen that T is a deductive system: $T = Cn(T)$. On the realistic interpretation T becomes the set of all actual facts.

Note that T is a *consistent and complete* deductive system: there are statements or facts *outside* T (false statements or facts), which means that T is *consistent*; and if any statement not in T is added to T, T becomes inconsistent, which means that T is *complete*. I shall later call any such consistent and complete deductive system (in "realistic" interpretation) a "*possible world.*" Thus T may be called "our own world."

The following notation will be used: AB will be the *intersection* of the two sets A and B; $A + B$ will be their *union*. Braces will indicate unit sets, so that $\{a\}$ will be the set containing the element a only. However, if a is a statement, the consequence class of a will, by way of abbreviation, be written "$Cn(a)$," instead of "$Cn(\{a\})$." Also "$\rightarrow$" is sometimes used in our metalinguistic definitions as shorthand for "only if," and "$\leftrightarrow$" for "if and only if."

I begin with some informal metalogical explanations. For simplicity's sake we interpret L as the class of all well-formed formulae (rather than of all expressions of L). Thus $a \epsilon L$ is taken to mean that a is either a well-formed statement or a well-formed statment function of L.

I now introduce my main auxiliary metalogical concept, the concept of *separateness*. This is closely related to *organicity* in the sense of Leśniewski and Wajsberg (and referred to by Tarski, op. cit. p. 45; see also Bolesław Sobociński, *Yearbook of the Polish Society for Arts and Sciences,* London, 1956, p. 7).

We write "$\sigma(a)$" for a "suffix" of the expression a, that is to say, for what remains of a after deletion of some or all of its quantifiers. We write "$a = b$" if a and b are the same expression, and "$\sigma(a) \not\subset b$" if and only if $\sigma(a)$ does not occur as a genuine part of the expression b.

Now we define:

(D_1) A is a class of separated axioms of D (in symbols, $A \epsilon a(D)$) if and only if

    (1) $D = Cn(D) = Cn(A)$
    (2) $(a)(b)(a \epsilon A \& b \epsilon D \rightarrow \sigma(b) \not\subset a)$

Note: The main point of this definition is to ensure that a "separated" system of axioms A consists of axioms none of which is written as a conjunction (or a conditional) of two members of $D = Cn(A)$.[1]

We next introduce the idea of a separated *basis* (that is, a separated *independent* axiom system):

(D_2) A is a separated basis of D (in symbols, $A\epsilon\beta(D)$), if and only if

$$A\epsilon\alpha(D)\&(a)(a\epsilon A\rightarrow(A-\left\{a\right\})\not\epsilon\alpha(D))$$

The purpose of these definitions—that is, of introducing the idea of a "*separated*" *basis*—is this. Suppose p is the statement, "All planets move very nearly in elliptic orbits," and that it is in N; and that m is a contingent statement like our moa-example (*L.Sc.D.,* p. 427: "All moas die before reaching the age of fifty years.") Then to be intuitively adequate, our definition must not put pm into N, since it is an obvious adequacy condition that N is a deductive system. To avoid this, we have to exclude such conjunctions from the set of "separated" bases.

The following terms G, H, and K, will be used as undefined terms.

G is, intuitively speaking, the set of *all* general statements (of some language L) or general facts (expressible in L), that is, of all statements or facts which are general by virtue of their logical form: G is supposed to contain, more especially, all physical theories, and not only all universal statements which are naturally or logically necessary in our world, but also all contingently true universal statements (such as our moa-example, m); and further, also all false universal statements. We may assume that G contains universal implications (or conditionals), beginning with a universal operator "for all x," where x may range over finite parts or regions of some world (or over all world points, or over all "occurrences" in the sense of *L.Sc.D.,* section 23, or a "realistic" interpretation of this section). The main thing is that in no statement or fact belonging to G may occur an individual constant or proper name (or an individual class name: cf. *L.Sc.D.,* section 14; or a predicate such as Quine's "Socratizes"), or anything that may specify an individual part or region of some world.

This explanation of G is not very satisfactory; a more precise explanation would be still more closely language-dependent, but it could be carried out by introducing some sufficiently rich artificial object language.

H is the set of all logically possible singular statements, including initial conditions I (see below). It will be interpreted broadly: I will assume that $H \subset L$ and that H may be infinite; also that it may include what are usually called "boundary conditions," that is to say, propositions or statements asserting the existence or non-existence of certain conditions in certain individual (*L.Sc.D.,* section 14) or singular parts or regions of the world. No member of the set H may assert, however, that such conditions exist in *all* parts of the world or in *no* parts of the world, since statements of this kind will be regarded as general or universal statements. But H may, for example, contain statements asserting that certain conditions—such as the

---

[1] There are other ways (and perhaps preferable ones) to achieve this purpose: we may define a concept of "separateness" adequate for our purpose using ideas other than organicity. (In fact I am not entirely happy about the utilisation, in my above definition of separateness, of what Sobociński says on organicity.)

existence of animals of a certain kind—are realised in certain finite parts of the world (e.g., in a certain spatio-temporal region), and *in no other part.* The class of statements of this kind I denote by "*K*," in contradistinction to initial conditions in the narrower sense, to be defined below, and denoted by "*I.*"

Note that although *G* and *H* are assumed to be exclusive (*GH* = O) they are not assumed to be exhaustive (*G* + *H* ≠ *L*). Neither of them is assumed to be consistent, and they are not deductive systems.

I shall make use of no undefined terms other than *G, H,* and *K.*

We now introduce a preliminary definition (Prel): we define the deductive systems *U* and *V*. The deductive system *U* is the system of all facts entailed by the set of all *true* general statements *not belonging* to *H*; and the deductive system *V* is the system of facts entailed by all *true* initial conditions.

(Prel 1) $U = Cn((TG)-H)$

Note that *U* contains elements which are not universal; for example, instantiations resulting from the substitution of individual names.

We now proceed to define the set *I* of initial conditions (in the narrower sense). To this end we first consider the set *J*, defined as the largest set of *conditionals* which belong to *UH*. Thus *J* may also be described as the largest set of (true) singular conditionals obtainable within *U* by instantiation. (Note that $a \supset b \epsilon J$ if and only if $\sim b \supset \sim a \epsilon J$.) The set of the *antecedents of J* belonging to *H* is the set *I* of initial conditions (in the narrower sense: *I* + *K* may be described as the set of initial conditions in the wider sense).

We are now ready to define the deductive system *V* as the system derivable from the *true* initial conditions in the wider sense:

(Prel 2) $V = Cn(T(I + K))$

Note also that although *U* and *V* are semantical terms, *they are not modal terms.*

With the help of *V* and $\beta(U)$, that is the class of all "*separated*" bases of *U*, we can now define *M* ("*M*" for "matrix"); that is to say, a "separated" (but not in general an independent) axiom system *M* for the system *N* (*N* = *Cn*(*M*)) of all *naturally or physically necessary facts or statements* (or statement functions).

(M) $a \epsilon M \longleftrightarrow (EA)A \epsilon \beta(U) \ \& \ a \epsilon A \ \& \ a \notin Cn((A - \{a\}) + V))$

Now we define the deductive system *N* of naturally necessary facts:

(N) $N = Cn(M)$

These definitions (Prel), (M), and (N) are, obviously, *technically* non-circular: none of the defining terms is in any sense a modal term. It is of some interest, however, to ask ourselves *in which sense* the definition of *N* is still circular. The answer is that we must assume our language *L* to be *adequate for the particular purpose of defining N.* That is to say, *L* must be sufficiently rich and articulate to allow a division of the true general and "separated" statements into two exclusive classes, one consisting of the naturally or physically necessary ones, and one of the naturally or physically contingent ones. Not every language will satisfy this condition. To take a trivial example, we assume that a language contains a primitive predicate *P* which is to be interpreted as "either planets or moas," and two predicates, *Q* and *R,* to be interpreted respectively as "always moving in near-elliptic orbits around a central body" and "dying before fifty." Then we have to express our two standard examples p and m by "$(x)((Px \cdot Qx) \rightarrow Qx)$" and "$(x)((Px \cdot Rx) \rightarrow Rx)$" respectively; and these will both be tautological, and therefore (logically) necessary.

Thus we cannot assert that our definition will be adequate for every language L in which we can express statements which are intuitively (or in intention) naturally necessary, or else contingent. We can only say that it will be adequate for every language which is adequate *for the particular purpose* of distinguishing between naturally or physically necessary statements and contingent statements. This means that our definition is circular in a sense; yet I regard this as a quite unexpectedly low degree of circularity.

Another difficulty is of a very different character. A strong assumption on which the success of our construction depends is that U is finitely or recursively axiomatisable. (If it is, it has obviously a basis and, in every appropriate language, a "separated" basis also.) Now, this question does not so much depend on L, but rather on T, that is to say, on our world. Since not even arithmetic is finitely axiomatisable, it appears that U will not be either. However, there are ways to get round this difficulty: for example, we might "subtract," as it were, the mathematics from U by including it among the logic (thus packing it, as it were, into the symbol "Cn" for logical consequence, or into $Cn(O)$; concerning the relativity of logical consequence, see Tarski, op. cit. chapter 16, pp. 418-20).

There is another method of dealing with this difficulty, which also utilises an idea of Tarski's (cf. Tarski, op. cit. p. 362, theorem 25). Tarski's idea allows us to represent any non-axiomatisable system D by the sum of some infinite series of strictly increasing axiomatisable systems X_i (and thus also of systems $X_i \, \epsilon\beta(Cn(X_i))$), that is to say, of bases). This suggests the following definition:

(D₃) A is a sequence of strictly increasing 'separated' bases of subsystems converging to D (in symbols, $A\epsilon\gamma(D)$) if and only if, for every natural number n, $(EB_n)(B_n \subset B_{n+1}$ & $B_n \neq B_{n+1}$ & $B_n \, \epsilon\beta(Cn(B_n))$ & $A = \sum_n B_n$ & $D = Cn(A))$.

Now we can replace (M) by (M')₂₂, which is exactly like (M) except that "β" is replaced by "γ."

III

It is clear from the start that our construction has no practical significance: my aim has been to see how far we can "rehabilitate" the concept of natural necessity, somewhat in the sense in which Tarski may be said to have rehabilitated the concept of truth. I am interested (as I am in the case of the concept of truth) not so much in finding a concept which is effectively applicable (except for very special languages, there is no criterion of truth), but rather in showing that we can use the concept intuitively without talking nonsense.

The deficiency of my old definition (N°) can best be seen by comparing it with the following definition (N') which incidentally also shows how my old definition can be repaired (and thus that it *can* be repaired). (N') is a close and, as it were, a largely "realistic" translation of (N).

(N')   *a* is a naturally or physically necessary fact (or statement, or statement
function) of our own world *T* if and only if *a* is satisfied in every *logically*
possible world which satisfies a set *M* of "separated" and universal facts,
consisting of every fact *b* such that to *b* corresponds an axiom *b'* with the
following properties: (1) *b'* belongs to one or another independent set *A*
of "separated" universal axioms *which are all satisfied in every possible
world differing from our own world (if at all) only with respect to initial
conditions (in the wider sense);* and (2) *b'* is *not* satisfied in every possible
world *W* in which all the other axioms of *A* are satisfied, even if it is
stipulated that *all those initial conditions* hold in *W* which hold *in our own
world.*

I wish to express again my gratitude to Messrs Nerlich and Suchting for
their criticism and to Dr Mary Hesse for spotting a mistake in an earlier version of
this note. As always, David Miller, my former research assistant, has been of the
greatest help in criticising and checking my efforts. But my greatest debt is to
William Kneale, who (in this *Journal* 12 (1961), 99-102) corrected some of my
formulations most convincingly and understandingly.

KARL POPPER

13. *Addendum, 1968*

Since this appendix was first published in 1959, there has been a very
interesting reply from William Kneale, *B.J.P.S.* 12, 1961, p. 99ff., and a criticism by
G. C. Nerlich and W. A. Suchting, *B.J.P.S.* 18, 1967, p. 233ff., to which I replied,
B.J.P.S. 18, 1967, p. 316ff. I do not now think that my reply is very good. In fact,
it is only after reconsidering Kneale's criticism that I realised what is at the bottom
of our disagreement.*

It is, I now think, the fact that most philosophers regard definitions as
important, and that they have never taken my assurance seriously that I do regard
them as unimportant. I neither believe that definitions can make the meaning of
our words definite, nor do I think it worth bothering about whether or not we can
define a term (though it may sometimes be moderately interesting that a term can
be defined with the help of terms *of a certain kind*); for we do not need undefined
primitive terms in any case.

I may perhaps sum up my position by saying that, while theories and the
problems connected with their truth are all-important, words and the problems
connected with their meaning are unimportant. (*Cp. Conjectures and Refutations,*
3rd edition, 1968, point (9) on p. 28.)

Reprinted by permission of the author and publisher from Karl Popper, *The Logic of
Scientific Discovery* (London: Hutchinson & Co., sixth impression, 1972), Appendix 10, p.
441.

*[All mentioned articles are reprinted in this text—Ed.]

For this reason I am not really interested in either the definition or in the definability of "natural necessity"; though I am interested in the fact (for I believe that it is a fact) that the idea is not meaningless.

Least of all am I interested in establishing the fact (if it is a fact, which I regard as doubtful) that a modal term can be defined with the help of non-modal terms. If I have given the impression that this is what I wanted to show, I have certainly given the wrong impression.

Suggested Readings for Part Two

Ayer, A. J. *The Foundations of Empirical Knowledge.* New York: Macmillan Company, 1940, chapter 4.

Ayers, M. R. *The Refutation of Determinism.* London, Eng.: Methuen and Company, 1968, chapters 4-5.

Blanshard, Brand. *Reason and Analysis.* La Salle, Ill.: Open Court Publishing Co., 1962, chapters 11-12.

Burks, A. W. "The Logic of Causal Propositions." *Mind* 60 (1951): 363-82.

Carnap, Rudolf. *Philosophical Foundations of Physics.* New York: Basic Books, Inc., 1966, chapters 19-21.

Cohen, L. Jonathon. *The Diversity of Meaning.* London, Eng.: Methuen and Company, 1966, chapter 10.

Ducasse, C. J. *Causation and the Types of Necessity.* New York: Dover Publications, 1969, Parts 2-3.

Ewing, A. C. *Idealism: A Critical Survey.* London, Eng.: Methuen and Company, 1934, chapter 4.

Kneale, William. *Probability and Induction.* Oxford, Eng.: Clarendon Press, 1949, sections 13-19.

Madden, E. H. and Hare, P. H. "The Powers that Be." *Dialogue* 10 (1971): 12-31.

Pap, Arthur. "Disposition Concepts and Extensional Logic." In *Minnesota Studies in the Philosophy of Science,* Volume 2, edited by H. Feigl, M. Scriven, and G. Maxwell. Minneapolis, Minn.: University of Minnesota Press, 1958, pp. 196-224.

Popper, K. *The Logic of Scientific Discovery.* London, Eng.: Hutchinson & Sons, 1959, Appendix 10, sections 1-13, 17.

Sellars, Wilfrid. "Counterfactuals, Dispositions, and the Causal Modalities." In *Minnesota Studies in the Philosophy of Science,* Volume 2, edited by H. Feigl, M. Scriven, and G. Maxwell. Minneapolis, Minn.: University of Minnesota Press, 1958, pp. 225-308.

Taylor, Richard. "Causation." *Monist* 47 (1963): 287-313.

PART THREE

MODERN REGULARITY THEORIES

INTRODUCTION

Modern Necessity Theories have forced defenders of the Regularity Theory to reconsider the basis for the distinction between universals of fact and nomological generalizations and also to explain the relation between laws and the counterfactual conditionals they support. Modern regularity advocates have generally agreed that these problems are genuine and that elucidation of the concept of lawlikeness merely in terms of "unrestricted universals of fact" is inadequate, whether the context is a scientific one or an ordinary context involving causal generalizations. Exponents of the regularity position have maintained with virtual unanimity, however, both that the necessity theorists' distinction between necessary universals and factual universals is misleading and that lawlikeness is explicable in terms of the type of support which unrestricted factual statements receive. Scientific contexts, where laws have direct inductive confirmation as well as support from other laws, are thought to be especially important.

The general direction of thought about causal necessity by modern defenders of this Regularity Theory may be described as follows: In causal contexts, the word "necessity" does not function to describe or to convey information about the facts as such. Rather, it marks a distinction between laws and accidental generalizations (segregating laws from non-laws), which is needed for certain activities that involve the use of predictive and subjunctive expressions. The facts referred to by both sorts of generalization do not differ in that only one sort refers to a modal fact; on the contrary, the two types of generalization differ primarily in the strength of our commitment to their unrestricted universality. General causal statements are not initially used for prediction because they are recognized by empirical study as distinctively lawlike; rather, general statements are recognized as lawlike because they draw our confidence by faithfully serving predictive functions. There are, then, pragmatic reasons for employing the notion of necessity, but there are no physical or metaphysical grounds for supposing that some objective feature of nature is denoted.

A. J. Ayer pursues this line of argument in a manner directly reminiscent of Hume's subjective account of necessity. Ayer admits that the distinction between nomological generalizations and unrestricted universals of fact cannot be explained by appeal merely to extensive inductive support; for the amount of factual information conveyed by the two types of universal may be substantially similar, and a contrary instance refutes both in the same way. He suggests that the distinction "lies not so much on the side of the facts which make [law statements] true or false as in the *attitude* of those who put them forward." The confidence placed in the factual evidence constitutes the decisive difference. The *treatment* which universal generalizations receive, then, is more important than the facts they express. Ayer's suggestion recalls Hume's explanation of his second definition of "cause." Hume pointed out that, in addition to the factual concomitance mentioned in his first definition, one who believes in a lawful sequence is mentally disposed to connect antecedent and consequent conditions for all similar situations. The extra strength of the connection in causal laws is not in the factual concomitance so much as it is in a mental preparation, including *belief,* which Hume characterized as an attitude of "reliance and security." This mental preparation is for Hume the source of the idea of necessity which distinguishes the lawlike from the non-lawlike, i.e., causal sequence from non-causal sequence. Ayer's article represents a return to this classical empiricist position.

 Ernest Nagel adopts the similar view that "the cognitive attitudes manifested toward a statement because of the nature of the available evidence" forms one important explanation of why statements are classified as laws of nature. He explicates nomological universals through analysis of the logical and epistemic conditions under which factual universals come to be accepted as lawlike. He maintains that whether or not a law sustains a counterfactual conditional depends as much on the predictive function served by the law in a particular setting of scientific explanation as on the truth of the law. He also argues a version of the now widely accepted view that counterfactuals should be analyzed as metalinguistic statements about what can be deduced from a system of statements S (which includes causal law statements and statements of assumed boundary conditions) when some antecedent condition statement A is introduced as a supposition. A consequent C follows necessarily from A and S, but this necessity is strictly logical. Introduction of natural necessity to account for counterfactuals seems gratuitous on this account; indeed no necessity is attributed at all other than the necessity of inferences warranted by the laws.

 J. L. Mackie's views reflect a somewhat different approach, though he clearly should be located in the regularity tradition. He concentrates on explicating the general meaning and use of counterfactuals in order to acquire perspective on their relevance for analysis of causal laws. He indicates complete dissatisfaction with interpretations which either construe counterfactuals as statements with truth values or as statements logically implied by other statements. He maintains instead that counterfactuals express imagined situations and have the form of condensed arguments which are *entertained* but not in fact *argued.* Mackie's point is that a number of factual premises and causal laws are presumed, no set of which is complete, in order to draw a counterfactual conclusion. Such a conclusion always has the status of an entertained supposition and not of an assertion. One proof of this is the fact that a counterfactual would always be given up if certain additional premises were added to the (always premise-incomplete) argument by means of which the law-governed counterfactual is derived. Since all the premises can never be entertained, the argument can never be completed. A relevant set of premises may sustain, but does not imply, the counterfactual conditional. Mackie would not deny that we ordinarily think both that counterfactuals are statements with truth values and, on a more sophisticated level, that laws entail counterfactuals. However, he will not admit that these common convictions count against his analysis; and he even suggests that quite ordinary counterfactuals are easily handled within his framework. For example, Mackie argues that the lawlike statement, "All defeated presidential candidates are disappointed," and the singular assertion, "Kennedy was a presidential candidate," sustain, but do not imply, "If Kennedy had been defeated, he would have been disappointed."

Mackie's theory is particularly inviting to a Humean because it helps resolve perhaps the major problem with counterfactuals: how to decide under what conditions one is justified in advancing them. Clearly one is justified if and only if the *beliefs* which support the counterfactual are justified. This problem in the case of law-governed counterfactuals is that of deciding when inductive generalizations held to be laws are justified—the problem of induction. Problems with counterfactuals, on Mackie's account, should not be regarded as somehow different from problems about induction. Also, it can be maintained on these grounds that general laws are thought to sustain counterfactuals while accidental universals do not, because the latter seem (for whatever reason) undermined by the supposition that there may be instances of the subject term not included in the evidence for the generalization. For example, an accidental universal might be based on a mere enumeration of a closed class and hence would be undermined if suppositions were made concerning objects outside the class. In the case of statements accepted as causal laws there is no such weakness. Contra necessity theorists, Mackie concludes that problems concerning the derivation of counterfactuals from laws are problems concerning why accidental universals are deficient; they are misconceived when taken as problems about the evidence for or logical strength of law statements.

George Molnar's article, "Kneale's Argument Revisited," is a tightly reasoned defense of Kneale's Necessity Theory of laws against Nagel, Mackie, and other recent philosophers. Molnar's article is, in effect, a rational reconstruction of Kneale's work which emphasizes the point that the Regularity Theory cannot fully account for our convictions concerning unrealized possibilities in nature. Molnar tries to show that on regularity theorists' principles it follows that no member of the set of contingent unrestricted existential statements [e.g., "There exists (somewhere, somewhen) a river of Coca Cola"] can be used to express an unrealized possibility. Specifically against the Nagel-Mackie-Ayer approach, Molnar argues that possibility is not an epistemic concept and that what is possible or impossible depends neither upon what someone or some group of scientists knows, nor upon the manner in which they acquire their knowledge, nor upon the evidential basis on which they accept hypotheses. Unknown nomic regularities, for example, define limits on what is possible no less than do known ones. Molnar reasons that:

> given the view of laws propounded by Nagel and Mackie, it is no longer laws alone which define possibilities. *p* will be a statement of possibility only if it is consistent with every law of nature *and with every proposition which is like a law in all respects except epistemic ones*. This is entailed by the knowledge-independence of possibilities in *re*. Thus if we accept both the epistemic restrictions on the definition of "law" and the idea of real empirical possibility, the definition of the latter has to be amended. . . .

Molnar concludes that no contemporary construal of laws other than Kneale's is satisfactory and that there are no manifest deficiencies in Kneale's Necessity Theory.

A. J. AYER

14. *What Is a Law of Nature?*

I

There is a sense in which we know well enough what is ordinarily meant by a law of nature. We can give examples. Thus it is, or is believed to be, a law of nature that the orbit of a planet around the sun is an ellipse, or that arsenic is poisonous, or that the intensity of a sensation is proportionate to the logarithm of the stimulus, or that there are 303,000,000,000,000,000,000,000 molecules in one gram of hydrogen. It is not a law of nature, though it is necessarily true, that the sum of the angles of a Euclidean triangle is 180 degrees, or that all the presidents of the third French Republic were male, though this is a legal fact in its way, or that all the cigarettes which I now have in my cigarette case are made of Virginian tobacco, though this again is true and, given my tastes, not wholly accidental. But while there are many such cases in which we find no difficulty in telling whether some proposition, which we take to be true, is or is not a law of nature, there are cases where we may be in doubt. For instance, I suppose that most people take the laws of nature to include the first law of thermodynamics, the proposition that in any closed physical system the sum of energy is constant: but there are those who maintain that this principle is a convention, that it is interpreted in such a way that there is no logical possibility of its being falsified, and for this reason they may deny that it is a law of nature at all. There are two questions at issue in a case of this sort: first, whether the principle under discussion is in fact a convention, and secondly whether its being a convention, if it is one, would disqualify it from being a law of nature. In the same way, there may be a dispute whether statistical generalizations are to count as laws of nature, as distinct from the dispute whether certain generalizations, which have been taken to be laws of nature, are in fact statistical. And even if we were always able to tell, in the case of any given proposition, whether or not it had the form of a law of nature, there would still remain the problem of making clear what this implied.

The use of the word "law," as it occurs in the expression "laws of nature," is now fairly sharply differentiated from its use in legal and moral contexts: we do not conceive of the laws of nature as imperatives. But this was not always so. For instance, Hobbes in his *Leviathan* lists fifteen "laws of nature" of which two of the most important are that men "seek peace, and follow it" and "that men perform their covenants made": but he does not think that these laws are necessarily respected. On the contrary, he holds that the state of nature is a state of war, and that covenants will not in fact be kept unless there is some power to enforce them. His laws of nature are like civil laws except that they are not the commands of any civil authority. In one place he speaks of them as "dictates of Reason" and adds

Reprinted by permission of the author and publisher from A. J. Ayer, "What Is a Law of Nature?" *Revue Internationale de Philosophie* Tome 10, Fascicule 2 (1956): 144-65. Also used by permission of St. Martin's Press, Inc., Macmillan & Co., Ltd. and reprinted from *The Concept of a Person*, by A. J. Ayer.
Note: Footnotes have been renumbered for the purposes of this text.

that men improperly call them by the name of laws: "for they are but conclusions or theorems concerning what conduceth to the conservation and defence of themselves: whereas Law, properly, is the word of him, that by right hath command over others." "But yet," he continues, "if you consider the same Theorems, as delivered in the word of God, that by right commandeth all things; then they are properly called Laws."[1]

It might be thought that this usage of Hobbes was so far removed from our own that there was little point in mentioning it, except as a historical curiosity; but I believe that the difference is smaller than it appears to be. I think that our present use of the expression "laws of nature" carries traces of the conception of Nature as subject to command. Whether these commands are conceived to be those of a personal deity or, as by the Greeks, of an impersonal fate, makes no difference here. The point, in either case, is that the sovereign is thought to be so powerful that its dictates are bound to be obeyed. It is not as in Hobbes's usage a question of moral duty or of prudence, where the subject has freedom to err. On the view which I am now considering, the commands which are issued to Nature are delivered with such authority that it is impossible that she should disobey them. I do not claim that this view is still prevalent; at least not that it is explicitly held. But it may well have contributed to the persistence of the feeling that there is some form of necessity attaching to the laws of nature, a necessity which, as we shall see, it is extremely difficult to pin down.

In case anyone is still inclined to think that the laws of nature can be identified with the commands of a superior being, it is worth pointing out that this analysis cannot be correct. It is already an objection to it that it burdens our science with all the uncertainty of our metaphysics, or our theology. If it should turn out that we had no good reason to believe in the existence of such a superior being, or no good reason to believe that he issued any commands, it would follow, on this analysis, that we should not be entitled to believe that there were any laws of nature. But the main argument against this view is independent of any doubt that one may have about the existence of a superior being. Even if we knew that such a one existed, and that he regulated nature, we still could not identify the laws of nature with his commands. For it is only by discovering what were the laws of nature that we could know what form these commands had taken. But this implies that we have some independent criteria for deciding what the laws of nature are. The assumption that they are imposed by a superior being is therefore idle, in the same way as the assumption of providence is idle. It is only if there are independent means of finding out what is going to happen that one is able to say what providence has in store. The same objection applies to the rather more fashionable view that moral laws are the commands of a superior being: but this does not concern us here.

There is, in any case, something strange about the notion of a command which it is impossible to disobey. We may be sure that some command will never in fact be disobeyed. But what is meant by saying that it cannot be? That the sanctions which sustain it are too strong? But might not one be so rash or so foolish as to defy them? I am inclined to say that it is in the nature of commands that it should be possible to disobey them. The necessity which is ascribed to these sup-

---

[1] *Leviathan*, Part I, chapter xv.

posedly irresistible commands belongs in fact to something different: it belongs to the laws of logic. Not that the laws of logic cannot be disregarded; one can make mistakes in deductive reasoning, as in anything else. There is, however, a sense in which it is impossible for anything that happens to contravene the laws of logic. The restriction lies not upon the events themselves but on our method of describing them. If we break the rules according to which our method of description functions, we are not using it to describe anything. This might suggest that the events themselves really were disobeying the laws of logic, only we could not say so. But this would be an error. What is describable as an event obeys the laws of logic: and what is not describable as an event is not an event at all. The chains which logic puts upon nature are purely formal: being formal they weigh nothing, but for the same reason they are indissoluble.

From thinking of the laws of nature as the commands of a superior being, it is therefore only a short step to crediting them with the necessity that belongs to the laws of logic. And this is in fact a view which many philosophers have held. They have taken it for granted that a proposition could express a law of nature only if it stated that events, or properties, of certain kinds were necessarily connected; and they have interpreted this necessary connection as being identical with, or closely analogous to, the necessity with which the conclusion follows from the premisses of a deductive argument; as being, in short, a logical relation. And this has enabled them to reach the strange conclusion that the laws of nature can, at least in principle, be established independently of experience: for if they are purely logical truths, they must be discoverable by reason alone.

The refutation of this view is very simple. It was decisively set out by Hume. "To convince us," he says, "that all the laws of nature and all the operations of bodies, without exception, are known only by experience, the following reflections may, perhaps, suffice. Were any object presented to us, and were we required to pronounce concerning the effect, which will result from it, without consulting past observation: after what manner, I beseech you, must the mind proceed in this operation? It must invent or imagine some event, which it ascribes to the object as its effective: and it is plain that this invention must be entirely arbitrary. The mind can never find the effect in the supposed cause, by the most accurate scrutiny and examination. For the effect is totally different from the cause, and consequently it can never be discovered in it."[2]

Hume's argument is, indeed, so simple that its purport has often been misunderstood. He is represented as maintaining that the inherence of an effect in its cause is something which is not discoverable in nature; that as a matter of fact our observations fail to reveal the existence of any such relation: which would allow for the possibility that our observations might be at fault. But the point of Hume's argument is not that the relation of necessary connection which is supposed to conjoin distinct events is not in fact observable: it is that there could not be any such relation, not as a matter of fact but as a matter of logic. What Hume is pointing out is that if two events are distinct, they are distinct: from a statement which does no more than assert the existence of one of them it is impossible to deduce anything concerning the existence of the other. This is, indeed, a plain tautology. Its importance lies in the fact that Hume's opponents denied it. They

---

[2] *An Enquiry concerning Humean Understanding*, iv. I.25.

wished to maintain both that the events which were coupled by the laws of nature were logically distinct from one another, and that they were united by a logical relation. But this is a manifest contradiction. Philosophers who hold this view are apt to express it in a form which leaves the contradiction latent: it was Hume's achievement to have brought it clearly to light.

In certain passages Hume makes his point by saying that the contradictory of any law of nature is at least conceivable; he intends thereby to show that the truth of the statement which expresses such a law is an empirical matter of fact and not an *a priori* certainty. But to this it has been objected that the fact that the contradictory of a proposition is conceivable is not a decisive proof that the proposition is not necessary. It may happen, in doing logic or pure mathematics, that one formulates a statement which one is unable either to prove or disprove. Surely in that case both the alternatives of its truth and falsehood are conceivable. Professor W. C. Kneale, who relies on this objection,[3] cites the example of Goldbach's conjecture that every even number greater than two is the sum of two primes. Though this conjecture has been confirmed so far as it has been tested, no one yet knows for certain whether it is true or false: no proof has been discovered either way. All the same, if it is true, it is necessarily true, and if it is false, it is necessarily false. Suppose that it should turn out to be false. We surely should not be prepared to say that what Goldbach had conjectured to be true was actually inconceivable. Yet we should have found it to be the contradictory of a necessary proposition. If we insist that this does prove it to be inconceivable, we find ourselves in the strange position of having to hold that one of two alternatives is inconceivable, without our knowing which.

I think that Professor Kneale makes his case: but I do not think that it is an answer to Hume. For Hume is not primarily concerned with showing that a given set of propositions, which have been taken to be necessary, are not so really. This is only a possible consequence of his fundamental point that "there is no object which implies the existence of any other if we consider these objects in themselves, and never look beyond the idea which we form of them,"[4] in short, that to say that events are distinct is incompatible with saying that they are logically related. And against this Professor Kneale's objection has no force at all. The most that it could prove is that, in the case of the particular examples that he gives, Hume might be mistaken in supposing that the events in question really were distinct: in spite of the appearances to the contrary, an expression which he interpreted as referring to only one of them might really be used in such a way that it included a reference to the other.

But is it not possible that Hume was always so mistaken; that the events, or properties, which are coupled by the laws of nature never are distinct? This question is complicated by the fact that once a generalization is accepted as a law of nature it tends to change its status. The meanings which we attach to our expressions are not completely constant: if we are firmly convinced that every object of a kind which is designated by a certain term has some property which the term does not originally cover, we tend to include the property in the designation; we extend the definition of the object, with or without altering the words which

---

[3] *Probability and Induction*, pp. 79ff.
[4] *A Treatise of Human Nature*, i. iii, vi.

refer to it. Thus, it was an empirical discovery that loadstones attract iron and steel: for someone who uses the word "loadstone" only to refer to an object which has a certain physical appearance and constitution, the fact that it behaves in this way is not formally deducible. But, as the word is now generally used, the proposition that loadstones attract iron and steel is analytically true: an object which did not do this would not properly be called a loadstone. In the same way, it may have become a necessary truth that water has the chemical composition H_2O. But what then of heavy water which has the composition D_2O? Is it not really water? Clearly this question is quite trivial. If it suits us to regard heavy water as a species of water, then we must not make it necessary that water consists of H_2O. Otherwise, we may. We are free to settle the matter whichever way we please.

Not all questions of this sort are so trivial as this. What, for example, is the status in Newtonian physics of the principle that the acceleration of a body is equal to the force which is acting on it divided by its mass? If we go by the text-books in which "force" is defined as the product of mass and acceleration, we shall conclude that the principle is evidently analytic. But are there not other ways of defining force which allow this principle to be empirical? In fact there are, but as Henri Poincaré has shown,[5] we may then find ourselves obliged to treat some other Newtonian principle as a convention. It would appear that in a system of this kind there is likely to be a conventional element, but that, within limits, we can situate it where we choose. What is put to the test of experience is the system as a whole.

This is to concede that some of the propositions which pass for laws of nature are logically necessary, while implying that it is not true of all of them. But one might go much further. It is at any rate conceivable that at a certain stage the science of physics should become so unified that it could be wholly axiomatized: it would attain the status of a geometry in which all the generalizations were regarded as necessarily true. It is harder to envisage any such development in the science of biology, let alone the social sciences, but it is not theoretically impossible that it should come about there too. It would be characteristic of such systems that no experience could falsify them, but their security might be sterile. What would take the place of their being falsified would be the discovery that they had no empirical application.

The important point to notice is that, whatever may be the practical or aesthetic advantages of turning scientific laws into logically necessary truths, it does not advance our knowledge, or in any way add to the security of our beliefs. For what we gain in one way, we lose in another. If we make it a matter of definition that there are just so many million molecules in every gram of hydrogen, then we can indeed be certain that every gram of hydrogen will contain that number of molecules: but we must become correspondingly more doubtful, in any given case, whether what we take to be a gram of hydrogen really is so. The more we put into our definitions, the more uncertain it becomes whether anything satisfies them: this is the price that we pay for diminishing the risk of our laws being falsified. And if it ever came to the point where all the "laws" were made completely secure by being treated as logically necessary, the whole weight of doubt would fall upon the statement that our system had application. Having deprived ourselves of the power of expressing empirical generalizations, we should have to make our existential statements do the work instead.

---

[5] Cf. *La Science et l'hypothèse*, pp. 119-29.

If such a stage were reached, I am inclined to say that we should no longer have a use for the expression "laws of nature," as it is now understood. In a sense, the tenure of such laws would still be asserted: they would be smuggled into the existential propositions. But there would be nothing in the system that would count as a law of nature: for I take it to be characteristic of a law of nature that the proposition which expresses it is not logically true. In this respect, however, our usage is not entirely clearcut. In a case where a sentence has originally expressed an empirical generalization, which we reckon to be a law of nature, we are inclined to say that it still expresses a law of nature, even when its meaning has been so modified that it has come to express an analytic truth. And we are encouraged in this by the fact that it is often very difficult to tell whether this modification has taken place or not. Also, in the case where some of the propositions in a scientific system play the rôle of definitions, but we have some freedom in deciding which they are to be, we tend to apply the expression "laws of nature" to any of the constituent propositions of the system, whether or not they are analytically true. But here it is essential that the system as a whole should be empirical. If we allow the analytic propositions to count as laws of nature, it is because they are carried by the rest.

Thus to object to Hume that he may be wrong in assuming that the events between which his causal relations hold are "distinct existences" is merely to make the point that it is possible for a science to develop in such a way that axiomatic systems take the place of natural laws. But this was not true of the propositions with which Hume was concerned, nor is it true, in the main, of the sciences of today. And in any case Hume is right in saying that we cannot have the best of both worlds; if we want our generalizations to have empirical content, they cannot be logically secure; if we make them logically secure, we rob them of their empirical content. The relations which hold between things, or events, or properties, cannot be both factual and logical. Hume himself spoke only of causal relations, but his argument applies to any of the relations that science establishes, indeed to any relations whatsoever.

It should perhaps be remarked that those philosophers who still wish to hold that the laws of nature are "principles of necessitation"[6] would not agree that this came down to saying that the propositions which expressed them were analytic. They would maintain that we are dealing here with relations of objective necessity, which are not to be identified with logical entailments, though the two are in certain respects akin. But what are these relations of objective necessity supposed to be? No explanation is given except that they are just the relations that hold between events, or properties, when they are connected by some natural law. But this is simply to restate the problem; not even to attempt to solve it. It is not as if this talk of objective necessity enabled us to detect any laws of nature. On the contrary it is only *ex post facto,* when the existence of some connection has been empirically tested, that philosophers claim to see that it has this mysterious property of being necessary. And very often what they do "see" to be necessary is shown by further observation to be false. This does not itself prove that the events which are brought together by a law of nature do not stand in some unique

---

[6] Cf. Kneale, *op. cit.*

relation. If all attempts at its analysis fail, we may be reduced to saying that it is *sui generis*. But why then describe it in a way which leads to its confusion with the relation of logical necessity?

A further attempt to link natural with logical necessity is to be found in the suggestion that two events E and I are to be regarded as necessarily connected when there is some well-established universal statement U, from which, in conjunction with the proposition *i*, affirming the existence of I, a proposition *e*, affirming the existence of E, is formally deducible.[7] This suggestion has the merit of bringing out the fact that any necessity that there may be in the connection of two distinct events comes only through a law. The proposition which describes "the initial conditions" does not by itself entail the proposition which describes the "effect": it does so only when it is combined with a causal law. But this does not allow us to say that the law itself is necessary. We can give a similar meaning to saying that the law is necessary by stipulating that it follows, either directly or with the help of certain further premises, from some more general principle. But then what is the status of these more general principles? The question what constitutes a law of nature remains, on this view, without an answer.

II

Once we are rid of the confusion between logical and factual relations, what seems the obvious course is to hold that a proposition expresses a law of nature when it states what invariably happens. Thus, to say that unsupported bodies fall, assuming this to be a law of nature, is to say that there is not, never has been, and never will be a body that being unsupported does not fall. The "necessity" of a law consists, on this view, simply in the fact that there are no exceptions to it.

It will be seen that this interpretation can also be extended to statistical laws. For they too may be represented as stating the existence of certain constancies in nature: only, in their case, what is held to be constant is the proportion of instances in which one property is conjoined with another or, to put it in a different way, the proportion of the members of one class that are also members of another. Thus it is a statistical law that when there are two genes determining a hereditary property, say the colour of a certain type of flower, the proportion of individuals in the second generation that display the dominant attribute, say the colour white as opposed to the colour red, is three quarters. There is, however, the difficulty that one does not expect the proportion to be maintained in every sample. As Professor R. B. Braithwaite has pointed out, "when we say that the proportion (in a non-literal sense) of the male births among births is 51 percent, we are not saying of any particular class of births that 51 percent are births of males, for the actual proportion might differ very widely from 51 percent in a particular class of births, or in a number of particular classes of births, without our wishing to reject the proposition that the proportion (in the non-literal sense) is 51 percent."[8]

---

[7] Cf. K. Popper, "What Can Logic Do For Philosophy?" *Supplementary Proceedings of the Aristotelian Society*, vol. xxii: and papers in the same volume by W. C. Kneale and myself.

[8] *Scientific Explanation*, pp. 118-19.

All the same the "non-literal" use of the word "proportion" is very close to the literal use. If the law holds, the proportion must remain in the neighbourhood of 51 percent, for any sufficiently large class of cases: and the deviations from it which are found in selected sub-classes must be such as the application of the calculus of probability would lead one to expect. Admittedly, the question what constitutes a sufficiently large class of cases is hard to answer. It would seem that the class must be finite, but the choice of any particular finite number for it would seem also to be arbitrary. I shall not, however, attempt to pursue this question here. The only point that I here wish to make is that a statistical law is no less "lawlike" than a causal law. Indeed, if the propositions which express causal laws are simply state-ments of what invariably happens, they can themselves be taken as expressing statistical laws, with ratios of 100 percent. Since a 100 percent ratio, if it really holds, must hold in every sample, these "limiting cases" of statistical laws escape the difficulty which we have just remarked on. If henceforth we confine our atten-tion to them, it is because the analysis of "normal" statistical laws brings in compli-cations which are foreign to our purpose. They do not affect the question of what makes a proposition lawlike: and it is in this that we are mainly interested.

On the view which we have now to consider, all that is required for there to be laws in nature is the existence of *de facto* constancies. In the most straight-forward case, the constancy consists in the fact that events, or properties, or processes of different types are invariably conjoined with one another. The attrac-tion of this view lies in its simplicity: but it may be too simple. There are objections to it which are not easily met.

In the first place, we have to avoid saddling ourselves with vacuous laws. If we interpret statements of the form "All S is P" as being equivalent, in Russell's notation, to general implications of the form "$(x) \Phi x \supset \Psi x$," we face the difficulty that such implications are considered to be true in all cases in which their ante-cedent is false. Thus we shall have to take it as a universal truth both that all winged horses are spirited and that all winged horses are tame; for assuming, as I think we may, that there never have been or will be any winged horses, it is true both that there never have been or will be any that are not spirited, and that there never have been or will be any that are not tame. And the same will hold for any other property that we care to choose. But surely we do not wish to regard the ascription of any property whatsoever to winged horses as the expression of a law of nature.

The obvious way out of this difficulty is to stipulate that the class to which we are referring should not be empty. If statements of the form "All S is P" are used to express laws of nature, they must be construed as entailing that there are S's. They are to be treated as the equivalent, in Russell's notation, of the conjunction of the propositions "$(x) \Phi x \supset \Psi x$ and $(\exists x) \Phi x$." But this condition may be too strong. For there are certain cases in which we do wish to take general implications as expressing laws of nature, even though their antecedents are not satisfied. Consider, for example, the Newtonian law that a body on which no forces are acting continues at rest or in uniform motion along a straight line. It might be argued that this proposition was vacuously true, on the ground that there are in fact no bodies on which no forces are acting; but it is not interpreted as being vacuous. But how then does it fit into the scheme? How can it be held to be descriptive of what actually happens?

What we want to say is that if there *were* any bodies on which no forces were acting then they *would* behave in the way that Newton's law prescribes. But we have not made any provisions for such hypothetical cases: according to the view which we are now examining, statements of law cover only what is actual, not what is merely possible. There is, however, a way in which we can still fit in such "non-instantial" laws. As Professor C. D. Broad has suggested,[9] we can treat them as referring not to hypothetical objects, or events, but only to the hypothetical consequences of instantial laws. Our Newtonian law can then be construed as implying that there are instantial laws, in this case laws about the behaviour of bodies on "which forces are acting, which are such that when combined with the proposition that there are bodies on which no forces are acting, they entail the conclusion that these bodies continue at rest, or in uniform motion along a straight line. The proposition that there are such bodies is false, and so, if it is interpreted existentially, is the conclusion, but that does not matter. As Broad puts it, "what we are concerned to assert is that this false conclusion is a necessary consequence of the conjunction of a certain false instantial supposition with certain true instantial laws of nature."

This solution of the present difficulty is commendably ingenious, though I am not sure that it would always be possible to find the instantial laws which it requires. But even if we accept it, our troubles are not over. For, as Broad himself points out, there is one important class of cases in which it does not help us. These cases are those in which one measurable quantity is said to depend upon another, cases like that of the law connecting the volume and temperature of a gas under a given pressure, in which there is a mathematical function which enables one to calculate the numerical value of either quantity from the value of the other. Such laws have the form "$x = Fy$," where the range of the variable y covers all possible values of the quantity in question. But now it is not to be supposed that all these values are actually to be found in nature. Even if the number of different temperatures which specimens of gases have or will acquire is infinite, there still must be an infinite number missing. How then are we to interpret such a law? As being the compendious assertion of all its actual instances? But the formulation of the law in no way indicates which the actual instances are. It would be absurd to construe a general formula about the functional dependence of one quantity on another as committing us to the assertion that just these values of the quantity are actually realized. As asserting that for a value n of y, which is in fact not realized, the proposition that it is realized, in conjunction with the set of propositions describing all the actual cases, entails the proposition that there is a corresponding value m of x? But this is open to the same objection, with the further drawback that the entailment would not hold. As asserting with regard to any given value n of y that either n is not realized or that there is a corresponding value m of x? This is the most plausible alternative, but it makes the law trivial for all the values of y which happens not to be realized. It is hard to escape the conclusion that what we really mean to assert when we formulate such a law is that there is a corresponding value of x to every *possible* value of y.

---

[9] "Mechanical and Teleological Causation" *Supplementary Proceedings of the Aristotelian Society,* vol. xiv, pp. 98ff.

Another reason for bringing in possibilities is that there seems to be no other way of accounting for the difference between generalizations of law and generalizations of fact. To revert to our earlier examples, it is a generalization of fact that all the Presidents of the Third French Republic are male, or that all the cigarettes that are now in my cigarette case are made of Virginian tobacco. It is a generalization of law that the planets of our solar system move in elliptical orbits, but a generalization of fact that, counting the earth as Terra, they all have Latin names. Some philosophers refer to these generalizations of facts as "accidental generalizations," but this use of the word "accidental" may be misleading. It is not suggested that these generalizations are true by accident, in the sense that there is no causal explanation of their truth, but only that they are not themselves the expression of natural laws.

But how is this distinction to be made? The formula "$(x)\ \Phi x \supset \Psi x$" holds equally in both cases. Whether the generalization be one of fact or of law, it will state at least that there is nothing which has the property Φ but lacks the property Ψ. In this sense, the generality is perfect in both cases, so long as the statements are true. Yet there seems to be a sense in which the generality of what we are calling generalizations of fact is less complete. They seem to be restricted in a way that generalizations of law are not. Either they involve some spatio-temporal restriction, as in the example of the cigarettes *now* in my cigarette case, or they refer to particular individuals, as in the examples of the presidents of France. When I say that all the planets have Latin names, I am referring definitely to a certain set of individuals, Jupiter, Venus, Mercury, and so on, but when I say that the planets move in elliptical orbits I am referring indefinitely to anything that has the properties that constitute being a planet in this solar system. But it will not do to say that generalizations of fact are simply conjunctions of particular statements, which definitely refer to individuals; for in asserting that the planets have Latin names, I do not individually identify them: I may know that they have Latin names without being able to list them all. Neither can we mark off generalizations of law by insisting that their expression is not to include any reference to specific places or times. For with a little ingenuity, generalizations of fact can always be made to satisfy this condition. Instead of referring to the cigarettes that are now in my cigarette case, I can find out some general property which only these cigarettes happen to possess, say the property of being contained in a cigarette case with such and such markings which is owned at such and such a period of his life by a person of such and such a sort, where the descriptions are so chosen that the description of the person is in fact satisfied only by me and the description of the cigarette case, if I possess more than one of them, only by the one in question. In certain instances these descriptions might have to be rather complicated, but usually they would not: and anyhow the question of complexity is not here at issue. But this means that, with the help of these "individuating" predicates, generalizations of fact can be expressed in just as universal a form as generalizations of law. And conversely, as Professor Nelson Goodman has pointed out, generalizations of law can themselves be expressed in such a way that they contain a reference to particular individuals, or to specific places and times. For, as he remarks, "even the hypothesis 'All grass is green' has an equivalent 'All grass in London or elsewhere is green.' "[10] Admit-

---

[10] *Fact, Fiction and Forecast*, p. 78.

tedly, this assimilation of the two types of statement looks like a dodge; but the fact that the dodge works shows that we cannot found the distinction on a difference in the ways in which the statement can be expressed. Again, what we want to say is that whereas generalizations of fact cover only actual instances, generalizations of law cover possible instances as well. But this notion of possible, as opposed to actual, instances has not yet been made clear.

If generalizations of law do cover possible as well as actual instances, their range must be infinite; for while the number of objects which do throughout the course of time possess a certain property may be finite, there can be no limit to the number of objects which might possibly possess it: for once we enter the realm of possibility we are not confined even to such objects as actually exist. And this shows how far removed these generalizations are from being conjunctions: not simply because their range is infinite, which might be true even if it were confined to actual instances, but because there is something absurd about trying to list all the possible instances. One can imagine an angel's undertaking the task of naming or describing all the men that there ever have been or will be, even if their number were infinite, but how would he set about naming, or describing, all the possible men? This point is developed by F. P. Ramsey who remarks that "the variable hypothetical '$(x) \Phi x$' resembles a conjunction (a) in that it contains all lesser, i.e., here all finite conjunctions, and appears as a sort of infinite product. (b) When we ask what would make it true, we inevitably answer that it is true if and only if every x has Φ; i.e., when we regard it as a proposition capable of the two cases truth and falsity, we are forced to make it a conjunction which we cannot express for lack of symbolic power."[1] But, he goes on, "what we can't say we can't say, and we can't whistle it either," and he concludes that the variable hypothetical is not a conjunction and that "if it is not a conjunction, it is not a proposition at all." Similarly, Professor Ryle, without explicitly denying that generalizations of law are propositions, describes them as "seasonal inference warrants,"[2] on the analogy of season railway-tickets, which implies that they are not so much propositions as rules. Professor Schlick also held that they were rules, arguing that they could not be propositions because they were not conclusively verifiable; but this is a poor argument, since it is doubtful if any propositions are conclusively verifiable, except possibly those that describe the subject's immediate experiences.

Now to say that generalizations of law are not propositions does have the merit of bringing out their peculiarity. It is one way of emphasizing the difference between them and generalizations of fact. But I think that it emphasizes it too strongly. After all, as Ramsey himself acknowledges, we do want to say that generalizations of law are either true or false. And they are tested in the way that other propositions are, by the examination of actual instances. A contrary instance refutes a generalization of law in the same way as it refutes a generalization of fact. A positive instance confirms them both. Admittedly, there is the difference that if all the actual instances are favourable, their conjunction entails the generalization of fact, whereas it does not entail the generalization of law: but still there is no better way of confirming a generalization of law than by finding favourable instances. To say that lawlike statements function as seasonal inference warrants is

---

[1] *Foundations of Mathematics*, p. 238.
[2] "'If,' 'So,' and 'Because,'" *Philosophical Analysis* (Essays edited by Max Black), p. 332.

indeed illuminating, but what it comes to is that the inferences in questions are warranted by the facts. There would be no point in issuing season tickets if the trains did not actually run.

To say that generalizations of law cover possible as well as actual cases is to say that they entail subjunctive conditionals. If it is a law of nature that the planets move in elliptical orbits, then it must not only be true that the actual planets move in elliptical orbits; it must also be true that if anything were a planet it would move in an elliptical orbit: and here "being a planet" must be construed as a matter of having certain properties, not just as being identical with one of the planets that there are. It is not indeed a peculiarity of statements which one takes as expressing laws of nature that they entail subjunctive conditionals: for the same will be true of any statement that contains a dispositional predicate. To say, for example, that this rubber band is elastic is to say not merely that it will resume its normal size when it has been stretched, but that it would do so if ever it were stretched: an object may be elastic without ever in fact being stretched at all. Even the statement that this is a white piece of paper may be taken as implying not only how the piece of paper does look but also how it would look under certain conditions, which may or may not be fulfilled. Thus one cannot say that generalizations of fact do not entail subjunctive conditionals, for they may very well contain dispositional predicates: indeed they are more likely to do so than not: but they will not entail the subjunctive conditionals which are entailed by the corresponding statements of law. To say that all the planets have Latin names may be to make a dispositional statement, in the sense that it implies not so much that people do always call them by such names but that they would so call them if they were speaking correctly. It does not, however, imply with regard to anything whatsoever that if it were a planet it would be called by a Latin name. And for this reason it is not a generalization of law, but only a generalization of fact.

There are many philosophers who are content to leave the matter here. They explain the "necessity" of natural laws as consisting in the fact that they hold for all possible, as well as actual, instances: and they distinguish generalizations of law from generalizations of fact by bringing out the differences in their entailment of subjunctive conditionals. But while this is correct so far as it goes, I doubt if it goes far enough. Neither the notion of possible, as opposed to actual, instances nor that of the subjunctive conditional is so pellucid that these references to them can be regarded as bringing all our difficulties to an end. It will be well to try to take our analysis a little further if we can.

The theory which I am going to sketch will not avoid all talk of dispositions; but it will confine it to people's attitudes. My suggestion is that the difference between our two types of generalization lies not so much on the side of facts which make them true or false, as in the attitude of those who put them forward. The factual information which is expressed by a statement of the form "for all x, if x has Φ then x has Ψ," is the same whichever way it is interpreted. For if the two interpretations differ only with respect to the possible, as opposed to the actual values of x, they do not differ with respect to anything that actually happens. Now I do not wish to say that a difference in regard to mere possibilities is not a genuine difference, or that it is to be equated with a difference in the attitude of those who do the interpreting. But I do think that it can best be elucidated by referring to such differences of attitude. In short I propose to explain the distinction between generalizations of law and generalizations of fact, and thereby to give some account of what a law of nature is, by the indirect method of analysing the distinction between treating a generalization as a statement of law and treating it as a statement of fact.

If someone accepts a statement of the form "$(x)\, \Phi x \supset \Psi x$" as a true generalization of fact, he will not in fact believe that anything which has the property Φ has any other property that leads to its not having Ψ. For since he believes that everything that has Φ has Ψ, he must believe that whatever other properties a given value of x may have they are not such as to prevent its having Ψ. It may be even that he knows this to be so. But now let us suppose that he believes such a generalization to be true, without knowing it for certain. In that case there will be various properties X, X_1 . . . such that if he were to learn, with respect to any value of a of x, that a had one or more of these properties as well as Φ, it would destroy, or seriously weaken his belief that a had Ψ. Thus I believe that all the cigarettes in my case are made of Virginian tobacco, but this belief would be destroyed if I were informed that I had absent-mindedly just filled my case from a box in which I keep only Turkish cigarettes. On the other hand, if I took it to be a law of nature that all the cigarettes in this case were made of Virginian tobacco, say on the ground that the case had some curious physical property which had the effect of changing any other tobacco that was put into it into Virginian, then my belief would not be weakened in this way.

Now if our laws of nature were causally independent of each other, and if, as Mill thought, the propositions which expressed them were always put forward as being unconditionally true, the analysis could proceed quite simply. We could then say that a person A was treating a statement of the form "for all x, if Φx then Ψx" as expressing a law of nature, if and only if there was no property X which was such that the information that a value a of x had X as well as Φ would weaken his belief that a had Ψ. And here we should have to admit the proviso that X did not logically entail not-Ψ, and also, I suppose, that its presence was not regarded as a manifestation of not-Ψ; for we do not wish to make it incompatible with treating a statement as the expression of a law that one should acknowledge a negative instance if it arises. But the actual position is not so simple. For one may believe that a statement of the form "for all x, if Φx then Ψx" expresses a law of nature while also believing, because of one's belief in other laws, that if something were to have the property X as well as Φ it would not have Ψ. Thus one's belief in the proposition that an object which one took to be a loadstone attracted iron might be weakened or destroyed by the information that the physical composition of the supposed loadstone was very different from what one had thought to be. I think, however, that in all such cases, the information which would impair one's belief that the object in question had the property Ψ would also be such that, independently of other considerations, it would seriously weaken one's belief that the object ever had the property Φ. And if this is so, we can meet the difficulty by stipulating that the range of properties which someone who treats "for all x if Φx then Ψx" as a law must be willing to conjoin with Φ, without his belief in the consequent being weakened, must not include those the knowledge of whose presence would in itself seriously weaken his belief in the presence of Φ.

There remains the further difficulty that we do not normally regard the propositions which we take to express laws of nature as being unconditionally true. In stating them we imply the presence of certain conditions which we do not actually specify. Perhaps we could specify them if we chose, though we might find it difficult to make the list exhaustive. In this sense a generalization of law may be weaker than a generalization of fact, since it may admit exceptions to the generalization as it is stated. This does not mean, however, that the law allows for exceptions: if the exception is acknowledged to be genuine, the law is held to be refuted. What happens in the other cases is that the exception is regarded as having been tacitly provided for. We lay down a law about the boiling point of water, without bothering to mention that it does not hold for high altitudes. When this is pointed out to us, we say this qualification was meant to be understood. And so in other instances. The statement that if anything has Φ it has Ψ was a loose formulation of the law: what we really meant was that if anything has Φ but not X, it has Ψ. Even in the case where the existence of the exception was not previously known, we often regard it as qualifying rather than refuting the law. We say, not that the generalization has been falsified, but that it was inexactly stated. Thus, it must be allowed that someone whose belief in the presence of Ψ, in a given instance, is destroyed by the belief that Φ is accompanied by X may still be treating "$(x)\,\Phi \supset \Psi x$" as expressing a law of nature if he is prepared to accept "$(x)\,\Phi x \cdot \sim Xx \supset \Psi x$" as a more exact statement of the law.

Accordingly I suggest that for someone to treat a statement of the form "if anything has Φ it has Ψ" as expressing a law of nature, it is sufficient (i) that subject to a willingness to explain away exceptions he believes that in a non-trivial sense everything which in fact has Φ has Ψ (ii) that his belief that something which has Φ has Ψ is not liable to be weakened by the discovery that the object in question also has some other property X, provided (a) that X does not logically entail not-Ψ (b) that X is not a manifestation of not-Ψ (c) that the discovery that something had X would not in itself seriously weaken his belief that it had Φ (d) that he does not regard the statement "if anything has Φ and not-X it has Ψ" as a more exact statement of the generalization that he was intending to express.

I do not suggest that these conditions are necessary, both because I think it possible that they could be simplified and because they do not cover the whole field. For instance, no provision has been made for functional laws, where the reference to possible instances does not at present seem to me eliminable. Neither am I offering a definition of natural law. I do not claim that to say that some proposition expresses a law of nature entails saying that someone has a certain attitude towards it; for clearly it makes sense to say that there are laws of nature which remain unknown. But this is consistent with holding that the notion is to be explained in terms of people's attitudes. My explanation is indeed sketchy, but I think that the distinctions which I have tried to bring out are relevant and important: and I hope that I have done something towards making them clear.

ERNEST NAGEL

15. Contrary-to-fact Universals

There are thus four types of considerations which seem relevant in classifying statements as laws of nature: (1) syntactical considerations relating to the form of lawlike statements; (2) the logical relations of statements to other statements in a system of explanations; (3) the functions assigned to lawlike statements in scientific inquiry; and (4) the cognitive attitudes manifested toward a statement because of the nature of the available evidence. These considerations overlap in part, since, for example, the logical position of a statement in a system is related to the role the statement can play in inquiry, as well as to the kind of evidence that can be obtained for it. Moreover, the conditions mentioned in these considerations are not asserted to be sufficient (or perhaps, in some cases, even necessary) for affixing the label "law of nature" to statements. Undoubtedly statements can be manufactured which satisfy these conditions but which would oridinarily not be called laws, just as statements sometimes called laws may be found which fail to satisfy one or more of these conditions. For reasons already stated, this is inevitable, for a precise explication of the meaning of "law of nature" which will be in agreement with every use of this vague expression is not possible. Nevertheless, statements satisfying these conditions appear to escape the objections raised by critics of a Humean analysis of nomic universality. This claim requires some defense; and something must also be said about the related problem of the logical status of contrary-to-fact conditionals.

1. Perhaps the most impressive current criticism of Humean analyses of nomic universality is the argument that *de facto* universals cannot support subjunctive conditionals. Suppose we know that there never has been a raven that was not black, that there is at present no raven that is not black, and that there never will be a raven that will not be black. We are then warranted in asserting as true the unrestricted accidental universal S: 'All ravens are black.' It has been argued, however, that S does not express what we would usually call a law of nature.[1] For suppose that in point of fact no raven has ever lived or will live in polar regions. But suppose further that we do not know whether or not dwelling in polar regions affects the color of ravens, so that as far as we know the progeny of ravens that might migrate into such regions may grow white feathers. Accordingly, though S is

From *The Structure of Science* by Ernest Nagel, copyright © 1961 by Harcourt Brace Jovanovich, Inc., and reprinted with their permission. Also reprinted by permission of Routledge & Kegan Paul, Ltd.

Note: Footnotes have been renumbered for the purposes of this text.

[1] William Kneale, "Natural Laws and Contrary-to-Fact Conditionals," *Analysis*, Vol. 10 (1950), p. 123 [Reprinted in this text]. Cf. also William Kneale, *Probability and Induction*, Oxford, 1949, p. 75. The impetus to much recent Anglo-American discussion of nomological universals and subjunctive as well as "contrary-to-fact" (or "counterfactual") conditionals was given by Roderick M. Chisholm, "The Contrary-to-fact Conditional," *Mind*, Vol. 55 (1946), pp. 289-307, and Nelson Goodman, "The Problem of Counterfactual Conditionals," *Journal of Philosophy*, Vol. 44 (1947), pp. 113-28, the latter also reprinted in Nelson Goodman, *Fact, Fiction, and Forecast*, Cambridge, Mass., 1955.

true, this truth may be only a consequence of this "historical accident" that no ravens ever live in polar regions. In consequence, the accidental universal S does not support the subjunctive conditional that if inhabitants of polar regions were ravens they would be black; and since a law of nature must, by hypothesis, support such conditionals, S cannot count as a law. In short, unrestricted universality does not explicate what we mean by nomic universality.

But though the argument may establish this latter point, it does not follow that S is not a law of nature because it fails to express an irreducible nomic necessity. For despite its assumed truth, S may be denied the status of law for at least two reasons, neither of which has anything to do with questions of such necessity. In the first place, the evidence for S may coincide with S's scope of predication, so that to anyone familiar with that evidence S cannot perform the functions which statements classified as laws are expected to perform. In the second place, though the evidence for S is by hypothesis logically sufficient to establish S as true, the evidence may be exclusively direct evidence; and one may refuse to label S as a law, on the ground that only statements for which indirect evidence is available (so that statements must occupy a certain logical position in the corpus of our knowledge) can claim title to the label.

But another consideration is no less relevant in this connection. The failure of S to support the subjunctive conditional mentioned above is a consequence of the fact that S is asserted to be true within a context of assumptions which themselves make dubious the subjunctive conditional. For example, S is asserted in the knowledge that no ravens inhabit polar regions. But it has already been suggested that we know enough about birds to know that the color of their plumage is not invariant for every species of birds. And though we do not know at present the precise factors upon which the color of plumage depends, we do have grounds for believing that the color depends at least in part on the genetic constitution of birds; and we also know that this constitution can be influenced by the presence of certain factors (e.g., high-energy radiations) which may be present in special environments. Accordingly, S does not support the cited subjunctive conditional, not because S is incapable of supporting *any* such conditional, but because the total knowledge at our command (and not only the evidence for S itself) does not warrant *this particular* conditional. It may be plausible to suppose that S does validate the subjunctive conditional that were any inhabitant of polar regions a raven not exposed to X-ray radiations, that raven would be black.

The point to be noted, therefore, is that whether or not S supports a given subjunctive conditional depends not only on the truth of S but also on other knowledge we may possess—in effect on the state of scientific inquiry. To see the point more clearly, let us apply the criticism under discussion to a statement generally counted as a law of nature. Suppose there are (omnitemporally) no physical objects that do not attract each other inversely as the square of their distances from each other. We are then entitled to assert as true the unrestricted universal S': 'All physical bodies attract each other inversely as the square of the distance between them.' But suppose also that the dimensions of the universe are finite, and that no physical bodies are ever separated by a distance greater than, say, 50 trillion light-years. Does S' support the subjunctive conditional that if there were physical bodies at distances from each other greater than 50 trillion light-years, they would attract each other inversely as the square of the distance between them? According to the argument under consideration, the answer must presumably be no. But is this answer really plausible? Is it not more reasonable to say that no answer is possible, either in the affirmative or negative—unless indeed some further assumptions are made? For in the absence of such additional assumptions, how can one adjudicate any answer that might be given? On the other hand, if such further assumptions were made—for example, if we assume that the force of gravity is independent of the total mass of the universe—it is not inconceivable that the correct answer may be an affirmative one.

In sum, therefore, the criticism under discussion does not undermine the Humean analysis of nomic universality. The criticism does bring into clear light, however, the important point that a statement is usually classified as a law of nature because the statement occupies a distinctive position in the system of explanations in some area of knowledge, and because the statement is supported by evidence satisfying certain specifications.

2. When planning for the future or reflecting on the past, we frequently carry on our deliberations by making assumptions that are contrary to the known facts. The results of our reflections are then often formulated as contrary-to-fact conditionals (or "counterfactuals"), having the forms 'If a were P, then b would be Q,' or 'If a had been P, then b would have been (or would be) Q.' For example, a physicist designing an experiment may at some point in his calculations assert the counterfactual C: 'If the length of pendulum a were shortened to one-fourth its present length, its period would be half its present period.' Similarly, in attempting to account for the failure of some previous experiment, a physicist can be imagined to assert the counterfactual C': 'If the length of pendulum a had been shortened to one-fourth its actual length, its period would have been half its actual period.' In both conditionals, the antecedent and consequent clauses describe suppositions presumably known to be false.

What has come to be called the "problem of counterfactuals" is the problem of making explicit the logical structure of such statements and of analyzing the grounds upon which their truth or falsity may be decided. The problem is closely related to that of explicating the notion of nomic universality. For a counterfactual cannot be translated in a straightforward way into a conjunction of statements in the indicative mood, using only the standard non-modal connectives of formal logic. For example, the counterfactual C' tacitly asserts that the length of pendulum a was not in fact shortened to one-fourth its actual length. However, C' is not rendered by the statement: 'The length of a was not shortened to a fourth of its actual length and if the length of a was shortened to one-fourth of its present length then its period was half its present period.' The proposed translation is unsatisfactory, because, since the antecedent clause of the indicative conditional is false, it follows by the rules of formal logic that if the length of a was shortened to a fourth of its present length, its period was *not* half its present period—a conclusion certainly not acceptable to anyone who asserts C'.[2] In consequence, critics of Humean

---

[2] This conclusion follows because of the logical rule governing the use of the connective "if-then." According to this rule both a statement of the form 'If S_1 then S_2' and the statement of the form 'If S_1 then not S_2' are true on the hypothesis that S_1 is false, no matter what S_2 may be.

analyses of nomic universality have argued that a distinctive type of nonlogical necessity is involved not only in universals of law but also in contrary-to-fact conditionals.

The content of counterfactuals can nevertheless be plausibly explicated without recourse to any unanalyzable modal notions. For what the physicist who asserts C' is saying can be rendered more clearly though more circuitously as follows. The statement 'The period of the pendulum a was half its present period' *follows logically* from the supposition 'The length of a was one-fourth its present length,' when this supposition is conjoined with the law that the period of a simple pendulum is proportional to the square root of its length, together with a number of further assumptions about initial conditions for the law (e.g., that a is a simple pendulum, that air resistance is negligible). Moreover, though the supposition and the statement deduced from it with the help of the assumptions mentioned are admittedly both false, their falsity is not included among the premises of the deduction. Accordingly, it does *not* follow from those premises that if a's length was a fourth of its present length then a's period was a half of its present period. In short, the counterfactual C' is thus asserted within some context of assumptions and special suppositions; and when these are laid bare, the introduction of modal categories other than those of formal logic is entirely gratuitous. More generally, a counterfactual can be interpreted as an implicit *metalinguistic* statement (i.e., a statement about *other* statements, and in particular about the logical relations of these other statements) asserting that the indicative form of its consequent clause follows logically from the indicative form of its antecedent clause, when the latter is conjoined with some law and the requisite initial conditions for the law.[3]

In consequence, disputes as to whether or not a given counterfactual is true can be settled only when the assumptions and suppositions on which it is based are made explicit. A counterfactual which is unquestionably true on one set of such premises may be false on another set, and may have no determinate truth-value on some third set. Thus, a physicist might reject C' in favor of the counterfactual 'If the length of pendulum a had been shortened to a fourth of its present length, the period of a would have been significantly more than half its present period.' He would be warranted in doing so if he is assuming, for example, that the arc of vibration of the shortened pendulum is more than $60°$ and if he also is assuming a modified form of the law for the periods of pendulums stated above (which is asserted only for pendulums with quite small arcs of vibration). Again, a tyro in experimental design may declare C' to be true, though he assumes among other things not only that the circular bob of the pendulum is three inches in diameter, but also that the apparatus enclosing the pendulum has an opening just a hairs-breadth wider than three inches at the place where the bob of the shortened pendulum has its center. It is obvious, however, that C' is now false because under the stated assumptions the shortened pendulum does not vibrate at all.

---

[3] Although the position adopted in the text has been reached independently, its present formulation is indebted to the views expressed in Henry Hiz, "On the Inferential Sense of Contrary-to-Fact Conditionals," *Journal of Philosophy,* Vol. 48 (1951), pp. 586-87; Julius R. Weinberg, "Contrary-to-Fact Conditionals," *Journal of Philosophy,* Vol. 48 (1951), pp. 17-22; Roderick M. Chisholm, "Law Statements and Counterfactual Inference," *Analysis,* Vol. 15 (1955), pp. 97-105; and John C. Cooley, "Professor Goodman's 'Fact, Fiction, and Forecast,' " *Journal of Philosophy,* Vol. 54 (1957), pp. 293-311.

The various assumptions under which a counterfactual is asserted are not stated in the counterfactual itself. The evaluation of the validity of a counterfactual may therefore be quite difficult—sometimes because we do not know the assumptions under which it is asserted or because we are not clear in our minds what tacit assumptions we are making, and sometimes because we simply lack the skill to assess the logical import even of the assumptions that we make explicit. Such difficulties frequently confront us, especially in connection with counterfactuals asserted in the course of everyday affairs or even in the writings of historians. Consider, for example, the counterfactual 'If the Versailles Treaty had not imposed burdensome indemnities on Germany, Hitler would not have come into power.' This assertion has been a controversial one, not only because those participating in the discussion of it adopt different explicit assumptions, but also because much of the dispute has been conducted on the basis of implicit premises that no one has fully brought into light. In any event, it is certainly not possible to construct a general formula which will prescribe just what must be included in the assumptions upon which a counterfactual can be adequately grounded. Attempts to construct such a formula have been uniformly unsuccessful; and those who see the problem of counterfactuals as that of constructing such a formula are destined to grapple with an insoluble problem.

J. L. MACKIE

16. Counterfactuals and Causal Laws

At the end of a recent article[1] Nicholas Rescher expresses the rash hope that the logical problem of contrary-to-fact conditionals may be allowed to rest in peace. But in saying that "nomological" or "law-governed" counterfactuals still "generate real problems for the proper understanding of the concept of law" he gives us an excuse for exhuming the logical problem too. For, as I shall argue, a more adequate account of the meaning and use of counterfactuals in general will resolve also the problems they raise for the concept of a law.

The most acute problems, I believe, are these. A law-governed counterfactual seems to be a non-logical, synthetic truth about an unrealized possibility, and therefore seems to extend the scope of a law beyond the actual facts. Also it seems that "generalizations of fact" or "accidental" universal propositions do not sustain counterfactuals in the way that causal laws do, so that causal laws must be

Reprinted by permission of the author from J. L. Mackie, "Counterfactuals and Causal Laws," in *Analytical Philosophy: First Series,* ed. by R. J. Butler (Oxford: Basil Blackwell, 1966), pp. 65-80. Footnotes included.

Note: Footnotes have been renumbered for the purposes of this text.

[1] "Belief-contravening Suppositions," *Philosophical Review,* LXX (1961), pp. 176-196.

something more than statements of actual universal sequence or concomitance.[2] If it just happens to be the case that everyone in this room understands English, it does not follow that if Mr. Khrushchev had been there he would have understood English, but if there is a causal law which connects being in this room with the understanding of English then this counterfactual conditional does follow. This seems to point to a distinction between what is asserted by a law-statement and by an "accidental" universal of the form "All A's happen, as a matter of fact, to be B's," which would compel us to reject a Humean or regularity theory of causation and admit that causal laws involve "connections" not reducible to concomitances and sequences. But such "connections" would constitute a difficulty for empiricism: how could we discover them, and what would they even *be*—for it will not do to define a connection simply as *that which* sustains a counterfactual?

I shall try to show that these problems can be solved within the framework of a regularity theory, and indeed that the very same interpretation of counterfactuals solves both them and the much-discussed logical problems which Rescher claims to have laid to rest.

I. GENERAL ACCOUNT OF THE MEANING AND USE OF COUNTERFACTUALS

A counterfactual such as 'If he had come he would have enjoyed himself' does two things: it has a conditional element and it asserts or hints that he did not come. It is of the conditional element that an account is needed, for clearly it does not state an entailment or strict implication, and yet there is in it something more than the material conditional (of the form $P \supset Q$) which is equivalent to "Either he did not come or he enjoyed himself." But an open conditional, such as "If he came he enjoyed himself," may likewise say more than the material conditional. Indeed its conditional element is just like the conditional element in the counterfactual: an open conditional is just like a counterfactual without the asserted or hinted denial of the antecedent. And similarly what Goodman has called a factual conditional, such as "Since he came he enjoyed himself," has still the same conditional element but also asserts or hints that the antecedent (and therefore the consequent also) is true. These three forms differ, then, only in what they say or suggest about the truth or falsity of the antecedent: in all there is also a conditional element, which makes some connection, over and above material implication, between the antecedent and the consequent, and it is of this that an account is needed. I shall offer an account of this element in counterfactuals, but it will be applicable with only minor modifications to other non-material conditionals as well.

Prima facie, a counterfactual seems to describe an imaginary situation, and to say or hint that it is imaginary. Consider "If you had had the brakes fixed, there would not have been a collision." A situation which, it is admitted has not come about, namely the brakes having been fixed, is further characterized by the absence of a collision. But this description is not a purely imaginative exercise; we imagine the brakes having been fixed but say that the absence of collision follows from this

---

[2] Cf. William Kneale, *Probability and Induction*, pp. 74-75, and "Natural laws and contrary-to-fact conditionals," *Analysis*, X (1950), reprinted in this text and in *Philosophy and Analysis*, ed. M. Macdonald; also "Universality and Necessity," *British Journal for the Philosophy of Science*, XII (1961), pp. 89-102, also reprinted in this text.

or goes with this non-imaginatively. How can we describe non-imaginatively an imaginary situation? Only by inference from something else that we know or believe. And yet to state a counterfactual is not to give an inference in full: we do not give all the premisses and intermediate steps. A counterfactual conditional, then, is a condensed and incomplete argument.[3]

For example, if we expanded the one about the brakes we might get something like this: "Suppose that you have had the brakes fixed. Then when the other car turns across your path you press the brake pedal. So your car stops quickly. So there is no collision." Though expanded, this is still incomplete: to complete it we should have to add further premisses describing the situation and laws connecting properly adjusted brakes with stopping, and stopping, in certain circumstances, with the absence of collision.

Something like this would be the ground on which one would advance this counterfactual. But we can understand it without being able to complete the argument: we can understand a counterfactual without knowing its grounds. It is therefore more like this incomplete argument: "Suppose that you have had the brakes fixed. Then (in view of certain unspecified true propositions) there is no collision."

But to advance the counterfactual is not to say that there is such an argument available; it is not to say, "There are true premisses from which together with the premiss 'You have had the brakes fixed' the conclusion 'There is no collision' follows." To advance the counterfactual is not to assert any proposition, even one about an argument; it is rather to run through a condensation of an argument. We can do this without being able to specify explicitly the other premisses and intermediate steps on which we are relying; we jump from the supposition to the conclusion in the light of knowledge and beliefs that we need not and commonly do not make explicit. Similarly we can understand as a condensed argument a counterfactual advanced by someone else, without being able to complete either his argument or one of our own. In either case the argument is not argued, but rather entertained: not all the premisses are asserted, nor is the conclusion. One premiss is merely supposed, and the argument from it to the conclusion lies within the scope of this supposition.

Since the argument is thus condensed or telescoped, there is inevitably some indeterminancy about the way in which it would be completed. Other premisses would have to be drawn from our other knowledge and beliefs, and, as Rescher has correctly stressed, the introduction of the belief-contravening supposition will compel us to reject some further beliefs if we retain others, but does not in itself determine which of the others are to be retained and which therefore rejected.

If we interpret counterfactuals, and other non-material conditionals, as arguments, we cannot say that they are true or false or that they are implied by other statements. But we can say that a non-material conditional is *sustained* by the premiss or premisses which, with the antecedent as a further premiss, entail the

---

[3] An interpretation of conditionals as arguments is given (in another content) by John Anderson in "Hypotheticals," *Australasian Journal of Philosophy,* XXX (1952), pp. 1-16. An interpretation of counterfactuals as incomplete arguments is developed by R. S. Walters in "The Problem of Counterfactuals," *Australasian Journal of Philosophy,* XXXIX (1961), pp. 30-46. My own account arises partly from discussion of an early draft of Walters's article, and I agree with much, but not all, of what he says.

consequent of that conditional. Thus "All defeated presidential candidates are disappointed" and "Kennedy was a presidential candidate" together sustain but do not imply "If Kennedy had been defeated he would have been disappointed" and similar pairs of statements sustain the open conditional (usable in October, 1960) "If Kennedy is defeated he will be disappointed" and the factual conditional "Since Nixon was defeated he was disappointed." It is true that if certain premises, together with a supposition P, entail a conclusion Q, then these premises alone entail the material conditional P ⊃ Q. So wherever true premises validly sustain a non-material conditional, the corresponding material conditional is true. But the non-material conditional corresponds not to the conclusion P ⊃ Q but rather to the whole argument within the scope of the supposition, from which we infer P ⊃ Q by the principle of conditional proof.

By treating counterfactuals as telescoped arguments we avoid the difficulties encountered by those who have tried to reduce them to statements of some other sort, and in particular to give a truth-functional analysis of them.[4] But we should expect that a statement (or consistent set of statements) of any sort could sustain a non-material conditional, since it could be the additional premiss (or set of premisses) which, with the antecedent, entails the consequent. And then if the sustaining statement (or statements) were true, the sustained conditional would be acceptable in the way in which an entertained argument is when its conclusion follows validly from premises of which one is the supposition and the others are true. But while this holds for open and for factual conditionals, it seems not to hold in all cases for counterfactuals: the problem from which we started was that accidental universals do not sustain these, and there are also other awkward cases. Since on this interpretation there is no question of counterfactuals being true or false we avoid the problem of finding adequate criteria for their truth;[5] but we are left with the two other problems of explaining in what circumstances we are prepared to advance a counterfactual and of saying when and why we are justified in doing so.

Now, as Rescher has stressed, a "belief-contravening supposition" always confronts us with the task of choosing which of our existing beliefs to retain in combination with it and which to reject, and this indicates a general solution of the above-stated problems: we use a counterfactual if and only if we are justified in thus sticking to the belief (or set of beliefs) that would sustain it. I shall show, in II below, how this principle explains the different bearing of causal laws and "accidental" universals on counterfactuals, and, in III below, how the same principle resolves other well-known difficulties.

II. LAWS AND "ACCIDENTAL" GENERALIZATIONS

If we· ask, "Why is it that causal laws sustain counterfactuals whereas generalizations of fact do not?" we are formulating the puzzle in a misleading way. We are suggesting that we must look for some special virtue in causal laws, over and above universality, that enables them to sustain counterfactuals, mysterious truths

---

    [4] *E.g.*, Roderick M. Chisholm, *Mind*, LV (1946), pp. 289-307, and F. L. Will, *Mind*, LVI (1947), pp. 236-249.

    [5] Discussed, *e.g.*, by Nelson Goodman, *Fact, Fiction and Forecast* (London, 1954), pp. 14-31.

that go beyond the actual world. My contention is that counterfactuals are not truths but condensed arguments, that so interpreted they cease to be mysterious, and that the premises that sustain them are just ordinary propositions, which may or may not be universals. The real puzzle is, "Why do some generalizations of fact, particularly those that are called 'accidental' generalizaitons, fail to sustain counterfactuals which a corresponding causal law would sustain?" The problem is not to find any extra virtue in causal laws, but to find what special deficiency there is in "accidental" universals.

Once we ask the right question it is comparatively easy to find the answer. Let us take it that we have discovered by complete enumeration, by checking each individual in turn, that all persons in this room understand English. To use this to sustain the counterfactual, "If Mr. Khrushchev were in this room he would understand English" would be to add the supposition "Mr. Khrushchev is in this room" and to use it along with the enumeratively established universal to derive the conclusion "Mr. Khrushchev understands English." But since our sole ground for believing the universal was an enumerative check, that ground disappears as soon as we add the supposition that someone *else* is in the room; someone, that is, who is not in fact in the room and whose understanding of English has not been checked. The adding of the supposition so changes the situation that the previous evidence for the universal completely fails to support it in the new situation. If the universal were true and Mr. Khrushchev were in the room then he would understand English, but our ground for believing the universal, the person-by-person check, evaporates as soon as we add the supposition, so we cannot take this universal *as we know it* and this supposition as joint premises in an argument. Because the supposition of Mr. Khrushchev's presence is contrary-to-fact, we have not checked the understanding of English of all the persons in the room in the supposed situation, and as the complete check was our only reason for believing the universal we are not justified in sticking to it when we add the supposition, and we are not in fact prepared to do so.

This account is confirmed if we contrast the counterfactual with an open conditional. The "accidental" generalization, "Everyone in this room understands English," does sustain the open conditional "If Mr. Khrushchev is in this room he understands English"—that is, one of the persons present may be Mr. Khrushchev disguised or unrecognised, and if so he has passed the check on his understanding of English. This is acceptable because the open supposition that he is here does not undermine our belief in the universal, whereas the supposition that he is here, coupled with the admission that in fact he is not, does undermine it. It is precisely the contrary-to-fact aspect of the antecedent that makes us unable to use it along with an enumeratively established universal.

This account can easily be extended to cover examples where the 'accidental' universal is known not by a complete enumeration but by some other, similar, process. If we know that none of the stones in this box is radioactive because a Geiger counter nearby shows no response, this universal does not sustain the counterfactual "If that other stone were in this box it would not be radioactive" because again the supposition that some *other* stone is in the box undermines the evidence of the Geiger counter as a reason for believing the universal along with the supposition.

On the other hand, a generalization sustains a counterfactual if our reason for adhering to it is not undermined when we add the supposition. This can come about in two ways, for these reasons may be either deductive or inductive ones.

Suppose it is known that all the pottery used at a certain period was unglazed. From this we can infer that all the pottery so far dug up in sites of that period is unglazed. The latter proposition, known thus by inference from the former, sustains the counterfactual that if some other site of that period had been excavated only unglazed pottery would have been found in it. And this holds even if the former proposition is itself only an "accidental" generalization; all that is essential is that it gives us a reason for adhering to the latter one which is not undermined when we add the contrary-to-fact supposition that a certain site of the period has been excavated—a site which has not in fact been excavated.

This is not, however, the only type of case. What is more interesting is that a causal law can sustain counterfactuals without being itself derivable from any wider generalization. This is the problem, for, it may be argued, if a causal law is a universal proposition that can be combined with a supposition that alters the extension of the subject term it must be something more than a generalization of fact. But I reply that the difference does not lie in the content of the proposition: it is not that a causal law asserts something of a different sort from what is asserted by any other universal. The difference lies first in the way we use them.[6] To use a proposition as a causal law is (i) to combine it with suppositions that go beyond cases for which the law has been checked, and so to advance open conditionals, and (ii) to combine it with suppositions that alter the extension of the subject term, and so to advance counterfactual conditionals. But secondly—and this is more important—the difference lies in the kinds of evidence we have. We are justified in using a universal as a causal law if we have good inductive evidence for it, so that our reasons for believing it are not impaired when it is combined with a supposition of kind (i) or (ii). We are also, of course, justified in thus using a universal that is derived from other causal laws, but only because they in turn are supported by good inductive evidence.

It may now be objected that I have shifted the problem to the realm of induction: to explain why a causal law sustains counterfactuals is to explain how there can be evidence for a universal proposition which is not impaired either (i) by a supposition that there is an instance of the subject term which has not been included in the evidence, or (ii) by a supposition which adds further (contrary-to-fact) instances of the subject term. To this charge I plead guilty: indeed what I claim to have shown is that the problem of the sustaining of counterfactuals by causal laws is nothing more than the general problem of induction. It is not my purpose to discuss this problem. If we can take it that there are good inductive reasons, that we can have evidence for generalizations which the supposition of further instances does not undermine in the way in which it undermines evidence which consists in a complete enumeration or anything of the same sort, then we have explained how causal laws differ from "accidental" universals in their ability to sustain counterfactuals without assuming that a causal law, in its content, is anything more than a simple universal.

---

[6] Cf. A. J. Ayer, "What is a Law of Nature?" *Revue Internationale de Philosophie*, 36 (1956), Fasc. 2. [Reprinted in this text.]

If we have inductive evidence for "All A are B," then this evidence supports the conclusion that an unobserved A is B, and thus it justifies the argument from the supposition that X is A to the conclusion that X is B, and the open conditional which is a condensation of that argument. But this evidence is logically related in exactly the same way to the argument from the supposition that Y is A to the conclusion that Y is B, even if we know that Y is not in fact A, and that is why it justifies the counterfactual which is a condensation of this argument. Formally all that is required to let a law sustain counterfactuals is that there should be the same logical relation (i) between the evidence and the proposed law (covering unobserved instances) as things are, and (ii) between the evidence and the proposed law with things otherwise the same but with additional instances of the subject term. And this holds for all ordinary inductive reasoning.

III. IMPLAUSIBLE AND COMPETING COUNTERFACTUALS

The principle I have used to explain why "accidental" generalizations fail to sustain certain counterfactuals will also explain why, among other counterfactuals, some are acceptable and others are not. Initially we might expect that the counterfactual "If A then C" would be acceptable wherever a statement (or set of statements) S was true (or believed to be true) and A and S would together entail C.[7] But some statements are not acceptable for the role of S, or are not acceptable in all circumstances, and some are more acceptable than others. It is my task to explain these differences, though this does not call for such hard and fast restrictions as would be needed if we wanted to call some counterfactuals true and others false.

If A is a contrary-to-fact supposition, then $\sim$A is true, and the conjunction A.$\sim$A entails any conclusion at all. Any counterfactual whatever would be justifiable on these grounds, and to avoid this trivialization we must not admit $\sim$A as an acceptable sustaining statement for the counterfactual "If A then C," and indeed we do not so use it. Our principle explains why this is so: since $\sim$A is the denial of the supposition A, we are not prepared to stick to $\sim$A when we introduce that supposition. Similarly, since $\sim$A is true, $\sim$A v C is also true, whatever C may be, and A together with $\sim$A v C entails C. But we do not advance the counterfactual "If A then C" on these grounds, for if our only reason for believing $\sim$A v C is that we believe $\sim$A, we have no reason for sticking to $\sim$A v C when we add the supposition A.

The competing counterfactuals "If Bizet and Verdi had been compatriots, Bizet would have been Italian" and "If Bizet and Verdi had been compatriots, Verdi would have been French" can be expanded respectively into these arguments:

"Verdi is Italian; suppose that Bizet and Verdi are compatriots; then Bizet is Italian."

"Bizet is French; suppose that Bizet and Verdi are compatriots; then Verdi is French."

Each of these by itself is unexceptionable. Each combines a true premiss with a contingent supposition and draws a conclusion which follows validly from them

[7] Cf. Goodman, op. cit., pp. 14-31.

(given certain linguistic rules about the term "compatriots" and nationality-descriptions such as "French," and "Italian"). But the three premisses "Verdi is Italian," "Bizet is French," and "Bizet and Verdi are compatriots" form, in the light of the linguistic rules, an inconsistent triad. Any two are compatible, so any two can be used in the same argument, but all three cannot be used together except in a *reductio ad absurdum,* and so we cannot use together, as direct arguments, the two arguments that need them as premisses. Corresponding comments apply to the counterfactuals that are condensations of the two arguments. There is a use for each of them separately, where we are prepared to stick to one or other of the nationality-statements along with the supposition, but there is no direct use for the combination of them into "If Bizet and Verdi had been compatriots Bizet would have been Italian and Verdi would have been French," because we cannot stick to both the nationality-statements along with the supposition. Since a counterfactual is not true or false, the competition between these two is no problem. Of any two competing counterfactuals we shall advance the one which is sustained by those of our other beliefs which in the actual context we are prepared to stick to when we add the supposition. In cases of the Bizet-Verdi sort, we would normally have no more reason for sticking to one rather than the other of the two beliefs when we add the supposition that brings them into conflict, and so we would not normally use either of the competing counterfactuals in such a case as this.

There is a similar formal pattern even where one of the relevant beliefs is or incorporates a causal law. The statements "Cyanide is a deadly poison," "Jones is alive," and "Jones took cyanide" form an inconsistent triad, and the first and second of these would sustain, respectively, the competing counterfactuals "If Jones had taken cyanide he would not be alive" and "If Jones had taken cyanide, cyanide would not have been a deadly poison." But these are not on level terms, as were the rivals in the Bizet-Verdi example. We are much more prepared to stick to the law that cyanide is a deadly poison than to the particular fact that Jones is alive. But it is not that the former generalization is "so secure that we are willing to retain it at all costs, and to let all else revolve about it when a belief-contravening supposition is made."[8] The point is that if it is definitely conceded that Jones did not take cyanide, then the supposition that he did take it so changes the situation that we have little reason to adhere, along with it, to the statement that Jones is alive. This is not because the law is secure, but merely because a situation containing a different temporal antecedent is a different situation, about which the observation that Jones is alive in the actual situation fails to inform us. It is not that we know the causal law about cyanide, but merely that we know there are causal laws, that a difference in a temporal antecedent is often followed by a different outcome. That this is the point is confirmed by the fact that the *open* conditional "If Jones took cyanide, cyanide is not a deadly poison" is quite natural and plausible. This is so because we can quite well combine the fact that Jones is alive with the supposition, considered as an open possibility, that he took cyanide, and use these as joint premisses in an argument. The corresponding counterfactual is not plausible because the contrary-to-fact supposition, just because it is contrary-to-fact, does away with our reason for adhering, along with it, to the statement "Jones is alive."

Similarly, if we have these five beliefs:[9]

(1) All dry matches located in an oxygen-containing medium light when struck.

(2) M is a dry match.

(3) M is located in an oxygen-containing medium.

(4) M has not been struck.

(5) M has not lit.

then when we introduce the supposition that denies (4) we must reject at least one of the others, so that there are four formally possible counterfactuals:

(a) If the match M had been struck, it would have lit.

(b) If the match M had been struck, it would not have been dry.

(c) If the match M had been struck, it would not have been located in an oxygen-containing medium.

(d) If the match M had been struck, it would not have been the case that all dry matches located in an oxygen-containing medium light when struck.

Of these, (a) is the most plausible, because, as in the cyanide example, the denial of (4) so changes the situation that we lose the ground we had for adhering to (5). But if we exclude (a) by making the antecedent "If the match M had been struck but not lit," there is then no general reason for preferring one rather than any other of the consequents of (b), (c), and (d), and which of the three counterfactuals we actually use on any occasion will depend on which of the beliefs (1), (2) and (3) we choose to retain. It is true that all of these are somewhat odd in another way. Counterfactuals are most naturally used to describe an imaginary course of events, where the antecedent of the conditional corresponds to a causal antecedent and the consequent to an effect, and of the four counterfactuals listed above only (a) conforms to this pattern. But this is only the most natural use, not the only possible one.

Goodman, in his search for adequate criteria for the truth of counterfactuals, has to introduce one restriction after another on the set S of statements that sustains the counterfactual, and it is in order to exclude such examples as (b) above that he finally lays it down[10] that S must be not merely compatible but "cotenable" with the antecedent A. Since cotenability depends on causal relations this criterion is circular, and involves Goodman in the "really serious" difficulty that we cannot determine whether S is cotenable with A without determining whether another counterfactual is true. Thus he faces the infinite regress that 'to establish any counterfactual . . . we first have to determine the truth of another."[11] But, as we have seen, once we reject the question of truth and confine ourselves to the tasks of explaining in what circumstances we are either prepared to use or justified in using a counterfactual we need not exclude absolutely such examples as (b), and we can explain our normal reluctance to use them without introducing the circular criterion of cotenability.

---

[9] Cf. Rescher's Example 13.

[10] Op. cit., p. 21.

[11] Op. cit., p. 23.

An argument from a supposition can be used either directly or indirectly. That is, we may use it *either* to say what would really happen (or have happened) if the supposition were (or had been) fulfilled, *or* to show that the supposition is false or in some sense impossible. There are two corresponding ways of using the open or counterfactual conditionals which are condensations of such arguments, and counterfactuals which conflict with one another in their direct use may be compatible when used indirectly. Thus although the competing counterfactuals about Bizet and Verdi cannot be used together directly, to say what would have been the case if the two really had been compatriots, they can be used together indirectly to show that in view of our other knowledge they could not have been compatriots. Similarly, two "law-governed" counterfactuals can be used together to show that their common supposition is causally impossible: "If there were a perpetual motion machine it would dissipate energy" and "If there were a perpetual motion machine it would not dissipate energy" can be used together by someone arguing that there could not be a perpetual motion machine.

IV. CONCLUSION

It may seem strange to say that non-material conditionals are condensed arguments, when on the face of it they are single statements. But what matters is not what they look like but how they work, and what kinds of logical commendation and disparagement are appropriate to them. We have seen that such conditionals, and especially counterfactuals, work like arguments, and that whereas we get into difficulties if we try to characterize them as true or false we avoid these difficulties by discussing the circumstances in which the correponding arguments can be used. Some of the difficulties would be met by saying that counterfactuals are ambiguous statements, but it seems impossible to say satisfactorily what straightforward statements a counterfactual is ambiguous between. We could perhaps say that non-material conditionals are just a special sort of statement and work not like other statements but like arguments; but if this much is conceded it is only a verbal issue whether we say that they are arguments or not.

It may be objected that the distinction between accidental and causal generalizations is a distinction between two sorts of thing that can be asserted, and not merely one between two ways of using and two ways of supporting what we assert. Granted that a certain generalization is true, there seems to be a real and objective issue whether it is causally true or only accidentally true. Without going back on what I have argued, I would admit that there are two sorts of objective issue that can be raised in these terms.

First, we can ask whether a universal is only accidentally true with implicit reference to some wider generalization. If it is true that all the pottery so far dug up in sites of a certain period is unglazed, we may say that this is accidentally true if not all the pottery used in that period was unglazed, but not only accidentally true if all the pottery used in that period was unglazed. In this sense an accidental generalization is simply one that is unrepresentative of a larger class of which we are implicitly taking it as a sample. In this sense it is an objective issue whether a generalization is accidental or not as soon as we have fixed the larger class with implicit reference to which the issue is raised.

Secondly, certain causal laws are sometimes distinguished from other universals in the following way.[12] Suppose that there were a closed deterministic system which we knew all about; then we could distinguish its fundamental laws of working from statements, even universal statements, of the collocations of things and properties at various times. This would not be a simple formal distinction, for collocation-statements might be put into a purely qualitative form. Nor would it coincide with our ordinary distinction of laws from mere facts, for statements which we should initially regard as causal laws might turn out to be derived from the conjunction of more fundamental laws with collocations. The distinction of which I am speaking could be made finally only in relation to complete knowledge of the system and of the relations among the true propositions that described it. Though not easily drawn, it would constitute an objective distinction between laws of working and collocations, and this is a possible sense in which the question whether a generalization is accidental or not could raise an objective issue: a non-accidental universal would be, in any system, a law of working which did not depend upon collocations. This distinction can in principle be drawn; but it does not mean that the laws of working are any more necessary, in any way logically stronger, than the collocation statements: these laws would be distinguished only negatively, by their freedom from any element of or dependence on collocation, not by any positive feature over and above their being true universal propositions.

I shall not pursue this question further, because it is not my purpose to attempt a full account of the nature of causal laws. All I have tried to do is to resolve those problems about the concept of a law which are raised by counterfactual conditionals. I claim that if we interpret such conditionals as condensed arguments we can both explain why some counterfactuals are acceptable while others are not and at the same time show that the supposed counterfactual core of causal statements, their applicability to unrealized possibilities, is nothing more than their being supported by inductive evidence and used accordingly. A proper analysis not only resolves the logical problem of counterfactuals but also reduces the problems raised by law-governed counterfactuals to the general problem of induction.

---

[12] Cf. H. Gavin Alexander, "General Statements as Rules of Inference?" in *Minnesota Studies in the Philosophy of Science*, Vol. II (1958), pp. 309-329, esp. p. 327.

GEORGE MOLNAR

17. Kneale's Argument Revisited

There exists an argument by William Kneale to the conclusion that on a certain account of laws of nature we cannot say of some propositions that they express unrealized empirical possibilities, although this is just what we would normally take them to express. Kneale has advanced the argument in two places,[1] but has not bothered to state the matter rigorously or in full detail. Nor has his contention been discussed in the copious recent literature on the subject of laws, with one marginal exception.[2] Considering the elegance and importance of the argument, this is surprising. In the first part of this article I shall essay a clear statement of what seems to be the essence of Kneale's argument. In doing so I am construing, rather than repeating, what he has said.[3] In the second part I describe four formally adequate ways of escaping the conclusion of the argument. In the third part I discuss these ways out, offering reasons for preferring one of them.

I

Consider the following definition of a law of nature:

D_1: p is a statment of a law of nature if and only if:

    (i) p is universally quantified; and

    (ii) p is omnitemporally and omnispatially true; and

    (iii) p is contingent; and

    (iv) p contains only nonlocal empirical predicates, apart from logical connectives and quantifiers.

This definition is plainly in the spirit of Hume, though not one offered by him. Whether anybody subscribes to it I do not know, but many modern philosophers accept definitions very similar to this one. I shall refer to it as the Regularity Theory of Laws of Nature.

A thing or state of affairs is empirically possible if its existence does not contravene any law of nature. A thing or state of affairs or event is an unrealized possibility if it is possible but does not exist, obtain, or occur. Hence:

Reprinted by permission of the author and the publisher from George Molnar, "Kneale's Argument Revisited," *The Philosophical Review* vol. 78, no. 1 (January 1969): 79-89. Footnotes included.

[1] William Kneale, "Natural Laws and Contrary to Fact Conditionals," *Analysis*, 10 (1950), reprinted in M. MacDonald (ed.), *Philosophy and Analysis* (Oxford, 1954); "Universality and Necessity," *The British Journal for the Philosophy of Science*, XII (1961). [Both reprinted in this text.]

[2] Karl Popper, *The Logic of Scientific Discovery* (London, 1959), pp. 426-441. [Reprinted in part in this text.]

[3] My formulation owes a great deal to an unpublished paper by Mr. D. C. Stove. The discussion, in Part III, of the non-deducibility requirement has benefited from talks with Dr. W. A. Suchting.

D_2: If p states that a thing exists (or that a state of affairs obtains, or that an event occurs) then what p states is possible if and only if p is consistent with every law of nature.

We call p a statement of possibility if and only if what p states is possible.

D_3: What p states is an unrealized possibility if and only if:

   (i) p is a statement of possibility: and

   (ii) p is false.

We call p a statement of unrealized possibility if and only if what p states is an unrealized possibility. D_2 and D_3 are uncontroversial. They capture Kneale's sense of "unrealized possibility" which of course is intended to correspond to the common notion of that which is neither actual nor impossible.

The argument can now be stated. Let "F" be an arbitrarily selected non-local empirical general term. Then:

1. "Something is F" is false.		(Assumption)
2. Nothing is F.		(1, Equivalence)
3. "Nothing is F" is a law of nature.		$(2, D_1)$
4. "Something is F" is inconsistent with "Nothing is F."		(Tautology)
5. "Something is F" is inconsistent with a law of nature.		(3, 4)
6. "Something is F" is not a statement of possibility.		$(5, D_2)$
7. If "Something is F" is false, then "Something is F" is not a statement of possibility.		(1-6, Conditional Proof)
8. It is not the case both that "Something is F" is false and that "Something is F" is a statement of possibility.		(7, Equivalence)
9. "Something is F" is not a statement of unrealized possibility.		$(8, D_3)$
10. For any x if x is an unrestricted empirical existential proposition, then x is not a statement of unrealized possibility.		(9, U.G.)

The conclusion of the argument is that for any contingent unrestricted existential proposition containing only empirical predicates, it logically cannot be the case both that the proposition is false and that it is consistent with every law of nature. Kneale's argument thus pits the Regularity Theory of Laws of Nature and the definition of a statement of unrealized possibility against each other. It shows that if the Theory and the definition are both accepted there will be a set of statements—namely, the set of contingent unrestricted existential statements, no member of which may be used to express a judgment of unrealized possibility. This conclusion is intuitively unpalatable. "There exists (somewhere, somewhen) a river of Coca Cola" is surely not a judgment of which we would want to be forced to say that either it is empirically impossible or it is actually true. We all believe that this statement is both false and possible, as are many others like it.

While the argument is potent enough to discredit the conjunction of D_1, D_2, and D_3, its strength should not be overestimated. Kneale's argument does not disbar those who accept these definitions from making any statements of unrealized possibility. For example, *restricted* existential statements may be so used. From the falsity of "There exists at time t, in place p, a river of Coca Cola" no unrestricted universally quantified proposition follows. Hence this judgment has not been shown to be such that it cannot be both false and consistent with every law of nature.

II

There are a number of formally adequate ways of evading commitment to the conclusion of the argument. I want to discuss four such ways out. All of them have wider metaphysical affiliations, and have been associated with different systematic analyses of lawlikeness. Thus while they all involve amending D_1 they are not mere *ad hoc* devices, but genuinely entertained positions.

1. *The Requirement of Non-Empty Terms.*   Laws of nature are sometimes thought of as statements of connection between items falling under distinct general terms. (By "statement of connection" is meant a quantification of a conjunction or disjunction of properties.) One may require of the general terms occurring in laws of nature that they be non-empty.[4] That is to say, one requires that with every law there be logically associated a true existential proposition asserting that the general terms occurring in the law are instantiated. These existential propositions may be either entailed by the laws or presupposed by them (in Strawson's sense of "presuppose"). Take entailment first. In this case the logical form of laws will be a conjunction of universally and existentially quantified propositions. If so, Kneale's argument fails to go through, since from the falsity of an existential proposition one can infer neither an unnegated existential proposition nor a conjunction one of whose conjuncts is an unnegated existential proposition. "There exists (somewhere, somewhen) a tame unicorn" can express a judgment of unrealized possibility since from its falsity we can only infer "Nothing is both a unicorn and tame" which is not a law on the view under discussion. The position is substantially similar with presupposition. It is a logical truth that if a proposition, p, presupposes another, q, then p cannot be derived from any proposition which is compatible with the negation of q. If laws of nature carry existential presuppositions, they cannot be derived from the falsity of existential propositions, for the negation of a given existential judgment is consistent with the negation of other existential judgments (assuming independence of terms). From the falsity of "There are tame unicorns" one cannot infer a universal proposition which presupposes the existence of unicorns; one can infer only, as in the entailment case, the presuppositionless "Nothing is both a unicorn and tame."

---

[4] The requirement is in the spirit of Humean empiricism as it is nowadays widely understood. For on a Humean account nomological generalizations are statements about what is actual. But some non-Humean empiricists have also embraced this requirement; e.g., John Anderson. See his *Studies In Empirical Philosophy* (Sydney, 1962).

2. *Epistemic Requirements.*   Some philosophers have argued that in addition to fulfilling syntactic and semantic requirements, a proposition has to satisfy certain epistemic conditions in order to be properly called a law of nature.[5] From this point of view D_1 is inadequate and needs to be supplemented by a clause requiring that p be known in a certain way, or that the evidence for it be of a certain kind, or that the evidence be acquired in a certain manner. If the definition of "law" is so supplemented, then the argument fails to go through, since from the falsity of an existential proposition we can infer only the truth of the universal proposition which is its negation; we cannot infer that this universal is known in a certain way. Hence what is entailed by the falsity of "Something is F" need not be a law, and thus it has not been shown that "Something is F" cannot be both false and consistent with every law of nature.

3. *Non-Deducibility Requirement.*   In trying to account for the distinction between nomological and accidental generalizations, some philosophers have introduced a distinction between basic laws, or fundamental laws, or laws properly so-called on the one hand, and other empirical generalizations on the other. One way of drawing the distinction is of special interest here. According to this view laws properly so-called are a subset of the set of propositions picked out by the Regularity Theory of Laws of Nature. The subset is distinguished by the fact that while many if not all empirical generalizations outside the subset are deducible from some member(s) of the subset in conjunction with some (singular) statements of initial conditions, no member of the subset is so deducible from any other generalization. The distinction between a law and another kind of generalization is that the latter can, but the former cannot, be exhibited as a special or limiting case of some more general nomological connection.[6] Given this restriction on what qualifies as a law, Kneale's argument fails to go through. From the falsity of "Something is F," where "F" is any empirical general term, we can derive only "Nothing is F," which need not be a law. (If it is deducible from other generalizations plus initial conditions, it will not be a law.) Hence we cannot prove that no unrestricted existential proposition can express an unrealized possibility.

4. *Strengthening the Modality of Laws.*   This is the way out which Kneale himself appears to favor, judging from some remarks in his *Probability and Induction* (1949). If we reject clause (iii) of D_1 and replace it by one requiring that laws be noncontingent, the argument no longer goes through. From the falsity of the contingent proposition "Something is F" one can infer only the contingent proposition "Nothing is F" which is not a law. " 'Something is F' is contingently false" does not entail " 'Nothing is F' is necessarily true." Consequently, "Something is F" can express an unrealized possibility, and it does express this in all those cases where "Nothing is F" is contingently, but not necessarily, true.

---

[5] E.g., Ernest Nagel, *The Structure of Science* (London, 1961), pp. 62-64; J. L. Mackie, "Counterfactuals and Causal Laws," in R. J. Butler (ed.), *Analytical Philosophy* (Oxford, 1962), esp. pp. 72-73. [Reprinted in this text.]

[6] The originator of this train of thought is John Stuart Mill (see *A System of Logic*, bk. iii, ch. xii *et seq.*). Among modern sources may be mentioned H. Reichenbach, *Elements of Symbolic Logic* (New York, 1947), ch. viii; C. G. Hempel and P. Oppenheim, "The Logic of Explanation," *Philosophy of Science*, 15 (1948), reprinted in H. Feigl and M. Brodbeck (eds.), *Readings in the Philosophy of Science* (New York, 1953).

III

The four ways out just described are formally adequate to evade the conclusion of Kneale's argument: someone who accepts one of the four amended definitions is in a position to reject the conclusion without contradiction. I now want to discuss their philosophical adequacy. Here I have in mind a negative criterion: a formally adequate way out is philosophically inadequate, I want to say, if it allows some *version* of Kneale's argument to go through to a conclusion which is unacceptable for the same sort of reasons which make the conclusion of the original argument unacceptable. I want to emphasize that I am not concerned with the intrinsic merits of these four suggestions. Whether any of them is true, or whether any of them contributes to a satisfactory account of lawlikeness will not be investigated here. What follows concentrates solely on whether these ways out effectively eliminate the unwanted philosophical implications of the argument.

1. *Non-Empty Terms.*   There is doubt about the general applicability of this way out. The proviso that laws should have non-empty terms can be applied only to propositions which affirm or deny connections. Prima facie not all laws of nature do this. Some laws are, formally, negative existential propositions, their content is the denial that a single general term is instantiated (for example, "Nothing travels faster than light"). If the apparent form of these laws is accepted, the requirement of non-emptiness simply cannot be applied. It may be held that the apparent form is misleading here, that laws of nature are always statements of connection, and that "Nothing is *F*" is never the true from of a law. Why this should be so has to my knowledge never been made clear. We seem to be committed to eliminating all lawlike propositions of the form "Nothing is *F*" in favor of statements of connection. This involves a substantial program of reductive analysis, success of which cannot be guaranteed in advance. One is entitled to remain skeptical about the general applicability of this way out.

Prescinding from the above, the important objection is this. The requirement that the terms of laws be non-empty still leaves a large subset of the set of unrestricted existential propositions such that no member of that subset can express an unrealized possibility. The subset consists of all those complex existential propositions which assert falsely that two or more *instantiated* attributes are possessed by something. Let "*F*" and "*G*" be any two non-empty empirical general terms. Then "Something is both *F* and *G*" cannot assert an unrealized possibility, for its falsity entails "Nothing is both *F* and *G*" which, since it has non-empty terms, is not to be reckoned as a law. The requirement of non-empty terms exempts from the conclusion of Kneale's argument only propositions which have at least one empty term. (That is why it was found natural, in expounding this way out, to use as example a proposition about unicorns.) To propositions with non-empty terms, the argument applies. This is unfortunate, for we are still not permitted to judge that "There exists a river of Coca Cola" is false but not empirically impossible.

2. *Epistemic Restrictions.*   Possibility is not an epistemic concept. The chief objection to this way out rests on this fact. In the sense of "possible" relevant to Kneale's argument, what is possible or impossible does not depend on what anyone knows, or on the manner in which knowledge is acquired, or on the evidential grounds on which hypotheses are accepted. Some simple considerations show this. There are, it is plausible to suppose, nomic regularities at present unknown to

anybody. It would be absurd to deny that they too limit what is possible. Or suppose that, contrary to fact, there exist no intelligent beings and that consequently nothing is known. In that case, too, certain things and states of affairs would be possible and others impossible; some events could happen and others could not. If it is true that the concept of law has epistemic criteria built into it, the conclusion to be drawn is that our definitions of "possibility" are in need of revision. For given the view of laws propounded by Nagel and Mackie, it is no longer laws alone which define possibilities. p will be a statement of possibility only if it is consistent with every law of nature *and with every proposition which is like a law in all respects except epistemic ones.* This is entailed by the knowledge-independence of possibilities in *re.* Thus if we accept both the epistemic restrictions on the definition of "law" and the idea of real empirical possibility, the definition of the latter has to be amended, and with these amendments to D_2 and D_3 Kneale's argument goes through in full to its unacceptable conclusion. This way out is therefore not philosophically adequate.

     3. *Non-Deducibility Requirement.*   The non-deducibility requirement can be illustrated by reference to Popper's example: "All moas die before reaching the age of fifty."[7] The reason why this omnitemporal truth is said not to be a law is that the death of moas before fifty can be attributed to the operation of certain local conditions—namely, the presence of viruses in the places where moas lived. "All moas die before reaching the age of fifty" is thus deducible from a conjunction of (1) generalizations stating connections between the life span of animals and the operation of factors such as viruses and (2) statements of initial conditions which bring the moas within the scope of these generalizations. What makes it reasonable to say that "There exists a sixty-year-old moa" is a statement of unrealized possibility is just that this proposition is inconsistent only with a general proposition whose truth depends on local conditions in certain places and at certain times having been what they were. The general idea behind the non-deducibility requirement is clear enough: propositions which do *not* limit possibilities are ones whose truth depends on local conditions, irrespective of the syntactical appearance of these propositions. Law, on the other hand—that is, propositions which *do* limit possibilities—are unconditional in their application and consequently cannot be deduced from any set of premises in which statements of initial conditions occur essentially. Another way of putting the matter is this: for an empirical proposition to satisfy the non-deducibility requirement, it is necessary and sufficient that its terms be what I dub "nomologically ultimate"—that is, such that what the law states with respect to them shall in no way depend on historical or geographical facts. That to which a true universal proposition ascribes a nomologically ultimate predicate satisfies the predication irrespective of what local conditions are anywhere. A true universal proposition containing only nomologically ultimate predicates states a cosmic regularity, something that is *just so,* whatever conditions are.

---

     [7] Popper, *op. cit.* pp. 427ff. Here only the example is used; Popper's proposed definition of "natural necessity" is not being discussed. There is reason to suppose that the definition as formulated in *The Logic of Scientific Discovery* is defective. See G. C. Nerlich and W. A. Suchting, "Popper on Law and Necessity," *The British Journal for the Philosophy of Science,* 18 (1967); K. R. Popper, "A Revised Definition of Natural Necessity," *ibid,* 18 (1968). [All reprinted in this text.]

It is evident that the non-deducibility requirement still leaves a subset of the set of unrestricted empirical existential propositions useless for stating unrealized possibilities. The unexempted subset consists of those existential propositions which contain only nomologically ultimate predicates. A statement to the effect that something is F, where being F is independent of local conditions, cannot be both false and possible. This remains as a defect in the proposed way out, unless it can be shown that lawlikeness and non-deducibility are the same.

Few would deny that nomological ultimacy is *necessary* for lawlikeness. For example, "has a maximum speed of no more than the speed of light" is a nomologically ultimate predicate of bodies, and it is reasonable to say that "There is a body which travels faster than light" is not a statement of unrealized possibility. This is so because "Nothing travels faster than light" is a law of nature. In general, for any law l, and for any unrestricted existential proposition e, if e is inconsistent with l, then e is inconsistent with a proposition which satisfies the non-deducibility requirement. We are, however, still left with the question: is nomological ultimacy *sufficient* for lawlikeness? The dispute about the adequacy of the non-deducibility requirement turns on the answer to this question. Proponents of the requirement argue that there is nothing more to lawlikeness than nomological ultimacy; critics of the requirement hold that there is.

How can this quarrel be resolved? I know of no argument that would settle the matter conclusively, one way or the other. But there is one consideration which tells strongly against the non-deducibility definition of "law," without constituting a disproof of it. That consideration is here brought out by reference to a fictitious case. Suppose that there is omnitemporally just one moa and that it dies before reaching fifty. Consequently, "All moas die before reaching fifty" is true. Suppose further that the death of this moa is neither causally nor scientifically explainable, not even "in principle." On the view of explanation accepted by all proponents of the non-deducibility definition of laws of nature, if a generalization has as its sufficient truth condition something inexplicable, then the generalization itself will not be deducible from a conjunction of further empirical generalizations and statements of initial conditions. Hence "All moas die before reaching fifty" will be a law, for it satisfies all criteria laid down by the non-deducibility analysis. Yet this generalization is not a law in the normal sense of the word. The objection to calling it a law is that what makes it true, in the case we postulated, is a purely accidental event. If Q is a generalization made true by the occurrence of a purely accidental event, then what Q rules out cannot be impossible. We have no grounds for thinking that the death of this moa before fifty could not have been otherwise; indeed the case as described leaves us little option but to say that it could have been otherwise, despite the fact that in our imaginary world "dies before reaching fifty" is a nomologically ultimate predicate of moas.

The crux of this case is the claim that the death of the lone moa is both inexplicable and accidental. Upholders of the non-deducibility definition are bound to deny this claim: they must say that if "All moas die before reaching fifty" is non-deducible, then what instantiates it is not accidental. Here one feels like digging in one's heels. For the ground on which it is declared that instances of non-deducibile generalizations are not accidental is just the belief that cosmic regularities *must be* lawful. This of course is a well-known consequence of Hume-inspired analyses of natural necessity.[8] It is a highly counterintuitive consequence, to say the least. We find it conceivable that an individual sequence should be accidental. We think that this is logically possible. We are also possessed of a deep conviction, articulated for a different purpose by Hume himself, that "repetition alone cannot give rise to a new idea." If it is conceivable that a particular sequence is accidental, then it is conceivable that a regular sequence should be accidental, even if the regularity is on a cosmic scale. This is the basis of our feeling that the description of laws as contingent empirical generalizations, true independently of local conditions, fails to reveal what it is about laws that enables them to limit possibilities. Such generalizations state that something is universally just so, and I cannot see, as Kneale could not see, how something's being just so can make its not being so impossible. The case of the inexplicable *and* accidental death of the lone moa therefore ought to be admitted as a counterexample to the analysis of law under discussion.

The above reasoning is persuasive rather than compulsive, for it rests at bottom on an appeal to intuition, and conceptual intuitions are not infallible. Fundamental theses in metaphysics, however, are often tested by such appeals, which are far from vitiated by the possibility of error of which they admit. The non-deducibility definition of "law" runs counter to one of our entrenched conceptual intuitions, and this fact constitutes a powerful though inconclusive objection to it.

4. *Strengthening Modality.*   This way out seems to allow of no loopholes. It is as far as I can see a completely adequate way of evading the conclusion. It should be stressed that in this article I have not offered any *conclusive* grounds for a necessitarian analysis of laws of nature. That analysis may be false, and there may be arguments to show its falsity. All I have claimed is that it alone of the four different ways out mentioned satisfactorily copes with the problem posed by Kneale's argument. That is certainly *one* reason in its favor. It is also a good reason for attempting a sympathetic reappraisal of the doctrine that laws of nature are necessary, despite the skeptical animus which moves so many contemporary thinkers to reject that doctrine.

---

[8] Cf. "Philosophers who treat suggestions of law as universal material implications say in effect that there is no sense in talking of historical accidents on a cosmic scale." Kneale, *B.J.P.S.*, p. 98. [Reprinted in this text.]

Suggested Readings for Part Three

Beauchamp, Tom L. "On Causal Irregularity: A Reply to Dretske and Snyder." *Philosophy of Science* 40 (June 1973).

Braithwaite, R. B. *Scientific Explanation.* Cambridge, Eng.: Cambridge University Press, 1963, chapter 9.

Chisholm, Roderick. "Law Statements and Counterfactual Inference." *Analysis* 15 (1954/55): 97-105.

Dretske, F. and Snyder, A. "Causal Irregularity." *Philosophy of Science* 39 (March 1972): 69-71.

Dretske, F. and Snyder, A. "Causality and Sufficiency: Reply to Beauchamp." *Philosophy of Science* 40 (June 1973).

Hartshorne, Charles. "Causal Necessities: An Alternative to Hume." *Philosophical Review* 63 (1954): 479-99.

Kim, Jaegwon. "Causes and Events: Mackie on Causation." *Journal of Philosophy* 68 (July 1971): 426-41.

Kim, Jaegwon. "Causation, Nomic Subsumption, and the Concept of Event." *Journal of Philosophy* 70 (April 1973): 217-36.

Mackie, J. L. "Causes and Conditions." *American Philosophical Quarterly* 2 (1965): 245-64.

Maxwell, Nicholas. "Can there be Necessary Connections between Successive Events?" *British Journal for the Philosophy of Science* 19 (1968): 1-25.

Mill, J. S. *A System of Logic.* London, Eng.: Longmans, 1961, Book 3, chapters 4-5, 10.

O'Connor, D. J. "The Analysis of Conditional Sentences." *Mind* 60 (1951): 351-62.

Pap, Arthur. *An Introduction to the Philosophy of Science.* New York: Free Press, 1962, Part Four.

Russell, Bertrand. "On the Notion of Cause." *Proceedings of the Aristotelian Society* 13 (1912-13). Reprinted in *Mysticism and Logic* and elsewhere.

Schlick, Moritz. "Causality in Everyday Life and in Recent Science." In *Readings in Philosophical Analysis,* edited by H. Feigl and W. Sellars. New York: Appleton-Century-Crofts, 1949, pp. 515-33.

Taylor, Richard. *Action and Purpose.* New York: Prentice-Hall, Inc., 1966, chapters 1-4.

Weinberg, Julius. "Contrary-to-Fact Conditionals." *Journal of Philosophy* 48 (1951): 17-22.

PART FOUR

THE MANIPULABILITY THEORY

INTRODUCTION

Regularity and necessity theorists agree that uniformity is an important and necessary condition of causation, but prior to the rise of modern science little emphasis had been placed on this criterion. Philosophers largely thought of causes in terms of individual powers or, in the case of animals, in terms of self-movement. The philosophers whose articles appear in this part of the text represent a sophisticated modern rendition of the belief that the model of self-movement, especially manipulative human actions, is basic for an adequate account of causation. These philosophers emphasize that we cite items called "causes" because they are controllable means to desired ends. The term "cause," in their view, *means* a state of affairs which human agents can control in order to produce or prevent another state of affairs (their "effect"). Accordingly, they analyze the causal relation in terms of a "production of *y* by manipulation of *x*" model. This manipulation model is thought to be the primitive notion of causation—others being somehow dependent upon or derivative from it.

Philosophers who propound this manipulability theory are primarily concerned with exploring the character of what may be called "the cause" judgments as distinguished from general causal judgments or law statements, though they certainly take their theories to apply the latter. In their view, a discerning analysis of actual causal judgments and their circumstances reveals more about causation than does a study of the laws which those judgments entail. Indeed, these philosophers find general judgments such as "All *X*'s cause *Y*'s" ambiguous because they seem subject to widely differing interpretations. "The cause," as distinguished from the complete set of causal conditions, they find to be selected in accordance with principles of controllability. This is no less true in science than elsewhere. However theoretical science might be, they argue, it is still a practical concern, and the term "causes" serves a practical function in scientific contexts. To understand this feature of the concept of causation is, in their judgment, to understand its most important aspect.

R. G. Collingwood argues that the term "cause," as ordinarily used, has at least three senses and possibly more. The first sense of "cause" is the one generally used by historians who speak of voluntary actions being caused by motives afforded to the acting agent. The second sense of "cause" is the manipulability sense discussed above. Collingwood finds this sense particularly ubiquitous in the practical sciences. The third sense of "cause" is roughly the one both regularity and necessity theorists are struggling to capture through precise definitions—a usage found most frequently in the theoretical sciences of nature. Collingwood maintains that the first sense is tied to the language of human responsibility, the second to language of controllability, and the third to language of theoretical explanation in terms of conditionship relations. But he thinks all three are connected with certain anthropomorphic understandings of nature, such as "compulsion" and "being within the power of human agency."

Collingwood's discussion of the second sense constitutes his manipulability theory. He argues that causes are recognized through a means-end model: agents can bring about or prevent certain ends (effects) by manipulating means (causes) to those ends. For this reason Collingwood finds causes analogous to handles of tools. The real producer or preventer, he suggests, is human action; but it is the handleable item selected for purposes of control that we denominate the cause, not the handler. For example, doctors prevent cancer through their actions, but to ask for the cause of cancer is to ask for conditions within the power of human beings to prevent, viz. the conditions which can be controlled in order to prevent cancer from occurring or spreading. Collingwood takes the producing-preventing feature to be essential to the meaning of "cause" in sense two. Only in his third sense does either lawlike regularity or necessity become significant.

From this general approach Collingwood derives the "principle of the relativity of causes." He argues that different persons who are differently situated in terms of their ability to control will give different answers to the question, "What is *the cause* of *y*?" Relativity of judgment occurs because the cause for any given person is that condition from among the set of relevant causal conditions which the person is capable of controlling or preventing, or at least the cause is that which he most naturally understands in terms of controllability. "The cause" judgments, on this analysis, are essentially relative to a specific context of investigation. Collingwood provides a graphic example:

> A car skids while cornering at a certain point, strikes the kerb, and turns turtle. From the car-driver's point of view the cause of the accident was cornering too fast, and the lesson is that one must drive more carefully. From the county surveyor's point of view the cause was a defect in the surface or camber of the road, and the lesson is that greater care must be taken to make roads skid-proof. From the motor-manufacturer's point of view the cause was defective design in the car, and the lesson is that one must place the centre of gravity lower.

Collingwood concludes that a person who is unable to control the conditions of an event's occurrence cannot use the term "cause" in sense two; there simply are not causes unless conditions are seen from the perspective of agent control. Mere spectators may make causal judgments, but not of this sort. (Some counterexamples intended to show deficiencies in Collingwood's relativity principle are found in section one of Gorovitz' article in Part Six.)

Douglas Gasking basically affirms Collingwood's position but argues to somewhat stronger conclusions. Gasking does not distinguish different senses of causation, yet he claims to have adequately "explained the 'cause-effect' relation in terms of the 'producing-by-means-of' relation." General causal expressions, such as "*A* causes *B*," he treats as recipes for producing things through manipulative operations. "Causes" here *means* "by applying to *x* the general technique for making things *B*, you will make it *C*." For example, we speak of causing iron to glow by making it hot. We have no means for making the iron hot by first making it glow; but if such a manipulative technique were available, we would view the glowing as the cause of the heat. Gasking maintains that a statement such as "A rise in the temperature of iron causes it to glow" *means* (roughly) "By applying to iron the general technique for making things hot you will also, in this case, make it glow." His example is intended to show how the concept of causation is essentially wedded to manipulative techniques for producing results.

Gasking also employs his analysis as a means for criticizing the Regularity Theory. He admits that causes can be spoken of apart from preventive or productive concerns in the case of some theoretical statements. But in such contexts he thinks it is always the case that one *can* produce events of the first sort as a means to producing events of the second sort. Hence, the causal relation is still analyzable in terms of recipes or manipulative techiniques. Gasking argues that whatever truth is to be found in the Regularity Theory, numerous cases exist where causes cannot be distinguished from effects by citing regularities (unless manipulative features are added) and other cases exist where the Regularity Theory would mistakenly lead us to attribute a causal relation when there is none. The former problem is said to be especially acute when causes and effects are simultaneous rather than successive (e.g., in the case of $1000°$ heat contemporaneously causing an iron bar to glow); the latter is troublesome in cases involving succession where we may regularly infer B from A and yet would only incorrectly say that A caused B (e.g., from knowledge of a freely falling body at 32 feet per second we may infer it will be moving at 64 feet per second one second later). Gasking's point seems to be that the Regularity Theory is useless in the second type of case and that if one removes the manipulability dimension from the first sort of case the causal relationship vanishes with it.

G. H. von Wright's concluding article continues the Gasking-Collingwood approach but examines causation from the perspective of recent work in action theory. Von Wright argues that there is a basic and significant difference between causation and action, but that there is nonetheless an important conceptual connection between the concepts of causation and action. Like Gasking, he regards regularity theorists' attempts to analyze causal notions by looking exclusively at refined scientific contexts as undue and misleading purification of the concept. Von Wright first attempts to clarify the notion of an action. He maintains that the connection between a cause and its effect is extrinsic, whereas the connection between an action and its result is logical and not causal. He suggests that when we say agents cause effects we should not understand this as meaning agents are causes. "Agents cause effects" is shorthand for saying agents create circumstances which become conditions productive of effects.

Von Wright applies this analysis to problems of causation by arguing that the distinction between cause-factors and effect-factors rests essentially on the distinction between things done and things brought about through human actions. On this analysis p is a cause and q its effect if and only if by doing p one could bring about q or by suppressing p one could remove or prevent q. This is both how we establish causal connections and how we come to mark global connections as nomological generalizations which support counterfactuals. (See Parts Two and Three for a discussion of the nature of counterfactuals.) Confirmation of law-governed counterfactual conditionals, according to von Wright, rests on a prior counterfactual conditional to the effect that "p would not have been there had we not produced it." But this kind of counterfactual is not a statement of causal conditionship relations; it has to do with action rather than causation. Von Wright concludes that the idea of a causal and nomic relationship depends essentially on the concept of action and that causal connections are established only when we are satisfied that by manipulating one factor we can bring about another.

Should one object that there are circumstances which we regard as causal and yet in which nothing can be manipulated, von Wright's answer is ready: "We can nevertheless *assume* that there is a causal bond between them. This would be tantamount to assuming, e.g., that *if we could* produce p as a result of action, we could also bring about q, viz. by producing p." This does not mean, he says, that whenever a cause can be truly said to operate some agent is involved, for causation operates in conditions unknown to man. It is simply to say that to think of a relation as causal is to think of it under the aspect of possible action. Only in this restricted sense does von Wright take action to be a more basic concept than causation.

R. G. COLLINGWOOD

18. Three Senses of the Word "Cause"

The term "cause," as actually used in modern English and other languages, is ambiguous. It has three senses; possibly more; but at any rate three.

Sense I. Here that which is "caused" is the free and deliberate act of a conscious and responsible agent, and "causing" him to do it means affording him a motive for doing it.

Sense II. Here that which is "caused" is an event in nature, and its "cause" is an event or state of things by producing or preventing which we can produce or prevent that whose cause it is said to be.

Sense III. Here that which is "caused" is an event or state of things, and its "cause" is another event or state of things standing to it in a one-one relation of causal priority: i.e., a relation of such a kind that (*a*) if the cause happens or exists the effect also must happen or exist, even if no further conditions are fulfilled, (*b*) the effect cannot happen or exist unless the cause happens or exists, (*c*) in some sense which remains to be defined, the cause is prior to the effect; for without such priority there would be no telling which is which. If C and E were connected merely by a one-one relation such as is described in the sentences (*a*) and (*b*) above, there would be no reason why C should be called the cause of E, and E the effect of C, rather than vice versa. But whether causal priority is temporal priority, or a special case of temporal priority, or priority of some other kind, is another question.

From R. G. Collingwood, *An Essay on Metaphysics* (Oxford at the Clarendon Press, 1940), pp. 285-87, 296-311. Footnotes included. Reprinted by permission of The Clarendon Press, Oxford.

Sense I may be called the *historical* sense of the word "cause," because it refers to a type of case in which both C and E are human activities such as form the subject-matter of history. When historians talk about causes, this is the sense in which they are using the word, unless they are aping the methods and vocabulary of natural science.

Sense II refers to a type of case in which natural events are considered from a human point of view, as events grouped in pairs where one member in each pair, C, is immediately under human control, whereas the other, E, is not immediately under human control but can be indirectly controlled by man because of the relation in which it stands to C. This is the sense which the word "cause" has in the *practical sciences of nature,* i.e., the sciences of nature whose primary aim is not to achieve theoretical knowledge about nature but to enable man to enlarge his control of nature. This is the sense in which the word 'cause' is used, for example, in engineering or medicine.

Sense III refers to a type of case in which an attempt is made to consider natural events not practically, as things to be produced or prevented by human agency, but theoretically, as things that happen independently of human will but not independently of each other: causation being the name by which this dependence is designated. This is the sense which the word has traditionally borne in physics and chemistry and, in general, the *theoretical sciences of nature.* . . .

In sense II that which is caused is an event in nature; but the word "cause" still expresses an idea relative to human conduct, because that which causes is something under human control, and this control serves as means whereby human beings can control that which is caused. In this sense, the cause of an event in nature is the handle, so to speak, by which human beings can manipulate it. If we human beings want to produce or prevent such a thing, and cannot produce or prevent it immediately (as we can produce or prevent certain movements of our own bodies), we set about looking for its "cause." The question "What is the cause of an event y?" means in this case "How can we produce or prevent y at will?"

This sense of the word may be defined as follows. *A cause is an event or state of things which it is in our power to produce or prevent, and by producing or preventing which we can produce or prevent that whose cause it is said to be.* When I speak of "producing" something I refer to such occasions as when one turns a switch and thus produces the state of things described by the position "the switch is now at the ON position." By preventing something I mean producing something incompatible with it, e.g., turning the switch to the OFF position.

Turning a switch to one or other position by finger-pressure is an instance of producing a certain state of things (the ON or OFF position of the switch) immediately, for it is nothing but a certain complex of bodily movements all immediately produced. These movements are not our means of turning the switch, they are the turning of the switch. Subject to certain indispensable conditions, the turning of the switch is our "means" of producing a further state of things, viz. incandescence or its absence in a certain filament. What is immediately produced (the position of the switch) is the "cause" in sense II of what is thus mediately produced.

The search for causes in sense II is natural science in that sense of the phrase in which natural science is what Aristotle calls a "practical science," valued not for its truth pure and simple but for its utility, for the "power over nature" which it gives us: Baconian science, where "knowledge is power" and where "nature is conquered by obeying her." The field of a "practical science" is the contingent, or in Aristotle's terminology "what admits of being otherwise." The light, for example, is on, but it admits of being off; i.e., I find by experiment that I am able to extinguish it by turning the switch to the OFF position. To discover that things are contingent is to discover that we can produce and prevent them.

Before the above definition of sense II is accepted, a preliminary question must be answered. I will put the question by distinguishing between two ideas, the idea of a "practical" science of nature and the idea of an "applied" science of nature, and asking to which of these ideas sense II belongs. By a "practical" science of nature I mean one whose relation to practice is more intimate than that of means to end: one whose practical utility is not an ulterior end for whose sake it is valued, but its essence. By an "applied" science of nature I mean one whose essence *qua* science is not practical utility but theoretical truth, but one which, in addition to being true, is useful as providing the solution for the practical problems by being "applied" to them. The Aristotelian and Baconian formulae might be understood as covering either of these two cases; but my present inquiry demands that they should be distinguished.

Sense II of the word "cause" is bound up with the idea of a "practical" science. An "applied" science, being *qua* science not practical but theoretical, uses the word cause in sense III: a sense in which it is only an "accident" (in the vocabulary of traditional logic) that knowing a cause enables some one to produce the effect, and in which, therefore, the statement "*x* causes *y*" would be in no way invalidated by the statement that *x* is a thing of such a kind as cannot be produced or prevented by human beings. I am not here denying that there is such a sense. What I am doing is to assert that there is another sense, recognizable in actual and long-established usage, in which it is not accidental but essential to the idea of causation that knowing the cause should enable some one to produce the effect, and in which the statement "*x* causes *y*" would be flatly contradicted by the statement that *x* is a thing of such a kind as cannot be produced or prevented by human beings.

This usage, representing sense II of the word "cause," can be recognized by two criteria: the thing described as a cause is always conceived as something in the world of nature or physical world, and it is always something conceived as capable of being produced or prevented by human agency. Here are some examples. The cause of malaria is the bite of a mosquito; the cause of a boat's sinking is her being overloaded; the cause of books going mouldy is their being in a damp room; the cause of man's sweating is a dose of aspirin; the cause of a furnace going out in the night is that the draught-door was insufficiently open; the cause of seedlings dying is that nobody watered them.

In any one of the above cases, for example the first, the question whether the effect can be produced or prevented by producing or preventing the cause is not a further question which arises for persons practically interested when the proposition that (for example) malaria is due to mosquito-bites has been established; it is a question which has already been answered in the affirmative by the establishment of that proposition. This affirmative answer is in fact what the proposition means. In other words: medicine (the science to which the proposition belongs) is not a theoretical science which may on occasion be applied to the solution of practical problems, it is a practical science. The causal propositions which it establishes are not propositions which may or may not be found applicable in practice, but whose truth is independent of such applicability; they are propositions whose applicability is their meaning.

Consider a (hypothetical) negative instance. A great deal of time and money is being spent on "cancer research," that is, on the attempt to discover "the cause of cancer." I submit that the word "cause" is here used in sense II; that is to say, discovering the cause of cancer means discovering something which it is in the power of human beings to produce or prevent, by producing or preventing which they can produce or prevent cancer. Suppose some one claimed to have discovered the cause of cancer, but added that his discovery would be of no practical use because the cause he had discovered was not a thing that could be produced or prevented at will. Such a person would be ridiculed by his colleagues in the medical profession. His "discovery" would be denounced as a sham. He would not be allowed to have done what he claimed to have done. It would be pointed out that he was not using the word "cause" in the established sense which it bears in a medical context. To use my own terminology, it would be pointed out that he was thinking of medicine as an applied science, whereas it is a practical science; and using the word cause in sense III, whereas in medicine it bears sense II.

This usage of the word is not exclusively modern. It can be traced back through Middle English usages to familiar Latin usages of the word *causa,* and thence to the Greek αἰτία and its equivalent πρόφασις in, for example, the Hippocratic writings of the fifth century before Christ.

A cause in sense II is never able by itself to produce the corresponding effect. The switch, as I said, only works the light subject to certain indispensable conditions. Among these are the existence of an appropriate current and its maintenance by insulation and contacts. These are called *conditiones sine quibus non.* Their existence, over and above the cause, constitutes one of the differences between sense II and sense III of the word "cause." . . .

A cause in sense III requires no such accompaniment. A cause in sense II is conditional, a cause in sense III is unconditional. This distinction was correctly understood by John Stuart Mill, whose formal definition of the term "cause" is a definition of sense III, but who recognizes that ordinarily when people speak of a cause they are using the word in sense II. A cause, he tells us, is the invariable unconditional antecedent of its effect. This antecedent, he thinks, is always complex, and any one of the elements that go to make it up is called a condition. But what people ordinarily call a cause is one of these conditions, arbitrarily selected, and dignified by a mere abuse of language with a name that properly belongs to the whole set.[1]

---

[1] "Since then, mankind are accustomed with acknowledged propriety so far as the ordinances of language are concerned, to give the name of cause to almost any one of the conditions of a phenomenon, or any portion of the whole number, *arbitrarily selected,* without excepting even those conditions which are purely negative, and in themselves incapable of causing anything; it will probably be admitted without longer discussion, that no one of the conditions has more claim to that title than another, and that *the real cause of the phenomenon is the assemblage of all its conditions.*" (J. S. Mill, *System of Logic,* Book III, chap. v, §3; ed. 1, vol. i, p. 403, my italics.)

Mill deserves great credit for seeing that the word "cause" was used in these two different ways. But his account of the relation between a cause in sense II and the conditions that accompany it is not quite satisfactory. Closer inspection would have shown him that the "selection" of one condition to be dignified by the name of cause is by no means arbitrary. It is made according to a principle. The "condition" which I call the cause (in sense II) of an event in which I take a practical interest is the condition I am able to produce or prevent at will. Thus, if my car fails to climb a steep hill, and I wonder why, I shall not consider my problem solved by a passer-by who tells me that the top of a hill is farther away from the earth's centre than its bottom, and that consequently more power is needed to take a car uphill than to take her along the level. All this is quite true; what the passer-by has described is one of the conditions which together form the "real cause" (Mill's phrase; what I call the cause in sense III) of my car's stopping; and as he has "arbitrarily selected" one of these and called it the cause, he has satisfied Mill's definition of what the word ordinarily means. But suppose an A.A. man comes along, opens the bonnet, holds up a loose high-tension lead, and says: "Look here, sir, you're running on three cylinders." My problem is now solved. I know the cause of the stoppage. It is *the* cause, just because it has not been "arbitrarily selected"; it has been correctly identified as the thing that I can put right, after which the car will go properly. If I had been a person who could flatten out hills by stamping on them the passer-by would have been right to call my attention to the hill as the cause of the stoppage; not because the hill was a hill but because I was able to flatten it out.

To be precise, the "condition" which is thus "selected" is in fact not "selected" at all; for selection implies that the person selecting has before him a finite number of things from among which he takes his choice. But this does not happen. In the first place the conditions of any given event are quite possibly infinite in number, so that no one could thus marshal them for selection even if he tried. In the second place no one ever tries to enumerate them completely. Why should he? If I find that I can get a result by certain means I may be sure that I should not be getting it unless a great many conditions were fulfilled; but so long as I get it I do not mind what these conditions are. If owing to a change in one of them I fail to get it, I still do not want to know what they all are; I only want to know what the one is that has changed.

From this a principle follows which I shall call "the relativity of causes." Suppose that the conditions of an event y include three things, a, β, γ; and suppose that there are three persons A, B, C, of whom A is able to produce or prevent a and only a; B is able to produce or prevent β and only β; and C is able to produce or prevent γ and only γ. Then if each of them asks "What was the cause of y?" each will have to give a different answer. For A, a is the cause; for B, β; and for C, γ. The principle may be stated by saying that *for any given person the cause in sense II of a given thing is that one of its conditions which he is able to produce or prevent.*

For example, a car skids while cornering at a certain point, strikes the kerb, and turns turtle. From the car-driver's point of view the cause of the accident was cornering too fast, and the lesson is that one must drive more carefully. From the county surveyor's point of view the cause was a defect in the surface or camber of the road, and the lesson is that greater care must be taken to make roads skid-proof. From the motor-manufacturer's point of view the cause was defective design in the car, and the lesson is that one must place the centre of gravity lower.

If the three parties concerned take these three lessons respectively to heart accidents will become rarer. A knowledge of the causes of accidents will be gained in such a sense that knowledge is power: causes are causes in sense II, and knowledge of the cause of a thing we wish to prevent is (not merely brings, but is) knowledge how to prevent it. As in the science of medicine so in the study of "accidents," where "accident" means something people wish to prevent, the word "cause" is used in sense II.

As in medicine, therefore, so in the study of "accidents" the use of the word in any other sense, or its use by some one who fails to grasp the implications of this sense, leads to confusion. If the driver, the surveyor, and the manufacturer agreed in thinking they knew the cause of the accident I have described, but differed as to what it was, and if each thought that it was a thing one of the others could produce or prevent, but not himself, the result would be that none of them would do anything towards preventing such accidents in future, and their so-called knowledge of the cause of such accidents would be a "knowledge" that was not, and did not even bring, power. But since in the present context the word "cause" is used in sense II, the reason why their "knowledge" of the "cause" of such accidents does not enable them to prevent such accidents is that it is not knowledge of their cause. What each of them mistakes for such knowledge is the following nonsense proposition: "the cause of accidents like this is something which somebody else is able to produce or prevent, but I am not." Nonsense, because "cause" means "cause in sense II," and owing to the relativity of causes "the cause of this accident" means "that one of its conditions which I am able to produce or prevent." Hence the folly of blaming other people in respect of an event in which we and they are together involved. Every one knows that such blame is foolish; but without such an analysis of the idea of causation as I am here giving it is not easy to say why.

In medicine the principle of the relativity of causes means that, since any significant statement about the cause of a disease is a statement about the way in which that disease can be treated, two persons who can treat the same disease in two different ways will make different statements as to its cause. Suppose that one medical man can cure a certain disease by administering drugs, and another by "psychological" treatment. For the first the "cause" of the disease will be definable in terms of bio-chemistry; for the second in terms of psychology. If the disease itself is defined in terms of bio-chemistry, or in terms that admit of explanation or analysis in bio-chemical language, the definition of its cause in terms of psychology may be thought to imply an "interactionist" theory of the relation between body and mind; and may be thought objectionable in so far as such theories are open to objection. But this would be a mistake. Definition of its cause in terms of psychology implies no theory as to the relation between body and mind. It simply records the fact that cases of the disease have been successfully treated by psychological methods, together with the hope that psychological methods may prove beneficial in future cases. To speak of this as "evidence for an interactionist theory" would be to talk nonsense.

A corollary of the relativity principle is that *for a person who is not able to produce or prevent any of its conditions a given event has no cause in sense II at all,* and any statement he makes as to its cause in this sense of the word will be a nonsense statement. Thus the managing director of a large insurance company once told me that his wide experience of motor accidents had convinced him that the cause of all accidnts was people driving too fast. This was a nonsense statement; but one could expect nothing better from a man whose practical concern with this affairs was limited to paying for them. In sense II of the word "cause" only a person who is concerned with producing or preventing a certain kind of event can form an opinion about its cause. For a mere spectator there are no causes. When Hume tried to explain how the mere act of spectation could in time generate the idea of a cause, where "cause" meant the cause of empirical science, that is, the cause in sense II, he was trying to explain how something happens which in fact does not happen.

If sciences are constructed consisting of causal propositions in sense II of the word "cause," they will of course be in essence codifications of the various ways in which the people who construct them can bend nature to their purposes, and of the means by which in each case this can be done. Their constituent propositions will be (*a*) experimental, (*b*) general.

(*a*) In calling them experimental I mean that they will be established by means of experiment. No amount of observation will serve to establish such a proposition; for any such proposition is the declaration of ability to produce or prevent a certain state of things by the use of certain means; and no one knows what he can do, or how he can do it, until he tries. By observing and thinking he may form the opinion that he can probably do a given thing that resembles one he has done in the past; he may, that is, form an opinion as to its cause; but he cannot acquire knowledge.

(*b*) Because the proposition "*x* causes *y*," in sense II of the word "cause," is a constituent part of a practical science, it is essentially something that can be applied to cases arising in practice; that is to say, the terms *x* and *y* are not individuals but universals, and the proposition itself, rightly understood, reads "any instance of *x* is a thing whose production or prevention is means respectively of producing or preventing some instance of *y*." It would be nonsense, in this sense of the word "cause," to inquire after the cause of any individual thing as such. It is a peculiarity of sense II that every causal proposition is a general proposition or "propositional function." In sense I every causal proposition is an individual proposition. In sense III causal propositions might equally well be either individual or general.

If the above analysis of the cause-effect relation (in sense II) into a means-end relation is correct, why do people describe this means-end relation in cause-effect terminology? People do not choose words at random; they choose them because they think them appropriate. If they apply cause-effect terminology to things whose relation is really that of means and end the reason must be that they want to apply to those things some idea which is conveyed by the cause-effect terminology and not by the means-end terminology. What is this idea? The answer is not doubtful. The cause-effect terminology conveys an idea not only of one thing's leading to another but of one thing's forcing another to happen or exist; an idea of power or compulsion or constraint.

From what impression, as Hume asks, is this idea derived? I answer, from impressions received in our social life, in the practical relations of man to man; specifically, from the impression of causing (in sense I) some other man to do something when, by argument or command or threat or the like, we place him in a situation in which he can only carry out his intentions by doing that thing; and conversely, from the impression of being caused to do something.

Why, then, did people think it appropriate to apply this idea to the case of actions in which we achieve our ends by means, not of other human beings, but of things in nature?

Sense II of the word "cause" is especially a Greek sense; in modern times it is especially associated with the survival or revival of Greek ideas in the earlier Renaissance thinkers; and both the Greeks and the earlier Renaissance thinkers held quite seriously an animistic theory of nature. They thought of what we call the material or physical world as a living organism or complex of living organisms, each with its own sensations and desires and intentions and thoughts. In Plato's *Timaeus*, and in the Renaissance Platonists whose part in the formation of modern natural science was so decisive, the constant use of language with animistic implications is neither an accident nor a metaphor; these expressions are meant to be taken literally and to imply what they seem to imply, namely that the way in which men use what we nowadays call inorganic nature as means to our ends is not in principle different from the way in which we use other men. We use other men by assuming them to be free agents with wills of their own, and influencing them in such a way that they shall decide to do what is in conformity with our plans. This is "causing" them so to act in sense I of the word "cause." If "inorganic nature" is alive in much the same way as human beings, we must use it according to much the same principles; and therefore we can apply to this use of it the same word "cause," as implying that there are certain ways in which natural things behave if left to themselves, but that man, being more powerful than they, is able to thwart their inclination to behave in these ways and make them behave not as they like but as he likes.

To sum up. Sense II of the word "cause" rests on two different ideas about the relation between man and nature.

1. The anthropocentric idea that man looks at nature from his own point of view; not the point of view of a thinker, anxious to find out the truth about nature as it is in itself, but the point of view of a practical agent, anxious to find out how he can manipulate nature for the achieving of his own ends.

2. The anthropomorphic idea that man's manipulation of nature resembles one man's manipulation of another man, because natural things are alive in much the same way in which men are alive, and have therefore to be similarly handled.

The first idea is admittedly part of what civilized and educated European men nowadays think about their relations with nature. The second idea is part of what they notoriously did think down to (say) four centuries ago. How they began to get rid of this idea, and how completely they have even now got rid of it, are questions I shall not raise. My point is that even to-day, when they use the word "cause" in sense II, they are talking as if they had not yet entirely got rid of it. For if the vocabulary of practical natural science were overhauled with a view to eliminating all traces of anthropomorphism, language about causes in sense II would disappear and language about means and ends would take its place.

DOUGLAS GASKING

19. *Causation and Recipes*

We sometimes speak of one thing, or of one sort of thing, causing another—of the second as being the result of or due to the former. In what circumstances do we do so?

If we start with some typical statements of causal connection—"The train-smash was due to a buckled rail"; "Vitamin B deficiency causes beri-beri"—two things are likely to strike us. First, the effect is something that comes into being after the cause, and secondly, we suppose that anyone fully conversant with the circumstances and the relevant causal laws could, from a knowledge of the cause, predict the effect. So it is very natural to suggest, as an answer to our question: We say that A causes B whenever a person with the requisite empirical information could infer from the occurrence of A to the subsequent occurrence of B. Or we might put it: We say that A causes B whenever B regularly follows A.

But this "regular succession" notion will not do. For there are cases where we would speak of A causing B where it is not the case that from the occurrence of A we may infer the subsequent occurence of B.

An example to illustrate this: Iron begins to glow when its temperature reaches a certain point. I do not know what that temperature is: for the sake of the illustration I will suppose it to be 1,000°C., and will assume that iron never glows except at or above this temperature. Now, if someone saw a bar of iron glowing and, being quite ignorant of the physical facts, asked: "What makes that iron glow? What causes it to glow?" we should answer: "It is glowing because it is at a temperature of 1,000°C. or more." The glowing, B, is caused by the high temperature, A. And here the B that is caused is not an event subsequent to the cause A. Iron reaches 1,000°C. and begins glowing at the same instant. Another example: Current from a battery is flowing through a variable resistance, and we have a voltmeter connected to the two poles of the battery to measure the potential difference. Its reading is steady. We now turn the knob of our variable resistance and immediately the voltmeter shows that the potential difference has increased. If someone now asks: "What caused this increase?" we reply: "The increase of the resistance in the circuit." But here again the effect was not something subsequent to the cause, but simultaneous.

Reprinted by permission of the author and the publisher from Douglas Gasking, "Causation and Recipes," *Mind* vol. 64, no. 256 (October 1955): 479-87.

So perhaps our account should be emended so as to read: We speak of A as causing B when the occurrence of B may be inferred from the occurrence of A and the occurrence of B is either subsequent to or simultaneous with the occurrence of A.

But this will not do either. For there are, first of all, cases where from the occurrence of A we may infer the subsequent occurrence of B, yet would not speak of A as causing B. And, secondly, there are cases where from the occurrence of A we may infer the simultaneous occurrence of B, yet would not speak of A as causing B.

Here is an example of the first case. Given (A) that at t_1 a body freely falling *in vacuo* is moving at a speed of 32 feet per second we can infer (B) that at t_2, one second later, it will be moving at 64 feet per second. We might be prepared to say that this inference was in some sense or other a causal inference. But it would be a most unnatural and "strained" use of the word "cause" to say that the body's movement at 64 feet per second at t_2 was caused by its moving at 32 feet per second at t_1. It would be even more unnatural, to take a famous example, to say that the day that will be here in twelve hours' time is caused by the fact that it is now night. Yet, from the present fact, we can certainly infer that in twelve hours' time it will be day.

An example to illustrate the second point. From the fact that a bar of iron is now glowing we can certainly infer (and it will be a causal inference) that it is now at temperature of $1,000°$C. or over. Yet we should not say that its high temperature was caused by the glowing: we say that the high temperature causes the glowing, not *vice versa*. Another example: watching the voltmeter and battery in the electrical circuit previously described, we see that the needle suddenly jumps, showing that the potential difference has suddenly increased. From this we infer that the electrical resistance of the circuit has, at that moment, increased. But we should not say that the rise in potential difference caused the increase in resistance: rather that the rise in resistance caused a rise in the potential difference. Or, again, knowing the properties of a certain sort of wax, we infer from the fact that the wax has melted that, at that very moment, it reached such and such a temperature. Yet we should not say that the wax's melting caused it to reach the critical temperature: rather that its reaching that temperature caused it to melt. Why do we speak of "cause" in some cases in which we can infer from A to B, but not in others?

The reason is not always of the same sort. Sometimes in such a case it would be nonsense to speak of A causing B, sometimes it would merely be false. Our very last example is a rather trivial instance of the first sort of reason. It is nonsense to speak of the melting of the wax causing the high temperature of the wax because "x melts" means "high temperatures causes x to become liquid." So, "the melting of the wax caused the high-temperature of the wax" is equivalent to the absurdity "the high temperature of the wax's causing of the wax to become liquid caused the high temperature of the wax."

But it is not for this sort of reason that we do not say that the glowing of the iron causes the high temperature of the iron. "Melting" is by definition an effect and not a cause of an increase in temperature, but the same is not true of "glowing." It is not logically absurd to say that the glowing of a piece of iron causes its high temperature; it is merely untrue. It is possible to imagine and to describe a world in which it would have been true. Here is an account of such an imaginary world.

"Our early ancestors many millennia ago discovered that you could make a large range of substances (wood, water, leaves, etc.) glow first blue, then purple, then red by a process of alternately covering them so as to exclude light, then rapidly letting light fall on them, then quickly covering them again, and so on. Wood, for instance, starts glowing after about six minutes of this treatment, and reaches the red stage in about ten minutes. If it is then left in constant daylight or in constant darkness, it gradually fades through purple to blue and then ceases glowing. A number of other substances behave similarly, though the time needed to produce the glowing effect differs somewhat from substance to substance. None of the things that early man thus learnt to make glow, however, suffered any change of temperature in the process. Then, about 1000 B.C., men got hold of samples of fairly pure iron, for the first time. They tried the covering-uncovering technique on it to see if it too, like wood and water, but unlike certain sorts of rock, would glow if manipulated in this way. They found that it would, but that, unlike other substances, iron began to get hot when it started glowing, got hotter still at the purple stage, and when glowing red was very hot indeed. Precise measurements in modern times showed that on reaching the red stage the temperature of iron was $1,000°C$. In other respects this imaginary world is just like our world, except that when you put a poker or other non-combustible object in a fire it does not begin to glow, however hot it gets."

Who can doubt that in this imaginary world we should have said that the glowing of the iron caused its temperature to rise, and not *vice versa*? What, then, are the essential differences between this world and ours, which would lead us to say one thing in one world and another in another?

Human beings can make bodily movements. They do not move their arms, fingers, mouths and so on by doing anything else; they just move them. By making bodily movements men can manipulate things: can lift them, hold them in certain positions, squeeze them, pull them, rub them against each other, and so on. Men discovered that whenever they manipulated certain things in certain ways in certain conditions certain things happened. When you hold a stone in your hand and make certain complex movements of arm and fingers the stone sails through the air approximately in a parabola. When you manipulate two bits of wood and some dry grass for a long time in a certain way the grass catches fire. When you squeeze an egg, it breaks. When you put a stone in the fire it gets hot. Thus, men found out how to produce certain effects by manipulating things in certain ways: how to make an egg break, how to make a stone hot, how to make dry grass catch fire, and so on.

We have a general manipulative technique for making anything hot: we put it on a fire. We find that when we manipulate certain things in this way, such as water in a vessel, it gets hot but does not begin to glow. But we find, too, that certain other things, such as bars of iron, when manipulated in this way do not only get hot, they also, after a while, start to glow. And we have no general manipulative technique for making things glow: the only way to make iron glow is to apply to it the general technique for making things hot. We speak of making iron glow by making it hot, i.e., by applying to it the usual manipulative technique for making things hot, namely, putting on a fire, which in this special case, also makes it glow. We do not speak of making iron hot by making it glow, for we have no general manipulative technique for making things glow. And we say that the high temperature causes the glowing, not *vice versa.*

In our imaginary world there is a general manipulative technique for making things glow—namely, rapidly alternating exposure to light and shielding from light. There is no other way of making them glow. In general, things manipulated in this way glow, but do not get hot. Iron, however, glows and gets hot. In this world we speak of making iron hot by making it glow, i.e., by applying to it the usual manipulative technique for making things glow, which, in this special case, also makes it hot. We do not speak of making iron glow by making it hot, for the general manipulative technique of putting things on fires, which makes them hot, does not, in this world, also make things glow. And, in this world, we should say that the glowing causes the high temperature, not *vice versa.*

What this example shows is the following: When we have a general manipulative technique which results in a certain sort of event, A, we speak of producing A by this technique. (Heating things by putting them on a fire.) When in certain cases application of the general technique for producing A also results in B we speak of producing B by producing A. (Making iron glow by heating it.) And in such a case we speak of A causing B, but not *vice versa.* Thus, the notion of causation is essentially connected with our manipulative techniques for producing results. Roughly speaking: "A rise in the temperature of iron causes it to glow" means "By applying to iron the general technique for making things hot you will also, in this case, make it glow." And "The glowing of iron causes its temperature to rise" means "By applying to iron the general technique for making things glow you will also, in this case, make it hot." This latter statement is, as it happens, false, for there is no general technique for making things glow, let alone one which, applied to iron, also makes it hot.

Thus, a statement about the cause of something is very closely connected with a recipe for producing it or for preventing it. It is not exactly the same, however. One often makes a remark of the form "A causes B" with the practical aim of telling someone how to produce or prevent B, but not always. Sometimes one wishes to make a theoretical point. And one can sometimes properly say of some particular happening, A, that it caused some other particular event, B, even when no one could have produced A, by manipulation, as a means of producing B. For example, one may say that the rise in mean sea-level at a certain geological epoch was due to the melting of the Polar ice-cap. But when one can properly say this sort of thing it is always the case that people can produce events of the first sort as a means to producing events of the second sort. For example, one can melt ice in order to raise the level of water in a certain area. We could come rather closer to the meaning of "A causes B" if we said: "Events of the B sort can be produced by means of producing events of the A sort."

This account fits in with the principle that an event, A, at time t_2 cannot be the cause of an event, B, at an earlier time, t_1. It is a logical truth that one cannot alter the past. One cannot, therefore, by manipulations at t_2 which produce A at t_2 also produce B retrospectively at t_1.

Let us turn now to the cases where, although from a state of affairs A we can infer a later state of affairs B, we nevertheless would not say that A causes B; e.g., to the case where from the speed of a freely falling body at t_1 we can infer its speed at t_2, or infer coming darkness from present daylight. These are cases where a process is taking place whose law we know, so that we can infer from one stage in the process a later stage. Our inference presupposes that nothing happens to interfere with the process; the falling body will not encounter an obstruction, the earth's spinning will not be stopped by, say, our sun becoming a super-nova. The difference between the earth's spinning and the body's falling is that in the latter case we can set the process going and arrange that nothing shall thereafter interfere with it for a certain time; in the former case we cannot. It is the same sort of difference as there is between melting ice in a bucket and the water-level rising in the bucket and melting Polar ice-caps and sea-level rising. We cannot set the earth spinning, but we can set a top spinning.

Imagine a world in which there is an exact correlation between the colour and the temperature of everything. Anything at a certain low temperature is a certain shade of, say, blue. If an object becomes warmer, its colour changes to purple, then red, then orange, then yellow and finally to white. Cold (or blue) objects can be made hot (or red) by putting them in a fire; after a long time in a very big fire they become very hot (yellow). In such a world we should very probably not have had two sets of words: "cold," "warm," "hot," "very hot" and also "blue," "purple," "red," "yellow"—but only one set—say, the words "blue," "purple," "red," and so on. We should have spoken of things "looking purple," or "being purple to the eyes" and of their "feeling purple" or "being purple to the touch." (In our actual world we talk of things being round or square whether we apprehend their shapes by the eye or by the touch: we do not have a special word meaning "round to the eye" and another quite different word meaning "round to the touch," since there is a correlation between these.)

In such a world we should speak of making purple things red by putting them on a fire, but should not normally speak of making something "red to the eye" (i.e., what we mean by "red") by putting it on a fire; nor of making something "red to the touch" (i.e., what we mean by "hot") by this method. Still less should we speak of making something "red to the eye" by making it "red to the touch," or of making it "red to the touch" by making it "red to the eye." (In our actual world we do not speak of making things "visibly round" by making them "tangibly round," not *vice versa*.) When a single manipulation on our part invariably produces two effects A and B, we do not speak of producing one by producing the other, nor do we speak of one as the cause of the other. (The visible roundness is neither cause nor effect of the tangible roundness of a penny.) It is only when we have a technique for producing A which in some circumstances but not in all also produces B that we speak of producing B by producing A, and speak of A as causing B.

When we set a process going—drop a stone from a tower, set a top spinning—we set the stage, see that nothing shall interfere (for a certain time at least) with the process we are about to start, and then set things going. After that, things take their own course without further intervention on our part—the stone gathers speed, the top loses it. There are successive stages in the process. At stage A at t_1 the stone is moving fairly fast, at a later stage B at t_2 the stone is going very fast. But, on the presupposition that the process continues undisturbed, the very same initial stage-setting and send-off C, which will produce fairly fast motion at t_1 (A), will always produce very fast motion at t_2 (B), and the initial stage-setting and send-off C, which will produce very fast motion at t_2 (B), will always produce fairly fast motion at t_1 (A). That is, the process being undisturbed, an initial send-off, C, will always produce both A and B: there is not a general technique for producing A which in some circumstances also produces B. Hence, we do not speak of producing B by producing A. There is not a general technique for bringing it about that, one second after the start, a stone is falling at 32 feet per second, which in some circumstances can also be used to bring it about that two seconds after the start it is falling at 64 feet per second. Hence, we do not speak of achieving the latter by means of the former, and do not speak of the former as causing the latter.

Of course one could, by attaching a rocket to the falling body, which fires one second after the start, secure that a body which is moving at 32 feet per second one second after departure is one second later travelling much faster than 64 feet per second. But this would contradict our presupposition that the process, after being started, was left uninterfered with. It is on this presupposition only that C always produces both A and B.

I have made two points:

First: that one says "A causes B" in cases where one could produce an event or state of the A sort as a means to producing one of the B sort. I have, that is, explained the "cause-effect" relation in terms of the "producing-by-means-of" relation.

Second: I have tried to give a general account of the producing-by-means-of relation itself: what it is to produce B by producing A. We learn by experience that whenever in certain conditions we manipulate objects in a certain way a certain change, A, occurs. Performing this manipulation is then called: "producing A." We learn also that in certain special cases, or when certain additional conditions are also present, the manipulation in question also results in another sort of change, B. In these cases the manipulation is also called "producing B," and, since it is in general the manipulation of producing A, in this case it is called "producing B by producing A." For example, one makes iron glow by heating it. And I discussed two sorts of case where one does not speak of "producing B by producing A." (1) Where the manipulation for producing A is the general technique for producing B, so that one cannot speak of "producing B by producing A" but only *vice versa*. (2) Where the given manipulation invariably produces both A and B, so that the manipulation for producing B is not a special case only of that for producing A.

The notion of "cause" here elucidated is the fundamental or primitive one. It is not the property of scientists; except for those whose work most directly bears on such things as engineering, agriculture or medicine, and who are naturally interested in helping their practical colleagues; scientists hardly ever make use of the notion. A statement about causes in the sense here outlined comes very near to being a recipe for producing or preventing certain effects. It is not simply an inference-licence. Professional scientists, when they are carefully stating their findings, mostly express themselves in functional laws, which are pure inference-licences, with nothing of the recipe about them (explicitly at least). Thus the formula $I = \dfrac{E}{R}$ tells you how to infer the current in a given circuit, knowing the electro-motive force and the resistance; it tells you how to infer the electro-motive force, knowing the resistance and current; and how to infer the resistance from current and electro-motive force. All these three things it tells you; and no one of them any more specially than any other—it works all ways, as an inference-licence. But while one might say a current of 3 amps. was caused by an e.m.f. of 6 volts across a resistance of 2 ohms, one would hardly say that a resistance of 2 ohms in the circuit was caused by an e.m.f. of 6 volts and a current of 3 amps. Why not? Given an e.m.f. of 6 volts, one could make 3 amps. flow by making the resistance equal to 2 ohms. But one could not, given an e.m.f. of 6 volts, make the resistance of the circuit equal to 2 ohms by making a current of 3 amps. flow.

From one point of view the progress of natural science can be viewed as resulting from the substitution of pure inference-licences for recipes.

There is, however, what might be called a "popular science" use of "cause" which may not exactly fit the account given—a use of the word by laymen who know some science and by some scientists in their less strictly professional moments. I have in mind such a locution as "Gravity causes unsupported bodies to fall." Such a statement is not quite on a par, logically, with "Great heat causes steel to melt." It would be fair to say, I think, that the use of the word "cause" here is a sophisticated extension from its more primitive and fundamental meaning. It is the root notion that I have been concerned with.

In accounts of causation given by philosophers in the past a specially fundamental role was often played by the motion of bodies. Every kind of change and every kind of natural law was often supposed to be "ultimately reducible to" or to be explicable in terms of it. In this account, too, though in a rather different way, the motion of bodies occupies a special position. Central to this account is the notion of a manipulation to produce A and thereby to produce B. When we manipulate things we control the motion of bodies; e.g., by rubbing sticks together (motion of bodies) men made them hot and thereby caused them to ignite. At least all those causal chains that are initiated by human beings go back to manipulations, that is, to matter in motion.

G. H. VON WRIGHT

20. Causality and Causal Explanation

When we say that the cause brings about the effect, we do not mean that the cause *by doing something* brings this about. Thanks to the fact that *it happens*, the cause achieves this. (The verbs "achieve," "bring about," "produce," are all loaded with metaphors from the language of action.) But by *making* the cause *happen,* we achieve or bring about the same as the cause does by happening. To say that we cause effects is not to say that agents are causes. It means that we do things which then as causes produce effects, "act" or "operate" as causes.

I now propose the following way of distinguishing between cause and effect by means of the notion of action: *p* is a cause relative to *q,* and *q* an effect relative to *p,* if and only if by doing *p* we could bring about *q* or by suppressing *p* we could remove *q* or prevent it from happening. In the first case the cause-factor is a sufficient, in the second case it is a necessary condition of the effect-factor. The factors can become "relativized" to an environment of other factors. Then the cause is not "by itself," but only "under the circumstances"; a sufficient or necessary condition of the effect.

But is it true that we always think of the cause as something that can be done? The eruption of Versuvius was the cause of the destruction of Pompeii. Man can through his action destroy cities, but he cannot, we think, make volcanoes erupt. Does this not prove that the cause-factor is not distinguished from the effect-factor by being in a certain sense capable of manipulation? The answer is negative. The eruption of a volcano and the destruction of a city are two very complex events. Within each of them a number of events or phrases and causal connections between them may be distinguished. For example, that when a stone from high above hits a man on his head, it kills him. Or that the roof of a house will collapse under a given load. Or that a man cannot stand heat above a certain temperature. All these are causal connections with which we are familiar from experience and which are such that the cause-factor typically satisfies the requirement of manipulability.

Could one not argue against our position as follows: *If* it is true that *p* is always and invariably accompanied by *q,* then surely *it follows* that also in the cases when *p* is done (produced "at will") *q* will be there as well. So causality does not *rest on* an idea of doing things, but itself provides a basis for possible manipulation. To argue thus, however, is to beg the question. For consider what the assumption of universal concomitance of *p* and *q* amounts to. Either it just *so happens* that *p* is always succeeded by *q* and the causal or nomic character of the uniformity is never

Note: Footnotes have been renumbered for the purposes of this text and appear at the end of the selection.

put to the test by doing p in a situation in which it would not "of itself" come about. (Perhaps p is something which we cannot do.) Then there is nothing which decides whether the truth of the general proposition is only accidental or whether it reflects a natural necessity. Or there have been such tests and they were successful. The assumption (hypothesis) that the concomitance of p and q has a nomic character contains *more* than just the assumption that their togetherness is invariable. It also contains the *counterfactual assumption* that on occasions when p, in fact, was not the case q would have accompanied it, had p been the case. The fact that it is a ground for counterfactual conditionals is what *marks* the connection as nomic.

It is logically impossible to verify on any single occasion when p was (is) not there, what would have been the case, had p been there. But there is a way of coming "very close" to such a verification. It is this:

Assume that p is a state of affairs which, on some occasions at least, we can produce or suppress "at will." This presupposes that there are occasions on which p is not already there and, we feel confident, will not come to be (on the next occasion), unless *we* produce it. Assume there is such an occasion and that we produce p. We are then confident that had we not done this, the next occasion would have been one when p was *not* there. But in fact it is one when p *is* there. If then q too *is* there, we should regard this as a confirmation of the counterfactual conditional which we could have affirmed had we not produced p, viz. that had p which was not there been there q would have been there too. This is as "near" as we can come to the verification of a counterfactual conditional.

The counterfactual conditional confirmed through the operation, be it observed, "rests" on another counterfactual conditional, viz. the one which says that p would not have been there had we not produced it. This counterfactual conditional is not a statement of a conditionship relation nor of a causal connection.

The above reasoning shows, I think, in which sense the idea of a causal or nomic relationship can be said to depend on the concept of action, i.e., on the factual conditions which make action *logically* possible.[1]

It is *established* that there is a causal connection between p and q when we have satisfied ourselves that, by manipulating the one factor, we can achieve or bring it about that the other is, or is not, there. We usually satisfy ourselves as to this by making experiments.

By "removing" p from a situation in which p occurs together with q and finding that q then vanishes as well, we aim at showing that p is a necessary condition of q. This has been established when we can confidently say: "We *can* make q vanish, viz. by removing p."

Similarly, we aim at showing that p is a (relative) sufficient condition of q by "introducing" p into a situation from which both p and q are missing, and finding that then q too comes about. The causal relation has become established when we can say: "We *can* produce q, viz. by producing p."

When we cannot interfere with p and q, we can nevertheless *assume* that there is a causal bond between them. This would be tantamount to assuming, e.g., that *if we could* produce p as a result of action, we could also bring about q, viz. by producing p. But only through experiments could this assumption be tested.

What has been said here does not mean that causal laws, nomic connections, can be "conclusively verified." But it means that their confirmation is not a mere matter of repeated lucky observations. It is a matter of "putting the law to a test." That such test is successful (with a view to the truth of the law) means that we learn how to do things by doing other things (which we already know how to do), that our technical mastery of nature is increased. One could say that we can be as certain of the truth of causal laws as we can be of our abilities to do, and bring about, things.[2]

We may be mistaken in thinking that we *can do* things. Sometimes we have to concede that it was only "by chance" that q appeared when we did p; further experiments fail. Or we may have to limit our initial claim to a more or less vaguely conceived frame of "normal circumstances." When an assumed connection (law) fails to hold in an individual case, we need not drop the law, but can make the circumstances responsible for an accidental failure. Sometimes a hypothesis is formed that there was a "counteracting cause." This is an assumption to the effect that it might be possible to control (part of the) circumstances under which a law is tested. The truth of the law can in principle always be placed entirely in our hands. This fact is a source of the position called "conventionalism."

The thesis that the distinction between cause- and effect-factors goes back to the distinction between things done and things brought about through action does not mean that whenever a cause can be truly said to operate some agent is involved. Causation operates throughout the universe—also in spatial and temporal regions forever inaccessible to man. Causes do their job whenever they happen, and whether they "just happen" or we "make them happen" is accidental to their nature as causes. But to think of a relation between events as causal is to think of it under the aspect of (possible) action. It is therefore true, but at the same time a little misleading to say that if p is a (sufficient) cause of q, then if I could produce p I could bring about q. For *that* p is the cause of q, I have endeavored to say here, *means* that I could bring about q, if I could do (so that) p.

No proof can decide, I think, which is the more basic concept, action or causation. One way of disputing my position would be to maintain that action cannot be understood unless causation is already intelligible. I shall not deny that this view too could be sustained by weighty arguments.

NOTES

1. The idea that action is conceptually prior to cause has a long ancestry in the history of thought. It also has a great many different variants. One of its champions was Thomas Reid. His opinion concerning the priority of the idea of action (active power) to that of causal efficiency is, however, rather different from the view taken here. According to Reid, our idea of *cause* and *effect* in nature is modeled on an *analogy* between the causal relation and that of an *agent* to his *action*. The notion of "active power" in a being, Reid says, is the idea that the being "can do certain things, if he wills" (Reid 1788, Essay I, Ch. V). A view of the relation between the notion of cause and that of action which is more akin to the view taken here is Collingwood's notion of the cause as "handle." Cf. Collingwood 1940, p. 296. The position most similar to mine which I have found in the litera-

ture is the one propounded in Gasking 1955. On Gasking's view, "the notion of causation is essentially connected with our manipulative techniques for producing results" and "a statement about the cause of something is very closely connected with a recipe for producing it or for preventing it" (p. 483). This is substantially true also of the cases when some particular event of a complex and global character, which no one could have produced by manipulation, is said to have caused another particular event. For example, when the rise in mean sea-level at a certain geological epoch is attributed to the melting of the Polar ice-cap. (Cf. our example about the eruption of Vesuvius and the destruction of Pompeii.) For "when one can properly say this sort of thing it is always the case that people can produce events of the first sort as a means to producing events of the second sort" (p. 483). This manipulative notion of cause Gasking calls "the fundamental or primitive one" (p. 486). He makes the observation, which seems to me correct and important, that this notion of a cause does not figure prominently in the theoretical statements of scientists (*ib.*). The progress of natural science can, from one point of view, be said to consist in the transition from "manipulative recipes" to "functional laws" (p. 487). This agrees with the view of Russell and others. But it should then be added that, for purposes of experiments and technical applications, these functional relationships provide a logical basis from which new recipes for producing or preventing things may be extracted. This accounts for the fact, noted by Nagel, that the notion of ("manipulative") causation continues to be "pervasive in the accounts natural scientists give of their laboratory procedures."

    2. For a forceful defense of the humean, "passivist," regular sequence view of causation and natural law see Hobart 1930. The author says that "mere sequence in events themselves generates necessity in them as characterized by us" (p. 298). *In a sense* this is also true of the view of causation which I am defending here. The idea of natural necessity, as I see it, is rooted in the idea that we can bring about things by doing other things. Our knowledge that things are done "bring about" other things rests, however, on observations of regular sequences. To say that things "bring about" other things is therefore misleading: *this* "bringing about things by doing other things. Our knowledge that things done "bring about" other things rests, however, on the observations of regular sequences. To say that things "bring about" other things is therefore misleading: *this* "bringing about is nothing but regular sequence. Our knowledge that we can do things, moreover, rests on our assurance that certain states of affairs will stay unchanged (or will change in a certain way), unless we interfere, productively or preventively, with the course of nature. Whence have we got this assurance? Obviously from experience. So, in the last resort the notion of action is rooted in our familiarity with empirical regularities.

Suggested Readings for Part Four

Aronson, Jerrold L. "On the Grammar of 'Cause.' " *Synthese* 22 (1971): 414-30.

Beauchamp, Tom L., and Robinson, Daniel N. "On von Wright's Argument for Backward Causation." *Ratio* 16 (December 1974).

Dray, William. *Laws and Explanation in History.* New York: Oxford University Press, 1957, chapters 4-5.

Dummett, Michael. "Bringing about the Past." *Philosophical Review* 73 (1964): 338-59.

Mackie, J. L. "The Direction of Causation." *Philosophical Review* 75 (1966): 447-49, section 4.

Rosenberg, Alexander. "Causation and Recipes: The Mixture as Before?" *Philosophical Studies* 24 (1973). [Critical of Gasking.]

Scriven, Michael. "The Logic of Cause." *Theory and Decision* 2 (1971): 49-66.

Walsh, W. H. "Collingwood and Metaphysical Neutralism." In *Critical Essays on the Philosophy of R. G. Collingwood,* edited by Michael Krausz. Oxford, Eng.: Clarendon Press, 1972, pp. 134-53.

Walsh, W. H. "Historical Causation." *Proceedings of the Aristotelian Society,* N.S., 63 (1963), 217-36. [Discusses Collingwood. Complement of Walsh above.]

PART FIVE

THE SINGULARIST THEORY

INTRODUCTION

In the introduction to Part Four it was pointed out that prior to Hume and to modern science, philosophers tended to particularize the notion of causal relatedness. They thought of the causal relation as analyzable in terms of a particular cause producing a particular change through its inherent power or transmission of energy. In effect, their conception was the reverse of Hume's. They thought of generalizations which express universal causal laws as established through repeated experience of sequences which are individually recognized as causal, whereas Hume argued both that individual causal sequences are analyzable in terms of laws and that power is analyzable in terms of imaginative association. Usually philosophers who advanced such a singularist analysis also appended a thesis about the *priority* of causal necessitation, according to which causes compel or necessitate effects in a directional manner in which effects could not necessitate their causes.

C. J. Ducasse's account of causation is a modern singularist theory with ties to traditional singularist theories but which attempts to expunge anthromorphic and unduly speculative elements. Ducasse maintains that the causal relation is ill-conceived when viewed as a relation involving only *two* terms, cause and effect. The *circumstances* constitute a third term. Any particular change occurs in a context of perhaps innumerable conditions. The occurrence might be an instance of a uniformity or it might occur in unique circumstances involving unique causally related items. Some of the circumstances are necessary for the causal occurrence, others are causally irrelevant.

Ducasse maintains from this triadic perspective that something is a "cause"—in the ordinary sense of the term—if it is a change followed sequentially by another change (the effect) when these are the only two changes in the circumstances. Ducasse augments this analysis with a theory that the cause is *etiologically sufficient* for the effect and the effect is *etiologically necessitated* by the cause. (Etiological necessity is not logical necessity since it is a relation between events and not between logical entities.) Other conditions required in the circumstances for the changes are said to be causally necessary but are to be distinguished from "the cause." In short, causal statements of the form "*x* caused *y*" *mean* (1) that *x* and *y* are both changes in the circumstances, (2) that *x* is the total set of changes sufficient for *y*, and (3) that *y* is the total set of changes necessitated by *x*.

Ducasse's singularism is perhaps best understood in terms of his specific objections to Hume's proposal that inquiry into causation involves inquiry into general laws without regard to individual instances. In his book *Causation and the Types of Necessity* Ducasse offers the following critique of Hume:

> If the engine of my car stops, and I ask "Why?," I am not asking for a
> statement of invariable succession or of a law, even though one may,
> conceivably, be inferable. . . . What I want to know is whether the latter
> occurrence was the single *difference* between the circumstances of the
> engine at the moment when it was running, and at the moment when it
> was not. . . . Constant conjunctions . . . would follow as a matter of
> course, if the cause and the conditions were repeated. But constant con-
> junction is then a possible corollary, not the definition, of causation. To
> have mistaken it for the latter was Hume's epoch-making blunder. . . .
> [Hume and Mill believe] inquiry into causation is inquiry into laws. The
> truth is on the contrary that it is directly and primarily an inquiry con-
> cerning *single, individual events.* *

Ducasse interprets Hume to mean that causal inquiry is directly concerned with
constant conjunctions and is not concerned, or is only indirectly concerned, with
single cases. Whether or not Hume held this view, Ducasse holds the opposite
opinion. A second disagreement concerns how we *know* what is asserted in causal
expressions. Hume's "epoch-making" epistemological twist, according to Ducasse, is
his claim that there is no recognition of a causal relation without an appropriate
backlog of experience. Ducasse disagrees. He thinks not only that a sequence occurring only once can be causal, but also that single differences can be *known through
observation* of genuinely unique cases.

The exact nature of this disagreement can be brought out by a more
precise analysis of Ducasse's singularist theory. He claims that a set of changes C,
composed of changes $c_1, c_2, \ldots c_n$, is the cause of an event E, in circumstances S
(composed of C, E, and the set of irrelevant causal conditions I), if and only if C
and E are the *only* two changes in S, and C can be distinguished from elements in I
by perception in singular cases. In any concrete case, he says, the causation which
occurred is as literally *perceived* as are the concrete events it connected. Ducasse
admits that mistakes are sometimes made, but these, he thinks, are attributable to
the fact that we have not made sure that the *only* change in the circumstances has
been isolated. Once *the* relevant change or changes are determined, the cause is
perceived.

Bernard Berofsky's defense of the regularity theory provides a critical look
both at Ducasse's polemic against Hume and at Ducasse's constructive defense of a
singularist analysis. Berofsky defends a "Humean theory of causation" to the effect
that analysis of singular causal statements entails either reference to general laws or
to the claim that there exist certain types of laws. Against Ducasse's claim that
causation is perceivable, he argues that in causal circumstances where few or no
restrictions are placed on causal relevance, we are frequently led either to mistaken
citations of the cause or to the discovery that one experiment is insufficient to
isolate the causal factors. Berofsky contends that Ducasse's analysis provides no
conceivable way of distinguishing causal relevance from causal irrelevance on the
basis of single cases, for we can always describe conditions under which we would
withdraw causal assertions (even though we might feel quite certain about their
correctness). Berofsky also hammers at the relevance of Ducasse's alleged counter-
examples by showing that they prove far less than Ducasse claims for them. He

---

*From the expanded edition, copyright 1969 by Dover Publications, Inc., pp. 19, 21.
Passages slightly rearranged.

concludes that although Ducasse's criticisms against Hume have some effect, a modern Regularity Theory can withstand all the objections raised by Ducasse and without conceding a significant point to the singularist analysis.

Arthur Pap's brief note is a criticism of Ducasse's singularist theory by a staunch regularity exponent. The chief object of Pap's discontent is Ducasse's claim that causation is completely analyzable and distinguishable from coincidental sequences without essential reference to regularity of sequence. He argues that Ducasse's definition of "cause" overlooks the fact that observation of solitary changes may warrant causal assertions only by tacitly presupposing key doctrines of the Regularity Theory. Pap maintains that analysis of the *meaning* of "cause" involves irreducibly the notion of changes regularly followed by other changes, and he claims that Ducasse's arguments are plausible only because they make an assumption to this fact. Pap also contends that Ducasse's treatment of the cause-condition distinction is thoroughly confusing and in no sense provides an adequate analysis of the *ordinary* meaning of "cause," as Ducasse had claimed. Pap even argues that Ducasse's analysis leads to the discomfiting circumstance that every specific causal statement is tautologous; they all say, in effect, that the total state of a spatial region at a particular time is immediately preceded by the total state of that region at the immediately preceding time.

Edward Madden and *James Humber* are non-Humean advocates of the Singularity Theory, and therefore are considerably more sympathetic to Ducasse than either Berofsky or Pap. Nonetheless, they argue that Ducasse's arguments are seriously deficient in at least four respects: First, the event ontology which Ducasse makes a necessary condition of causal relatedness is so broad that it includes everything we would normally refer to as a non-event and does not seem to be necessary anyway. Second, like Hume, Ducasse confuses a method of verification of causal statements (the method of single difference) with the meaning of "cause." Third, the nonlogical necessity theory propounded by Ducasse is both analytically weak and also infected by a failure to explain how "etiological necessity" can be perceived (rather than simply inferred). Fourth, Ducasse's analysis suffers the embarrassment of not ruling out anything significant the Humean wants to say.

In the last section of their article Madden and Humber attempt to show how singularism can nonetheless be revived and developed into a significant anti-Humean theory. Madden further develops this perspective in his individual article. According to this view, causal language expresses the powers that singular items have by virtue of their natures to make certain events occur. The relationship between the nature of a particular and its powers and capacities is held to be non-contingent, in the sense that particulars cannot lose their relevant powers and capacities and still remain the same particulars. This account of causation is summarized as follows: there is "a relation of natural necessity between what a thing is and what it is capable of doing and undergoing, and it is this relation of natural necessity that the conceptual necessity of the concept of cause reflects." Moreover, it is held that this argument is not inconsistent with Hume's view that there may be changes in the course of nature. Suppose such change is both logically and empirically possible, they hypothesize; it does not follow that it is in any sense impossible that there be nonlogically necessary connections in the world, for the connections are between individually related items.

   Donald Davidson attempts to provide a reconciliation "within limits" between regularity theorists and Ducasse. The Humean view that all singular causal statements entail laws and that justification for a singular causal statements requires grounds for a law can, in Davidson's judgment, consistently coexist with Ducasse's position that singular causal statements entail no law and can be known to be true without knowledge of a law. His reconciliation depends on a distinction he draws between knowing that there exists a law and knowing what the law is. He paradoxically maintains that "Ducasse is right that singular causal statements entail no law; Hume is right that they entail there is a law." Davidson is arguing both (1) that singular causal statements entail no *known* law, even though they do entail that there is a law, and (2) that we frequently justify our acceptance of singular causal statements by appealing to a reason why we think an appropriate law exists, even though the law itself is not actually known.

   Davidson criticizes Hume for failing to distinguish between a strong and a weak manner of interpreting general causal statements. On a strong interpretation, says Davidson, a general causal statement consists of those predicates 'X' and 'Y' which are specifically used in singular statements to describe particular objects or events x and y (which are instances of the general law). The singular statement "x caused y," in other words, entails a particular law incorporating the predicates actually used in describing x and y. On a weak interpretation, there might be *some* true descriptions of x and y such that the sentence derived by substituting these descriptions for 'x' and 'y' in the singular statement "x caused y" follows logically from *a* true nomological generalization. The second interpretation is weaker because no particular law using the predicates 'X' and 'Y' is directly entailed by ordinary singular causal statements and the latter can be defended without having to defend any particular law. The predicates initially employed to describe individuals or events x and y may not even appear in the entailed statement. Davidson's suggestions focus attention on the simple, but easily overlooked, point that a distinction must be firmly drawn between *causes* (those properties of objects which actually bring about an effect and which would be mentioned in one or more true causal laws) and those *features of causal occasions* which are generally cited in our descriptions of a cause and its effect. This line of argument parallels some of Ducasse's attacks on Hume, but Davidson's strategy is to use it as a means of reconciliation between the two.

   Davidson's article is of considerable philosophical significance independently of discussions of singularity theories. But the elucidation and justification of singular causal statements, such as "The short circuit caused the fire," is certainly one of his major objectives. He is looking for a proper analysis of the *logical form* of singular causal statements, a task he here limits to analysis of the logical or grammatical functions of key causal terms in singular sentences. Davidson denies that singular causal statements are illuminated by appeal to necessary and sufficient conditionship relations, a favorite device of some regularity theorists and of singularists such as Ducasse. His point seems to be that an analysis of causation in terms of conditions prejudices issues of causation in favor of lawlikeness by inhibiting expression of the *relation* in particular cases. His analysis of logical form also leads to interesting criticisms of those necessity theorists who advocate a modal strengthening of laws.

The latter point could be used to give a different perspective to part Five. The whole part could be read as an extension of the debate witnessed in Parts Two and Three between defenders of the Regularity Theory and defenders of the Necessity Theory. Whereas Ducasse, Madden, and Humber are all explicitly defending necessity theses, Berofsky, Pap, and Davidson are somewhat more covertly defending the regularity point of view.

C. J. DUCASSE

21. *Analysis of the Causal Relation*

The problem of the nature of causality is that of discovering the right or a right definition of the term "cause" as actually employed. And the data of this problem—the empirical facts the definition sought must fit—consist of *phrases that are actual instances of the employment of that term as predicate* (whether affirmatively, negatively, or interrogatively); that is, of its employment to designate the relation asserted, denied, or queried, as between the events the given phrase mentions.

I take it, however, that the usage of the term "cause" we are now interested to analyze is not any of the odd usages it may happen to have in the language of crude or careless speakers or of deliberate innovators, but is its ordinary, common usage when confident rather than hesitant and strict rather than loose. The phrases constituting data relevant to the analysis we are interested to undertake will then be such as that the 1938 New England hurricane caused the death of a number of persons; that its tidal wave caused a number of yachts to become lodged on the top of a bridge; that it caused to fly away numerous shingles from the roof of my house; that it broke, i.e., caused to break, a large branch of an old tree in my garden; that my writing these words just now did not cause the ring of the door bell that followed it; that the starting of the furnace just now was caused by the closing of the electric contact in the thermostat; that the failure of the engine of my car to start as usual this morning was caused by the fact that the spark plugs had become covered with dew; and so on. Indeed, the data will include also phrases employing any of the innumerable verbs of physical or psychological operation, such as to push over, to blow off, to break, to kill, to uproot, to bend, to dissolve, to remind one of, to inhibit, to encourage, etc.—all of which signify causation of particular kinds of effects.

The question we seek to answer about these data is then, what definition of "cause" fits the employment of the term in these and similar phrases—the test of "fitting" or "not fitting" being whether the *definiens* of a proposed definition can or cannot, in such phrases, be substituted for the word "cause" without altering what is admittedly entailed by the propositions the given phrases formulate.

From C. J. Ducasse, *Nature, Mind and Death* (La Salle, Ill.: Open Court Publishing Co. 1951), pp. 102-9, 113-25. Footnotes included. Reprinted by permission of The Open Court Publishing Co., La Salle, Illinois.

Note: Footnotes have been renumbered for the purposes of this text.

It is important in this connection to be clear that data statements employing the verb "to cause"—e.g., that the wind caused a branch of my tree to break—are not given as being true rather than false, but only as being ones in which as a matter of English, the verb "to cause" was the proper one to describe the relation which the utterer of the statement had in mind, and which he presumably *believed* to have obtained between the wind and the breaking of the branch; whereas to have used for this (instead of "caused"), for instance the word "motivated," or "bribed," or "planned," would have been improper—not suitable to express in English what was meant.[1]

It will be noticed that the statements I listed as samples of the data of our problem do not include any such ordinary statement as that the swallowing of arsenic causes death. My reason for excluding this statement and others like it would be that it is elliptical, and that the literal statement of what it means, viz., that ingestion of arsenic in some cases causes the death of the animal that ingested it, does not specify either by general description of by individual mention the cases it summarizes and therefore does not enable us to decide whether a proposed definition of cause does or does not fit them.

DEFINITION OF CAUSALITY IN TERMS
OF THE FACTORS OF EXPERIMENTS

The methodological nature of our first and fundamental problem being now clear, let us turn to the problem itself. The general character of the account of the causal relation which I would submit may already have been surmised from my criticisms of Hume's views, and in particular from the described classroom experiment with the paper parcel. Broadly stated, my contention is that the relation of cause and effect is rightly defined not, for the reasons stated, as by Hume in statistical terms (viz., as sequence empirically 100 percent regular), but in terms of what is called an experiment; and that an experiment is the sort of thing we observe when we observe a state of affairs S in which only two changes occur: one, a change C introduced in S at a time T_1, and the other, a change E spontaneously following in S at a time T_2. The first change may be introduced by ourselves, or by someone else, or by the natural course of events as for example in an eclipse; and of course a change in the given state of affairs at a given time cannot be the only change in it at that time unless it is the total change in it at that time.

If it should be objected that "introduced" is itself a causal verb, and therefore cannot legitimately be employed in a definition of causality, the reply

---

[1] Bertrand Russell states that although it is customary to give the name "effect" only to an event which is later than the cause, there is no kind of reason for this restriction. "We shall do better," he writes, "to allow the effect to be before the cause or simultaneous with it, because nothing of any scientific importance depends on its being after the cause." (*Scientific Method in Philosophy*, p. 226). It may well be granted that, on the basis of knowledge of the relevant causal law and of minutely detailed observation of a given event, the cause of that event could be inferred no less well than its effect. But the fact that *inference* can be from effect to cause as well as from cause to effect does not warrant the assertion that a cause may be after its effect. To assert it is either to confuse cause with premise and effect with conclusion, or else deliberately and needlessly to rob the words "cause" and "effect" of a part of the meaning they certainly have as employed in ordinary usage.

would be that what is being defined is, specifically, causation *of a change E in S by an earlier change C in S*. This is defined by the specification that C and E are the only two changes in S. In the face of this definition of causation within S, it is perfectly legitimate (although not obligatory) to suppose an earlier, partially overlapping, state of affairs Z in which C was the *second* of two only changes, B and C, and in which C was therefore caused by B in the same generic sense of "to cause." We could then say that C was introduced into S by change B in Z; for C figures *both in Z and in S*, but in Z as effect (of B) and in S as cause (of E).

But as stated above, even the supposition just described is not obligatory, for the word "introduced" can be left out of the definition altogether. It then reads that causality is the relation which obtains between an event C at a time T_1, and another event E at a later time T_2 if C and E are two changes in a given state of affairs S and are the only two changes in it.

If, however, it should now be objected that change E in S might not be the effect of change C in S at all, but might have been introduced into S by some cause outside of S, the reply would then be, first, that to suppose this is simply to reject outright, but not to criticize or invalidate, the proposed definition of causation in S of E by C. For if C and E do, as supposed, meet the conditions that definition lays down, then C was, *by definition,* the cause of E. Secondly, however, the statement of the above objection itself employs the verb "introducing" or "causing," but without defining it. That statement therefore leaves us wholly in the dark as to *what the supposition is,* which it purports to formulate and the possibility of the truth of which is alleged by the objector to invalidate the definition proposed.

Let us now return to what occurs when we perform or witness an experiment. If we believe that the first change we observe supervening in the state of affairs constituted by the setup of the experiment is the only change at the time in it, then we declare that it was the proximate cause of the change which followed it in that state of affairs, and that the latter change was the proximate effect of the former. We are aware, of course, that we might be mistaken in believing that the first change we observed was the only change that occurred in the given state of affairs at that time; but we are quite sure that *if* it was the only change, then it was what caused the change which followed it; *for just this is what it means, to say that it "caused" the latter.* That is, the sort of relation described is not a *sign* that a causal relation (in some other sense of the term) hiddenly exists between the two changes concerned. Rather, the relation described is *the causal relation itself.*

The canon of what Mill called the method of difference is thus a description of the very sort of relation which is called causation of a sequent event by an immediately antecedent one. Accordingly, that canon is not, as Mill thought, the description of a *method* for discovery or proof of the existence, as between the two events, of some relation *other* than the one that canon actually describes, such perhaps as the relation of invariable regularity of sequence. What that canon furnishes can be called a "method" for the ascertainment of causal connections only in the sense in which the police description of some fugitive from justice can be said to be or to provide a method for identifying him; that is, that canon furnishes us with a description of the specific sort of relation we are to look for when cases of the relation called "causality" are what we look for.

As more than one critic has pointed out, Mill's formulation of the canons of Difference and of Agreement—to say nothing of the others—is, for a variety of reasons, hardly felicitous. Before attempting to improve on them, however, I must point out that although discussions of causality are generally worded as if the term covered nothing but the relation of cause to effect, it covers in fact also another relation, viz., that of a *condition* to what is dependent, but only in part, upon it—fulfilment of the condition thus permitting, or contributing to the possibility of, the dependent event, but not necessitating the event. Mill notwithstanding, common sense is right in distinguishing between the effect of an event and the contingencies—the possibilities—to which the event gives rise.[2] The distinctions are as follows:

The *cause* of an event B was an event A which, in the then existing circumstances, was *sufficient to* the occurrence of B; and therefore, conversely,

The *effect* of an event A was an event B which, in the then existing circumstances, was *necessitated by* the occurence of A. Again:

A *condition* of an event B was an event A which, in the then existing circumstances, was *necessary to* the occurrence of B; and therefore, conversely,

A *resultant* of an event A was an event B which, in the then existing circumstances, was *contingent upon* the occurrence of A.

An "event," let it be noted, may be either a *change* of some feature of a state of affairs, or (to use Dr. Charles Mercier's term), an *unchange,* i.e., the *persistence unchanged* during some time, of such a feature. For example, the question "What occurred then?" could, with equal propriety, be answered by mention of a change, e.g., "He got up," or of an unchange, e.g., "He remained motionless." Either answer reports the occurrence of an event. But a cause is always a *difference* occurring in a state of affairs S in which the effect is another and later *difference*. If the event is a change, then its cause is a change in a state of affairs otherwise unchanging at the time; whereas if the event is an unchange, then its cause is an unchange in a state of affairs otherwise consisting of changes. Thus, should a state of affairs be contemplated in or about which no change was occurring or had ever occurred, then questions of cause or effect concerning it would be incongruous. To avoid expanding our discussion unnecessarily, we shall at most places word it hereafter, as up to this point, in terms of examples where the cause-event and the effect-event are changes, rather than unchanges.

---

[2] There seems to be no unambiguous or special term in common use to designate an event B qua made possible or contributed to by another event A; that is, no definite term for the relational status of B when the relation between B and A is "unless A, not B." To say that this is the relation between A and B is to say, about A, that it is *necessary to* (but not that it is sufficient to) occurrence of B; and, about B, that it is *contingent upon* (but not that it is necessitated by) occurrence of A. The common name of the relational status of A in such a case is "condition of"; A is said to be a condition of B. To designate the then corresponding relational status of B, the best term available would seem to be "resultant of" (in a sense analogous to that which this term has when used in connection with the composition of forces); or "dependant of" (employing, for this usage, the optional spelling "dependant" instead of the more common "dependent"). Let us therefore agree that when B is contingent upon A, we shall call B a resultant or a dependant of A. For a pointed criticism of Mill's criticism of the common distinction between cause and condition, see Dr. Charles Mercier's *Causation and Belief,* pp. 49, 50.

In defining above the distinction between cause and condition, and between effect and resultant, use was made of the notions of sufficiency and necessity. Reasons will be given farther on to show that it is legitimate to speak not only of *logical* but also of physical, of psychological, or more generally of what we shall call *etiological* necessity and sufficiency; that is, of necessity and sufficiency *as between events,* instead of as between logical entities. At this point, I wish to emphasize only two things. One is that "necessitated by" is the converse of "sufficient to," and "contingent upon" the converse of "necessary to," irrespective of whether the necessity concerned be logical or etiological. The other thing is that causal relations are not, as often assumed, two-term relations, but that, as indicated in what precedes, some *set of circumstances*—some *state of affairs*—always enters in as a third term. This point too will be more fully considered later. . . .

ETIOLOGICAL NECESSITY DISTINGUISHED FROM LOGICAL

It is true that sometimes one meets the contention that "necessity" is something found only among logical entities, not among physical or psychical entities. But this contention is rooted only in a tacit and arbitrary decision to restrict "necessity" to what is only *logical* necessity; for common sense and common language recognize types of necessity other than logical. When, for instance, we speak of "the necessities of life" we mean certain physical things— food, water, etc.—without which life ceases; and the impossibility of its being maintained without them is not logical—not a matter of contradiction in terms—but physiological. Again, it would commonly be said that cutting off the head of a living man suffices to kill him (or, synonymously, that his dying is rendered inevitable, or is necessitated, by it); or that explosion of a certain specifiable quantity of dynamite is sufficient to blow up a given tree stump; or that the sound of finger nails grating on a blackboard is sufficient to give some persons the shivers, etc.; and the sufficiency and necessitation meant in these cases are similarly not logical but (respectively) physiological, physical, psychological. It is in each case *causal* sufficiency—sufficiency of the occurrence of a phenomenon A to occurrence of another phenomenon B, and therefore necessitation of occurrence of B by A. It is a relation between *events,* not between timeless logical entities. To designate necessity as between events—whether physical, physiological, psychical, or other—I shall, as stated earlier, use the inclusive term "etiological necessity." The adjective "etiological" is chosen for this purpose in preference to certain others, e.g., "ontological," "real," "natural," "eventual," which also suggest themselves, but each of which seems more liable to misconstruction in certain contexts.

In this general connection, mention must be made of a paper by R. B. Braithwaite, in which he argues for a theory of causation of the same general type as Hume's and criticizes, among others, the theory I maintain.[3] He seems to assume, however, that only logical necessity is "genuine" necessity. I say "seems" because he defined "genuine," as used in such contexts, only as "not to be analyzed in a Pickwickian sense" (p. 468, note); and the question might thus well reduce to

---

[3] R. B. Braithwaite, "The Idea of Necessary Connection," *Mind,* Oct. 1927 and Jan. 1928.

whether a given analysis—for example, mine, or his—is or is not Pickwickian. Like him, I agree with G. E. Moore "in thinking that the task of philosophy is to analyze propositions which are universally accepted, not to reject the propositions of common sense because they cannot be analyzed in a particular way" (p. 469). But it seems to me that common sense, in all the statements I have given as examples, does mean to assert necessity as between certain events. Common sense would say, for instance, that, to kill Charles I, it was *enough*—i.e., it was *sufficient*—to cut off his head. And the converse of "sufficient to" is "necessitated by"; that is, cutting off his head necessitated his dying. But, apparently because this necessitation cannot be analyzed as *logical* necessitation, Braithwaite denies that it is "genuine"; asserting that "if causal propositions are taken as asserting a genuine necessary connexion between events then . . . there are no true causal propositions" (p. 468). And he then offers an analysis of causation in terms of two universal propositions of fact (*vs.* "of law") which—just because it leaves out the very necessitation common sense means to assert when it asserts causation—seems to me to be an analysis of causation only in a Pickwickian (or Humean) sense. Moreover, the force of Braithwaite's discussion is weakened throughout by the fact that his examples are for the most part *general* causal propositions, whereas the causal propositions of the truth of which common sense is most confident are singular propositions. In such a causal proposition as that swallowing a pound of arsenic always causes death, physical or physiological necessitation is of course not to be found; but this is because the proposition is simply false. If the man's stomach is immediately pumped out, he may not die; or, if someone immediately shoots him through the heart, his death is caused by this not by the arsenic. Any general causal proposition which, like this one about arsenic, omits to specify what the circumstances at the time are assumed to be (and thus presents the causal relation erroneously as dyadic instead of triadic) is almost certain to be false. Even in the much stronger example of cutting off a man's head it is conceivable that the science of the future might discover some way of preventing this from killing him. But when we pick as examples singular instead of general propositions of causation, the circumstances are thereby automatically given. The supposition, for instance, that some way exists by which Charles I's head could have been stuck on again and his life preserved is then irrelevant; for what common sense asserts about his death is no universal proposition, but is only that, in the circumstances *that were present at the time* (which included the fact that no such surgical feat occurred), the beheading did suffice to cause his death.

Braithwaite's reference to the possibility that a definition may be Pickwickian raises the important methodological question as to how one can find out whether or not a proposed definition of what a term means is really what it means. For after all, one might attack skeptically even Hume's own contention as to the nature of *logical* necessity. One might ask him how he knows, for instance, that from "This man is tall and handsome" it necessarily follows that "This man is tall." For, conceivably, this might not be really, but only seemingly, an example of logical necessitation. And, if the reply were that to suppose the first true and the second false is to suppose a contradiction, one might still ask whether this very sort of relationship between two propositions is *really* what logical necessitation of the second by the first consists in.

The answer, of course, is that, ultimately, this is a matter of the meaning which the words "contradiction" and "logical necessitation" *in fact* have in the language. And it seems to me, similarly, that when the question is instead as to whether the definition I proposed, of "causation" or "necessitation among events," is what these terms really mean, the answer is ultimately again a matter of whether the proposed definition fits the use the language does in fact make of those terms.

To show that it does fit, and thus that it is not Pickwickian, I now ask what in fact one would do if one wished to discover, for instance, whether or not, in order to bring a certain chair from the other side of the room, it is enough, i.e., is sufficient, to say "Chair, come here!" Evidently, one would not proceed by asking whether the supposition that the chair does not come implies a contradiction. Rather, one would simply make the experiment, i.e., one would utter the command. Then, if the chair did not come, this single experiment would have proved that, under the circumstances which existed, uttering that command was not enough, was not sufficient; i.e., that it did not cause, did not necessitate, movement of the chair.

On the other hand, if the chair had then immediately come (and one's command really was, as it is assumed to have been, the single change then in the circumstances), then I submit that one would likewise have proved, and again by a single experiment, that the command was enough, sufficed, i.e., that under the circumstances then existing, it caused, necessitated, the coming of the chair.

The evidence that the definition of causation I have proposed is what causation, i.e., event-necessitation, really means is thus that when we desire to find out whether a given event will, under the circumstances existing at the moment, suffice to cause, i.e, necessitate, the occurrence of a certain other, we actually proceed as the definition proposed would require us to proceed, and the definition does not call for repetition of the experiment. In practice, it is true, one would repeat the experiment a few times, but this would be done only to minimize the chance that the change introduced, e.g., the command, was not really the only change that occurred at the time in the given state of affairs; and evidently, to do this would not be to proceed on a different definition of causation, but on the contrary to increase the probability that one really complied with the requirements of the given definition.

In the case of terms such as sufficiency and necessity, which are in common use, the philosopher's business is not to restrict or to expand arbitrarily either their application or their implication, but first to classify the variety of instances in which they are actually employed, and then to discover analytically the intension which corresponds to each class of employments. Occasion for ruling instead of analyzing arises only at the "edges" of such classes, where ordinary language hesitates and where ruling therefore does not violate any established usage. That is, the philosopher's business, where such terms are concerned, is not to make over existing language, but only to perfect it—to purge it of defects, such as vagueness, ambiguity, or inconsistency, which it happens still to contain.

IS CAUSATION OBSERVABLE?

The analysis we have now made of the nature of the causal relation shows that this relation is not, as sometimes assumed, a mysterious one, hidden behind what we are able to observe in any instance of it. The truth is only that it is hard and often impossible to attain certainty that the relation we actually observe in given cases really conforms to the definition; that is, in the main, that the change we observe in the state of affairs constituted by the setup of a given experiment is the *only* observable change in that setup at the time.[4]

The difficulty of making sure of this, however, is of a type not at all peculiar to causality, for it is of the same type as, and theoretically neither greater nor less than, in any other case where we are called upon to establish through observation the truth of a *universal negative* proposition. The proposition in the case of causality is that no observable change other than a certain observed one occurred at a given time in a given set of circumstances. It is difficult to make sure that no other occurred; but it is likewise difficult to make sure by observation that there is at a given time no mosquito in a given room, or no flea on a given dog. All we really know in any such case is that we have searched and not found any; that our method of search was one capable of revealing cases of the sort of thing we were looking for; and that the more thorough and careful was our search with such a method, the less likely it is that a case of what we look for would have escaped our observation. Thus, theoretically, all that observation can yield is probability, in higher or lower degree, that the universal negative proposition we are concerned with is true; but actually, there are cases where the thing searched for, and the method of search used, are such that the supposition that the thing might have eluded our search retains no plausibility whatever. If, for example, the statement had been that there is no horse or, more specifically, no horse of ordinary size in a given room, then, if the room were well lighted, not too large and not encumbered with large objects, and our eyesight reasonably good, the probability that we should not have found a horse if one had been in the room would, it may fairly be claimed, be zero.

The bearing of these remarks on the question of the observability of the causal relation is that this relation is not in principle, or even in practice, unobservable, but that in many cases it is difficult or impossible to attain certainty that what we observe really conforms to the definition of the relation. However, if any specific doubt as to its conformity arises, additional observation can often dispose of the doubt and thus increase the probability that the given case conforms to the definition. That the conditions under which experimentation is carried on are in many cases so favorable that a causal connection is conclusively established by it is the harder to deny when one remembers that experiments performed under laboratory conditions are the very foundation of the imposing achievements of which natural science can boast today. But, for instances where causation is really observed, we need not go outside common experience: I submit that, when Charles I lost his head, it would have been mere silly perversity on the part of the executioner or of other close spectators to maintain that the blow of the axe was not certainly but only probably what caused the head to come off.

Upon analysis, Hume's contention that causation, in the sense of necessitation of an event by another, is never observable among events, ultimately reduces to two propositions, one true and the other false. One is:

---

[4] Changes of kinds or magnitudes not amenable to observation are of course never observed but only postulated; and the need to postulate them arises only if no cause, or no effect, of a given event is observable, and if we assume that one nevertheless exists.

(*a*) That *logical* necessitation is not observable among events. This is true, for events themselves are not logical entities, but physical or psychological entities. The other proposition is:

(*b*) That "necessitation" always means logical necessitation. This is simply false; for it is a proposition about language as it actually is—a proposition as to what the word "necessitation" or its cognates are in fact used to mean in ordinary language. And physical or psychological necessitation is undeniably what common usage means in innumerable instances—whenever, for example, such expressions as "physically impossible," "psychologically inevitable," "physiologically necessary," etc., occur; and in all verbs of physical or psychological causation, such as to break, to bend, to cure, to kill, to drag, to annoy, to induce, etc.—all of which in fact are used in the sense of "to make occur" an event of this or that specific sort. Moreover, it would be only by using "to observe" in a Pickwickian sense that it would be possible to deny that we ever observe one thing breaking, or bending, or killing, or dragging, etc. another thing.

What the correct analysis of *physical* or *psychological* necessitation is, is of course a distinct question; but that a given analysis does not reduce it to *logical* necessitation is not the least evidence that it is an incorrect analysis. Rather, if it did so reduce it, this would be evidence that the analysis is Pickwickian.

CAUSALITY A RELATION BETWEEN CONCRETE INDIVIDUAL EVENTS

The relation which an experiment seeks to exhibit is, as we have analyzed it, a relation between two concrete, individual events and a set of concrete circumstances: the definition of the relation does not employ the notion of collections or kinds of events.

Accordingly, if the requirements specified in the definition are really met by the relation between two concrete events in a given case, then the two events concerned really are cause and effect even if each of them should happen to be completely unique in the history of the universe. Just because the definition does not employ the notion of recurrence of the sequence, the observing of such recurrence is theoretically unnecessary to the identification of cases of causation. There is need to repeat an experiment only in order to make certain or more probable that the requirements of the definition were actually met. Moreover, as pointed out earlier, regularity of sequence does not at all guarantee that the earlier of the two events concerned causes the other, but only suggests that perhaps it does; and we can be said to have observed that indeed it does, only when we have succeeded in testing that suggestion by means of an experiment, as described in what precedes.

It was to avoid having to say, as Hume's definition would require, that day was the cause of night and night was the cause of day, that Mill added, in his own definition of causation, the requirement of "unconditionality" to that of invariability of sequence—without perceiving, however, that as soon as "unconditionality" was introduced, the requirement of invariability became superfluous. For if an event B "unconditionally" followed from an antecedent event A, i.e., if the event A was indeed *sufficient* without additional conditions to the event B, then obviously as often as A might recur identically, B would necessarily recur also. But this "unconditionality" is the very thing which Mill had declared was not revealed by mere regularity of sequence. Hence it has to be ascertained experimentally, and therefore in some individual case, by the "method of difference." Mill, however, never seems to see that this means that the canon of difference is then the very definition of the relation called causation, not the description of a sign of that relation; and that it defines this relation in terms of *one* experiment.

His failure to see this is perhaps due mainly to the fact that he never clearly perceived the difference between experimentation itself and comparison of two (or more) experiments for purposes of generalization by abstraction.[5] He never was adequately conscious that it is one thing to introduce an only change into the set of concrete circumstances of a given concrete entity and note what change, if any, this entity then undergoes; and a very different thing to compare two or more or less similar such experiments which yielded an effect of the same kind, and to note in what respects alone the change introduced in each case, and also the circumstances in each case, agreed, i.e., were alike, in the two experiments. To compare in this way the two experiments is indeed to use the "method of agreement," but as so used it is a method of *abstraction* for purposes of generalization of the results of experiments, not at all itself a method of experimentation. Discrimination of the *concrete event* which caused a given event in a given case is one thing, and discrimination of a *common kind,* to which the cause event in each of several cases belonged, is quite another thing.

The *experimental* use of the method of agreement, on the other hand, would consist in taking a concrete set of circumstances, under which a certain phenomenon *P* continues, and *altering* the circumstances, one by one, without this causing the phenomenon to cease, until a single one remains unaltered; which, one concludes, must be the cause. It is perhaps needless to say that causation is not often discovered in this way. What this procedure actually is good for is to eliminate wrong hypotheses as to what is the cause.

AMBIGUITY OF "THE CAUSE OF AN EVENT"

To the definition I have given of the term "cause" it might be objected that we cannot, without violation of it, refuse to regard as part of the cause of a given change in a given state of affairs any part of the change antecedent to it in that state of affairs; but that on the contrary we very frequently in ordinary language seem to use the word cause in such a way as to do just that. For example, at the instant a brick strikes a window pane, the pane is also struck perhaps by the air waves due to the song of a canary near by. Yet we usually would say that the cause of the breakage was the impact of the brick, and that the impact of the air waves, although it was part of the prior total change in the given state affairs, was no part of the cause. This being the way in which the word "cause" actually is sometimes used, how then can a definition which forbids us to call the cause anything less than *the whole* of the prior change in the given state of affairs be regarded as a correct analysis of the meaning which the term "cause" actually possesses?

---

[5] This has been noted by W. S. Jevons, *Pure Logic and Other Minor Works,* p. 251; and is apparent even in Mill's formulation of the canon of difference.

But the incompatibility of this use of "cause" with the definition is only apparent, and the appearance of it depends on a confusion between two different questions, due in turn to the fact that the phrase "the cause of an event" is used in one case in the sense of "the *concrete* event which caused a given *concrete* event," and in the other in the sense of "the *kind* of event an instance of which caused a given event *of a stated kind.*"

Explicitly stated, the first of the two questions is then, *What did cause the whole of the completely determinate change which occurred at the given time T_2 in the given state of affairs?* The second question, on the other hand, assumes the answer to the first as already obtained by observation, and goes on to ask, *What part of what caused it is left if we subtract from that cause such portions and specificities as were unnecessary to causation of the part, described not more determinately than as "breakage of window pane," of what occurred at time T_2?*[6]

When the question faced is the first, then the song of the canary, the precise mass, shape, position and speed of the brick, and every other part and specificity of what occurred at time T_1 is causally relevant to one or another part or feature of what occurred at time T_2. Hence, when events and states of affairs are taken thus in their full determinateness and entirety, the earlier of the two only changes in the given state of affairs is not only sufficient but also necessary to the later change, and the later not only necessitated by but also contingent upon the earlier.

On the other hand, consider the situation when the question faced is the second one. Since the whole of the earlier event is sufficient to the whole of the later, it is sufficient to all its parts and all their features,—in particular, to the part described abstractly only as "breakage of window pane." But not the whole of the earlier event is necessary to this part of the later. The canary's singing, for example, is not necessary to it, although the singing too had effects, and these too were parts, but *other* parts, of the whole later event.

Thus, whenever that of which we ask for the cause is an event not taken in its full determinateness and entirety, but only described, (i.e., taken only in so far as it has the features needed to make it an instance of the abstract kind the description names), then, in every such case, what is asked is identification of its cause *similarly by abstract description only,* i.e., identification of it *only as instance of a certain kind of event,* namely, a kind such that any instance of it, in any circumstances of a certain kind, causes an event of the given kind (e.g., of the kind "breakage of window pane").

Moreover, since in the great majority of cases we *put a name* on the event whose cause we ask for, the second of the two questions distinguished above is the one we are asking in such cases. The question we ask is then a call not literally for the cause of the event occurring, but a call to *abstract,* i.e., to *extract,* from its cause such parts of it as alone are causally relevant to those parts which we select and abstract out of the occurring event by the mere act of *putting a name* on that

---

[6] The words "determinate," and "determinable," or "indeterminate," are used here and throughout in W. E. Johnson's sense (*Logic,* Vol. I, Ch. XI). For example, the description "breakage of window pane" specifies a less determinate kind of event than would the description "breakage of window pane into five pieces," and the latter description in turn a less determinate kind than would be specified by "breakage of window pane into three large and two small pieces"; and so on.

of which we seek the cause. It is to be noted that the abstractive problem so set concerns not solely the one event occurring, but essentially also at least one other occurrence. For it is the problem of discovering the respects in which the concrete cause of the concrete event occurring resembles the concrete causes of one or more certain other concrete events that resemble the given concrete event in the respects implied by the name we put on this event.

BERNARD BEROFSKY

22. *Causality and General Laws*

Although I would not want to defend Hume's theory of causation, I am prepared to defend a Humean theory of causation. As is so often the case, philosophers use a particular philosopher's name to characterize a set of closely related views each one of which bears only some resemblance to the philosopher's view. By a "Humean" theory of causation I mean the view that the analysis of particular causal propositions must include a reference to general laws or the claim that there exist general laws of a certain kind. (I am specifically—and arbitrarily—excluding from consideration the further thesis that general laws are, in no sense, necessary truths.) I shall now state more specifically the thesis to which I subscribe, by listing and commenting upon various versions of the Humean theory.

1. '*C* is the cause of *e*' means " 'All *c*'s are *e*'s' is a law." This is clearly unacceptable. 'Smith's kick caused the football to travel 50 yards' does not mean "Every time Smith kicks the football, it travels 50 yards' is a law."

2. '*C* is the cause of *e*' means "There is a law one of whose antecedent condition terms is '*c*' and whose consequent term is '*e*'." This, also, is too strong; for there is no law that contains the expression 'Smith's kick'.

3. '*C* is the cause of *e*' means "There is a law one of whose antecedent condition terms is true of the same event as *c* and whose consequent term is true of the same event as *e*." One should take " '*x*' is true of the same event as *y*" as entailing *y*. Then, since we normally take "*c* is the cause of *e*" (where '*c*' and '*e*' are particular-designating terms) as entailing '*c*' and '*e*', this same entailment relation will also hold of the analysans.

One crucial difficulty, though, is that 'Harry got ptomaine because he ate lunch quickly' (*Q*) expresses a different causal proposition from 'Harry got ptomaine because he ate last week's fried fish' (*F*) although 'Harry's eating lunch quickly' designates the same event as 'Harry's eating last week's fried fish', since he ate the fried fish for lunch quickly. Hence, the analysis of *F* may assert the existence of a law about food spoilage, whereas *Q* clearly does not assert the existence of a law of this kind.

Nor will it do to demand that the two event descriptions be connected by law, for it may be entailed by a psychological law plus antecedent conditions that

Reprinted by permission of the author and the publisher from Bernard Berofsky, "Causality and General Laws," *The Journal of Philosophy* vol. 63, no. 6 (March 17, 1966): 148-57.

Harry always eats fried fish for lunch quickly; but our attitude toward the example would not change. We must, therefore, demand that the event descriptions be connected by definitions, meaning postulates, or rules (semantic, correspondence).

Moreover, it seems clear that, if we accept an analysis like 3, we do suppose that the situation in which c and e occur is an instance of the law. We thus assert that any other conditions besides the one designated by 'c' which are postulated by the law hold in the way that they must in order for the effect to have occurred. (Thus, if the law refers to magnitudes, the variables must take values in the particular case which are compatible with the effect's being what it is, e.g., "traveling 50 yards from the point of the kick.") We shall try to solve these problems by the following formulation.

4. 'C is the cause of e' means "There is a set of conditions described by the conjunction 'S' (one conjunct of which is 'c') each conjunct of which holds of the situation in which c and e occur and a set of laws L and a set of meaning postulates M (definitions, semantic rules, etc.), such that $S \cdot M \cdot L$ entails e and e is not entailed by any of the following: $S, M, L, S \cdot M, M \cdot L, T \cdot M \cdot L$, where T is any proper subset of S."

On this view, one's decision that some condition is relevant entails that that condition appears in some form in the law; for, if it does not appear there, then the deduction of e does not require it, and it would not, therefore, appear in 'S'. It may also be the case that the law tells you whether or not some condition is "in the same situation as c and e." For example, the law should tell you whether some condition must be simultaneous with c.

5. There is, finally, a weaker position, according to which statistical laws are allowed. This view would not, then, demand that e be deducible from $S \cdot M \cdot L$. It would simply demand the deduction, roughly, of "e is probable" or "e is highly probable."

Neither 4 nor 5 is a sufficient analysis, though, for at least two reasons: (1) *Any* condition of some event would be "the cause" if we assume equivalence. But a complete analysis of 'cause' would have to explain how we make the distinction between "cause" on the one hand and "condition," "occasion," etc. on the other. (2) Not any type of law will do. Laws that take the form "Objects that have characteristics c_1, c_2, and c_3 will also have characteristic c_4" do not always assert causal connection between the possession of these characteristics. But it is not necessary to allow only "causal" laws in the analysans, if we think of the Boyle-Charles' law, for example, as noncausal (on the grounds that there is no claim as to which magnitude is the cause). For this law does enter into an analysis of 'the change in temperature caused a change in the pressure'. One must, therefore, make the appropriate distinctions without introducing the word 'cause'.

It will be recalled, though, that the Humean theory holds only that analyses like 4 or 5 state necessary conditions. When I speak of the Humean theory from now on, therefore, I shall be referring to 4 or 5 construed in this way.

Since I am not concerned in this paper with a detailed defense of 4 or 5 I shall neither present a further clarification of these views nor examine the tenability of holding the stronger of the two. I shall rather do the following:

I. I shall briefly examine Ducasse's alternative to the Humean theory. Ducasse's most recent statement of his theory was his presentation to the American

Philosophical Association, Eastern Division, at Boston in 1964, an abstract of which appears in this *Journal,* 61, 21 (Nov. 12, 1964). Its title is "Causation: Perceivable? Or Only Inferred?"

II. I shall then examine Ducasse's criticisms of Hume's theory in the present paper to see whether or not they apply to the Humean theory. (It is, of course, no criticism of Ducasse to point out that a legitimate criticism of Hume is inapplicable to the Humean theory.)

I

In the APA paper Ducasse argues that the causal relation is perceivable and not a matter of inference. To formulate the problem in these terms, though, may introduce problems that are best put aside as irrelevant. For example, to assert that the causal relation is perceivable is not to assert that a single observation suffices to warrant an incorrigible causal proposition, at least in the sense that no evidence from distinct situations may be brought to bear upon the causal proposition. (Of course, in this sense, redness as a property of physical objects is not perceivable either.) Ducasse correctly grants the relevance of such evidence. But if the word 'incorrigible' is dropped, the thesis becomes so vague as to admit of interpretations that the staunchest Humean (including Hume) could accept. When I, therefore, contend that Ducasse has not shown that the causal relation is perceivable, I shall be using the term roughly in the same way he uses it although, undoubtedly, there are many problems involved in defining that use.

One may formulate Ducasse's contention that the causal relation is perceivable as the following conjunction: (1) 'C is the cause of e in S' means (and is, therefore, entailed by): (a) c occurs at t_0; (b) e occurs at t_1; (c) c and e are the only changes in S (where c and e are particular and distinct changes, S is a particular state of affairs, and t_1 is a time shortly after t_0). (2) What is described by (a), (b), and (c) is, in each case, perceivable. The first conjunct is simply a restatement of Ducasse's analysis of causality, and the second conjunct is implicit in the view that the causal relation is perceivable. For if one of the propositions that enters into the analysis does not refer to a "perceivable fact," then, clearly, the causal relation is not perceivable. (This is the same reason that Ducasse appeals to when he denies that the causal relation is perceivable if the terms of the relation are not perceivable.)

Let us suppose the following very common situation. A change e occurs and is preceded by two other changes, c and d. Let us assume, moreover, that each change is perceivable. Now, on the analysis under examination, if we say, as we sometimes do, that c alone is the cause of e in S, we imply that d is not in S, i.e., d is causally irrelevant to e. This follows from the stipulation that cause and effect are the only changes in the situation. But, what are we to say if, in a subsequent experiment, c occurs, but d and e do not? (Strictly, we should replace each letter by 'an event of the same type as c (or d or e)'.) If we believe that no other factor is causally relevant in either case, we would conclude either that d or that $c \cdot d$ was the cause of e in the first case. (This is Mill's method of difference.) But, on Ducasse's analysis, this is impossible.

If we conclude that d was the cause of e in the first case, then d and e would have to have been the only changes in S. Thus, we were wrong when we said that c and e were the only changes in S. c never was in S. But we did not discover this by finding out that there was something wrong with our perceptions, that the first experiment was not conducted strictly, or that the outcome was not accurately observed. It is absolutely impossible to discover that c never was in S unless more than one experiment is performed. Hence, propositions like "c and e are the only changes in S" are not "known by perception"—at least in the sense intended by Ducasse, whereby two experiments are necessary only for the purpose specified. Putting this in a better way, one experiment is not sufficient to define S, i.e., to specify the changes that are or are not in S.

Matters are no better if we conclude that $c \cdot d$ was the cause of e in the first experiment; for this too would entail that c and e were not the only changes in S. In this case, c *was* in S; but d was also. Again, more than one experiment is necessary in order to specify S, not simply to make sure that the first experiment was properly performed.

Evidently, when we are allowed few or no restrictions on causal relevance, an indefinite number of experiments may be required simply, to use Ducasse's analysis, to define S.

If one were to argue that the causal relation might still be perceivable even if several experiments are required to define S, one might just as well argue that general facts (what make general laws true) are perceivable and that one repeats experiments only to specify the state of affairs of the first experiment. Nor can one rebut this analogy by pointing out that general laws of the form "All p's are q's" entail that there will be no cases of $p \cdot \sim q$ and, hence, do not simply describe a single instance; for another way to express the point I wish to make is that causal inferences from a perceived situation do just the same. The claim, for example, that c, not d, is the cause of e in S entails that there are no cases of $c \cdot \sim e$ (assuming either that c is causally sufficient for e or that all other relevant conditions of e are satisfied, assumptions that are required by the fact that causal propositions are weaker than claims that a specific law is instantiated).

As a matter of fact, one may use certain aspects of Ducasse's analysis to defend the Humean theory. To specify S is to reject as causally irrelevant all changes that are roughly simultaneous with the change distinguished as the cause. But without appeal to matters distinct from S, there will be no way of doing this. Hence propositions of the form "D is causally irrelevant to e" must be inferences from laws or from propositions describing other situations via, perhaps, laws or, at least, general considerations. We saw earlier that this fact is included in the Humean analysis.

The nonperceivable character of the causal relation can be brought out even if one disregards the problems raised by the notion of the state of affairs. Given simply that e follows c and that we affirm that c caused e, how can Ducasse explain (1) the fact that we may surrender this particular causal judgment if e's do not succeed c's in subsequent cases and (2) the fact that we certainly would surrender the belief that c is causally sufficient for e if we found just one case of $c \cdot \sim e$? The first experiment may have been performed perfectly, and we may even have known of the existence of the other factors that turned out later to be relevant. The point is that there is no conceivable way to ascertain causal relevance from a single case.

Finally, may one not argue that I know very well why I cut myself shaving this morning without performing subsequent tests? In the first place, one must in such cases specify two distinct events; for the notion of causality in which Ducasse is interested is the notion of a relation between distinct events. If e is the opening in the skin and c the motion of the blade on my skin, then the claim that c caused e may be understood as a tacit elimination of other possible candidates (splashing water does not cause skin openings) together with the knowledge that, under certain conditions which may have held in this case, c's do bring e's about. (To call it a "cut," as Ducasse pointed out to me, is to imply information about the cause. We, therefore, avoid this question-begging description.) Can one not describe conditions under which we would reject this particular causal proposition? We discover later that we are victims of a strange skin disease, etc. Although this is highly unlikely, the fact that it might occur is incompatible with Ducasse's thesis.

II

1. The first difficulty in Hume's theory cited by Ducasse in the present paper concerns Hume's contention that causation may be detected by a single experiment. Hume argues that an inference to a law is justified by the assumption, roughly, of determinism, an assumption which we do make.

Ducasse points out that, given Hume's views about induction, the assumption of determinism is not justified and cannot, therefore, ground the inference.

First of all, one who accepts a Humean theory is not saddled with Hume's skepticism. Thus, he may ground an inference to a law on another general proposition.

Secondly, although it may be psychologically the case that people do suppose determinism (in some sense) to be true when they make inferences to laws, a Humean need only suppose that a weaker assumption is made. If "c is the cause of e" is affirmed, then one is supposing (since it is part of the analysis) that there exists some law connecting c to e. (This supposition is to be understood as an abbreviated version of the Humean theory.) Regardless of the way this assumption should enter into a reconstruction of inductive inference, it is a fact (and the Humean theory requires it) that its rejection would necessitate the rejection of the causal proposition. We indicated the reasons for believing this fact earlier. The shaving example was intended to illustrate the general point that one can describe situations that would entitle us to withdraw causal propositions. It is true that at the time the causal proposition in question, viz., "The opening in the skin is caused by the motion of the razor blade," is affirmed we have an overwhelming amount of evidence that we shall not have to withdraw it. For we have tacitly adduced general considerations to limit the possibilities, have no reason to believe that any other possible cause is present, and have many positive instances of a law connecting the motion of sharp blades and skin openings (or a general theory of which this law is but one of many lower-order generalizations). We, therefore, have a great deal of evidence for "There is a law connecting c to e" and, *therefore*, are entitled, given information about this particular case, to affirm "c is the cause of e." If, therefore, we have enough background information, we are entitled to make a causal judgment on the basis of a single experiment.

2. Ducasse points out that Hume does not distinguish legitimate generalizations from a single case of sequence from illegitimate ones. I have tried to point out that Ducasse cannot do this either without appealing to general considerations. This is evidenced by the fact that we often do infer the cause and discover that we are mistaken. We had not known that some other factor might be relevant or we did not know that some other factor which turned out to be the cause was even present.

There are many problems that Ducasse may be alluding to here. Since the Humean theory uses the notion of law, one may wish to burden it with all the problems involved in analyzing this concept. It will suffice to show here that Ducasse's alternative faces the same problems and that the Humean theory is at least necessary to suppose in order to deal with some of these problems. Thus, the only "criticism" that remains is: "The Humean theory uses the notion of law and there are aspects of this notion which have not been fully clarified."

a. There are the linguistic problems of Goodman. Granted that "x is grue and x is soothing to Jones" does not warrant "All grue things are soothing to Jones" and that one must show why this is so, it is also the case that Ducasse must show that the same situation does not warrant "Jones is soothed because x is grue." Nor can Ducasse say that the causal proposition is true since Jones is soothed because x is green, but the general proposition false since next year (when grue = blue) Jones will not be soothed by blue things. If 'grue' is admissible, then, should we discover that next year Jones does not find blue things soothing, we would have to replace "Jones is soothed because x is grue" with "Jones is soothed because x is green." This is exactly the same sort of situation that arises with normal predicates. We discover that Jones was frightened not because the animal was a dog, but rather because it was a dachshund.

b. There are sequences of many different kinds. The distinction "accidental-causal" is far too gross.

i. There are sequences which are accidental and the generalization of which would be false and unwarranted. "I type the letter 't'—it begins to rain" is an example. A Humean would not generalize this sequence because there is no reason to believe that any law connects the two. I have tried to argue that Ducasse can provide no better reason for not affirming a causal connection, since he must stipulate that the terms of the sequence do not belong to the same state of affairs, a stipulation he cannot make in the absence of general considerations.

ii. There are sequences which are accidental and the generalization of which would be unwarranted, but true. Every so often a social scientist discovers a bizarre correlation, the terms of which have nothing to do with each other. If so, our belief that this is the case is explained as in (i). He who generalizes does not affirm a law, but simply a true generalization that he has no reason to believe.

iii. There are sequences the generalizing of which is warranted even though the generalization is neither lawlike nor causal nor true. An example is "Hooter of factory hoots in Manchester at noon—workers of factory in London leave for lunch." I am warranted in generalizing this sequence under certain conditions although there is no causal connection between the terms of the sequence. Moreover, although it does not follow from the fact that there is no causal connection here that the generalization is not a law, I would be prepared nevertheless to say that the generalization is not a law because it is not lawlike. Finally, I may have no reason to believe that the London lunch hour will be changed to 11 a.m., although it will be, thereby falsifying the generalization. Evidently some of the information that grounds the inference is general, e.g., the way people respond to prearranged signals. The details may be difficult to specify; but surely Ducasse's theory provides no better explanation. Thus, in (i) and (ii) above, it is not sufficient to believe that no law connects the terms. Sometimes generalizations are warranted by citing laws that connect *other* terms, together with information about the particular case, e.g., there is a hooter in the London factory that hoots at the same time as the one in Manchester.

iv. The same comments apply to cases identical with iii in all relevant respects except that the generalizations are true rather than false. Since the "true-false" distinction in itself makes no difference to the "warranted-unwarranted" distinction, I shall no longer draw the former distinction.

v. There are lawlike, noncausal sequences. We observe that characteristic c_1 is found with characteristic c_2 and infer the noncausal law that these characteristics will always appear together. It is not clear that Ducasse has anything to say about this sort of case, since no causal relationship exists. Although there is a real problem, as we pointed out earlier, in distinguishing sequences of this sort from causal sequences, the claim that a sequence is lawful rather than accidental rests upon general considerations not so very different in character from those which warrant causal inferences. If Ducasse's theory were applied to these cases, it would surely run into the same problems we discovered in the causal cases.

vi. There are lawlike, causal sequences. We discussed these in replying to Ducasse's first objection to Hume's theory. Notice (1) that we may or may not be prepared to specify the actual law governing the sequence, and (2) that there is the problem of distinguishing these sequences from the noncausal variety referred to in v.

I conclude that the Humean theory can withstand all objections arising from the distinction between legitimate and illegitimate inferences from a single case of sequence.

3. Ducasse criticizes Hume for using rules to pick out the cause of an event which cannot be justifiably employed if we accept Hume's skepticism about inductive inference. But, as was pointed out earlier, a Humean theory of causation is compatible with the rejection of Hume's skepticism.

4. Hume gets into difficulty by supposing that identical effects must be the results of identical causes. But a Humean theory does not require this assumption. There is no contradiction or problem in supposing that there are two laws with identical consequent-conditions.

5. Although a Humean is not committed to the principle "same cause—same effect," he is committed to the principle "same cause plus same relevant conditions—same effect." But Ducasse's alleged counterexample is not even a counterexample of the simple principle, since "unintentionally stepping on a man's foot" is a different cause from "intentionally stepping on a man's foot."

I conclude that Ducasse has neither offered a tenable theory of causation nor presented any arguments that warrant the rejection of the Humean theory of causation.

ARTHUR PAP

23. A Note on Causation and the Meaning of "Event"

Critics of the regularity theory of causation usually point out that two events may be "constantly conjoined" without being causally connected, as shown by such examples as the succession of day and night or the succession of the states of one clock upon the corresponding states of another clock which is nearly synchronized with it and goes at the same rate. But most of them are silent about an alternative *analysis* of the concept of causation; some of them, indeed, hold it to be an unanalyzable "category." There is, however, a noteworthy exception to this trend: C. J. Ducasse, whose Carus lectures, *Nature, Mind, and Death,* are a veritable mine of thorough, sober analyses of fundamental concepts, is to my knowledge the only recent critic of the regularity theory who has offered an alternative analysis according to which causal judgments are empirically verifiable (or at least confirmable) and do not involve postulation of perceptually unobservable "ties" between events. He claims nothing less than to be able to analyze the difference between a purely coincidental sequence of events in time and a causal sequence of events without any reference to *regularity* of sequence. But his analysis seems to me completely untenable, for the reasons to be presented forthwith.

According to Ducasse, to assert that an event *e* was caused by an antecedent event *c* in a situation *S,* is to assert that *c* is the only change in *S* which immediately preceded *e.* He seems to have arrived at this analysis by a tacit application of the verifiability theory of meaning to ordinary uses of the word "cause": what people do in order to verify that *c* caused *e,* is not usually to observe other events resembling *c* in order to see whether they are followed by events resembling *e;* rather they try to make sure that *c* was the only change in *S* that preceded *e.* He reports an experiment performed with his students whose outcome is alleged to confirm his analysis of the meaning of "cause":

> I bring into the room and place on the desk a paper-covered parcel tied with string in the ordinary way, and ask the students to observe closely what occurs. Then . . . I put my hand on the parcel. The end of the parcel the students face then at once glows. I then ask them what caused it to glow at that moment, and they naturally answer that the glowing was caused by what I did to the parcel immediately before. [*Op. cit.,* p. 95.]

Since the evidence on which the causal judgment is based is just that nothing else happened to the parcel before the glowing except its being touched by Ducasse's hand, the causal judgment must *mean,* so Ducasse argues, that this contact was "the only change introduced into the situation immediately before glowing occurred." But Ducasse overlooks that the observation of a solitary change preceding the event to be explained may not be the sufficient ground of the causal judgment, that it may warrant the causal judgment only in the context of a tacit argument from elimination of alternatives. In order to show this, let us analyze the idea of one

Reprinted by permission of the publisher from Arthur Pap, "A Note on Causation and the Meaning of 'Event'," *The Journal of Philosophy* vol. 54, no. 6 (March 14, 1957): 155-59. Footnotes included.

change being caused by another change in "substance language" as follows: the fact that a thing A has a property Q at time t_1 (which property A does not have at the slightly earlier time t_0) is caused by A having property P at t_0 (which A did not have immediately before t_0). Suppose, now, that this causal proposition in turn were analyzed as follows: A had P immediately before it acquired Q, and for any t, and for any x, if x has P at t, then x has Q at $t + dt$. From this analysis it follows at once that if at some time t_i x has P without having Q at $t_i + dt$, then the fact that x has Q at some time cannot be caused by the fact that x had P immediately before. In other words, the analysis entails the impossibility of (x having Q) being caused by (x having P) if there is a finite time-interval (more exactly, a time interval that is large relative to dt) during which x has P invariably but does not have Q. Suppose, to illustrate, it had occurred to Ducasse's students that perhaps it was the contact with the desk which caused the parcel to glow; surely the observation that the parcel had the property of being in contact with the desk for quite a while without acquiring the property of glowing would have been sufficient to eliminate the causal hypothesis if it means what it means according to the regularity theory. In general, if R_1, $R_2 \ldots R_n$ are properties with respect to which x does not change during a certain time-interval within which x acquires Q, i.e., within which there are instants when x does not have Q and later instants when x has Q, then no hypothesis of the form "for any t, if $R^i (x,t)$, then Q $(x,t + dt)$" can be true. On the assumption that some change of A (with respect to some property) which immediately preceded A's acquisition of Q caused the latter, and that P is the only property[1] with respect to which A changed immediately before, it follows indeed that it is *this change* which caused the effect.

It should be obvious, then, that Ducasse's argument in support of his analysis of "cause" as corresponding to what people mean by the word is invalid. If his students meant by "cause" a change of a kind that is *regularly* followed by the effect and further believed in universal causation, then they would, as they did, identify the cause with what they believed to be the only immediately preceding change undergone by the parcel. What Ducasse adduces as evidence disconfirming the regularity analysis, therefore, in fact confirms it. A single experiment may highly confirm a causal hypothesis interpreted as an assertion of regular sequence, the degree of confirmation being, within the framework of causal determinism, proportional to the probability that all the relevant variables except one were constant. In short, Ducasse's argument assumes that if the regularity theory is correct, then only induction by enumeration, not induction by elimination of alternative hypotheses, can increase the antecedent probability of a given causal hypothesis.

So far I have only argued against Ducasse's *argument* in support of his alternative analysis of causation, not against the analysis itself. But I propose to show further that (a) his analysis is incorrect, (b) his defense of his analysis against the obvious *prima facie* objection involves a radical departure from the way "event" is used when one speaks, both in everyday life and in science, of the causes and effects of events. And he could not afford to ignore this sort of criticism, which flourishes especially in contemporary Oxford and is greatly disliked by many philosophers who consider "ordinary usage" unworthy of philosophers' attention,

---

[1] "Property" is here used in the broad sense customary in logic which covers *relations*.

for what he claims for his theory, as against the regularity theory, is precisely conformity to the ordinary meanings of words.

(a) On Ducasse's analysis it is self-contradictory to suppose that an event which is immediately preceded by more than one change in its neighborhood is caused at all. If one antecedent event is causally irrelevant to *e*, then all of them are, since a change which is one of several concurrent changes in *S* cannot be said to be the only change in *S*. But surely the supposition is not self-contradictory according to the ordinary meaning of "cause."

(b) Ducasse is aware of this objection. He supplies himself a good illustration: Nobody would call the breaking of a window pane an uncaused event just because the impact of the stone was not the only immediately preceding change going on in the neighborhood; if at the same time a bird was singing nearby, in consequence of which air waves spread from the bird's location towards the window, we would say that this change was causally irrelevant and that the stone's impact caused the breaking (*cf. op. cit.*, p. 123). Ducasse answers the objection by distinguishing between *concrete events* and *kinds of events.* His analysis is intended, he says, as an analysis of "cause" taken as a relational predicate applicable to concrete events. Such concrete events "are specifiable only in terms of their time and place, i.e. only by means of some such phrase as 'what is occurring here now', or 'what occurred at place P at time T' " (p. 151). The breaking of the window pane, then, is not a concrete event, but an abstracted part of the concrete event which occurred at that time and place; another part of this concrete event consists in the approach of the air waves, and to this part of the concrete event the bird's singing was not causally irrelevant. And since what we describe as the impact of a brick is again only a part of the concrete event which preceded the effect, and the word "cause" is applied by Ducasse to concrete events, it follows of course that the approach of the air waves was part of the cause.

Now, if the words "cause" and "effect" were applied to such concrete events which cannot be described by characterizing predicates since, by definition, whatever is so described is an event *of a certain kind,* then all causal judgments would be monotonously similar and in fact tautologous: What caused the event in the spatial region S at time *t*? The *a priori* answer is: the event which occurred in S at $t - dt$! No doubt, the concrete event which immediately preceded in S the concrete event which occurred in S at *t* is—the concrete event which immediately preceded the latter in S. No surprise that Ducasse succeeds in proving that "every event has a cause" is analytic (*cf.* pp. 151*ff.*): to suppose that more than one concrete event occurred in S at $t - dt$ is contradictory since a "concrete" event occurring in a spatial region at a given time is defined as the *total state* of the region at that time; and when we regard it as logically conceivable that no change at all may precede a given change, that up to the latter there is just a lapse of pure time, we overlook, Ducasse argues correctly, that at least a clock must have gone through a succession of states. But Ducasse could have gone further and drawn from his analysis of "cause" the conclusion that every *specific* causal statement about concrete events is analytic. They all amount to the same sort of tautology: that the total state of a spatial region at a given time *t* is immediately preceded by the total state of that region at $t - dt$.

Clearly, in any ordinary and significant use the words "cause" and "effect" are applied to instances of definite kinds of events, not to what Ducasse calls "concrete events." Causal questions do not have the form "why did the event with space-time coördinates x, y, z, t happen?," but "why did the event *of kind K* with space-time coördinates x, y, z, t happen?" Suppose that we distinguish between coördinate-descriptions and *characterizing* descriptions of events. An example of a characterizing event-description is "the breaking of a window pane which occurs at time t at place (x, y, z)." Then we may say that any conceivable contingent causal statement that is ever made and that it could ever be useful to make involves characterizing event-descriptions. And since Ducasse can defend his analysis against the above objection only by shifting from characterizing descriptions to coördinate-descriptions, he has failed to analyze the ordinary meaning of "cause."

EDWARD H. MADDEN
JAMES HUMBER

24. Nonlogical Necessity and C. J. Ducasse

For over forty years C. J. Ducasse effectively criticized Humean views of causality, though he was never content simply to be a critic. We owe to his ingenuity and precision one of the most attractive non-Humean alternatives to be found in twentieth-century philosophy. *Causation and the Types of Necessity* was the first published statement of his views, and this book, long out of print, has been republished recently with more recent articles appended.[1] His second major statement, changed in details but essentially the same, appears as Part II of *Nature, Mind, and Death,* his contribution to the Carus Lecture Series.[2] His later articles on causality are included in the recently published collection of essays *Truth, Knowledge and Causation,*[3] where he thoughtfully answers the questions raised by serious-minded critics of his two books.

Professor Ducasse's work is now complete, and the publication of the two books provides the occasion for an overall assessment of his contribution to the philosophy of causality—a not inconsiderable one, as we shall see, and one from which Humeans and non-Humeans alike have much to learn. This holds true for

Reprinted by permission of the authors and the publisher, Basil Blackwell, from Edward H. Madden and James Humber, "Nonlogical Necessity and C. J. Ducasse," *Ratio* vol. 13, no. 2 (December 1971): 119-38. Footnotes included.

[1] *Causation and the Types of Necessity* (New York: Dover Publications, Inc., 1969). This new edition has an Introduction by Vincent Tomas. The book was originally published by the University of Washington Press in 1924. All references in this paper are to the Dover Edition. The abbreviation *CTN* will be used.

[2] *Nature, Mind, and Death* (La Salle, Ill.: Open Court Publishing Company, 1951). The abbreviation *NMD* will be used.

[3] *Truth, Knowledge and Causation* (London: Routledge and Kegan Paul, 1968). The abbreviation *TKC* will be used.

method as well as substantive results. His analyses of causal concepts provide models of precision and clarity rarely achieved by those who most ardently declare their devotion to these virtues. Ducasse had that rare genius of *being* clear, as well as stressing the need for it.

Though we agree wholly with Ducasse's rejection of the Humean tradition, we find it equally impossible to accept his causal alternative, dependent, as it is, upon an event ontology. A close study of his work, however, will throw considerable light on the new directions that discussions of causality have recently taken. Given these facts, we will proceed in the following way: (1) state his analyses succinctly, yet hopefully with the same precision found in his own work; (2) give reasons for rejecting his analysis of causality and non-logical necessity, at the same time indicating what we find of lasting value in it; and (3) indicate briefly the direction in which we believe a more successful non-Humean analysis must proceed.

1

First, only an event, and not an object, thing, or substance, can be a cause or an effect. It is the exploding of the gasoline in the cylinders that causes the car to move and the running out of gasoline that causes it to stop on the highway. It is the lightning striking the tree that caused the forest fire, and the snapping of the beam that caused the bridge to collapse. Whenever we say that an object caused something to happen that is only an elliptical way of referring to an event causing something to happen. Thus when we say that the carpenter caused the table to exist what we must mean is that certain movements of the carpenter caused the table to exist. These examples are all intuitively clear, for what we ordinarily mean by an event is a "happening," which, in turn, means a change in a state of affairs. Clearly this is what Ducasse means by "event," but he also intends something more. A change in a state of affairs is an event, to be sure, but, according to Ducasse, so is *the continued existence of a state of affairs* an event. The question "What happened then?" can be answered reasonably either by saying "He got up," a change in a state of affairs, or "He remained seated," an "unchange" in a state of affairs, and hence the latter qualifies as an event just as much as the former. Thus Ducasse defines "event" inclusively as "either a change or unchange in a state of affairs."[4]

Second, Ducasse identifies the causal relation between events as that which holds between the three terms of any strict experiment. Usually he describes an experiment only in terms of a change in a state of affairs. An experiment, he says, is a state of affairs S in which only two changes occur: one, C, occurring in S at t_1, and the other, E, occurring spontaneously and immediately following C in S at t_2. The first change may be introduced by human beings or by the natural course of events as in an eclipse. The only change at t_1 must be the *total* change, and C, consequently, may be either simple or complex. Since the elements of S and the changes at t_1 and t_2 are all observable (or insofar as they are all observable), the causal relation itself can be said correctly to be directly perceivable and, upon occasion, directly perceived. The strict experiment, Ducasse continues, is what the logician calls the method of single difference and, like the other "experimental

---

[4] *NMD*, pp. 108-9.

methods," is usually construed as a way of discovering or confirming causal relations. However, it is not in fact simply a method for discovering causes in some
other sense of "cause" but itself constitutes the *definition* of that concept. The
principle provides a method for identifying a cause only in the sense in which the
description of a fugitive from justice can be said to be or to provide a method for
identifying him. Ducasse's last and most concise definition of the causal concept is
this:

> Causation is the observable relation which obtains between the
> three terms of any strict experiment: If, in a given state of affairs *S*, *only*
> *two* changes (whether simple or complex) occur during a given period, one
> of them *E* occurring immediately after and adjacent to the other *C*, then,
> *eo ipso*, *C* proximately *caused E*, and *E* was the proximate *effect* of *C*.[5]

From this definition of "cause" various important consequences follow.[6]

(i) Causality is an irreducibly *triadic* relationship between *C* and *E in S*.
The analysis of "cause" as "whole set of necessary conditions" is necessarily mistaken, since such an analysis is dyadic in nature. It collapses the commonsensical
distinction between cause and condition by making the whole of *S C* of *E*. Com-
monsensically, Ducasse says, we distinguish between dry underbrush as a condition
for the occurrence of a forest fire—a condition without which the effect would not
occur—and the striking of the tree by lightning as the cause of it—that change in a
state of affairs sufficient to bring about another single change in the same *S*. When
the string by which a weight is suspended is cut and the weight falls, it was the
cutting of the string that caused the weight to fall and not the attraction of the
masses of the object and the earth. The attraction was just as much a fact before
the string was cut as after; hence while it is a condition for the occurrence of the
effect it is not the cause of it.

(ii) If the total change *C* at t_1 is simple, the only point in repeating an
experiment is to check that all the factors in the control and experimental groups
were indeed held constant. If the total change *C* is complex, however, repetition is
required to discover if *C(a,b)* was just sufficient to *E* or more than sufficient.
Another experimental set-up would be needed where *C(a)* is repeated without *C(b)*
in a state of affairs otherwise identical to *S*. If *E* did not occur at t_2, then we are in
a position to say that *C(b)* is just sufficient to *E* while *C(a,b)* is more than sufficient. According to Ducasse, when we now say that *C(b)* is the cause of *E* we are
using a "generalized" concept of cause and cannot be said to directly perceive
causes in this sense. This generalized sense has important practical functions and is
the sense usually involved in ordinary usage. However, it still remains true that in
perceiving the concrete, unique *C(a,b)* in *S* one perceived the only change in *S* prior
to *E* at t_2 and hence observed the causal relation. To perceive what was more than
sufficient to *E* was also to perceive what was sufficient to *E*.

(iii) Regularities are causal when each individual case subsumed under the
generalization is causal. Relations are not causal simply because they are regular;

---

[5] C. J. Ducasse, 'Minds, matter and bodies' in *Brain and Mind*, ed. J. R. Smythies
(London: Routledge and Kegan Paul, 1965), p. 84. Cf. *CTN*, pp. 51-61; *NMD*, pp. 101-49; and
TKC, pp. 1-14.
    [6] All these implications are to be found in the material cited in the previous footnote.

they are regular because they are causal. Causality explains regularity, not the other way around. A sequence could be unique in the history of the world and still be causal, while a regular recurring sequence, like that of night and day, might not be causal at all.

(iv) To ask how one given event caused another can only mean, "What other intermediary causal steps were there?" Such a question if asked of proximate instead of remote causes is absurd—implicitly self-contradictory. It makes sense to ask why taking a pill removes the symptoms of an illness. Such a question amounts to asking for a specification of the in-between steps between taking the pill and the disappearance of the symptoms. The answer consists in specifying certain chemical changes brought about by the dissolution of the pill and the distribution of its ingredients throughout the system. But it does not make sense, except in terms of a higher-order chemical theory, to ask why the chemical ingredients have the power to remove the symptoms—as if there were still further in-between processes which, by hypothesis, there are not.

(v) The causal relation is wholly neutral about whether cause and effect events are physical or mental, or whether one term of the relation is one type while the other is the opposite. Ducasse eventually claims that all possible combinations of cause-and-effect relationships occur: (1) physico-physical (the snapping of the beam caused the bridge to collapse); (2) physico-psychical (the stimulation of the central nervous system caused the person to have a percept of the table); (3) psycho-physical (his desire for the orange caused him to pluck it off the tree); and (4) psycho-psychical (his intense interest in things past caused him to write his memoirs).

(vi) One might be mistaken in believing that C at t_1 was the only change in S prior to E at t_2, and hence mistaken in ascribing C as the cause of E, but one cannot be mistaken about this: if C was the only change prior to E then it was the cause of E, for this is precisely what is meant by saying that anything is the cause of anything else.

> When any philosophically pure-minded person sees a brick strike a window and the window break, he judges that the impact of the brick was the cause of the breaking, *because* he believes that impact to have been the only change which took place then in the immediate environment of the window. He may, indeed, have been mistaken, and acknowledge that he was mistaken, in believing that impact to have been the only change in the environment. But if so he will nevertheless maintain that *if* it had been the only change, it would have been the cause. That is, he will stand by the definition of cause, and admit merely that what he perceived was not a true case of what he meant and still means by cause.[7]

The precariousness of causal assertions, however, should not be over-emphasized. They are no more precarious than any universal negative proposition established through observation. It is admittedly difficult to make sure that no other change than C occurred at t_1 in S, but it is also difficult to make certain by observation that at any given time there is no mosquito in a given room or no flea on a given dog. "All we really know in any such case is that we have searched and not found any; that our method of search was one capable of revealing cases of the sort of thing we were looking for; and that the more thorough and careful was our

---

[7] *TKC*, p. 8.

search with such a method, the less likely it is that a case of what we look for would have escaped our observation."[8] That the experimental methods of science are excellent methods of search is attested to by the imposing achievements of modern science. Certainly experiments performed under strict laboratory conditions help ease the precariousness of causal judgments. And in cases of the direct perception of causality there are times when it would be strange indeed to insist upon the precariousness of such judgments: "I submit that, when Charles I lost his head, it would have been mere silly perversity on the part of the executioner or of other close spectators to maintain that the blow of the axe was not certainly but only probably what caused his head to come of."[9]

2

Ducasse's definition of causality and its implications raise almost every substantive issue that has been debated by Humeans and non-Humeans, and we cannot hope to consider even all the major issues here. We will limit ourselves to what seem to be four of the most fundamental and interesting issues and will show where we think Ducasse is wrong. Our criticisms will in no way depend upon Humean assumptions, but will reflect either inconsistencies in Ducasse's view or our own brand of non-Humean commitments. Other crucial issues will be discussed later when we consider Ducasse's analysis of nonlogical necessity. There our own positive views will become increasingly evident.

(i) There is an initial difficulty with Ducasse's inclusive definition of an event as a change or unchange in a state of affairs. The first half of the definiens seems faultless, but the latter half strained and difficult to justify. What we ordinarily and intuitively mean by an event is a "happening," and this meaning can be formulated technically as a change in a state of affairs, this concept referring in turn to objects (or particulars of any other justifiable sort), properties of objects, and relations among them. Examples of an event would be the snapping of a beam, the breaking of a glass, the exploding of gasoline, and the recalling of a forgotten name. Ducasse, however, extends this intuitively clear notion of event to "unchanges" in states of affairs as well. According to Ducasse, the question "What occurred then?" or "What happened then?" could be answered equally sensibly either by "He got up," a change in a state of affairs, or "He remained seated," an "unchange" in a state of affairs, and hence the latter qualifies as an event just as much as the former.[10]

This argument seems weak, however, since it gives unusual meanings to the words "occur" and "happen" while supposedly using them in ordinary ways. These words have the general dynamic sense of "to take place" or "to come about," which suggests the basic notion of change in a state of affairs rather than unchange. The same suggestion is involved in the colloquial exclamation, "That was some event!" where "event" means "some change in routine of a dramatic sort." So there is something quite artificial in saying that the man's continued sitting is an occurrence or happening and hence an event. It would seem more reasonable to say that

[8] *NMD*, p. 119. [Reprinted in this text.]
[9] *NMD*, p. 120. [Reprinted in this text.]
[10] *NMD*, pp. 108-9. [Reprinted in this text.]

in this case the man did nothing that could be construed as a happening and, in fact, nothing happened to him. To the question asked after a severe storm, "What happened to the barn?" it is correct to say that in spite of what happened to it, the pounding rain and hurricane-force winds, the barn still stands intact. The continued standing of the barn, then, in spite of what happened to it, is not a "happening" itself, but the continued existence through time of certain particulars, their properties, and their relations.

The strangeness of Ducasse's definition of "event" can be brought out in yet another way. On his view, one may legitimately ask, "What is not an event?" "Event" must be construed as including everything, for there is nothing with which it may be contrasted. It is as though one defined a new color "brello" as being "blue or non-blue"; of what use is such a concept? So too with the supposedly empirical concept event; if it is to have any utility it must mark off some distinction. But it does not. When this fact is taken in conjunction with the fact that ordinary usage contrasts an event with an unchange in a practicable and serviceable manner, one cannot help but feel that Ducasse has uselessly redefined "event." We are forced to conclude that if unchanges can properly and meaningfully be designated causes and effects, as Ducasse maintains, then he should really give up the view that only events can be causes.

(ii) There seems to be no good reason for insisting that a cause is always an event, as distinct from a standing condition, and that Hume, Mill, and their modern counterparts are simply flying in the face of commonsense when they define "cause of y" as "whole set of conditions necessary for occurrence of y." That commonsense supports his claim and not theirs is, in fact, the only reason Ducasse ever gives for the correctness of the former and the falsity of the latter. In spite of his commitment to ordinary contexts, however, Ducasse unfortunately is not sufficiently attentive to the complexity of such contexts. Paying attention to such complexity quickly convinces one that there is no point in looking for *the* meaning of "cause" supported by ordinary usage as if the term were somehow being used in the same sense throughout. There are numerous occasions when we do usefully refer to an event and only an event as the cause of y, and the reasons for doing so are usually practical, prudential, or legal in nature. We say that running out of gasoline caused the car to stop and removing the center beam caused the barn to collapse. Such talk makes perfectly good sense by drawing attention to a change in a situation which was under the control of human intelligence, and the point of drawing attention to just these conditions is prudential in nature: check the tank before starting next time, and learn something about construction before you try your hand at remodeling. Sometimes the point of such ascriptions is to assert legal responsibility; the guide on a desert tour whose car runs out of gas and the contractor who pulls the wrong beam may well be liable for damages. There are, however, numerous other occasions, both scientific and commonsensical, when we usefully refer to what Ducasse calls a "standing condition" as a cause, or to a whole set of conditions, including both events and standing conditions, as the cause of y. For example, we sometimes ask "What was the cause of y?" when what we want is an explanation as complete as possible of this particular occurrence of y, an explanation which shows, without taking anything for granted, why it is that y had to occur at t_1 rather than something else. In response to such a question as this one it would not be enough to mention either those conditions alone which have prudential or legal significance or those which have scientific significance, but it would be necessary to mention the set of conditions without which the effect at t_1 would not occur. To explain why the car stopped it is necessary to mention both that the car ran out of gasoline and that friction was no longer overruled, just as it might be necessary another time to mention both that the driver put on the brakes and that friction was reinforced.

The first context is the one that gives rise to the ordinary distinction between cause and standing condition (though the distinction is not always or necessarily made by using these specific words), and Ducasse is rightly sensitive to this important distinction. He errs, however, in elevating the concept of cause involved in it into *the* meaning of the concept cause—claiming, as he does, that only changes in S (whether introduced by a person or simply occurring in nature) count as causes—and then justifying this claim by reference to usage as if it were the only sense used.

The second context is the one that gives rise to the definition of "cause," given by Hume, Mill, and their modern counterparts, as "whole set of necessary conditions"; and they are rightly sensitive to *this* explanatory sense of the word.[11] They err as much as Ducasse, however, by elevating *this* definition of "cause" into *the* definition—claiming, e.g., that it is always arbitrary and capricious to single out one necessary condition and call it the cause of y. That such selections are far from arbitrary and capricious should be abundantly clear from the examples and contexts given above.

(iii) Strangely enough, Ducasse and Hume both seem to fall victim to the same error, though, of course, not in identical ways. They both confuse the *reasons* we have for saying that two objects or events are causally related with the *meaning* of the term "cause." They both mistakenly presuppose that if we discover how causal statements are verified we would automatically have discovered the meaning of such assertions. (This claim refers to the positivistic and not the skeptical interpretation of Hume's work.) Hume sees the method of agreement as the primary way causal propositions are verified and so interprets the meaning of "cause" as "constant conjunction." Ducasse, on the other hand, sees the method of single difference as the primary way causal assertions are known to be true (that is, *identified* as causal assertions) and hence interprets the meaning of "cause" as "the only change in S immediately prior to E." No doubt both methods provide upon occasion perfectly good reasons for saying that x is the cause of y, but in that case they cannot also be construed as definitions of the concept cause. If I say that John is Carol's brother and someone asks how I know this, what reason I have for saying it, the reply "because John is Carol's male sibling" would be rejected as either irrelevant or enjoyed as a jest. Specifying a definiens and giving a reason are not only two different things but are incompatible. If x is used as one, it cannot be used as the other, and vice versa. The confusion between giving the meaning of x and giving a reason why x is the case could never be more beautifully signalled than in the conflict between Ducasse and Hume. Both operate on the assumption that meaning and verification are intimately connected and, operating on this assump-

---

[11] Cf. S. Gorovitz, "Causal judgments and causal explanation," *Journal of Philosophy*, Vol. LXII (1965), pp. 695-711. [Reprinted in this text.]

tion, produce two incompatible definitions of the concept of causality. Indeed, this anomaly points up nicely how the meaning of a proposition could not possibly be the sum total of its experienced consequences or effects, since such consequences in the case of causality would lead to incompatible elements in a generalized definition.

(iv) Ducasse seems mistaken in claiming that when we perceive what was more than sufficient to E we have nonetheless directly observed the causal relation. The situation referred to, it will be recalled, is this: The complex change $C(a,b)$ is the only change perceived in S at t_1 while later experiments show that $C(b)$ was just sufficient to E and $C(a,b)$ more than sufficient to E. Now the question is, in perceiving the complex change $C(a,b)$ in S at t_1 and then perceiving E at t_2, did we directly observe the causal relation? Ducasse answers "yes" because we experienced what was in fact sufficient to E, even though what we experienced was more than sufficient. It seems to us, however, that the correct answer is "no" because there is a difference between experiencing the cause of E and experiencing something as the cause of E. Ducasse confuses the two notions. He is right in saying that one has perceived what is the cause of E but wrong in thinking that one thereby has perceived x as the cause of E. Given any complex change, one cannot claim to have experienced the whole of it or any part of it as the cause of E because what the cause of E is can be known in such cases only inferentially. Take the case of a football player being hit by tacklers on both sides and falling to the ground. Being hit by the two tacklers is the only change in S immediately prior to the player's falling, and we directly perceived this (complex) change in S. Consequently we perceived what in fact made the runner fall to the ground, though we did not perceive anything as making him fall. The runner may have fallen because of one impact or the other, or their combined impact; and since we cannot know which is the case we cannot be said to perceive $C(a,b)$ as the cause of E. The case might be otherwise for the runner. He may have felt the impact of the second tackler knocking him to the ground just a second after he weathered the impact of the first. Being hit simultaneously by both, however, he might be in no better position than an observer to know if this complex change in S was just sufficient or more than sufficient to knock him to the ground.

3

Thus far there has been no mention of Ducasse's concept of nonlogical necessity, certainly one of the most interesting strands of his causal theory and one which takes us to the heart of current discussions of causality. Having cleared the ground, so to speak, we can now proceed to an examination of this crucial concept and can indicate the direction we think a more adequate non-Humean analysis than Ducasse's must take.

Ducasse's analysis of "causal necessity" is not as clear and unambiguous as most of his writing. Even so, certain facts are undeniable. It is clear that Ducasse's notion of causal necessity entails the view that necessity is not limited in its meaning to logical necessity. Logical necessity, by definition, is found only between logical entitites; it dictates the relationships which concepts or propositions may or may not have to one another. Causal necessity, on the other hand, holds only between *events;* it dictates the relationships which events, whether physical, physiological, or psychological, may or may not have to one another. Thus "causal necessity," as understood by Ducasse, cannot have "logical necessity" as all or any part of its meaning. In order to distinguish causal necessity from logical, and in an attempt to make the term broad enough to cover its presence between events of dissimilar types (e.g., the blow of the hammer physically necessitates the breaking of the vase, chopping off a man's head physiologically necessitates his death, and thinking of "two plus two" psychologically necessitates some people to think of "four"), Ducasse refers to such necessity as *etiological.* He introduces this concept through the prior one of etiological sufficiency. When one perceives a situation in which C at t_1 is the only change prior to a second only change E at t_2, he has perceived a situation in which C was etiologically sufficient to E. Conversely, he has perceived a state of affairs in which E was etiologically necessitated by C in S.[12]

Now the above facts are helpful but fall short of telling us what Ducasse takes to be the precise meaning of "etiological necessity." Scattered throughout his works there is evidence to support either of two possible interpretations. The first interpretation is that Ducasse sees this concept as denoting some perceivable "power" or "force" which is present in the cause, thus *making* the effect occur. Certain examples tend to indicate that such is his meaning, not the least of which is the reference to King Charles I losing his head. Recall that telling quotation:

> I submit that, when Charles I lost his head, it would have been mere silly perversity on the part of the executioner or of some other close spectators to maintain that the blow of the axe was not certainly but only probably what caused the head to come off.[13]

In this passage it would certainly seem that Ducasse is taking "etiological necessity" to mean "a perceivable power present in the axe-swing which *forced* King Charles' head to separate from his body."[14] To the objection that it is conceivable that the science of the future might discover some way of preventing decapitation from killing a person, Ducasse aptly replies that the assertion about the death of Charles is no universal proposition and what the science of the future might discover is irrelevant to both its meaning and truth. All that commonsense asserts about his death is that "in the circumstances *that were present at the time* (which included the fact that no such surgical feat occurred), the beheading did suffice to cause his death."[15] In the most recent statement of his views, Ducasse writes that "the spectators *perceived* the blow's *making* the head come off."[16] Scattered elsewhere throughout his writings on causality are similar statements that lend themselves to the same interpretation. " 'Produces' is substantially synonymous with 'causes,' and has no more anthropomorphic implication than has the latter term."[17] And the plain fact is that "every person has *perceived*—and I say *perceived,* not *inferred*— that, for example, a particular tree branch was *being caused to bend* by a particular

---

[12] *NMD*, pp. 113-21. [Reprinted in this text.]

[13] *NMD*, p. 120. [Reprinted in this text.]

[14] Sterling Lamprecht clearly understood Ducasse in this sense at first but through an interchange of notes came to realize that Ducasse really meant something quite different. Cf. *CTN*, pp. 131-6.

[15] *NMD*, p. 116. [Reprinted in this text.]

[16] Ducasse, "Minds, matter and bodies," p. 84.

[17] *NMD*, p. 144.

bird's alighting; that a particular bottle was *being caused to break* by the fall on it of a particular rock; that a particular billiard ball was *being caused to move* by a particular other billiard ball's rolling against it; [and] that a particular match was *being caused to ignite* by friction of it on a particular rough surface . . ."[18] And, the favorite example again, "To say that the movement of the axe *made* the head come off means that *causation not logical entailment,* of the second by the first is *what occurred then."*[19]

Ducasse's examples and statements lend themselves to an interpretation of nonlogical necessity interestingly akin—though superior—to that taken by the otherwise divergent philosophers William James, F. C. S. Schiller, G. F. Stout, A. N. Whitehead, Charles Hartshorne, and W. R. Boyce-Gibson.[20] They all agree that 'causal necessity' is undefinable but denotatively meaningful from the direct experience we have of it in volitional contexts. Then they (or most of them) extrapolate this relationship to the physical world and say it holds between physical objects also, thus getting involved in a panpsychism which is wholly objectionable to most contemporary philosophers. Some writers avoid volitional contexts, thus hoping to avoid panpsychism, though they retain the person as one term of the causal relation: we directly experience the hurricane wind bending us, the falling boulder crushing our leg, and the waves tumbling us smartly into shore. But it is not clear how this strategy successfully avoids panpsychism, since it also extrapolates the relation to physical contexts where neither term refers to a conscious being. The significance of Ducasse's statements and examples is that they suggest we are directly aware of causal necessities in the physical world itself and hence that there is no need of projecting anything whatsoever onto the physical world. According to Ducasse, we directly experience the blow of the axe severing Charles' head from his body, the alighting of the bird bending the branch, the falling rock breaking the bottle, and the hitting and moving of the second billiard ball by the first.

Ducasse's examples of the striking of a match on a rough surface causing it to burst into flame and the gasoline exploding in the cylinders causing the car to move also suggest a second interpretation of the concepts power and nonlogical necessity, wholly compatible with the first, which has been increasingly advocated in recent literature.[21] Scratching the match on a rough surface is what made the phosphorus sulfide tip burst into flame at that moment and thus exhibit the power of igniting it always had by virtue of its nature. The chemical structure of phosphorus sulfide explains why it has the power to ignite under certain conditions, and chemical theory, in turn, can explain the structure of phosphorus sulfide. Turning on the ignition, etc., is what made the gasoline exhibit at that moment the power of exploding it always had by virtue of its nature. The chemical structure of gasoline explains why it has the power to explode and chemical theory, again, can explain why it has that structure, though it is not necessary that a particular have *its* nature

---

[18] *TKC,* p. 26.

[19] *TKC,* p. 31.

[20] Cf. E. H. Madden and P. H. Hare, "The powers that be," to appear in *Dialogue, Canadian Philosophical Review.*

[21] Rom Harré, "Powers and qualities," to appear in *British Journal for the Philosophy of Science;* E. H. Madden, "A third view of causality," *Review of Metaphysics,* Vol. 23 (1969), pp. 67-84; and M. R. Ayers, *The Refutation of Determinism* (London: Methuen, 1968). [Madden reprinted in this text.]

explained before that nature is capable of explaining the powers and capacities of that particular. The weight of the air and the pressure of the atmosphere explain why water goes up a pump when air is evacuated from the cylinder even though the weight of the air is not explained, in turn, though it could be, by gravitational attraction. Again, the weight of the bird, the weight of the stone, and the pressure of the deep water—all characteristics of the nature of some particular—explain why the bird's alighting makes the branch bend, the stone break the glass, and the pressure crush the submarine—where "bending," "breaking," and "crushing" are causal verbs expressing powers to make certain events occur under specific releasing occasions of alighting, falling, and submerging.

Though Ducasse's examples and use of phrases like "x produces y," "x makes y happen," and "causal necessity is directly perceived suggest the above analyses, he draws back from their implications. There are two reasons for this, one which he explicitly gives and one which hovers in the background and needs to be made explicit. Any "power" analysis of causality, Ducasse charges, introduces a mysterious, ineffable element into causality and thus must be rejected. It would do no good simply to add such a concept to the definition of "cause" as an unanalysed element, since such a procedure would guarantee nothing about what is supposedly referred to. We need no St. Anselms in the philosophy of causality.[22]

It is also necessary for Ducasse to reject power interpretations of etiological necessity because they sometimes lead to ascriptions of causality incompatible with his claim that causes are always events and never standing conditions. Instances of this conflict are not difficult to find. If a car runs out of gasoline and comes to a halt on the highway, the question arises of whether the disappearance of the gasoline or the friction of the tires on the road surface was the cause of the stopping (assuming that one is not holding that the whole set of necessary conditions was the cause). Given his definition of causality, Ducasse would have to say that the event consisting of the disappearance of the gasoline, as distinct from the standing condition of friction, was the cause, for this was the only change in S prior to the occurrence of E. However, as one critic points out,

> There is strictly no causal connection between the absence of something and the failure of an event to happen. . . . The friction of the moving car with the surrounding air and the road down which it was proceeding caused the car to come to a stop.[23]

Ducasse, however, was unmoved by his critics and resolutely and finally equated "etiological necessity" with his formal definitions of "sufficient to" and "necessitated by" and insisted that necessity in this sense was directly perceivable. If C is the only change in S at t_1 and E the only change at t_2, and the times are immediately successive, then C is causally sufficient to E in S, and anyone who has perceived this only change has perceived causal sufficiency. Conversely, if C was the only change in S immediately prior to E, then E was necessitated by (as distinct from necessary to) C in S, and anyone who had perceived this only change and its result had perceived causal necessity.

---

[22] C. J. Ducasse, "Of the nature and efficacy of causes," *Philosophical Review*, Vol. XLI (1932), p. 397, and *CTN*, pp. 131-6.

[23] Sterling Lamprecht, "Causality" in *Essays in Honor of John Dewey*, ed. John Cross (New York: Henry Holt, 1937), pp. 201-2.

This definition of etiological necessity, it should be clear, runs into all the difficulties of the definition of causality pointed out earlier, but the claim that etiological necessity is literally perceivable raises additional fascinating epistemic problems. There is no problem in saying that changes C and E are directly perceived in some cases at least, like the snapping of the beam and the falling of the bridge; nobody would reject this contention. The problem, however, is to make sense out of the claim that we can directly perceive C as the *only* change in S immediately prior to E. There is clearly inference rather than perception involved here: we infer, e.g., that C was the only change in S at t_1 because we observed it and did not observe any other change even though we were alert and looked carefully. Surprisingly enough, Ducasse would admit that this description precisely fits the case, but nevertheless would claim that it still counts as perception. The reason for this is that he thinks some sort of inference is involved in all perception as distinct from a sensory given.[24] When one perceives a bird, one's "perceiving" consists not only in having certain visual sensations but in addition in *interpreting* these sensations, semiotically, as *signs* of the existence, at that time and place, of all that being a bird includes (being tangible, having blood, beak, wings, feathers, etc.). The same is supposedly true in the case of perceiving etiological necessity. When one perceives C as the only change in S at t_1, one's "perceiving" consists not only in having visual representations of C but, in addition, in interpreting these visual sensations as referring to the only change in S at t_1 by virtue of the fact that no other change was observed, etc.

Fascinating as this view may be, there seem to be fatal difficulties with Ducasse's claim that etiological necessity is directly perceivable. In the first place, his whole causal theory of perception would be rejected by most contemporary epistemologists. The immediate objection to his theory of perception, and all such examples like "perceiving" a bird, is that we are never aware of any inferential dimension in perceiving. Always and in every case we seem directly aware of the attributes of physical things, though the grounds for retrospectively justifying such perception may well refer to specific ways the object appeared to us. Ducasse's reply is that such inferences are automatic, telescoped, non-discursive, and unconscious, and hence pass unnoticed. To an ear unprejudiced by theory, such a reply is unconvincing since rejecting all the ordinary criteria of inference seems to amount to the admission that there is not any inference present after all.

The situation is even more problematic in the case of perceiving etiological necessity since a discursive element seems genuinely involved. I may perceive C and no other change at t_1 but not go through any inferential process to the effect: "I saw C; I did not see any other change; I was alert and looked carefully; hence C is (probably) the only change in S at t_1." If the answer is given that the inference went unnoticed because it was automatic, telescoped, non-discursive, and unconscious, the previous reply is again appropriate—such a response seems to deny any inferential nature in the process of ascribing it. Moreover, a person *may* go through a genuinely discursive process to establish this causal claim. A person may

---

[24]C. J. Ducasse, "How literally causation is perceivable," *Philosophy and Phenomenological Research*, Vol. 28 (1967-8), pp. 271-3, and *NMD*, pp. 304-99 (especially pp. 332-3). Cf. Nani L. Rankin, "A note on Ducasse's perceivable causation," *Philosophy and Phenomenological Research*, Vol. 28 (1967-8), pp. 269-70.

observe C in S at t_1 and really say to himself, "look around carefully," do so, find nothing, and conclude that C is indeed the only change in S at t_1. But then we have a case of actually inferring that C is the only change, in which case, however, we have not perceived C's being the only change in S.

It is particularly difficult to see how Ducasse can claim that etiological necessity can be directly perceived when the paradigm case for his very definition of causality requires that such necessity be inferred. The experimental method of single difference provides Ducasse with his definition of causality. Now the whole point in equating all factors except one in the control group and the experimental group is to have good reason for saying that C in S at t_1 was the only change in S and hence must be the cause. But great precaution and expert knowledge is required in setting up such a controlled experiment; the whole procedure is elaborately inferential and renders the claim that C is directly perceived as the *only* change, even in Ducasse's extended sense of "perceive," completely untenable. Ducasse might admit that in such a case the inference genuinely is too long-drawn-out to be accommodated even within his extended sense of "perceive" but still insist that in other cases etiological necessity can be directly perceived. We have already thrown doubt on this latter claim, and the point we would urge now is this: Ducasse's claim that etiological necessity can be directly perceived cannot apply where it crucially needs to apply, namely, in the paradigmatic case that gives his concept of nonlogical necessity its very meaning.

Another fundamental difficulty with Ducasse's discussion of nonlogical necessity centers around his assumption that "x caused y" simply entails "y is necessitated by x." Whence the justification of his identification of the causal relation with necessary connections between matters of fact? The main reason Ducasse gives for identifying the two is that there are perfectly good examples of causal talk in everyday life which imply nonlogical necessity. These expressions are clear and precise and serve perfectly good purposes. Hence there is no point in flying in the face of such usage as Hume does by insisting that all necessity is conceptual or logical in nature. Such a performance misses the whole point of philosophy. The job of the philosopher is to frame definitions which fit the ways in which crucial terms like "cause" are actually used in ordinary life and not invent prescriptive senses of such terms that satisfy the needs of ontological commitments which are, in principle, indefensible.[25] Ducasse offers many examples of ordinary usage to support his view: "When, for instance, we speak of 'the necessities of life' we mean certain physical things—food, water, etc.—without which life ceases; and the impossibility of its being maintained without them is not logical—not a matter of contradiction in terms—but physiological."[26] Again, we would say, and correctly so, that it is physiologically impossible for a man to live after his head has been severed from his body; it was physically impossible for the stump to be unmoved by the explosion of a certain amount of dynamite; and that it was psychologically impossible for Smith to hear fingernails grating on a blackboard without shivering. It would simply by flying in the face of linguistic facts to insist

---

[25] *NMD*, pp. 3-87; *TKC*, pp. 238-55; and *Philosophy As a Science* (New York: Oskar Piest, 1941).

[26] *NMD*, p. 114. [Reprinted in this text.]

that the necessity meant in all these cases was conceptual or logical in nature; rather the sufficiency and necessity involved here are relations between matters of fact.

The trouble with Ducasse's argument is that it contains little which a Humean need deny. The Humean willingly admits that we employ nonlogical concepts of necessity in ordinary discourse, but he offers a very simple and powerful argument to show that it is impossible to take these usages at face value. It is in principle impossible, he says, that C and not E be self-contradictory because it is always logically possible that nature might change its course. Then he has the problem of explaining why we mistakenly think there are necessary connections between matters of fact. Hume offers the projecting-habit-onto-events explanation, a poor one, to be sure, and one which contemporary Humeans reject, though they are no more able to produce a convincing explanation than he. But poor as these explanations are, the in-principle argument of Hume remains and nothing Ducasse writes even tends to rebut it. And unless the Humean argument is rebutted, Ducasse's contention that "x caused y" entails "y was etiologically necessitated by x" collapses. Moreover, as far as we can see, Ducasse's event ontology has no resource whatever for rebutting the Humean argument. Had he followed the lead of his examples and phrases and analysed the concepts of power and capacity in terms of the natures of particulars, he would have had the ingredients for an adequate reply to the in-principle argument. We shall return to this point later and discuss it in some detail.

4

While we have been critical of Ducasse's philosophy of causality, we believe that he has made contributions of permanent value to this topic. Though he never countered Hume's in-principle argument against nonlogical necessity, he criticized the positive doctrines of the Humeans in numerous incisive ways. His claim that any adequate analysis of "cause" must leave the meaning and truth value of ordinary causal assertions unchanged is sound and crucial, even though, in the face of Hume's argument, he does not show how such an analysis is possible. It should be pointed out that Ducasse advocated this sort of analytical meta-philosophy long before it was fashionable to do so and continued to insist upon it even though it became fashionable.

Moreover, Ducasse's distinction between cause and condition is more precise and sophisticated than any previous one and can usefully be accepted by one who nevertheless rejects the absolute nature of the distinction. His insistence upon the fact that we are sometimes directly aware of causal necessity, that we genuinely *perceive* upon occasion the causal relation, is also useful in drawing attention to the neglected non-Humean views of James and Whitehead, though, of course, the nature of the causal necessity allegedly perceived in all these cases is different. Ducasse's examples, in fact, suggest a way in which James' interesting view could be rephrased so that it would avoid the panpsychistic consequences James dreaded.

While we believe strongly that the non-Humean view of causality held by Ducasse has its virtues, we also believe that the view he almost held—the one suggested by his examples and phraseology—has far greater merit. We had a brief glimpse of this view in the previous section and will not amplify it much more in the present one. We have given detailed explanations and defenses of it else-where.[27] Suffice it to show here that, unlike Ducasse's view, it yields a funda-mental answer to Hume's in-principle argument against the possibility of nonlogical necessity.

Recall Ducasse's examples of a match bursting into flame, gasoline ex-ploding in the cylinders of a car, the branch bending, the glass breaking, and the crushing of the submarine. The atomic structure of phosphorus sulfide and gasoline, the weight of the bird and the falling stone, and the pressure of the deep water—all characteristics of the nature of some particular—explains why scratching the match on a rough surface made it burst into flame, turning on the ignition made the gasoline explode, the bird's alighting made the branch bend, the stone's falling made the glass break, and the deep water crushed the submarine—where "igniting," "exploding," "bending," "breaking," and "crushing" are causal verbs expressing the powers that particulars have by virtue of their natures to make certain events occur under specific releasing occasions like scratching, alighting, falling, and submerging.

The question immediately arises of what sort of relationship there is between the nature of a particular and the powers and capacities this nature helps explain. It cannot be a contingent one in the sense that particulars could lose all their powers and capacities, or special sets of them, and still be said to remain the same particulars in the sense that they still have the same natures. A liquid that smelled like gasoline but would not explode no matter what means of ignition were applied would not count as gasoline any longer, since a cluster of interrelated concepts and explanations would have broken down; just as a bird that was so diaphanous as never to bend a limb, or twig, however small, would not count as a bird any longer, but would necessarily turn out to be something seen in an ani-mated cartoon or the inhabitant of our dream world. The claim that atmospheric pressure failed to raise water in a pump, given the appropriate conditions in the cylinder of the pump, but nevertheless that air has weight and the atmospheric blanket remains, is simply self-contradictory, just as the claim that falling stones left all glasses in their paths unbroken even though the stones retained their weight and motion, and the glasses were not reinforced, is self-inconsistent. To talk about the nature of a particular remaining the same even though p loses the powers and capacities this nature helps explain, is to assert and deny at once that p has nature N. There is, in short a relation of natural necessity between what a thing is and what it is capable of doing and undergoing, and it is this relation of natural neces-sity that the conceptual necessity of the concept of cause reflects.

While a relation of nonlogical necessity exists between N of p and the powers and capacities of p, there is nothing self-contradictory, it is true, about the possibility of a change in N of p. Some changes in N of p, of course, do not count since they occur in a theoretical structure which explains the identity of p though change. Such a theoretical structure, however, presupposes certain fundamental p's which do not change themselves since these p's constitute an explanatory frame of reference (S). These p's are the ones that count. Now the crucial point is that there is nothing self-contradictory about the notion of change even in these fundamental p's, since no actual or possible S's entail the falsity of each other. Though there is a

[27]Madden, "A third view of causality," and Madden and Hare, "The Powers That Be."

necessity corresponding to the nature of the actual, this necessity does not imply that the actual is itself necessary in the sense that its meaning implies its existence. We happen to have the universe we do, though within any possible universe certain things would be bound to happen.

Now we are able to see the crucial fact that Hume's in-principle argument against the possibility of nonlogical necessity is mistaken. The argument, again, is this. If there were a necessary connection between C and E, then the conjunction of $C \cdot \sim E$ would be self-contradictory; but clearly it is not so, since there is nothing self-inconsistent about the concept of a change in the course of nature. Hence there can be no nonlogical necessity between C and E. However, it follows from our analysis that the conjunction of $C \cdot \sim E$ *is* self-consistent even though there is nothing self-contradictory about the notion of a change in the course of nature when this phrase is taken to mean a change in the nature of a fundamental p. There *is* something self-inconsistent in the conjunction of $C \cdot \sim E$ unless one puts double quotes around C to indicate that while "C" $\cdot \sim E$ is not self-contradictory the concept of x as C of E has been relinquished. It would simply be self-defeating to say that x has nature y which helps explain the occurrence of E, and hence is part of C of E, and yet x still has nature y when C occurs without E. This would be equivalent to saying that x at once both has and does not have nature y. The great error of Hume was to think mistakenly that " 'C' $\cdot \sim E$ is never self-contradictory" entails "$C \cdot \sim E$ is never self-contradictory." Or saying the same thing in a better way, and one that is closer to the historical facts, he never saw the ambiguity of the phrase "change in the course of nature" and so erroneously thought that because it is logically possible for nature to change at all it is impossible for there to be any nonlogical necessary connections in the world.

EDWARD H. MADDEN

25. A Third View of Causality*

There have been a number of alternatives offered to the Humean position on causality but they have not seemed very satisfactory, trying, as they usually do, to prove too much and ignoring much of value in what the historical Hume had to say. In what follows I will sketch a third view of causal necessity that seems more plausible to me than either the Humean or entailment theories we are generally offered as the only reasonable alternatives. I will show also what I take to be insurmountable difficulties in the contemporary Humean analysis of 'nomic necessity,' as well as trying to rebut certain objections that are bound to arise against my own view.

Reprinted by permission of the author and the publisher from Edward H. Madden, "A Third View of Causality," *The Review of Metaphysics* vol. 23, no. 1 (September 1969): 67-84. Footnotes included.

*Revised version of a paper read at the Dartmouth College Philosophy Colloquium, April 12, 1968. Discussions with Barry Cohen, James Humber, Kevin Traynor, and Eric Dayton were a help to me in formulating my ideas.

I

To begin with, there is a conceptual necessity implied in the very concept of cause itself, and in all concepts that have a causal element; and this definitional "must," far from being conventional or arbitrary, reflects the natural necessity of those physical systems which in fact constitute the nature of our universe.[1] The conceptual necessity of the concept of cause can be pointed up in the following way. Assume that we have good reason for saying at t_0 that f, g, h, and i are jointly sufficient to E and hence C of E. What would we say at t_1 if f, g, h, and i occurred but not E? We would clearly *not* say then, or ever, that while ordinarily these conditions are jointly sufficient for E, this time they were not; rather we would say that somehow we were mistaken in thinking that f, g, h, and i at t_1 were identical (except for location in space and time) with f, g, h, and i at t_0. We might have been mistaken in either of two ways. We might have mis-identified one of the conditions at t_1, erroneously thinking, say, that p was an f; or one or more of the conditions might have had its nature altered, losing some capacity or power it once had. In either case, we would withdraw the claim at t_1 that C was the cause of E. Since we would withdraw the use of C at t_1 and would never admit that f, g, h, and i at any t, if genuine instances of f, g, h, and i, would not produce E, we are clearly using C in such a way that actually producing E is part of its meaning. On the assumption that the conditions are genuinely the same (except for location in space and time), it follows, so to speak, from the principle of identity that they must produce the same effect.

So far we have seen how the concept of cause involves conceptual necessity, but the question immediately arises whether this necessity is only stipulative and conventional in nature or whether it actually tells us something about the nature of physical systems. The latter, it seems to me, is clearly the case if we take seriously our ordinary ways of thinking and see no compelling reason to depart from them. These ways have been taken seriously by such prima facie diverse thinkers as Aristotle, American radical empiricists, and certain Oxonian analysts, all of whom produce interestingly similar, though not identical, concepts of physical systems.[2]

To see that the conceptual necessity of 'cause' reflects the necessity of physical systems, consider the case of a suction pump. Let us say that the pressure of the air on the reservoir and the partial vacuum in the cylinder of the pump are the conditions jointly sufficient for raising the water up the pump and out the spigot. Ordinarily we would say that the atmosphere has the ability or power to push the water up the cylinder, when there is no counteracting pressure there, and that the water has the capacity, or disposition, to be pushed up the cylinder in the absence of air there. The power or ability of the atmosphere, in turn, would be

---

[1] Cf. E. H. Madden, "Causality and the Notion of Necessity," in forthcoming volume of *Boston Studies in the Philosophy of Science*.

[2] Among the radical empiricists, I have in mind particularly Sterling P. Lamprecht and among the Oxonian analysts Rom Harré and M. R. Ayers. See Lamprecht's *The Metaphysics of Naturalism* (New York, 1967), pp. 1-33, 112-145, and his "Of a Curious Reluctance to Recognize Causal Efficacy," *The Philosophical Review*, Vol. XXXIX (1930), pp. 403-414; Ayers' *The Refutation of Determinism* (London, 1968); C. J. Ducasse's *Nature, Mind, and Death* (La Salle, Ill., 1951), Chapter 8; and Richard Taylor's *Action and Purpose* (Englewood Cliffs, N.J., 1966).

explained by referring to the nature of the atmosphere—the atmosphere is a blanket of air around the surface of the earth; air has weight and so exerts pressure; and the farther down in the blanket of air the greater the weight and the greater the pressure, etc. While the power or ability of the atmosphere to raise water is understood by referring to its nature, such reference does not explain away the power. A Jaguar XK-E has the ability (is able, has the power) to do 120 m.p.h., and this ability is explained in terms of its having six cylinders, a certain kind of fuel injection pump, etc.—that is, in terms of the nature of the car.[3] But such explanations in terms of the nature of the car scarcely eliminate the notion that the car has power. 'Power', 'ability', and 'nature' are intimately interwoven and any effort to assign ontological priorities among them is as futile as trying to assign priorities among the concepts of particulars, properties, and relations. The ineliminability of 'power' and 'ability' shows up again on the highest level of explanation where one can only ascribe power without any understanding of a nature that helps explicate that power. Confining ourselves to classical physics, we would say, e.g., that the masses of the earth and the atmosphere have the power of attracting each other, but we do not know anything in the nature of the masses that explains the ability of mutual attraction. The ineliminable but non-mysterious powers and abilities of particular things, then, and not an ontological "tie that binds" causes and effects together is what the conceptual necessity of 'cause' reflects. The power is in the atmosphere, though it will not produce an effect unless the partial vacuum in the cylinder exists, just as the power is in the attraction of the barn and the earth when the latter collapses, though this effect would not have occurred unless the center beam had been removed. Running out of gasoline and the friction of tires on pavement are jointly sufficient for stopping the car, though it was the latter that had the power to stop the car, just as previously it was the exploding of the gasoline in the cylinder that provided the power to overcome that of friction.[4]

The concept 'x has the power to do y', it is interesting to note, catches what might be called the strong sense of 'potentiality', namely, 'what would automatically happen if interfering conditions were absent or taken away'. As long as gasoline is exploding in the cylinders, power is produced to overcome the normal operation of friction; and as long as the center beam is intact the attraction of the barn and earth is kept in check. But as soon as the gasoline runs out or the beam rots, the operation of these powers, a function of the structural and basic nature of our universe, comes into play. They finally produce the effect which had been held in abeyance by interfering conditions. Since interfering conditions cannot last forever, such potential events must eventually occur, though if the removal of the obstacles is under the control of man, the events need not occur at any given time.

In addition to the conceptual necessity involved in the concept of cause itself, there is conceptual necessity built into any concept whatever that has a causal component. Take, for example, the case of 'copper'.[5] For the scientist this term refers to something having the properties malleability, fusibility, ductility,

---

[3] Ayers, *The Refutation of Determinism*, pp. 84ff.

[4] It is this point which illuminates the discussions between Lemprecht and Ducasse. Cf. Lamprecht, *The Metaphysics of Naturalism*, p. 141, and Ducasse, "Of the Spurious Mystery in Causal Connections," *Philosophical Review*, Vol. XXXIX (1930), pp. 398-403.

[5] I am indebted here to Professor Ducasse's letters in the Ducasse-Dickinson Miller correspondence in my possession.

electric conductivity, density 8.92, atomic weight 63.54, and atomic number 29 (properties both dispositional and explanatory in nature, be it noted). If an O lacked any of these features it would not be called C, or, if one thought O was C but it turned out not to have one of these features one would withdraw the ascription of C. In short, the ascription of C to O at any given time necessarily implies the presence of a cluster of properties. The reason for this conceptual necessity is clear: all the dispositional properties are interwoven closely with the concepts of atomic structure and hence with each other, so that if any part were missing the whole conceptual framework would be vitiated and the ascription of the concept C would be pointless. Again, this conceptual necessity, far from being stipulative in nature, has important ontological implications.

The first thing to note is that we are dealing here with capacities to undergo rather than abilities to do, with dispositions to react in certain ways under given conditions rather than powers to act in certain ways when the occasion arises. The copper wire has a disposition to flatten out when struck by a hammer, to melt when heated to $1,083°$C., and to conduct an electric charge. Yet the dispositional concepts of malleability, fusibility, and conductivity are just as much explained by the atomic structure of copper as the power of the atmosphere to raise water is explained by the nature of the atmosphere. Capacities just as much as powers, what particulars or substances are able to undergo as well as what they are able to do, are explained as dimensions of what the thing is itself.[6] Both what particulars are able to undergo and to do are determined by their natures—or, better, are manifestations of their natures—and hence to talk about particulars remaining the same and yet lacking their capacities and powers is to assert and deny at once that O has nature C. If we had compelling reason to believe we were not mistaken in identifying O as continuous from t_0 to t_1, but at t_1 O was not malleable, then we would correctly conclude that O had different capacities and powers at t_1 and hence had undergone a change in nature and was no longer the particular C it was at t_0. It is physically impossible for a substance to act or react incompatibly with its own nature. It is not impossible for O to act and react differently at t_1 than at t_0, but what is impossible is for it to do so and remain the same substance. In short, there is a natural necessity between what a thing is and what it is capable of doing and undergoing, and it is this natural necessity that the conceptual necessity of 'copper' reflects.

There seems, however, to be an immediate problem with this view, since some individuals do gain or lose certain capacities or powers but do not thereby lose their identity—they still have the same nature.[7] A drug may lose its effectiveness over a period of time, photographic paper will not make prints after a while, and a person may lose his capacity to remember names; but the drug, paper, and person do not thereby lose their identities. This is only a *prima facie* problem, however, since such changes in powers and capacities themselves occur in some theoretical ambit within which they are explained, and hence the overall theory provides the invariable and identical nature of x which continues constant throughout the changes while explaining them. Such theoretical structures also presuppose

---

[6] Cf. Rom Harré, "Powers and Qualities," part of a full scale work in production. I am indebted to Professor Harré for letting me see this article.

[7] *Ibid.* Cf. Ayers, *The Refutation of Determinism*, pp. 84-89.

what might be called the nature of some "fundamental particulars," space and time, etc., in the sense that their natures are taken as unchanging in order to explain those particulars which are held to be identical through changes.

II

The notion of causal or physical necessity is far from simple in nature and needs to be seen from different angles to be fully understood. Two new angles will be introduced in the present section—the direct experience of causal power or efficacy, on the one hand, and an examination of the nature of scientific explanation, on the other. There is a vast literature on both questions, so I will restrict myself severely to clarifying what I take to be fundamental issues.

To begin with, there is a great deal of confusion surrounding the claim that we are sometimes directly aware of causal power or efficacy. Critics often dismiss the claim out of hand because no one, including Hume, they say, denies we have an experience of causal connection—the question is: what is the correct philosophical analysis of this fact?[8] Critics are also suspicious of the claim because it seems to lead inevitably to pan-psychism or animism.[9] However, both of these criticisms are misguided and reflect a lack of appreciation of what a sophisticated formulation of the direct-experience-of-causality view would be.

Hume, it is true, never doubted that we have an experience of causal connectedness, and provided the following philosophical analysis of it. Since we do not have the idea of necessary connection between events, it must be derived somehow from experience. However, we are unable to find the original of this idea either in the impressions of the senses or in the internal impressions of volition. Since we do not see, feel, or hear causal necessity the idea of it cannot be derived from the impressions of our senses. Nor can it be traced to any single "internal impression," not even to our consciousness of the influence of the will. We are never able, after all, to predict with certainty that an act of willing will have its expected results. Moreover, we are not directly aware of the causal power that raises the arm because the cause includes, besides willing to raise the arm, many other neural and muscular conditions and events with which we cannot be directly acquainted. Hume concludes that the original of the idea of necessary connection, since it does not arise from a single impression, must arise from a repetition of similar instances which produces the habit or customary transition of the imagination from one object to its usual attendant. One comes to *feel* the events to be connected, though they are not, for all that, shown to be actually connected.

The advocate of direct experience claims that Hume's analysis is faulty and provides an alternate one of his own—where 'analysis', however, is not equivalent to 'providing a definition'.[10] In briefest of outlines the strategy of the most sophisti-

---

[8] T. R. Miles, "Michotte's Experiments and the Views of Hume," in A. Michotte, *The Perception of Causality* (New York, 1963), pp. 410-415; and D. W. Hamlyn, *The Psychology of Perception* (London, 1957), pp. 76ff.

[9] A. J. Ayer, *The Foundations of Empirical Knowledge* (London, 1964). SML edition, pp. 183-199.

[10] Lamprecht and Ducasse are the most sophisticated of the direct-experience-of-causality advocates. William James states the position well but cannot see how to avoid pan-psychism. Alfred North Whitehead also defends this view and unenthusiastically accepts certain pan-psychic implications.

cated direct-experience advocate has three parts. First, he rejects Hume's associa-
tionistic explanation of how we come to have an idea of necessary connection. This
part of Hume's thesis is factual in nature and can be seen to be clearly mistaken in
the light of modern psychological investigations of the origin of the concept of
causality. Second, he rejects Hume's claim that "internal impressions" cannot yield
the concept of physical necessity. In the case of voluntarily raising my arm I do
experience directly a power of will involved in producing the effect. It is true that I
do not experience a power relation between the whole set of conditions jointly
sufficient to moving my arm, but Hume's assumption that if power is to be experienced at all it must be experienced between all necessary conditions and the effect
is simply unwarranted—just as Hume's assumption that the only legitimate sense of
'cause' is 'set of conditions jointly sufficient for e' is unwarranted. Third, the
advocate of direct perception must avoid the claim that only in volitional cases is he
directly aware of causal power. If he does not avoid the "inferential predicament"
he will inevitably land in pan-psychism and animism. One gets into the inferential
predicament by arguing in the following way. I feel the force of the wind bending
me and conclude that it must also be the force of the wind bending the slanting
tree. There is, however, much psychological and common-sense evidence (including
the use of causal expressions) to suggest that we directly apprehend the operation
of power between objects and events even before we experience it between objects
or events and ourselves. The paradigm for direct experience of power is wind-
bending-tree not wind-bending-me. It is instructive to compare the inferential
predicament in causality with its counterpart in the causal theory of perception,
where one has a visual impression, a tactual impression, and so on, and then "in-
fers" somehow the physical object which causes all the impressions. The "inference" here, however, is just as evanescent and unlocated as the supposed inference
in causal experience from wind-bending-me to wind-bending-tree.

Now let us turn our attention briefly to the nature of scientific explanation and see what implications it has for the concept of causal necessity. Recall
again the power of the atmosphere to raise water in the cylinder of a pump. Call
gravitational theory U' and the water going up the pump U. U must occur relative
to U', we say, because the latter, plus information to the effect that there is a
partial vacuum in the cylinder, explains why U happens rather than something else,
say, the water's turning purple. If something else like this could have happened, we
would not have succeeded in explaining why U happened rather than it. Conversely,
we have good reason for believing that U' is the case because it is indirectly and
independently established by various U sets of events and laws that it conceptually
unites. Hence, the necessity in a body of knowledge follows from what must be the
case if U' is true, and we have good reason for believing that U' is the case. It does
not follow, however, that U' is necessarily true in the sense that its meaning entails
its existence. U' is not necessarily true in the sense that it is the only possible
physical framework. Rather the point is that given U', certain U's are "hypothet-
ically necessary" in the sense that, given U', the denial of these statements would
produce inconsistencies in the theory. Even though this universe is not the only
possible one, the unifications of U's suggest that it is the actual one, and the
adequacy of the theory means that it reflects the nature of *this* universe. Insofar as
this theory is adequate, it is necessary, since a change in the physical universe would
involve a change in the nature of the particulars of that universe; and, supposing

such a change to occur, there would be a new universe with a new nature, a new adequate theory, etc. So there is a necessity corresponding to the nature of the actual, though this necessity does not imply that the actual is itself necessary in the sense that its denial is self-contradictory.

III

The contemporary Humean himself believes that there are "nomic universals" which are more than mere generalizations over time, but insists that such universals can be analyzed adequately within his own frame of reference without requiring the concept of physical necessity.[11] I believe he does not sustain the claim, and in principle cannot, though it will take a bit of digging to show why not.

Roughly stated, the dominant contemporary Humean account of a particular causal statement would be: 'x is the cause of y' means 'there is a set of initial conditions x, a set of subsequent conditions y, and there is a law or set of laws L, and a set of meaning postulates M (definitions, semantical rules, etc.), such that $L \cdot M \cdot x$ entails y and y is not entailed by any of the following: $x, M, L, x \cdot M, x \cdot L$, $M \cdot L$, or $Z \cdot M \cdot L$, where z is any proper subset of x'. If statistical laws are included in L, then $L \cdot M \cdot x$ entails only 'y is probable' or 'y is highly probable'. L, in turn, is characterized as a "nomic universal" and distinguished from accidental and summative universals in the following way. Nomic universals are those which in addition to being true are *lawlike;* and universals are lawlike whenever in addition to being true they share some intrinsic characteristic like 'contain only purely qualitative predicates', 'are unrestricted in scope', 'have a scope not closed to further argumentation', and 'the evidence for which does not coincide with the scope of predication'; or when they have certain epistemic relations to some corpus of scientific or common-sense knowledge. While nomic universals of this sort give the required sense of universality beyond mere generality over time, they do not commit one to any non-Humean concept of physical or causal necessity. One has, so to speak, the cash equivalent of 'necessity' without any ontological mortgages.

There are, however, a number of difficulties with this contemporary formulation of the Humean thesis, some of which, like difficulties with the deduction requirement, have been pointed out endlessly. There are also difficulties with the proposed definition-in-use because it confuses the meaning of a causal assertion with certain reasons that legitimately might be given for saying that some x is the cause of y. It is also perfectly legitimate in various prudential, legal, and scientific contexts to single out one of the antecedent conditions as cause, though this is no striking criticism since essentially the same Humean analysis could be reformulated to fit such contexts.[12] The criticism I am interested in pressing centers rather around the concepts of "nomic universal" and "lawlikeness." The latter concept is itself untenable and hence no adequate substitute for the former. Conclusive counter-examples have been given for all the intrinsic characteristics which have been suggested as the common factor of nomic universals, and various counter-

---

[11] In what follows, by "contemporary Humean" I mean especially Professors Hempel and Nagel.

[12] Cf. Bernard Berofsky, "Causality and General Laws," *Journal of Philosophy*, Vol. LXIII (1966), p. 150. [Reprinted in this text.]

examples destructive of different strands in the epistemic characteristic have been offered.[13] It is sometimes argued against the latter counter-examples that they are inadequate because no theoretical terms are involved in their "higher-order laws," but Murray Kitely and I have constructed in detail a hypothetico-deductive system with theoretical terms which, nevertheless, has no vestige of "nomic universality" about it.[14]

The overall result of these discussions is that the whole concept of lawlikeness is hopeless. Every criterion proposed has a counter-example which eliminates it as the characteristic which all laws, plus being true, have in common. To be sure, it is possible that there are other criteria, but one has a tired feeling that they too would have counter-examples. The plain truth of the matter is that there is nothing that all laws have in common which, plus being true, makes them nomic universals. There is no set of necessary and sufficient conditions which a universal must meet before it can be called a "nomic universal." Some universals are called laws by scientists for a variety of reasons, none of which is necessary and any one of which may be sufficient if it does not conflict with the others. Some of these reasons are partially related, others mutually independent. Universals are sometimes called laws, depending upon the context, e.g., when they fit into an established body of knowledge or connect well with what we already know, when they have predictive or explanatory power, when they contain theoretical terms or are logically related to an assertion that does, when they occur in a model theory, when their initial conditions fill in spatio-temporal gaps, when different types of instances confirm them, and even when only the multiplication of instances confirms them, if they do not conflict with any of the other criteria. The presumption, in short, is that any generalization counts as a law unless there is good counter-evidence. Epistemic relations in a given context, thus, are important in deciding not only what counts as a law but what counts as an accidental universal also.

The contemporary Humean might reply by saying that he is convinced that searching for what all laws have in common is a mistake and will abandon the concept of lawlikeness. He also agrees that a body of knowledge is necessary both to characterize a universal as accidental and as a law. But given the fact that in specific contexts we *can* distinguish laws from accidents we have, he says, all the Humean needs. Such laws are nomic universals and support counter-factual inferences while accidental universals do not.

Although this new position would be a great improvement over the previous one, nevertheless it is not without difficulties itself. Take the case of the suction pump again. Here we say that 'whenever there is a partial vacuum, water goes up the cylinder' is a nomic universal because it can be inferred from what we know about atmospheric pressure and gravitational attraction. However, as we indicated, there are counter-examples from which we can infer non-nomic universals from a body of integrated knowledge, whether or not theoretical terms are

[13] Roderick M. Chisholm, "Law Statements and Counterfactual Inference," *Analysis*, Vol. XV (1955), pp. 97-105; Edward H. Madden, "Definition and Reduction," *Philosophy of Science*, Vol. 28 (1961), particularly pp. 390-394, and "Discussion: Ernest Nagel's *The Structure of Science*," *Philosophy of Science*, Vol. 30 (1963), pp. 64-70.

[14] Edward H. Madden and Murray Kiteley, "Postulates and Meaning," *Philosophy of Science*, Vol. 29 (1962), pp. 66-78.

involved in the higher-order "laws." Now what distinguishes the pump case as genuinely nomic as contrasted with the counter-examples? It is that the counter-examples have no power to explain in fact why any particular conclusion must follow rather than something else. The counter-examples are destructive only of alleged formal characteristics shared by all instances of 'law'; they are not counter-examples of genuine laws. The only counter-example of a law would be to show that in fact there was some negative case, and we did not have a law after all. In a genuine case of nomic universality like that of the pump, however, there is an actual explanation in terms of the powers, capacities, and natures of substances why one result rather than another had to be the case—why, that is, the water must go up the cylinder rather than turning purple. But if a common-sense or scientific explanation genuinely shows why something must be the case rather than something else, then the Humean position must be abandoned as inadequate for explicating 'nomic necessity'.

Humeans sometimes try to salvage the concept of nomic necessity by giving a sense of "must" with one hand and taking it away with the other. It is true, they say, that x has to occur, or "must" occur, rather than something else because some system of knowledge requires or explains it. However, the most fundamental hypothesis of all, whatever constitutes the framework in which this "must" relation gets its meaning, is itself not necessary but only contingent and hence the whole system ultimately is contingent and not causally or physically necessary.

Here certainly the effort to get the cash value of nomic necessity without ontological mortgages is most jarring. The major error of the Humean consists in thinking that because the whole system is contingent what happens within the system is also contingent. But the latter is a non sequitur. It is true that there is an infinite number of possible universes and a contingent fact that we happen to have the one we do. To say our universe is contingent is to say that there is nothing about its nature that renders its existence necessary. But from the fact that our universe is not a necessary one it does not follow that, given our universe, what happens within it is not necessary. If something else could happen within it, then our actual universe would have a different constitution than it does have. And if something else than what must happen could happen within any system, then no explanation within that system could ever occur because one would not have succeeded in explaining the occurrence of one event rather than another.

IV

We have rejected the Humean analysis of "nomic necessity" as in principle untenable and have put in its place the concept of physical or causal necessity, a notion, we have claimed, which is internally sound and dovetails with our intuitions, common sense, and the structure of scientific explanation. However, there can be little doubt that contemporary Humeans would return the compliment by rejecting the present analysis as not simply false in detail but unsound in principle. So it is necessary for me to meet these complaints before it can be said I have mounted anything like an adequate defense of my third view of causality. What criticism the Humean would offer is not difficult to guess, since any notion of physical necessity goes against what he sees as eternal verities—principles which, he feels, have been established beyond doubt by now.

(i) In principle there can be no concept of necessity in the causal relation because the conjunction of C·~E is never self-contradictory. This insight supposedly applies to all efforts to show that physical necessity is an irreducible concept. There is no self-contradiction in saying that water in the reservoir turns purple instead of going up the cylinder when a partial vacuum is created there, or that water freezes when heated, or that air pressure decreases with depth, no matter how unexpected these results might be. The reason that asserting C·~E is never self-contradictory is that the notion of a change in the course of nature is not self-contradictory.

The question immediately arises of what a Humean means by 'a change in the course of nature is not self-contradictory'. The only plausible answer is this: there are logically consistent systems of statements of the form *if x, then y* which do not conform to the way things are, and there is nothing in these systems and in the system U' which does fit our universe which *entails* the falsity of each other. But there is nothing in this analysis which counts against my position. The fact that all possible U's do not entail the falsity of each other is equivalent to saying that no U' is necessarily true in the sense that its meaning entails its existence. Not only does this view not conflict with what I hold, but indeed I have urged this point myself. However, while it is perfectly true that there is nothing self-contradictory about the notion of a change in the course of nature, there is something self-contradictory in the conjunction of C·~E unless one puts double quotes around C to indicate that while "C"·~E is not self-contradictory the notion of x as C of E has been relinquished. If "C"·~E occurred there was a change in the nature of x, and it is no longer C. It *would be* self-contradictory to say that x has nature y which explains the occurrence of E, and hence is C of E, and yet x still has nature y when E occurs without C. All of these points can be applied in detail to the example of 'copper' by the reader. There is a conceptual and physical necessity between the nature of O and how it acts and reacts, so that if the latter changes so has the former. Hence it is quite true that physical systems must always produce their results, though the Humean would be quite right in insisting that there is nothing self-contradictory in the concept of a change in the nature of a fundamental particular. There is nothing in what I have said that entails the necessity of the nature of any O remaining unchanged throughout time.

(ii) Even if the notion of causal necessity were acceptable, nothing could ever be known to be so related, since it is always logically possible to be mistaken whatever causal claim is made. There may be good evidence that eating strawberries caused my rash, but then I discover a case of "C"·~E and conclude that it was not strawberries after all. There seems to be good evidence now that C is some ingredient found in several foods, one of which was always eaten before the rash appeared. But it is always possible that this causal claim too is false, since others like it for which there seemed to be good evidence have turned out to be false (the rash, after all, always appeared after eating strawberries before t_1), and so on, until the limit is reached—it is logically possible that every claim to the effect that x is the cause of y may be mistaken, no matter what x and y may be. Now it does not follow that because it is always possible to be mistaken about causal claims, that x and y are not necessarily related; but it does follow that they can never be known to be so related.

This argument, seemingly dependent only on the Humean insight that 'C·~E' is never self-contradictory, in fact proves too much, and leads to skepticism about any knowledge claims whatever.[15] The isomorphs of this type argument are unlimited. Even though there are accepted techniques for distinguishing veridical and illusory perception, it is always possible that the allegedly verdical ones are illusory or hallucinatory beyond the range of the accepted techniques to discover. While it would not follow that because it is always possible to be mistaken about perceptual claims that there are no physical objects, it would follow that they could never be known to exist. Again, even though there are accepted techniques for distinguishing a fair sample from a biased one, it is always possible that the allegedly fair sample is biased beyond the range of the accepted sampling techniques to discover. While it would not follow from this argument that there are no fair samples, it would follow that one could never know he had one.

To the assumption in this argument that 'to know x' is equivalent to 'being able to demonstrate x', a tempting but nevertheless mistaken reply is often given, though less frequently in recent years. According to this reply, key terms of the "skeptic's" argument are being used in a self-contradictory way. This type of reply has many variants of which the following is one extremely condensed variation.[16] Take the case of 'fair sample'. Though the specifications in the definiens are far from definite and precise, and though it is over-simplified in other ways, this definition of 'fair sample' is apparently correct: 'sample that has been randomly selected, stratified, etc.'. Now if the skeptic uses 'fair sample' in this regular sense, he is referring to a kind of sample revealed by one of the vague requirements or some refinement thereof. If he does utilize this meaning, but also talks about a "fair sample" which one can never know he has, or have good reason to believe he has, no matter how many or refined the requirements it meets, then his use of the term is self-inconsistent, meaning that at once it both does and does not satisfy the regular requirements of a fair sample. If the use of the term is to avoid self-inconsistency, it must function in some new sense. Since no new sense is provided, however, if it is not self-inconsistent, it is vacuous.

The decisive difficulty with this reply, it is important to see, is one that it shares, strangely enough, with the Humean tradition itself, namely, the confusion between the meaning of a term and evidence for its justifiable application. Except for one who wants to prove a point, 'fair sample' does not mean 'sample that has been stratified . . .' but rather 'sample that reflects the ratio of 'x's to y's in the whole population'. Random selection and stratification, then, can be seen as reasons for claiming that any given sample is a fair one. By identifying the meanings of 'fair sample' and 'sample that is stratified . . .', a person would be unable to give as a reason why a given sample is a fair one the facts that it has been stratified, randomly selected, etc.; but this, of course, is precisely what one wants to be able to do.

The beginning of a more appropriate reply to the Humean consists in pointing out that the possibility of being mistaken is no good reason for thinking one is mistaken. Recall the problem of distinguishing between accidental and nomic universals. Any universal counts as a law unless there is counter-evidence which

---

[15] Madden, *The Structure of Scientific Thought* (Boston, 1960), pp. 340-342.
[16] *Ibid.*, pp. 291-292, 312-317.

shows why it must be construed as accidental. And so it is with any fundamental distinction, whether it be between accidental and nomic universals, veridical and illusory experiences, or fair and biased samples—a body of knowledge is presupposed in which the distinctions themselves make sense. To call x accidental, illusory, or biased, and to call x nomic, veridical, or fair, all require positive reasons drawn from this frame of reference; simply pointing out that it is logically possible to be mistaken wholly leaves open the question whether one is or not, just as simply pointing out that it is logically possible one is correct wholly leaves open the question whether one is or not. One fears he has been shown to be wrong in his basic beliefs by the skeptic's argument, but he has only been shown that it is impossible to *demonstrate* their correctness. But we are reassured when we remember that a framework is presupposed for saying either that x is mistaken or is correct.

The historical Hume, it must be noted finally, can be interpreted in such a way that he is both an epistemic skeptic and yet draws back from this position partially by arguments similar to the one above. According to this interpretation of Hume, he is only claiming that constant conjunction is all we *perceive* of the causal relation, not that this constitutes the ontological *nature* of the relation. Hume rejects the principle that "nothing exists but experience" but concludes that what 'cause' might denote beyond constant conjunction must forever remain unknown. Although we ordinarily mean 'necessary connection' when we use the concept of causation, and believe that such a connection has ontological status, neither the definition nor the belief can be justified by reason or experience. And yet, Hume says, just as one believes in the existence of the external world by instinct, so nature has seen fit to set up within one's thought processes a habit or custom which impels one to accept causation as necessary. The reasonings concerning cause and effect thus are "more properly an art of the sensitive than of the cognitive part of our natures." And though reason is unequal to the task of proving that the external world exists and that there are necessary connections between objects and events, still it is equally incapable of proving these things impossible. This, plus the fact that the instinct which compels us to believe these things is useful, shows that it would be foolhardy to believe otherwise.

The moral of this historical excursion is twofold. It suggests that Hume himself would not accept the last "in principle" argument against my position and that, in general, Hume would not make a good contemporary Humean. It should be clear that, given this interpretation of Hume, my views on causality are no further from this historical Hume on one side than contemporary Humeans are from him on the other.

DONALD DAVIDSON

26. *Causal Relations**

What is the logical form of singular causal statements like: 'The flood caused the famine', 'The stabbing caused Caesar's death', 'The burning of the house caused the roasting of the pig'? This question is more modest than the question how we know such statements are true, and the question whether they can be analyzed in terms of, say, constant conjunction. The request for the logical form is modest because it is answered when we have identified the logical or grammatical roles of the words (or other significant stretches) in the sentences under scrutiny. It goes beyond this to define, analyze, or set down axioms governing, particular words or expressions.

I

According to Hume, "we may define a cause to be an object, followed by another, and where all the objects similar to the first are followed by objects similar to the second." This definition pretty clearly suggests that causes and effects are entities that can be named or described by singular terms; probably events, since one can follow another. But in the *Treatise,* under "rules by which to judge of causes and effects," Hume says that "where several different objects produce the same effect, it must be by means of some quality, which we discover to be common amongst them. For as like effects imply like causes, we must always ascribe the causation to the circumstances, wherein we discover the resemblance." Here it seems to be the "quality" or "circumstances" of an event that is the cause rather than the event itself, for the event itself is the same as others in some respects and different in other respects. The suspicion that it is not events, but something more closely tied to the descriptions of events, that Hume holds to be causes, is fortified by Hume's claim that causal statements are never necessary. For if events were causes, then a true description of some event would be 'the cause of *b*', and, given that such an event exists, it follows logically that the cause of *b* caused *b*.

Mill said that the cause "is the sum total of the conditions positive and negative taken together . . . which being realized, the consequent invariably follows." Many discussions of causality have concentrated on the question whether Mill was right in insisting that the "real Cause" must include all the antecedent conditions that jointly were sufficient for the effect, and much ingenuity has been spent on discovering factors, pragmatic or otherwise, that guide and justify our

Reprinted by permission of the author and the publisher from Donald Davidson, "Causal Relations," the *Journal of Philosophy* vol. 64, no. 21 (November 9, 1967): 691-703. Footnotes included.

*Presented in APA symposium of the same title, December 28, 1967.

I am indebted to Harry Lewis and David Nivison, as well as to other members of seminars at Stanford University to whom I presented the ideas in this paper during 1966/67, for many helpful comments. I have profited greatly from discussion with John Wallace of the questions raised here; he may or may not agree with my answers. My research was supported in part by the National Science Foundation.

choice of some "part" of the conditions as the cause. There has been general agreement that the notion of cause may be at least partly characterized in terms of sufficient and (or) necessary conditions.[1] Yet it seems to me we do not understand how such characterizations are to be applied to particular causes.

Take one of Mill's examples: some man, say Smith, dies, and the cause of his death is said to be that his foot slipped in climbing a ladder. Mill would say we have not given the whole cause, since having a foot slip in climbing a ladder is not always followed by death. What we were after, however, was not the cause of death in general but the cause of Smith's death: does it make sense to ask under what conditions Smith's death invariably follows? Mill suggests that part of the cause of Smith's death is "the circumstance of his weight," perhaps because if Smith had been light as a feather his slip might not have injured him. Mill's explanation of why we don't bother to mention this circumstance is that it is too obvious to bear mention, but it seems to me that if it was Smith's fall that killed him, and Smith weighed twelve stone, then Smith's fall was the fall of a man who weighed twelve stone, whether or not we know it or mention it. How could Smith's actual fall, with Smith weighing, as he did, twelve stone, be any more efficacious in killing him than Smith's actual fall?

The difficulty has nothing to do with Mill's sweeping view of the cause, but attends any attempt of this kind to treat particular causes as necessary or sufficient conditions. Thus Mackie asks, "What is the exact force of [the statement of some experts] that this short-circuit caused this fire?" And he answers, "Clearly the experts are not saying that the short-circuit was a necessary condition for this house's catching fire at this time; they know perfectly well that a short-circuit somewhere else, or the overturning of a lighted oil stove . . . might, if it had occurred, have set the house on fire" (*ibid.*, 245). Suppose the experts know what they are said to; how does this bear on the question whether the short circuit was a necessary condition of this particular fire? For a short circuit elsewhere could not have caused *this* fire, nor could the overturning of a lighted oil stove.

To talk of particular events as conditions is bewildering, but perhaps causes aren't events (like the short circuit, or Smith's fall from the ladder), but correspond rather to sentences (perhaps like the fact that this short circuit occurred, or the fact that Smith fell from the ladder). Sentences can express conditions of truth for others—hence the word 'conditional'.

If causes correspond to sentences rather than singular terms, the logical form of a sentence like:

(1) The short circuit caused the fire.

would be given more accurately by:

(2) *The fact that* there was a short circuit *caused it to be the case that* there was a fire.

In (2) the italicized words constitute a sentential connective like 'and' or 'if . . . then . . .'. This approach no doubt receives support from the idea that causal laws are universal conditionals, and singular causal statements ought to be instances of

---

[1] For a recent example, with reference to many others, see J. L. Mackie, "Causes and Conditions," *American Philosophical Quarterly*, II, 4 (October 1965): 245-264.

them. Yet the idea is not easily implemented. Suppose, first that a causal law is (as it is usually said Hume taught) nothing but a universally quantified material conditional. If (2) is an instance of such, the italicized words have just the meaning of the material conditional, 'If there was a short circuit, then there was a fire'. No doubt (2) entails this, but not conversely, since (2) entails something stronger, namely the conjunction 'There was a short circuit *and* there was a fire'. We might try treating (2) as the conjunction of the appropriate law and 'There was a short circuit and there was a fire'—indeed this seems a possible interpretation of Hume's definition of cause quoted above—but then (2) would no longer be an instance of the law. And aside from the inherent implausibility of this suggestion as giving the logical form of (2) (in contrast, say, to giving the grounds on which it might be asserted) there is also the oddity that an inference from the fact that there was a short circuit and there was a fire, and the law, to (2) would turn out to be no more than a conjoining of the premises.

Suppose, then, that there is a non-truth-functional causal connective, as has been proposed by many.[2] In line with the concept of a cause as a condition, the causal connective is conceived as a conditional, though stronger than the truth-functional conditional. Thus Arthur Pap writes, "The distinctive property of causal implication as compared with material implication is just that the falsity of the antecedent is no ground for inferring the truth of the causal implication" (212). If the connective Pap had in mind were that of (2), this remark would be strange, for it is a property of the connective in (2) that the falsity of either the "antecedent" or the "consequent" is a ground for inferring the falsity of (2). That treating the causal connective as a kind of conditional unsuits it for the work of (1) or (2) is perhaps even more evident from Burks' remark that "p is causally sufficient for q is logically equivalent to $\sim q$ is causally sufficient for $\sim p$" (369). Indeed, this shows not only that Burks' connective is not that of (2), but also that it is not the subjunctive causal connective 'would cause'. My tickling Jones would cause him to laugh, but his not laughing would not cause it to be the case that I didn't tickle him.

These considerations show that the connective of (2), and hence by hypothesis of (1), cannot, as is often assumed, to be a conditional of any sort, but they do not show that (2) does not give the logical form of singular causal statements. To show this needs a stronger argument, and I think there is one, as follows.

It is obvious that the connective in (2) is not truth-functional, since (2) may change from true to false if the contained sentences are switched. Nevertheless, substitution of singular terms for others with the same extension in sentences like (1) and (2) does not touch their truth value. If Smith's death was caused by the fall from the ladder and Smith was the first man to land on the moon, then the fall from the ladder was the cause of the death of the first man to land on the moon. And if the fact that there was a fire in Jones's house caused it to be the case that the pig was roasted, and Jones's house is the oldest building on Elm street, then the fact that there was a fire in the oldest building on Elm street caused it to be the

---

[2] For example by: Mackie, *op. cit.*, p. 254; Arthur Burks, "The Logic of Causal Propositions," *Mind*, LX, 239 (July 1951): 363-382; and Arthur Pap, "Disposition Concepts and Extensional Logic," in *Minnesota Studies in the Philosophy of Science*, II, ed. by H. Feigl, M. Scriven, and G. Maxwell (Minneapolis: Univ. of Minnesota Press, 1958), pp. 196-224.

case that the pig was roasted. We must accept the principle of extensional substitution, then. Surely also we cannot change the truth value of the likes of (2) by substituting logically equivalent sentences for sentences in it. Thus (2) retains its truth if for 'there was a fire' we substitute the logically equivalent '$\hat{x}$ ($x = x$ & there was a fire) = $\hat{x}$ ($x = x$)'; retains it still if for the left side of this identity we write the coextensive singular term '$\hat{x}$ ($x = x$ & Nero fiddled)'; and still retains it if we replace '$\hat{x}$ ($x = x$ & Nero fiddled) = $\hat{x}$ ($x = x$)' by the logically equivalent 'Nero fiddled'. Since the only aspect of 'there was a fire' and 'Nero fiddled' that matters to this chain of reasoning is the fact of their material equivalence, it appears that our assumed principles have led to the conclusion that the main connective of (2) is, contrary to what we supposed, truth-functional.[3]

Having already seen that the connective of (2) cannot be truth-functional, it is tempting to try to escape the dilemma by tampering with the principles of substitution that led to it. But there is another, and, I think, wholly preferable way out: we may reject the hypothesis that (2) gives the logical form of (1), and with it the ideas that the 'caused' of (1) is a more or less concealed sentential connective, and that causes are fully expressed only by sentences.

II

Consider these six sentences:

(3) *It is a fact that* Jack fell down.
(4) Jack fell down *and* Jack broke his crown.
(5) Jack fell down *before* Jack broke his crown.
(6) Jack fell down, *which caused it to be the case that* Jack broke his crown.
(7) *Jones forgot the fact that* Jack fell down.
(8) *That* Jack fell down *explains the fact that* Jack broke his crown.

Substitution of equivalent sentences for, or substitution of coextensive singular terms or predicates in, the contained sentences, will not alter the truth value of (3) or (4): here extensionality reigns. In (7) and (8), intensionality reigns, in that similar substitution in or for the contained sentences is not guaranteed to save truth. (5) and (6) seem to fall in between; for in them substitution of coextensive singular terms preserves truth, whereas substitution of equivalent sentences does not. However this last is, as we just saw with respect to (2), and hence also (6), untenable middle ground.

Our recent argument would apply equally against taking the 'before' of (5) as the sentential connective it appears to be. And of course we don't interpret 'before' as a sentential connective, but rather as an ordinary two-place relation true of ordered pairs of times; this is made to work by introducing an extra place into

---

[3] This argument is closely related to one spelled out by Dagfinn Føllesdal [in "Quantification into Causal Context" in *Boston Studies in the Philosophy of Science*, II, ed. R. S. Cohen and M. W. Wartofsky (New York: Humanities, 1966), pp. 263-274] to show that unrestricted quantification into causal contexts leads to difficulties. His argument is in turn a direct adaptation of Quine's [*Word and Object* (Cambridge, Mass.: MIT Press, 1960), pp. 197-198] to show that (logical) modal distinctions collapse under certain natural assumptions. My argument derives directly from Frege.

the predicates ('*x* fell down' becoming '*x* fell down at *t*') and an ontology of times to suit. The logical form of (5) is made perspicuous, then, by:

> (5') There exist times *t* and *t'* such that Jack fell down at *t*, Jack broke his crown at *t'*, and *t* preceded *t'*.

This standard way of dealing with (5) seems to me essentially correct, and I propose to apply the same strategy to (6), which then comes out:

> (6') There exist events *e* and *e'* such that *e* is a falling down of Jack, *e'* is a breaking of his crown by Jack, and *e* caused *e'*.

Once events are on hand, an obvious economy suggests itself: (5) may as well be construed as about events rather than times. With this, the canonical version of (5) becomes just (6'), with 'preceded' replacing 'caused'. Indeed, it would be difficult to make sense of the claim that causes precede, or at least do not follow, their effects if (5) and (6) did not thus have parallel structures. We will still want to be able to say when an event occurred, but with events this requires an ontology of pure numbers only. So 'Jack fell down at 3 P.M.' says that there is an event *e* that is a falling down of Jack, and the time of *e*, measured in hours after noon, is three; more briefly, $(\exists e) (F \text{ (Jack, } e) \ \& \ t(e) = 3)$.

On the present plan, (6) means some fall of Jack's caused some breaking of Jack's crown; so (6) is not false if Jack fell more than once, broke his crown more than once, or had a crown-breaking fall more than once. Nor, if such repetitions turned out to be the case, would we have grounds for saying that (6) referred to one rather than another of the fracturings. The same does not go for 'The short circuit caused the fire' or 'The flood caused the famine' or 'Jack's fall caused the breaking of Jack's crown'; here singularity is imputed. ('Jack's fall', like 'the day after tomorrow', is no less a singular term because it may refer to different entities on different occasions.) To do justice to 'Jack's fall caused the breaking of Jack's crown' what we need is something like 'The one and only falling down of Jack caused the one and only breaking of his crown by Jack'; in some symbols of the trade, '$(\imath e) F \text{ (Jack, } e)$ caused $(\imath e) B \text{ (Jack's crown, } e)$'.

Evidently (1) and (2) do not have the same logical form. If we think in terms of standard notations for first-order languages, it is (1) that more or less wears its form on its face; (2), like many existentially quantified sentences, does not (witness 'Somebody loves somebody'). The relation between (1) and (2) remains obvious and close: (1) entails (2), but not conversely.[4]

III

The salient point that emerges so far is that we must distinguish firmly between causes and the features we hit on for describing them, and hence between the question whether a statement says truly that one event caused another and the

---

[4] A familiar device I use for testing hypotheses about logical grammar is translation into standard quantification form; since the semantics of such languages is transparent, translation into them is a way of providing a semantic theory (a theory of the logical form) for what is translated. In this employment, canonical notation is not to be conceived as an improvement on the vernacular, but as a comment on it.

For elaboration and defense of the view of events sketched in this section, see my "The Logical Form of Action Sentences" in *The Logic of Action and Preference*, ed. Nicholas Rescher (Pittsburgh: University Press, 1967).

further question whether the events are characterized in such a way that we can deduce, or otherwise infer, from laws or other causal lore, that the relation was causal. "The cause of this match's lighting is that it was struck.—Yes, but that was only *part* of the cause; it had to be a dry match, there had to be adequate oxygen in the atmosphere, it had to be struck hard enough, etc." We ought now to appreciate that the "Yes, but" comment does not have the force we thought. It cannot be that the striking of this match was only part of the cause, for this match was in fact dry, in adequate oxygen, and the striking was hard enough. What is partial in the sentence "The cause of this match's lighting is that it was struck" is the *description* of the cause; as we add to the description of the cause, we may approach the point where we can deduce, from this description and laws, that an effect of the kind described would follow.

If Flora dried herself with a coarse towel, she dried herself with a towel. This is an inference we know how to articulate, and the articulation depends in an obvious way on reflecting in language an ontology that includes such things as towels: if there is a towel that is coarse and was used by Flora in her drying, there is a towel that was used by Flora in her drying. The usual way of doing things does not, however, give similar expression to the similar inference from 'Flora dried herself with a towel on the beach at noon' to 'Flora dried herself'. But if, as I suggest, we render 'Flora dried herself' as about an event, as well as about Flora, these inferences turn out to be quite parallel to the more familiar ones. Thus if there was an event that was a drying by Flora of herself and that was done with a towel, on the beach, at noon, then clearly there was an event that was a drying by Flora of herself—and so on.

The mode of inference carries over directly to causal statements. If it was a drying she gave herself with a coarse towel on the beach at noon that caused those awful splotches to appear on Flora's skin, then it was a drying she gave herself that did it; we may also conclude that it was something that happened on the beach, something that took place at noon, and something that was done with a towel, that caused the tragedy. These little pieces of reasoning seem all to be endorsed by intuition, and it speaks well for the analysis of causal statements in terms of events that on that analysis the arguments are transparently valid.

Mill, we are now in better position to see, was wrong in thinking we have not specified the whole cause of an event when we have not wholly specified it. And there is not, as Mill and others have maintained, anything elliptical in the claim that a certain man's death was caused by his eating a particular dish, even though death resulted only because the man had a particular bodily constitution, a particular state of present health, and so on. On the other hand Mill was, I think, quite right in saying that "there certainly is, among the circumstances that took place, some combination or other on which death is invariably consequent . . . the whole of which circumstances perhaps constituted in this particular case the conditions of the phenomenon . . ." (*A System of Logic,* book III, chap. V. § 3). Mill's critics are no doubt justified in contending that we may correctly give the cause without saying enough about it to demonstrate that it was sufficient; but they share Mill's confusion if they think every deletion from the description of an event represents something deleted from the event described.

The relation between a singular causal statement like 'The short circuit caused the fire' and necessary and sufficient conditions seems, in brief, to be this.

The fuller we make the description of the cause, the better our chances of demonstrating that it was sufficient (as described) to produce the effect, and the worse our chances of demonstrating that it was necessary; the fuller we make the description of the effect, the better our chances of demonstrating that the cause (as described) was necessary, and the worse our chances of demonstrating that it was sufficient. The symmetry of these remarks strongly suggests that in whatever sense causes are correctly said to be (described as) sufficient, they are as correctly said to be necessary. Here is an example. We may suppose there is some predicate '$P(x,y,e)$' true of Brutus, Caesar, and Brutus's stabbing of Caesar and such that any stab (by anyone of anyone) that is P is followed by the death of the stabbed. And let us suppose further that this law meets Mill's requirements of being *unconditional*—it supports counterfactuals of the form 'If Cleopatra had received a stab that was P, she would have died'. Now we can prove (assuming a man dies only once) that Brutus's stab was sufficient for Caesar's death. Yet it was not the cause of Caesar's death, for Caesar's death was the death of a man with more wounds than Brutus inflicted, and such a death could not have been caused by an event that was P (P' was chosen to apply only to stabbings administered by a single hand). The trouble here is not that the description of the cause is partial, but that the event described was literally (spatio-temporally) only part of the cause.

Can we then analyze 'a caused b' as meaning that a and b may be described in such a way that the existence of each could be demonstrated, in the light of causal laws, to be a necessary and sufficient condition of the existence of the other? One objection, foreshadowed in previous discussion, is that the analysandum does, but the analysans does not, entail the existence of a and b. Suppose we add, in remedy, the condition that either a or b, as described, exists. Then on the proposed analysis one can show that the causal relation holds between any two events. To apply the point in the direction of sufficiency, imagine some description '$(\imath x) Fx$' under which the existence of an event a may be shown sufficient for the existence of b. Then the existence of an arbitrary event c may equally be shown sufficient for the existence of b: just take as the description of c the following: '$(\imath y) (y = c \; \& \; (\exists! x) Fx)$'.[5] It seems unlikely that any simple and natural restrictions on the form of allowable descriptions would meet this difficulty, but since I have abjured the analysis of the causal relation, I shall not pursue the matter here.

There remains a legitimate question concerning the relation between causal laws and singular causal statements that may be raised independently. Setting aside the abbreviations successful analysis might authorize, what form are causal laws apt to have if from them, and a premise to the effect that an event of a certain (acceptable) description exists, we are to infer a singular causal statement saying that the event caused, or was caused by, another? A possibility I find attractive is that a full-fledged causal law has the form of a conjunction:

$$\text{(L)} \begin{cases} \text{(S)} & (e) \, (n) \, ((Fe \; \& \; t(e) = n) \rightarrow (\exists! F) \, (Gf \; \& \; t(f) = n + \epsilon \; \& \; C(e,f))) \; and \\[2ex] \text{(N)} & (e) \, (n) \, ((Ge \; \& \; t(e) = n + \epsilon) \rightarrow (\exists! f) \, (Ff \; \& \; t(f) = n \; \& \; C(f, e))) \end{cases}$$

---

[5] Here I am indebted to Professor Carl Hempel, and in the next sentence to John Wallace.

Here the variables 'e' and 'f' range over events, 'n' ranges over numbers, F and G are properties of events, '$C(e,f)$' is read 'e causes f', and 't' is a function that assigns a number to an event to mark the time the event occurs. Now, given the premise:

(P) $(\exists!e)\ (Fe\ \&\ t(e) = 3)$

(C) $(\imath e)\ (Fe\ \ \&\ t(e) = 3)$ caused $(\imath e)\ (Ge\ \&\ t(e) = 3 + \epsilon)$

It is worth remarking that part (N) of (L) is as necessary to the proof of (C) from (P) as it is to the proof of (C) from the premise '$(\exists!e)\ (Ge\ \&\ t(e) = 3 + \epsilon))$'. This is perhaps more reason for holding that causes are, in the sense discussed above, necessary as well as sufficient conditions.

Explaining "why an event occurred," on this account of laws, may take an instructively large number of forms, even if we limit explanation to the resources of deduction. Suppose, for example, we want to explain the fact that there was a fire in the house at 3:01 P.M. Armed with the appropriate premises in the form of (P) and (L), we may deduce: that there was a fire in the house at 3:01 P.M.; that it was caused by a short circuit at 3:00 P.M.; that there was only one fire in the house at 3:01 P.M.; that this fire was caused by the one and only short circuit that occurred at 3:00 P.M. Some of these explanations fall short of using all that is given by the premises; and this is lucky, since we often know less. Given only (S) and (P), for example, we cannot prove there was exactly one fire in the house at 3:01 P.M. that was caused by the short circuit. An interesting case is where we know a law in the form of (N), but not the corresponding (S). Then we may show that, given that an event of a particular sort occurred, there must have been a cause answering to a certain description, but, given the same description of the cause, we could not have predicted the effect. An example might be where the effect is getting pregnant.

If we explain why it is that a particular event occurred by deducing a statement that there is such an event (under a particular description) from a premise known to be true, then a simple way of explaining an event, for example the fire in the house at 3:01 P.M., consists in producing a statement of the form of (C); and this explanation makes no use of laws. The explanation will be greatly enhanced by whatever we can say in favor of the truth of (C); needless to say, producing the likes of (L) and (P), if they are known true, clinches the matter. In most cases, however, the request for explanation will describe the event in terms that fall under no full-fledged law. The device to which we will then resort, if we can, is apt to be redescription of the event. For we can explain the occurrence of any event a if we know (L), (P), and the further fact that $a = (\imath e)\ (Ge\ \&\ t(e) = 3 + \epsilon)$. Analogous remarks apply to the redescription of the cause, and to cases where all we want, or can, explain is the fact that there was *an* event of a certain sort.

The great majority of singular causal statements are not backed, we may be sure, by laws in the way (C) is backed by (L). The relation in general is rather this: if 'a caused b' is true, then there are descriptions of a and b such that the result of substituting them for 'a' and 'b' in 'a caused b' is entailed by true premises of the form of (L) and (P); and the converse holds if suitable restrictions are put on the descriptions.[6] If this is correct, it does not follow that we must be able to

---

[6] Clearly this account cannot be taken as a definition of the causal relation. Not only is there the inherently vague quantification over expressions (of what language?), but there is also the problem of spelling out the "suitable restrictions."

dredge up a law if we know a singular causal statement to be true; all that follows is that we know there must be a covering law. And very often, I think, our justification for accepting a singular causal statement is that we have reason to believe an appropriate causal law exists, though we do not know what it is. Generalizations like 'If you strike a well-made match hard enough against a properly prepared surface, then, other conditions being favorable, it will light' owe their importance not to the fact that we can hope eventually to render them untendentious and exceptionless, but rather to the fact that they summarize much of our evidence for believing that full-fledged causal laws exist covering events we wish to explain.[7]

If the story I have told is true, it is possible to reconcile, within limits, two accounts thought by their champions to be opposed. One account agrees with Hume and Mill to this extent: it says that a singular causal statement '*a* caused *b*' entails that there is a law to the effect that "all the objects similar to *a* are followed by objects similar to *b*" and that we have reason to believe the singular statement only in so far as we have reason to believe there is such a law. The second account (persuasively argued by C. J. Ducasse[8]) maintains that singular causal statements entail no law and that we can know them to be true without knowing any relevant law. Both of these accounts are entailed, I think, by the account I have given, and they are consistent (I therefore hope) with each other. The reconciliation depends, of course, on the distinction between knowing there is a law "covering" two events and knowing what the law is: in my view, Ducasse is right that singular causal statements entail no law; Hume is right that they entail there is a law.

IV

Much of what philosophers have said of causes and causal relations is intelligible only on the assumption (often enough explicit) that causes are individual events, and causal relations hold between events. Yet, through failure to connect this basic *aperçu* with the grammar of singular causal judgments, these same philosophers have found themselves pressed, especially when trying to put causal statements into quantificational form, into trying to express the relation of cause to effect by a sentential connective. Hence the popularity of the utterly misleading question: can causal relations be expressed by the purely extensional material conditional, or is some stronger (non-Humean) connection involved? The question is misleading because it confuses two separate matters: the logical form of causal statements and the analysis of causality. So far as form is concerned, the issue of nonextensionality does not arise, since the relation of causality between events can

---

[7] The thought in these paragraphs, like much more that appears here, was first adumbrated in my "Actions, Reasons, and Causes," this Journal, LX, 23 (Nov. 7, 1963): 685-700, especially pp. 696-699; reprinted in *Free Will and Determinism*, ed. Bernard Berofsky (New York: Harper & Row, 1966). This conception of causality was subsequently discussed and, with various modifications, employed by Samuel Gorovitz, "Causal Judgments and Causal Explanations," this Journal, LXII, 23 (Dec. 2, 1965): 695-711, and by Bernard Berofsky, "Causality and General Laws," this Journal, LXIII, 6 (Mar. 17, 1966): 148-157. [Both reprinted in this text.]

[8] See his "Critique of Hume's Conception of Causality," this Journal, LXIII, 6 (Mar. 17, 1966): 141-148; *Causation and the Types of Necessity* (Seattle: University of Washington Press, 1924); *Nature, Mind, and Death* (La Salle, Ill.: Open Court, 1951), part II. I have omitted from my "second account" much that Ducasse says that is not consistent with Hume.

be expressed (no matter how "strong" or "weak" it is) by an ordinary two-place predicate in an ordinary, extensional first-order language. These plain resources will perhaps be outrun by an adequate account of the form of causal laws, subjunctives, and counterfactual conditionals, to which most attempts to analyze the causal relation turn. But this is, I have urged, another question.

This is not to say there are no causal idioms that directly raise the issue of apparently non-truth-functional connectives. On the contrary, a host of statement forms, many of them strikingly similar, at least at first view, to those we have considered, challenge the account just given. Here are samples: 'The failure of the sprinkling system caused the fire', 'The slowness with which controls were applied caused the rapidity with which the inflation developed', 'The collapse was caused, not by the fact that the bolt gave way, but by the fact that it gave way so suddenly and unexpectedly', 'The fact that the dam did not hold caused the flood'. Some of these sentences may yield to the methods I have prescribed, especially if failures are counted among events, but others remain recalcitrant. What we must say in such cases is that in addition to, or in place of, giving what Mill calls the "producing cause," such sentences tell, or suggest, a causal story. They are, in other words, rudimentary causal explanations. Explanations typically relate statements, not events. I suggest therefore that the 'caused' of the sample sentences in this paragraph is not the 'caused' of straightforward singular causal statements, but is best expressed by the words 'causally explains'.[9]

A final remark. It is often said that events can be explained and predicted only in so far as they have repeatable characteristics, but not in so far as they are particulars. No doubt there is a clear and trivial sense in which this is true, but we ought not to lose sight of the less obvious point that there is an important difference between explaining the fact that there was *an* explosion in the broom closet and explaining the occurrence of *the* explosion in the broom closet. Explanation of the second sort touches the particular event as closely as language can ever touch any particular. Of course this claim is persuasive only if there are such things as events to which singular terms, especially definite descriptions, may refer. But the assumption, ontological and metaphysical, that there are events, is one without which we cannot make sense of much of our most common talk; or so, at any rate, I have been arguing. I do not know any better, or further, way of showing what there is.

---

[9] Zeno Vendler has ingeniously marshalled the linguistic evidence for a deep distinction, in our use of 'cause', 'effect', and related words, between occurrences of verb-nominalizations that are fact-like or propositional, and occurrences that are event-like. [See Zeno Vendler, "Effects, Results and Consequences," in *Analytic Philosophy,* ed. R. J. Butler (New York: Barnes & Noble, 1962), pp. 1-15.] Vendler concludes that the 'caused' of 'John's action caused the disturbance' is always flanked by expressions used in the propositional or fact-like sense, whereas 'was an effect of' or 'was due to' in 'The shaking of the earth was an effect of (was due to) the explosion' is flanked by expressions in the event-like sense. My distinction between essentially sentential expressions and the expressions that refer to events is much the same as Vendler's and owes much to him, though I have used more traditional semantic tools and have interpreted the evidence differently.

My suggestion that 'caused' is sometimes a relation, sometimes a connective, with corresponding changes in the interpretation of the expressions flanking it, has much in common with the thesis of J. M. Shorter's "Causality, and a Method of Analysis," in *Analytic Philosophy,* II, 1965, pp. 145-157.

Suggested Readings for Part Five

Anscombe, G. E. M. *Causality and Determination.* New York: Cambridge University Press, 1971.

Anscombe, G. E. M. "Causality and Extensionality." *Journal of Philosophy* 66 (1969): 152-59.

Berofsky, Bernard. *Determinism.* Princeton, N.J.: Princeton University Press, 1971, chapters 4, 7-8.

Davidson, Donald. "Actions, Reasons, and Causes." *Journal of Philosophy* 60 (1963): 685-700. Reprinted in B. Berofsky, ed., *Free-Will and Determinism,* New York: Harper & Row, 1966, pp. 221-40.

Ducasse, C. J. "Concerning Berofsky's 'Causality and General Laws.'" *Journal of Philosophy* 63 (1966): 524-27.

Ducasse, C. J. "How Literally Causation is Perceivable." *Philosophy and Phenomenological Research* 28 (1967): 271-73. [A reply to Ranken.]

Ducasse, C. J. *Truth, Knowledge, and Causation.* London: Routledge Kegan Paul, 1968), Articles 1-5.

Furlong, E. J. "The Powers that Be." *Dialogue* 10 (1971): 768-69. [Regularity response to Madden-Humber-Hare arguments.]

Harré, R. "Powers." *British Journal for the Philosophy of Science* 21 (1970): 81-101.

Harré, R. and Madden, E. H. "In Defense of Natural Agents." *The Philosophical Quarterly* 23 (April 1973): 117-32.

Harré, R. and Madden, E. H. "Natural Powers and Powerful Natures." *Philosophy* 48 (July 1973).

Martin, Raymond. "Singular Causal Explanations." *Theory and Decision* 2 (1972): 221-37.

Ranken, Nani L. "A Note on Ducasse's Perceivable Causation." *Philosophy and Phenomenological Research* 28 (1967): 269f.

Vendler, Zeno. "Causal Relations." *Journal of Philosophy* 64 (1967): 704-13. [Response to Davidson.]

PART SIX

CAUSAL EXPLANATION AND CAUSAL CONTEXT

INTRODUCTION

Philosophers have long believed that problems of causation are closely connected to problems of explanation. Undoubtedly this is because effects traditionally have been regarded as explainable or understandable in terms of the cause which produced them. Aristotle's influential account of the "four causes" was clearly intended as an analysis of basic principles of explanation, as well as of types of causal relatedness. And throughout the history of philosophy specific theories of causation have been linked to particular types of explanation which philosophers have employed in attempting to solve such basic philosophical problems as induction, free will, time, the existence of God, and the nature of human action.

Recently there has been a growing tendency in philosophy to assimilate or even to reduce analysis of the causal relation to analysis of causal explanation. Several philosophers included in Part Six exhibit this tendency, though the extent to which they could actually be said to *reduce* the category of causation to the category of explanation varies significantly. But the majority does seem convinced that the concept of causation should be analyzed, at least in some contexts, in terms of an analysis of explanation rather than by the reverse procedure. Perhaps this latter way of expressing their position is an overstatement, but minimally it can be said that they attempt to analyze significant features of the concept of causation through an analysis of explanation, even if a full account of causation is not attempted. These philosophers might also be called causal contextualists, since each argues that selection of the cause is in some crucial way relative to a particular context of inquiry and to a set of assumed explanatory principles.

Norwood Hanson's theory is perhaps the most radical of these recent accounts. He is primarily concerned with scientific explanation, but there can be little doubt that he is advancing a general thesis about causation. He takes the view that Hume and his followers have made a major mistake by conceiving of causes and effects as chains of sequential events and another in requiring that cause and effect be logically distinct, individually describable items. Hanson argues that a close look at actual causal language shows it to be "theory-loaded." His point seems to be that the very concepts used to identify an item as a cause or as an effect of a certain type tacitly incorporate semantical connections (which presume a background of theory) between any cause item and effect item of that type. Hanson indicates that if the background knowledge of the linkage were not present, the request for an explanation of an effect item would not even be intelligible.

As an example, Hanson points out that an effect can be conceptually understood only in terms of its cause in statements such as "The scar on his arm was caused by a wound he received when thrown from his carriage." In this context, "wound" is an explanatory word and "scar" denotes the explained item. To simply *see* something as a wound is already to diagnose it through at least an embryonic knowledge of pathology. The identification itself, says Hanson, commits one to a causal judgment. In other contexts these words might function differently; and in the present context other theory-loaded concepts might provide an explanation of the scar. Hanson thinks there are as many *causes* of the scar as there are *explanations* of it; and which is a cause-word and which an effect-word is determined by a specific context of explanation.

"Causes certainly are connected with effects," says Hanson, "but this is because our theories connect them, not because the world is held together by cosmic glue." Theories, he reasons, become so deeply imbedded in our terminology that specific effect-words follow inevitably upon the utterance of related cause-words. Such language functions to put guarantees on inferences from causes to effects. Contra necessity theorists, Hanson maintains that this semantic relation is the "whole story" about necessary connection and is the sole way in which lawlike connections are distinguished from merely accidental ones. Apparently he is claiming that causal laws derive their peculiar character of "necessity" from a logical or semantical connection between cause and effect—a connection made by a general theory. And, since theory-loading is contextually determined, words which might ordinarily lack theoretical dimensions may obtain them in a new context. Unfortunately, Hanson's expressions are often metaphorical, and it is left to the reader to grasp the precise logical character of the inference guarantees between cause-terms and effect-terms as well as the relationship between laws of nature and counterfactual expressions.

David Braybrooke and *Alexander Rosenberg* find more to criticize in Hanson than mere obscurity. They point out that Hanson first conflates "causal chain" accounts with detection of causal relations by "normal vision" and then tends uncritically to associate both with the Regularity Theory. They maintain that once one separates these conflated elements it is possible to see the innocuous character of Hanson's critique of regularity accounts as well as the confusions embedded in his own doctrine of theory-loaded relations. Of special importance, they claim, is Hanson's unfounded belief that causal chain or regularity accounts obscure the role of theories in the detection of causal relations. Hanson's argument, they say, trades on a confusion of (1) the role of theories in the *identification* of causally related items with (2) the notion that causes and effects are *constituted* by theories. Whereas the former and quite respectable view is a claim for which Hanson does argue, (2) is an entirely different claim and is never really argued for at all. Part of Hanson's alleged confusion is illustrated, they claim, by his assertion that *events* are theory-loaded, when he surely has no right to claim more than that the *terms* used in a causal explanation or in the expression of a causal relation are theory-loaded. Moreover, Braybrooke and Rosenberg claim that it does not follow, even if (1) is true, that events cannot be explained by causal chain explanations which reflect different "theoretical levels" and which are perfectly compatible with the Regularity Theory.

    H. L. A. Hart and *A. M. Honoré* draw heavily upon uses of the term "cause" in legal, historical, and practical contexts. They have a special interest in "the cause" judgments of ordinary thought. They contend that careful attention to terms such as "cause," "effect," "result," and "consequence" shows dimensions of meaning completely neglected by most philosophical treatments of causation, especially by the Regularity Theory. They find, for example, that causal notions such as "provision of reasons," "provision of opportunity," and "human intervention" go unaccounted for by other theories. They argue against the Regularity Theory by drawing a distinction between causal conditions and non-causal conditions in circumstances where the non-causal factors may as uniformly accompany effects as do the causes. They hold that non-regularity principles for discriminating the cause govern the judgments of lawyers, historians, and the plain man. And they claim that the principles which guide their thought have more to do with the context of causal inquiry than with causal generalizations which might be used for the purpose of justifying causal judgments.

    In their constructive analysis, Hart and Honoré argue that a cause in practical life is a condition which deviates from the normal or reasonably expected course of events, whereas a mere condition is that which is normal and inconspicuous. Clearly criteria of normalcy are relative to a context of inquiry. This indicates, as they note, that use of the word "cause" is closely tied to the need for explanation of a puzzling or unusual occurrence. At several points their analysis parallels Collingwood's. They are contextualists who find the concept of causation to involve a cluster of related concepts and who also find the manipulability model illuminating. However, they consider Collingwood's general analysis to be too narrow and paradoxical. He has missed, in their estimation, the close connection between explanation and causation and also has missed the crucial insight that causes are departures from the normal course of events.

    Samuel Gorovitz' analysis of causation is indebted to Hart and Honoré's but makes significant departures. The first part of Gorovitz' article contains a brief critical exploration of the causal theories of Mill, Ducasse, and Collingwood, especially their treatment of the cause-condition distinction. He is attracted to Collingwood's contentions that there are various levels of talk about causation, each requiring a different analysis, and that there are non-arbitrary but contextual principles by means of which "the cause" is selectively discriminated from other conditions. But he also finds Collingwood's account of the principles of the selection process subject to damaging counterexamples. He then sets out to remedy these deficiencies through his own analysis of "the cause" statements.

    Gorovitz' proposals derive directly from the Hart-Honoré thesis that causes are relative to context and are selected because they are deviations from the circumstantially normal. Gorovitz finds the notion of "normality" both obscure and incomplete, however. He suggests that a sufficiently comprehensive account requires the following "differentiating-factor analysis": A cause c of an event e is selectively distinguishable from a mere condition of e by contrasting the situation S of the effect's occurrence with some other similar type of situation T (not necessarily a normal circumstance) in which c and e do not occur; *the cause* is the condition which differentiates S (where e occurs) from T (where e does not occur). Gorovitz' theory appears basically to be a novel synthesis of the analyses by

Ducasse and Hart and Honoré—presumably minus their deficiencies. In the final part of his article Gorovitz discusses his differentiating-factor analysis in relation to a number of those theories which appear in earlier parts of the present work, especially those theories concerned with the relation between singular causal statements and causal laws.

NORWOOD RUSSELL HANSON

27. Causality

We do not have a simple event A *causally connected with a simple event* B, *but the whole background of the system in which the events occur is included in the concept, and is a vital part of it.*

BRIDGMAN[1]

A

"For want of a nail a shoe was lost; for want of a horse a rider was lost; for want of a rider a battalion was lost; for want of a battalion a battle was lost; for want of a victory a kingdom was lost—all for the want of a nail." Here is a persistent view of causality. All of us hold it some of the time; some hold it all of the time. But it is inadequate for appreciating causal situations in physics.

The view can be put forward in several ways. One of these is the causal-chain figure. Consider Galileo with his inclined plane. The balls, terminating their descent and subsequent roll, collect in a loose formation at the far end of the floor. Down comes a brass sphere. It collides with another ball, which moves off with a predictable velocity. Again another ball is nudged: another, and another, always with a predictable velocity.

A better causal-chain account could not be found; but Russell comes close:

> Inferences from experiences to the physical world can . . . be jus-
> tified by the assumption that there are causal chains, each member of
> which is a complex structure ordered by the spatio-temporal relation of
> compresence. . . .[2]
> The chain of causation can be traced by the inquiring mind from
> any given point backward to the creation of the world.[3]

Reprinted by permission of the publisher from Norwood Russell, *Patterns of Discovery*, Cambridge, Eng.: Cambridge University Press, 1961, pp. 50-65. Footnotes included.
Note: Footnotes have been renumbered for the purposes of this text.

[1] *The Logic of Modern Physics* (New York, 1927), p. 83.

[2] *Human Knowledge* (London, 1948), p. 244.

[3] *Book Review, Observer*, 4 April 1954.

It is not language with which we are concerned. It is the concepts under-lying this language.

Causal chains consist of links. They are discrete events, bound to neigh-bour-events very like themselves. "All the members of such a chain are similar in structure . . ." (Russell).[4] Why did this ball move? That other ball struck it. Why did that ball strike the first? Because it was hit by another at a right angle. What made the third ball move? The brass sphere hit it after rolling down the plane. And so on. A variation is the genealogical-tree account. Broad appeals to this in his lively phrase "causal ancestry." Galilei senior was the father of Galileo and the son of Galileo's grandfather, X. X, in turn, was the son of W, Galileo's great-grandfather, who was the son of V. Thus back to A, Adam. Bachelors break chains of succession, but in causal ancestry, every event has a cause and some effect: there are no bachelor-events. Note our temptation to think of nature as divisible into discrete happenings, each of which has one "father" (cause) and one, or several "sons" (effects).

This way of looking at the world leads to bewiskered questions. Y caused Z, X caused Y, W caused X, V caused W. Thus back to A. What caused A? Dryden makes the standard answer pleasing to the ear:

> . . . Some few, whose Lamp shone brighter, have been led
> From Cause to Cause, to Nature's secret head;
> And found that one first principle must be;
> But what or who, that Universal He;
> Whether some Soul encompassing this Ball,
> Unmade, unmov'd; yet making, moving All. . . .[5]

Laplace claimed that, were he but supplied with an account of the state of the universe at one moment, plus a list of all the causal laws, he could predict and retrodict every other moment of the world's history—a dictum which is of a piece with the view to be examined.[6] However, for Laplace a causal chain was just a deductive chain. This complication merits special treatment.

Causes are related to effects as are the links of a chain, or the generations of a genealogical tree. It is all one plot with two themes, ancestry and progeny, like a novel by one of the Brontës. But this simplicity is unreal; and it springs from the same source as did the views of observation and facts examined earlier. Whatever else Galileo did, he did not dig up clues about the world in this simple fashion. Laboratory work seldom proceeds like the following-out of instructions on a treasure-map: "ten steps north from the dead oak, four paces left, do this, now

---

[4] *Op cit.* (note 2 above), *loc. cit.*

[5] *Religio Laici.* And see Russell's discussion of "causal ancestry" in *Human Knowl-edge*, p. 483. Cf. R. B. Braithwaite, *Scientific Explanation* (Cambridge, 1953), pp. 308, 321.

[6] "Une intelligence qui pour un instant donné, connaîtrait toutes les forces dont la nature est animée, et la situation respective des êtres qui la composent, si d'ailleurs elle était assez vaste pour soumettre ces données à l'analyse, embrasserait dans la même formule, les mouvements des plus grands corps de l'univers et ceux du plus léger atome: rien ne serait incertain pour elle, et l'avenir comme le passé serait présent a ses yeux. L'esprit humaine offre dans la perfection qu'il a su donner a l'astronomie, une faible esquisse de cette intelligence" [Laplace, *Essai philosophique sur les probabilités* (Paris, 2nd ed. 1814), pp. 3-4].

that, until at last the treasure, the cause."[7] The tracts, treatises and texts of the last three hundred years of physics rarely contain the word *cause,* much less *causal chain.* In their prefaces and their *obiter dicta* physicists may get expansive;[8] nonetheless the concept is used infrequently in the actual practice of physics, and this fact is important.[9]

Why should this be? Because in so far as the chain analogy dominates a physicist's off-duty thinking about causation, he will find little in his work for which "cause" seems the appropriate word. If he is free from thinking about causation in this way, other expressions may still seem more appropriate to his research. The elements of that research are less like the links of a chain and more like the legs of a table, or the hooks on a clothes pole. They are less like the successive generations of an old family and more like the administrative organisation of an old university.

Causal-chain accounts are just plausible when we deal with fortuitous occurrences, a series of striking accidents. Imagine Galileo at sunset packing his instruments. His telescope slips and begins to roll down the hill. The shrubs will stop it, he thinks, or the ravine. He sets off in pursuit. He does not notice a hole before him. He falls, and gets to his feet just as the telescope rolls past where the shrubs *had* been. (So that was what the gardener was up to.) And the ravine? Yes, it has been filled in too. Into the river goes the telescope. If only he had not been so clumsy; if only that hole had not been there, or at least had been seen; if only the shrubs had not been cut and the ravine had not been filled in. Galileo might even muse: for want of a ravine or a shrub there was nothing to stop the rolling telescope, for want of light I did not see the hole. So the instrument slipped into the river, all for the want of a ravine or a shrub.

Or suppose that Galileo's carriage strikes a pedestrian in the darkened streets of Padua. The coroner might consider the circumstances: if only that banana skin had not been on the kerb; if only the driver had not been glancing back; if only the rivets in the brakeblocks had been secure. He too might set out his report: for want of a rivet a brakeblock was lost, for want of a brakeblock the distracted driver could not stop in time, for want of this control the carriage struck the Paduan who had slipped into the street because of the banana skin; this resulted in death—all for want of a rivet.

Furthermore, except in a context like the inclined plane experiment it would have been fortuitous that there was another ball *in situ* for the brass sphere to hit as it came off the plane, fortuitous that yet another ball was in the path of the ball set moving by the brass sphere. . . . Do good billiards players achieve their results by accident? If they do not, causal-chain accounts of their performances are

---

[7] This is not to say that research never proceeds in this way, e.g., Kepler, Boyle, Faraday, Röntgen, Mme Curie certainly endured painstaking hunts for "disturbing factors" in much of their work.

[8] Thus Newton's conclusion of the *Opticks,* Bk. III, I. And cf. Dirac, *Quantum Mechanics* (Oxford, 1930), p. 4.

[9] Cf. Galileo, "Discourses," *Opere,* vol. VII, p. 202 and Newton, "I have not been able to discover the cause of those properties of gravity . . . it is enough that gravity does really exist, and act according to the laws which we have explained" [*Philosophiae Naturalis Principia Mathematica* (3rd ed.), Conclusion].

oversimplified. The "for-want-of-a-nail" story is a chapter of accidents,[10] as are the "for-want-of-a-ravine" and "for-want-of-a-rivet" stories. An inquest of the street accident would consist in a coroner's recital of accidental happenings. Event A would not normally result in event B, but only in these exceptional circumstances; likewise for B and C, C and D, etc. The best materials for the causal-chain model are series of unparalleled events. But there are no inquest-laws of physics, for physics is not just a recording of dramatic accidents. Philosophers whose thinking about science is chained down to this notion of causation make laboratory research sound like an inquest.

B

Reference to one link of a chain *simpliciter* explains nothing about any other link—why, how, or from what it was made, etc. It does not even entail the existence of any other link. However, to know why the ball in Galileo's experiment was moved as it was, it is not enough to know that the brass ball was moving towards it just before a "click" was heard. One must also know what are some of the properties of brass balls, and those made of other materials.[11] A familiarity with the dynamics of elastic bodies is involved too. Few would expect a head-on collision to result in both spheres moving off as one. All of us know enough dynamics to play golf, tennis, cricket, and to be able to make general comments about the spheres of Galileo's experiment (for example, we expect them to roll down the plane, not melt down it like hot wax, or transport themselves down like a water droplet on an oily slope).

To know why the kingdom was lost it is not enough to know that a battle was fought, that a battalion and a rider fared badly, that a horseshoe-nail was missing. It is also necessary to be familiar with the frictional properties of nails imbedded in cartilaginous substances, to know why horses are happier when shod, why dispatch carriers require horses, how helpless an isolated battalion can be, how much an army's fortunes can depend on one battalion, and the ways in which the security of kingdoms can depend on military success. To understand how the Paduan pedestrian came to grief, it is not enough to know that certain incidents were strung out in temporal order t_0, t_1, t_2, t_3 .... One must know what usually happens when people step on banana skins, when drivers are distracted at dusk, when the rivets on brakeblocks are insecure.

The primary reason for referring to the cause of x is to explain x. There are as many causes of x as there are explanations of x. Consider how the cause of the death might have been set out by a physician as "multiple haemorrhage," by a barrister as "negligence on the part of the driver," by a carriage-builder as "a defect in the brakeblock construction," by a civic planner as "the presence of tall shrub-

---

[10] "A chapter of lucky accidents" is Toynbee's happy phrase. Cf. *A Study of History* (Oxford, 1934-54), vol. VII.

[11] Alice learned this much from her croquet game: "It was very provoking to find that the hedgehog had unrolled itself, and was in the act of crawling away" [Lewis Carroll, *Alice in Wonderland* (London, 1897), ch. VIII].

bery at that turning."[12] The chain analogy obscures this feature of causation. Examples adduced in favour of the analogy (billiard balls colliding and levers opening switches) are tacitly loaded with assumptions and theoretical presuppositions. Without these the examples would not be intelligible, much less support one view against another. Only its simplicity and familiarity makes this background knowledge fade before the spectacular linkage of the attention-getting events.

Nothing can be explained to us if we do not help. We have had an explanation of *x* only when we can set it into an interlocking pattern of concepts about other things, *y* and *z*. A *completely* novel explanation is a logical impossibility. It would be incomprehensible (just as a completely sense-datum visual experience is a patchwork of colours, wholly without consequences); it would be imponderable, like an inexpressible or unknowable fact.

The chain model encourages us to think that only normal vision is required to be able to see the brass sphere causing another ball to recoil away; apparently one has only to look and see the linkage between the missing nail and the collapsing kingdom, or the loose brakeblock rivet and the untidy Paduan street.[13] But in fact what we refer to as "causes" are theory-loaded from beginning to end. They are not simple, tangible links in the chain of sense experience, but rather details in an intricate pattern of concepts. Seeing the cause of the movement of the stars, or the coolness of the night air, is less like seeing flashes and colours and more like seeing what time it is, or seeing what key a musical score is written in, or seeing whether a wound is infected, or seeing if the moon is craterous. Let us consider this further.

---

[12] Or is there but one favoured type of causal explanation? What is it? That of classical mechanics? Cf. Du Bois: "The cognition of nature is the reduction of changes in the material world to motions of atoms, acted on by central forces, independent of time ... wherever such a reduction is successfully carried through our need for causality feels satisfied" [*Über die Grenzen des Naturerkennens* (Leipzig, 1872), vol. I]. Helmholtz: "The task of physical science is to reduce all phenomena of nature to forces of attraction and repulsion. ... Only if this problem is solved are we sure that nature is conceivable" [*Über die Erhaltung der Kraft* (Leipzig, 1847)]. Or is it the explanations of quantum mechanics to which all others must be reducible? In his passionate attack on the thesis of this chapter (expressed in my article "Causal Chains," *Mind*, LXIV, 255) Mr David Braybrooke works hard to miss the point (cf. "Vincula Vindicata," *Mind*, LXVI, 262). He succeeds completely. Braybrooke writes: "It would be ridiculous to claim that scientists ... do not often confront particular questions to which chain-like causal accounts are appropriate answers" (*ibid.* p. 224). Of course it would. It would also be ridiculous to claim that scientists never confront anything *but* such questions, which was the burden of my article and of this chapter, and which was apparently too much of a burden for Mr. Braybrooke to support. As to what scientists do or do not do, however, perhaps we ought to hear it from a couple of them, rather than have Mr Braybrooke as our spokesman: "Consider a wheeled vehicle accelerating on a level road. What is the cause of this motion? For the magistrate it is the driver in charge of the vehicle; for the engineer it is the engine which provides the propulsive power; but for the applied mathematician it is the forward thrust exerted by the road on the wheels or tyres" [Professor G. Temple, "The Dynamics of the Pneumatic Tyre," in *Endeavor* (1956), p. 200]. And, "in biology ... when we speak of *the cause* of an event we are really over-simplifying a complex situation. ... The cause of an outbreak of plague may be regarded by the bacteriologist as the microbe he finds in the blood of the victims, by the entomologist as the microbe-carrying fleas that spread the disease, by the epidemiologist as the rats that escaped from the ship and brought the infection into the port" [Professor W. I. B. Beveridge, *The Art of Scientific Investigation* (Heinemann, London, 2nd ed.)].

[13] All one *does* do is look and see; that was the argument of ch. 1. The operation is psychologically uncomplicated, in one sense, but logically it is complex.

"The scar on his arm was caused by a wound he received when thrown from his carriage." Here "wound" is an explanatory word; "scar" serves (here) not as an explanation, but as an *explicandum*. What we call "wounds" and "scars" are seldom strung on the same chain of discourse by a repetitive linkage: the situation is more complicated. What is the difference here between "scar" and "wound"? What is it for a man to have been wounded?

Is a wound just a more-than-superficial incision? Let us agree that it is. Minor scratches and nicks will not count as wounds. However, surgeons do considerably more than scratch and nick their subjects; yet it is not usual to speak of a surgeon as wounding his patients.[14] Does an operation on a fully anaesthetized patient count as wounding when the incision has been planned after consultation with other experts? No. Does the surgeon inflict a wound when he drops a scalpel, cutting a patient's arm? Perhaps. More must be known about the situation. Does the plantation owner wound the rubber tree when he carves the V-shaped trough deep into its bark? Again, perhaps. More needs to be learned about *Ficus elastica* before we can say. We can be certain of this, however: the Eskimo hacking blubber off a dead whale is not wounding the whale. Nor will throwing darts at a stuffed moose head upset the R.S.P.C.A. The carpenter does not wound the timber, however much he slices, gouges, and drills it. Only living things can be wounded; no incision in dead matter is a wound.[15] Nor would every deep incision in a living organism be a wound. An anaesthetized man undergoing appendectomy is not being wounded. A deep cut in a calloused foot is not a wound. Carving identification marks in the horns and hoofs of cattle is not wounding them.

A wound, therefore, is not *any* sort of deep incision: it is one which endangers the life, or impairs the functions of the wounded. That is why it cannot be said whether the ministrations of the plantation owner constitute wounding *Ficus elastica*. His slicing may impair the plants' functioning and endanger their lives; more information about the species is required before we can decide.

For the person who asks "What caused that man's scar?," the scar is a visible datum: it can be seen. It is an *explicandum* about which he asks this and other questions. He could sketch the scar. But for that same man a sketch of the original wound may be nothing more than a picture of a deep incision. To see it as a wound is to identify it. It is to diagnose it as endangering life or impairing function. To see a wound at all requires knowing a modicum of pathology. In other contexts seeing scars requires knowing some dermatology and neurology. For instance, "What caused the instrument-maker's retirement?" His fingertips were scarred in a carriage-accident." To see his scarred fingertips is to see why he could no longer build instruments. Merely to see his fingertips as rough and calloused is still to require information about the effects of such tissue on one's dexterity.

This feature of causation and explanation gets lost when concepts are forged in the causal-chain mould. The scar on a man's arm is explained by reference to the wound which caused it, because a wound is the sort of deep incision that would leave a scar like that. To hang the wound and the scar on the same causal line fails to mark how scars are explained by reference to wounds. "Scar" and "wound" are words on different theoretical levels.

---

[14] We are not discussing the technical sense of "wound" as used in surgical theory.

[15] Sometimes "wound" is appropriated for ships and aircraft: "She plunged on despite her wounds." But this is pure metaphor.

Galileo often studied the moon. It is pitted with holes and discontinuities; but to say of these that they are craters—to say that the lunar surface is crater-ous—is to infuse theoretical astronomy into one's observations. Is a deep, natural valley a crater? Miners dig steeply and deeply, but is the result more than a hole? No; it is not a crater. An abandoned well is not a crater; nor is the vortex of a whirlpool. To speak of concavity as a crater is to commit oneself as to its origin, to say that its creation was quick, violent, explosive: artillery explosions leave craters, and so do falling meteors and volcanoes. Sketches of the moon's surface would just be sketches of a pitted, pock-marked sphere; but Galileo saw craters.

Again, a liquid is tasted and is declared to be bitter. That is all the tongue can tell, but we, perhaps, say that it is poison. To say of a liquid that it is poison is to diagnose it as capable of doing all the things poisons do. "What caused the death?" We might answer "poison." When would we answer "a bitter liquid," and leave it at that?

A wound is a cut which endangers life or impairs function. A scar is a dermal discontinuity which lessens sensitivity, and sometimes dexterity. Lunar craters are superficial pits resulting from explosion or impact. Poison is lethal. Words like "wound," "scar," "crater" and "poison," are often expressed with medical, biological, geological, and chemical overtones. Diagnoses, analyses, prog-noses, are built into them. That is why in certain contexts they explain scars, clumsiness, rough surfaces and death; why it is natural to refer to the wound as the cause of the scar, to the scar as the cause of clumsiness, to the crater as the cause of uneven surface reflexion, to volcanoes or meteors as the cause of the crater, and to poison as the cause of death. Scars are what most wounds result in; hence it explains a man's scar to say that it was caused by a wound incurred in a carriage accident. (Most words which serve in this explanatory capacity are loaded in a similar way: for instance, particle, elastic, vector, acid copper, eclipse, light . . . there is no end.)

The terms of physics thus resemble "pawn," "rook," "trump" and "off-side"—words which are meaningless except against a background of the games of chess, bridge and football. To one ignorant of what happens as a rule in bridge, "finesse" will explain nothing. Even though nothing escapes his view while the finesse is made, he will not *see* the finesse being made. To one ignorant of what happens as a rule with chemical solutions, "laevo-rotatory" will explain nothing, though his gaze be fixed on all the laboratory equipment when the chemist makes his announcement. Similarly "wound" explains the man's scar only against the implicit background of theory brought out here. So too with "crater" and "poi-son." The diagnostic and prognostic quality of these causal substantives reflects in the verbs with which they combine, verbs which are loaded in the same way: "inhale," "perforate," "dissolve," "charge," "expand," "stretch," etc.

Consider "stretch." We stretch rubber, elastic bands, springs, shrunken clothing, our arms and legs. Do we stretch butter from one corner of a scone to the other? Do we stretch seed from one corner of the garden to another? Does the gas escaping from the cooker stretch into the atmosphere? Does a cloud stretch when caught by a wind? Perhaps these are all cases of stretching; there are times when these might be natural ways of speaking. Still, there are differences between stretch-ing rubber and springs on the one hand and stretching butter, sand and gas on the other. In the former cases, when we stop stretching, the body returns to its original shape; but this is not so with butter, sand or gas. The cloud does not snap back to its earlier shape when the wind dies. Shrunken socks do not return to their diminutive shapes after stretching; but yet we cannot stretch socks as we might "stretch" butter, or sand, or gas. Waterfalls are not stretching water. A spreading population is not stretching.

Though rarely explicit, the diagnosis built into "stretch" will differ, than, according to whether it is rubber, sand or the truth that we are stretching. There are many theoretical backcloths against which "stretch" can show up.

To improve a clock's action a clock-maker may stretch its mainspring. He may stretch the lubricant available for the clock, and he may stretch the truth when showing the clock to a buyer. Doubtless he knows what behaviour is appropriate in each case. He possesses knowledge of mainsprings, stress, strain, and elastic limit; of lubricants, viscosity and the oil requirements of this clock; and of people who inquire after "olde Englishe clocks."

The fact that x has been stretched can explain some event y. Or, x's having been stretched can be the *cause* of y. This is saying more than that if we had opened our eyes and looked, a picture of x-being-stretched-and-causing-y would have registered in our visual space. These suggestions may be reinforced by some further remarks on *seeing that*.

C

One of Galileo's apprentices (Viviani or the young Toricelli) may see how gears, rachets and levers of a clock engage each other. He may portray this in a diagram; and in this the apprentice may excel his old master (whose vision was weak and failed late in life). But Viviani may not yet see that the force transmitted by the weighted drum is passed on to the driving gear, and thence through the gear-train, to "escape" by measured degrees through the escapement—something which old Galileo is sure to see. The young apprentice may not appreciate the dynamics of the weight suspended from the driving drum, nor how these are related to the instrument's activity.[16] That most of us *do* appreciate this—*do* see the weight which pulls the string which turns the drum which drives the gear train— does not make such knowledge less essential to our comprehension of "The driving weight is the cause of the escapement's action." The statement is intelligible only in terms of knowing something about the properties of metals, the elements of mechanics, and the principles of horology.

Seeing what causes a clock's action requires more than normal vision, open eyes and a clock: we must learn what to look for. We do not recite the lessons of this training each time we see the cause of some event, but their content is indispensable in the search. The chain account obscures this by ignoring it: it treats the world as a simple Meccano construction where observers are cameras. But causes are no more visual data *simpliciter* than are facts. Nothing in sense-datum space could be labelled "cause," or "effect."[17]

---

[16] Just as some school students do not understand the action of Atwood's machine.

[17] This seriously damages Michotte's thesis. Cf. *La perception de la causalité* (Louvain and Paris, 1946).

Yet, unmistakably, the old Galileo sees what causes the clock's action. " 'I see,' said the blind man, but he did not see at all." A blind man cannot see how a timepiece is designed, or what distinguishes it from other clocks. Still, he may see that, if it is a clock at all, it will embody certain dynamical principles; and may explain the action to his young apprentice. The latter, however keen his vision, can describe only the pertubations of the clock; he cannot say what causes it to behave as it does. Galileo can say what causes it (and any other similarly constructed clock) to do what it does, because the blind Galileo has what his apprentice lacks—a knowledge of horological theory. Though the apprentice has what Galileo lacks, normal vision, he cannot detect the cause of the clock's motion.

Notice the dissimilarity between "theory-loaded" nouns and verbs, without which no causal account could be given, and those of a phenomenal variety, such as "solaroid disc," "horizoid patch," "from left to right," "disappearing," "bitter." In a pure sense-datum language causal connexions could not be expressed. All words would be on the same logical level: no one of them would have explanatory power sufficient to serve in a causal account of neighbour-events. But it is here that the causal-chain should work best, for at the sense-datum level all events *are* like the links of a chain. They meet Russell's requirement by being similar in structure. Yet they elude the language of causality.[18] The chain analogy is appropriate only where genuine causal connexions cannot be expressed. How could explanations be advanced in a sense-datum language?

It is not that certain words are absolutely theory-loaded, whilst others are absolutely sense-datum words. Which are the data-words and which the theory-words is a contextual question. Galileo's scar may at some times be a datum requiring explanation, but at other times it may be part of the explanation of his retirement. "Wound" helped to explain Galileo's scar, but it might also express a datum, something observed yet requiring explanation—as when a medical classroom is bedecked with pictures of several varieties of wound, all awaiting commentary by the Professor of Surgery. "Red now," "smooth," "disappearing" are not once-for-all unladen with theory. Such language could function within sophisticated explanations, rather than as mere verbal records of immediate experience. "Red now" in an astrophysical context (involving the Döppler effect) might explain celestial phenomena. "Smooth" in a statistical context, "disappearing" in a cathode-ray tube context (involving, say, Crooke's dark space), likewise contain volumes. We can infer an effect from some cause only when the "cause-word" guarantees the inference; but which words are cause-words and which effect-words is for the context to determine.

Causal connexions are expressible only in languages that are many-levelled in explanatory power. This is why causal language is diagnostic and prognostic, and why the links-in-a-chain view is artificial. This is why within a context the cause-words are not "parallel" to the effect-words, and why causes explain effects but not vice versa. For "cause"-words are charged: they carry a conceptual pattern with

---

[18] 'Of the sense data we cannot know more . . . than that they are in agreement . . .' (Leibniz, *Die Philosophische Schriften* (Berlin, 1875-90), vol. IV, p. 356). Contrast 'The elementary proposition consists of names. It is a connexion, a concatenation, of names' (Wittgenstein, *Tractatus*, 4. 22). 'From an elementary proposition no other can be inferred' (*ibid*. 5. 134).

them. But "effect"-words, being, as it were, part of the charge, are less rich in theory, and hence less able to serve in explanations of causes. Galileo might explain the action of the clock hands by reference to the weight-driven main gear, the gear train, the escapement, the pendulum. (Note how "theory-loaded" are each of these expressions; how extensive are their horological and dynamical implications.) He might say that the main gear, the train, escapement, and pendulum cause the motion of the hands. Explanation would not proceed in the opposite way: Galileo would not explain the action of these parts by describing the motion of the hands. Neither the system of dynamics nor any system of horology unfolds in that order.

When the apprentice says "pendulum-escapement," he may mean little more than "tick-tock, to-and-fro." Much may follow from that, but not what follows for Galileo when these same words leave his lips. When the youngster says "lightning and thunder," he probably means "flash and rumble." Again, a lot may follow, but what follows for him is different from what follows for the meteorologist—for whom "lightning and thunder" probably means "electrical discharge and aerial disturbance." Ask the shepherd "what caused that thundering noise?" and the response may be "rain is on the way.' The meteorologist says: "The noise originates near that cumulus cloud. In principle the cloud is an electrostatic generator. The ice crystals within it produce, by friction between themselves, electric charges, the separation of which leads to a concentration of positive charge in one region of the cloud and of negative charge in another. As charge separation proceeds, the field between these charged centres (or between one of them and the earth) grows. Finally, electrical breakdown of the air occurs; we see this as lightning. It leads to a partial vacuum in the atmosphere. Surrounding air rushes in. The result is a disturbance not unlike the breaking of a lamp bulb; we hear this as thunder."

One might regard this as an example of causal-chain talk. Rather, it is a deductive chain. Each step in this account does follow the one before, but not like links in a chain or sheep over a log. This is not the single-file following of children's games but the following of entailment; it is details following a pattern, elements following a scheme. Much more than normal vision is involved in seeing a flash as lightning, and in hearing a rumble as thunder.

The "wider" a word is theoretically, the more loaded it can be causally. The more widespread its net of effect-words, the more fertile its explanatory possibilities. ["... ('The sky looks threatening': is this about the present or the future?) Both; not side-by-side, however, but about the one *via* the other."][19]

Cause-words resemble game-jargon, as was noted earlier. "Revoke," "trump," "finesse" belong to the parlance system of bridge. The entire conceptual pattern of the game is implicit in each term: you cannot grasp one of these ideas properly while remaining in the dark about the rest. So too "bishop," "rook," "checkmate," "gambit" interlock with each other and with all other expressions involved in playing, scoring and writing about chess.

Likewise with "pressure," "temperature," "volume," "conductor," "insulator," "charge" and "discharge," "wave-length," "amplitude," "frequency," "elastic," "stretch," "stress" and "strain" in physics; "ingestion," "digestion,"

[19] Wittgenstein, *Phil. Inv.* p. 179e.

"assimilation," "excretion" and "respiration" in biology; "wound," "poison," "threshold" in medicine; "gear-train," "escapement," "pendulum" and "balancer" in horology. To understand one of these ideas thoroughly is to understand the concept pattern of the discipline in which it figures. This helps to show how cause-words are theory-loaded in relation to their effect-words. It is something like the way in which "trump," a bridge-loaded word, explains "beat my ace" which is not bridge-loaded, but merely more thinly game-loaded. "You beat my ace" might be said in many card games; "you trumped me" will be heard only in bridge and whist. The more "phenomenal" a word, the less "theoretical" it is. We are more capable of understanding these low-level words independently of the language-system in which they figure. Children in the nursery, after learning a few object-names[20] do quite well with "cold," "hot," "red." The more their experiences vary, the greater the demands put on the language they are learning to use. When explanation, causation and theorizing have become their daily fare, each element of their speech will have worked into a comprehensive language-pattern, buttressed and supported in many ways by the other elements. Questions about the nature of causation are to a surprising degree questions about how certain descriptive expressions, in definite contexts, coupled together, complement and interlock with a pattern of other expressions.

D

Context has been stressed. The background information, the "set" that makes an explanation stand out, derives as much from what is obvious in a situation as from discursive knowledge gained through training. If someone opened the door and shouted "Fire!," you would not have to rummage through your memory before suitable action suggested itself. This is connected with the remark that a body of theory and information guarantees inferences from cause-*words* to effect-*words*. Cause-words, in appropriate contexts, unleash much more than an isolated word in an indefinite context. If, in the blank pages of a next year's diary we find the word "fire" in the place reserved for St Valentine's day, no action would suggest itself. Consider another man shouting "Fire!"; but now he is in uniform, hovering over a busy gun crew. Were we members of that crew, our response would be automatic. (One thing we should not do would be to scurry for shelter.) In other contexts "fire" might herald a worker's dismissal, or the entrance of a Wagnerian soprano amid pyrotechnics. It can signal a phase in the making of pottery, describe how an actress reads her part, or designate some primitive rite.[21] From these utterances (in specific contexts) much can be inferred. "Fire" has, in each situation, a propositional force; it is shorthand for complex statements whose nature is clear from the contexts of utterance.[22] We are not born able to recognize such contexts, any more than we are to see eclipses and escapements. For that we need education.

---

[20] "The first and oldest words are names of 'things' " (Mach, *Science of Mechanics*, p. 579).

[21] No ambiguity results when contexts are thus specified. This parallels the bird-antelope, which is not "ambiguous" when set into contexts (ch. 1). Cf. Wittgenstein's "Green is green" (*Tractatus*, 3. 323). "The silent adjustments to understand colloquial language are enormously complicated" (*Tractatus*, 4. 002).

[22] Cf. Wittgenstein, *Tractatus*, 4. 032.

This is more familiar than it appears. After moving his stethescope over a patient the physician exclaims "valvular lesion"; his nurse understands this as an intelligible assertion. The chemist who knowingly labels a flask of water "inflammable" will be pressed for an explanation. Words like "lesion" and "inflammable" in these contexts, like "pendulum," "wound," and "lightning" in others, do the service of complete propositions. And propositions are the stuff of inference.

In a similar way, though not in the same way, "cause" words show their family connexions in the contexts of their employment. They draw explanatory force from conceptual patterns underlying the situations in which they are used, somewhat as "fire" draws propositional force from contexts in which it might be uttered. "It takes a particular context to make a certain action into an experiment. . . . But if a sentence can strike me like a painting in words, and the very individual word in the sentence as like a picture, then it is not such a marvel that a word uttered in isolation and without purpose can seem to carry a particular meaning in itself" (Wittgenstein).[23]

Further, if a man shouts "Fire!," pointing to a blazing dynamite warehouse, and then adds "Run for your life!," we might say "Naturally—what else?" Part of the force of "Fire!" here is that he who hesitates is lost. The added "Run for your life!" is compellingly obvious. Who could hear and understand such an alarm and fail to run? Effect-words dovetail with cause-words like this. That the clock-hands are moved by the weighted gear-train will seem obvious if we know what gear-trains and clock-hands are. One may even feel that, in a sound clock, the hands, being what they are, *must* be moved by the gear-train—for would there not be something unsound about the clock if they were not? (The weight actuates the gear-train, and ultimately the hands. This is what we mean by "clock," "gear-train," "weight," and "hands.")

This is the whole story about necessary connexion. "Effect" and "cause," so far from naming links in a queue of events, gesture towards webs of criss-crossed theoretical notions, information, and patterns of experiment. In a context and by way of a theory, certain effect-words inevitably follow the utterance of certain cause-words: "main-spring uncoils—hands move," "lightning flashes—thunder rumbles," "rain falls—wet pavement," "summer—heat," "fire—destruction."

Causes certainly are connected with effects; but this is because our theories connect them, not because the world is held together by cosmic glue. The world *may* be glued together by imponderables, but that is irrelevant for understanding causal explanation.[24] The notions behind "the cause x" and "the effect y" are intelligible only against a pattern of theory, namely one which puts guarantees on inferences from x to y. Such guarantees distinguish truly causal sequences from mere coincidence. There is no connexion between the swings of Galileo's pendulum and the synchronous ringing of the distant church-bell. Nor is there a causal connexion between baby's first taste of banana and a simultaneous eclipse of the sun, though this may put the child off bananas. Similarly there is no causal relation between my winding the clock and then going to sleep, though no two

---

[23] *Phil. Inv.* p. 215.
[24] All that matters is that certain systems of concepts can help us to understand what there is. Cf. *Tractatus*, 6. 342 and 6. 3432, two profound observations on the philosophy of physics.

events occur with more monotonous regularity. One could predict my going to sleep from watching me wind the clock, or retrodict my having wound the clock from observing me asleep. But this is risky, like amateur weather-forecasting or angling advice. No conceptual issue is raised by the failure of such a prediction or retrodiction. Our understanding of nature receives no jar from guessing wrong here on one occasion.

This shows what we expect of a causal law. These are not built up in the manner: $(A \text{ then } B)_1$, $(A \text{ then } B)_2$, $(A \text{ then } B)_3$, therefore all A's are followed by B's. This obscures the role of causal laws in our conceptions of a physical world. It is not merely that no exceptions have been found. We are to some extent conceptually unprepared for an exception: it would jar physics to its foundations; the pattern of our concepts would warp or crumble. This is not to say that exceptions do not occur, but only that when they do our concepts do warp and crumble.[25] It is all or nothing. The causal structure of the universe, if such a thing there be, cannot be grasped simply by counting off event-pairs, Noah-fashion, and then summarizing it all with an umbrella formula.[26]

The difference between generalizing the repeated occurrence of contiguous, propinquitous, asymmetric event-pairs and understanding the "causal" structure of a natural phenomenon is like the difference between having a visual impression of a lunaroid patch and observing the moon. It is like the difference between contemplating a concavity on the lunar surface, and appreciating the fact that the moon is craterous.

Coincidental event-pairs are bound by no reputable theory, and we would feel little unsettlement if one occurred without the other. That happenings are often related as cause and effect need not mean that the universe is shackled with ineffable chains, but it does mean that experience and reflexion have given us good reason to expect a Y every time we confront an X. For X to be thought of as a cause of Y we must have good reasons for treating "X," not as a sensation word like "flash," "rumble," "bright," "solaroid," "bitter" or "red," but rather as a theory-loaded, explanatory term like "wound," "crater," "stretch," "pendulum," "discharge" or "elastic impact."

This is obscured by the links-in-a-chain, ancestry-progeny view of cause and effect. How could such a view ever grip us? Why do we so often think of physical events as clicking off in single file?

---

[25] Cf. ch. v.

[26] "A hypothesis to be regarded as a natural law must be a general proposition which can be thought to *explain* its instances; if the reason for believing the general proposition is solely direct knowledge of the truth of its instances, it will be felt to be a poor sort of explanation of these instances" (Braithwaite, *Scientific Explanation*, p. 302).

DAVID BRAYBROOKE
ALEXANDER ROSENBERG

28. Vincula Revindicata

Hanson, flamboyant and irrepressible man, striding in seven-league boots over the ordinary limits of academic roles, has now, regrettably, been dead for some time. Those who knew him, including those who engaged in unfinished controversy with him, might well be content to remember him pleasantly and let him rest in peace. One might think, however, that he would himself have preferred, rather than be treated merely as an object of fragrant memory, to have the controversies which he stirred up continue. So long as his chapter[1] on causality continues to be of interest to philosophers, which it does, it invites controversy; and in particular, controversy respecting his treatment of the notion of causal chains.

For the chapter takes the form of a sustained attack on the notion or analogy of causal chains. One might wonder, why does Hanson attribute so much importance to this analogy, which seems innocuous and even unimportant? We, in fact, argue that the analogy is innocuous and that its claim to importance is tenuous, consisting mainly in the unnecessary confusion that is created by repudiating it for the wrong reasons. Hanson, however, ascribes to the analogy a pervasive influence which affects (in his view, for the worse) all, or almost all, the central issues raised by the concept of causality. He contends that the analogy (1) suggests that causal relations can be detected simply at sight, by "normal vision"; (2) casts into the shade the inadequacies of the constant conjunction view of causation; (3) in effect gives fortuitous occurrences, to which alone it applies, an unwarranted place among the topics of scientific inquiry (and thus leads us to misconceive what the true topics or some of their important features are); (4) obstructs us from perceiving the use of theories and theoretical notions in the detection of causes; (5) failing itself to accommodate any difference in "theoretical" level between a cause and its effect, distracts us from providing this accommodation in any case; (6) distracts us equally from accommodating the fact that there is a steady decline in theoretical "richness" of levels as we move from higher to lower levels in a causal hierarchy.

We think that the notion of causal chains is innocent of any of these alleged crimes; but clearly the charges are serious ones, and deserve examination. Examining them will, moreover, bring us face to face with some critical questions about the adequacy of Hanson's own view of causality.

Hanson alleges that causal chain explanations are unsatisfactory because they somehow make causes out to be "visual data simpliciter" [p. 59 (211)]: "The chain model encourages us to think that only normal vision is required to be able to see [a causal connection]" while in fact causes and effects "are not simple tangible

This article appears here for the first time. An earlier article by Braybrooke entitled "Vincula Vindicata" appeared in *Mind* vol. 66 (1957). Hanson's reply to that article is found in the footnotes to his article "Causality," reprinted in this text.

[1] "Causality," *Patterns of Discovery* (Cambridge: Cambridge University Press, 1958) p. 50-69. [All page references initially are to the original chapter; references in parentheses are to the corresponding page numbers for the selection, as printed in this text.]

links in the chain of sense experience . . ." [p. 54 (208)]. Hanson nowhere substantiates this charge. What, indeed, does causal chaining have to do with any thought about normal vision? Hanson's "normal vision" theme may reflect oversimplified treatments of causation in terms of pairs of events, taken one pair at a time. But are these treatments committed to the chain analogy? Or it, to them or their suggestions about "normal vision"? If one has to explain why an elastic gas-filled container expands on heating, one can recount a chain of events that happen, some of them to things—molecules—quite outside the reach of "normal vision." Even were causal chain accounts taken to suggest implicitly that all causal connections are to be appreciated on an analogy with the connections displayed in paradigm cases of observable causal relations, like the collision and recoil of billiard balls, the original charge would not follow.

Hanson wants to show that the alleged reliance of the chain analogy on the view that causes and effects are visible data is a defect because it obscures the fact that "what we refer to as causes are theory-loaded from beginning to end. They are not simple tangible links in the chain of sense experience, but rather details in an intricate pattern of concepts" [p. 54 (208)]. Notice that literally taken, Hanson is saying that events, the relata of causal relations, are "theory-loaded," that events are "details in an intricate pattern of concepts." What he must mean to say is that the *terms* in which a causal explanation is offered or the terms in which a causal relation is expressed are theory-loaded, are details in an intricate pattern of concepts, without surrendering the view that both causal explanations and causal relations can fall into chain-like sequences. Let us at least reserve judgment: In the end, we may need do no more than acknowledge that in some chains some links differ somewhat in character.

Hanson's second charge is that the causal chain model obscures the inadequacies of the constant conjunction view of causality. "There is no causal relation between my winding the clock and then going to sleep, though no two events occur with more monotonous regularity" [p. 64 (215)]. According to Hanson, the view that causal explanation proceeds by reference to chains encourages us to entertain and perhaps even sanction the claim that there is a causal relation between these two events. Hanson simply assumes that any causal chain account comes hand-in-glove with a regularity or constant conjunction view of causation. If if it did (and, as will become clear later, we see no connection), it would hardly follow that a constant conjunction or regularity theory (such as Mackie's, for example) is committed to maintaining that there is a causal relation between the events in Hanson's bedroom. For one thing the counterfactual "If Hanson wound his clock at noon, he would then immediately go to sleep" is not sustained (to use Mackie's language) by any available nomological generalization.

Since chain-like accounts are suited only to fortuitous occurrences, to accidents, "the chain analogy," Hanson says, "is appropriate only where genuine causal connexions cannot be expressed" [p. 59 (212)]. But, of course, this is a *non sequitur*. Even if Hanson were correct in claiming that the analogy works only when we have in mind "a series of striking accidents" [p. 59 (212)], this would be no ground for suggesting that the causal chain model never suits the expression of genuine causal explanations and relations. Accidents themselves are the results of perfectly genuine *causal* connections and have equally genuine causal explanations, both in ordinary life and science (consider Hanson's remark about the work of Kepler, Boyle, Faraday, Röntgen, Curie, note 3, p. 190). Moreover, it is interesting that many philosophers (for example, Gorovitz, Honoré and Hart, Mackie, Collins) invite us to consider causal enquiry, whether in science or in everyday life, as enquiry into the difference between the normal situation and the abnormal one in which a cause is sought. Situations in which we search for causes, claims one typical author, are "deviations from what is to be expected."[2] And Hanson says as much himself, in another place:

> . . . we ask [what is the cause?] only when we are confronted with some breach of routine . . . On being told that [Galileo] had cut his arm, Sagredo might then ask for the cause of the cut. It is unlikely, however, that on an ordinary Tuesday morning Sagredo would ask after the cause of Galileo's moderate good health. Why should he? Only if he expected Galileo to be otherwise would the question be in place [p. 69].

Hanson charges that the causal chain analogy, partly because of its alleged reliance on visible data, obstructs us from perceiving the use of theories and theoretical notions in the detection of causes. However, it turns out that this charge is no more seaworthy than the others. "Galileo can say what causes [the clock] to do what it does, because the blind Galileo has . . . a knowledge of horological theory. Though the apprentice has what Galileo lacks, normal vision, he cannot detect the cause of the clock's motion" [p. 59 (212)]. Whether Galileo would have an advantage in theory in respect to every sort of cause we might doubt; but let us admit he has an advantage here, which enables him to detect a cause that his apprentice cannot. Does it follow that his findings cannot be expressed in a chain-like account? Not at all. Does it follow that if we express his findings in a chain-like account, we shall be obstructed from appreciating the difference that Galileo's theoretical insight made in detecting the cause? Not at all; and even a tendency to obstruct seems unlikely if we consider that Galileo may have applied the notion of a causal chain in applying his theoretical advantage: "The second hand moves forward one second because the escape wheel moves forward one notch; the escape wheel moves forward one notch because the pendulum at one end of its swing pulls the anchor momentarily off the escape wheel." Of course, we may miss the importance of Galileo's theoretical advantage if we have too simple an idea of causation; but the causal chain analogy lends itself equally to simple ideas and to complex ones. Hanson mistakes the simplicity—even naivete—of some of its applications for a persistent limitation.

The fifth of Hanson's complaints about the chain analogy rests on the allegation that it fails to accommodate the difference in "theoretical level" between a cause and its effect. "Level" is a slippery notion here as elsewhere. Suppose e_1 is on a different level from e_2, which e_1 causes. May not e_2 be in turn a cause itself, the cause of say e_3? Does this fact elevate e_2's status? Perhaps, just by its entitlement as a cause, it has a claim to be admitted (generally speaking, day in and day out) to the same level as e_1. We suppose, however, that Hanson would reserve a higher, more exclusive level for e_1. Perhaps, in his view, there is a general hierarchy of levels to which events are assigned, with cause-events always assigned to a level

---

[2] Gorovitz, S. "Causal Judgments and Causal Explanations," *Journal of Philosophy*, vol. 62, p. 699 [Reprinted below.]

higher than the effects to which they directly relate; alternatively, there is such a hierarchy for all the types of events within the scope of a given theory. As they stand, both of these suppositions, illuminating or not, are quite consistent with the chain analogy. Can chains not be hung up vertically? Are there not chains in which the higher links are heavier, larger, perhaps even more ornately wrought than links at lower levels? Indeed we could hardly have a causal hierarchy of more than two levels without opening up room for applying the chain analogy.

The relata of a causal relation, it is supposed, are always hierarchically ordered, in that events on the causal level can only be described in a language theoretically richer than events at the effect level below. But can this be true? Complex servomechanisms and feedback loops (organic, electronic, or mechanical) are composed of causes and effects which can satisfy this requirement only on pain of contradiction. In such systems e_1 causes e_2, which causes e_3, where e_1 and e_3 are not the same event, but are identified and described in language of identical theoretical richness. On Hanson's view e_3 is both uniquely at the same theoretical level as e_1 and uniquely below it, which is plainly impossible. Consider a specific mechanical example, which might have come as a discovery from Masters and Johnson, but which we have in fact taken from Bunge;[3] an account of the automatic control of a steam engine:

> One of the oldest devices for automatic control is the governor . . . invented by Watt (1788). When the engine runs too fast [event e_1], balls [attached to drive shaft] move outward [event e_2], and by doing so they tend to close the throttle [event e_3], thus slowing down the speed of the machine [event e_4]. And when the engine runs too slowly, the balls tend to open the throttle.

The events in this example—e_1 . . . e_4, connected in a feedback loop—can be represented as connected in a causal chain. (There is a loop and chain also, though not a feedback loop, in the clock example: The motion of the pendulum causes the forward motion of the escape wheel; but the forward motion of the escape wheel, under the pull of the weight attached to it, in turn causes the motion of the pendulum.) Such applications of the chain analogy suffice to reject Hanson's final complaint that the chain model fails to accommodate the fact that there is always a steady decline in theoretical richness of concepts as we move down a causal hierarchy. There is no such fact (and no reason, again, to suppose that the chain analogy could not accommodate such a fact). In our example there are perfectly genuine causal connections which lead from e_1 to e_4. But there is no hierarchy in which e_1 is richer or higher than e_4 (save a temporal one). Theoretically e_1 is the same type of event as e_4; they both amount to changes in the rate of revolutions per minute of the drive shaft. Moreover, reverting to an earlier point, though there is a causal chain explanation available for the self-regulation of the engine, surely this event, state, fact, or whatever it is, is not a fortuitous occurrence.

Let us consider more fully whether any of Hanson's arguments are effective against the constant conjunction or regularity view of causal relations which he impetuously associates with the causal chain analogy. We do not believe so. Suppose we concede that there are causal relations expressed both in daily life and in science in which the terms that we hit on for describing the causes are theory-

---

[3] Bunge, M., *Causality* (Cambridge, Mass: Harvard University Press, 1959) p. 154.

loaded and the terms we hit upon for describing the effects are not. We should say "relatively" theory-loaded and "relatively" not; it must be recognized that the difference is dependent entirely on the contexts in which these terms figure. Hanson writes: "to hang the wound and the scar [a cause and its effect] on *the same causal line* fails to mark how scars [the effects] are explained by reference to wounds [the causes]. 'Scar' and 'wound' are words on different theoretical levels" [p. 56 (209)]. Are we to infer that scarrings and woundings are metaphysically different? That the latter is on a higher level, or is theoretically richer, or is an item of an altogether different sort from the former? Of course not.

> It is not that certain words are absolutely theory-loaded, whilst others are absolutely sense-datum words. Which are the data-words and which the theory-words is a contextual question. Galileo's scars may at some times be a datum requiring explanation but at other times it may be part of the explanation of his retirement. "Wound" helped to explain Galileo's scar, but it might also express a datum, something requiring explanation . . . [p. 59f (212)].

Differences in theory-loadedness turn out to be differences in the attention that we give to the theory-load of a term, depending on whether (in our search for causes) we treat it as referring to a cause that is to do the explaining or as an effect that is to be explained. When we treat "wound" as referring to a candidate for identification as as cause, we are alive to the fact that *ex vi termini* a wound breaks the skin and makes an opening which the body will normally cover in time with a scar. When we treat it as referring to an effect, our attention (searching for causes) will have shifted elsewhere; and the fact that the wound in question will probably (like other wounds) be succeeded by a scar recedes from our view.

The events in question keep their characters all along. *They* do not change, even relatively, in theory-loadedness, as contexts change and our attention shifts. As particular events, if they are conjoined in pairs—or in chains—they remain conjoined; as generic events, if they are constantly conjoined, they remain constantly conjoined. Moreover, not all causal relations are even capable of being expressed in terms that are theory-loaded and as theory-loaded subject to shifts in "load" with changes in context and attention. Suppose we examine an entirely new set of events, for which we have as yet no theory, nor even a settled set of descriptions. We may still discover that the relations manifest among the events are of a causal sort, and (often) determine which of the events is cause and which effect. It is just in such novel connections that the constant conjunction theory comes into its own, furnishing at least part of the analysis of causal relations.

We have illustrated, besides, well-established descriptions of causal relations in which theoretical loads are not differentially distributed in accordance with Hanson's demands and could not be, without rendering the relations described unintelligible. These examples are perfectly amenable to a regularity theory analysis of the causal chains asserted in them.

Finally, there are reasons to believe that no causal relations need be expressed in terms manifesting a hierarchical distribution of theory-loads. So long as we recognize that such relations are always and everywhere contingent, we must admit that any two compossible events can without contradiction be said to be respectively cause and effect, even where the cause is the reappearance of a particular large and active sun spot and the effect is the rise in the Canadian index of industrial activity from 146.5 to 147.3. To object, perhaps with Hanson, that this claim presupposes the contingency of causal claims, is simply to recognize that the strongest point in favor of the constant conjunction theory is our well-grounded belief that causal connections are *contingent*.

H. L. A. HART
A. M. HONORÉ

29. *The Analysis of Causal Concepts*

Preoccupation with the familiar pair of terms "cause and effect" may make us think that there is a *single* concept of "causation" awaiting our inspection and that the huge range of other causal expressions "consequence," "result," "caused by," "due to," "lead to," "made," are mere stylistic variants. Sometimes indeed expressions of this group may be substituted without alteration of meaning. It matters little, for example, whether we say that a fire was *caused by* a short circuit, or was *due to* it or that a short circuit *led* to the fire. Yet very often this substitution cannot be made without change of meaning or gross incongruity of expression. The use of the term "effect" is in fact fairly definitely confined to cases where the antecedent is literally a *change* or *activity* of some sort (as distinct from a persistent state or negative condition), and where the event spoken of as the effect is a change brought about in a continuing thing or person. Thus though the icy condition of the road, or a failure to signal may be the cause of an accident, this is not spoken of as the "effect" of these causes. Again, though we say a person fined for driving a car at an excessive speed that this was the *consequence* of his speeding it is not the effect of it. The expression "the effect of speeding" calls to mind (because its standard use is to refer to them) such things as the heating of the engine, or the nervous fatigue of the driver. "Effects" as distinct from "consequences" are usually "on" something, brought about as the terminus of a series of changes which may or may not be deliberately initiated by human agents but involve no deliberate intervention by others. "Consequences" has a much wider application, though it cannot always be used where "effects" is appropriate, since it is not normally used of the terminus of a very short series of physical or physico-chemical changes. Hence the incongruity in speaking of, for example, the melting of wax in a flame as the consequence of heating it: it is its effect. "Results" has also special implications and so a characteristic sphere of application different from either of the other two expressions. It is typically used of what emerges as the culminating phase or outcome of a process which is complex and consciously designed. So we speak of the "result" of a game, a trial, or an experiment. Here no substitution of "effect" or "consequence" could be made without change of mean-

From H. L. A. Hart and A. M. Honoré, *Causation in the Law* (Oxford at the Clarendon Press, 1958), pp. 25–41. Footnotes included. Reprinted by permission of the authors and by permission of The Clarendon Press, Oxford.

Note: Footnotes have been renumbered for the purposes of this text.

ing. The prisoner's acquittal is the *result* of a trial, the public excitement caused may be one of its *effects*, and the eventual change in the law one of its *consequences*. It is clear that "cause and effect" have caught too much of the limelight of philosophical attention; for they are in fact not as frequently used as this has led us to think.

These few examples of what can be done to draw out differences between various causal expressions perhaps suffice to show that there is not a single concept of causation but a group or family of concepts. These are united not by a set of common features but by points of resemblance, some of them tenuous. Of this group the correlatives "cause and effect" mark off one member which is of fundamental importance in practical life and for that reason, if no other, has a claim to be considered the central notion, by comparison and contrast with which the other related notions can be best characterized and understood. In this chapter we shall first exhibit certain salient features of the central notion and, secondly, show how analogies with these characterize the common-sense identification of causes in a wider field and the way in which the contrast between the cause and mere circumstances or conditions is drawn there. We shall then examine the cases where the language of "cause" and "consequence" is also used to refer to the interpersonal transactions mentioned in Chapter I and to certain other relationships even more distantly related to the central notion of "cause and effect."

CAUSE AND EFFECT: THE CENTRAL NOTION

Human beings have learnt, by making appropriate movements of their bodies, to bring about desired alterations in objects, animate or inanimate, in their environment, and to express these simple achievements by transitive verbs like push, pull, bend, twist, break, injure. The process involved here consists of an initial immediate bodily manipulation of the thing affected and often takes little time. Men have, however, learnt to extend the range of their actions and have discovered that by doing these relatively simple actions they can, in favourable circumstances, bring about secondary changes, not only in the objects actually manipulated, but in other objects. Here the process initiated by bodily movements and manipulation may be protracted in space or time, may be difficult to accomplish and involve a series of changes, sometimes of noticeably different kinds. Here we use the correlative terms "cause" and "effect" rather than simple transitive verbs: the effect is the desired secondary change and the cause is our action in bringing about the primary change in the things manipulated or those primary changes themselves. So we cause one thing to move by striking it with another, glass to break by throwing stones, injuries by blows, things to get hot by putting them on fires. Here the notions of cause and effect come together with the notion of means to ends and of producing one thing by doing another. Cases of this exceedingly simple type are not only those where the expressions cause and effect have their most obvious application; they are also paradigms for the understanding of the causal language used of very different types of cases. This is so for two reasons: first some important point of resemblance, or at least analogy, with these simple cases is traceable in the wider range to which causal language is extended; and, secondly, expressions which have a literal use in the simple cases have come to be used in a metaphorical and sometimes baffling way in cases far outside their scope. It is therefore important to consider certain prominent features of these simple cases which affect the general use of causal language in this way.

Human action in the simple cases, where we produce some desired effect by the manipulation of an object in our environment, is an interference in the natural course of events which *makes a difference* in the way these develop. In an almost literal sense, such an interference by human action is an intervention or intrusion of one kind of thing upon another distinct kind of thing. Common experience teaches us that, left to themselves, the things we manipulate, since they have a "nature" or characteristic way of behaving, would persist in states or exhibit changes different from those which we have learnt to bring about in them by our manipulation. The notion, that a cause is essentially something which interferes with or intervenes in the course of events which would normally take place, is central to the common-sense concept of cause, and at least as essential as the notions of invariable or constant sequence so much stressed by Mill and Hume. Analogies with the interference by human beings with the natural course of events in part control, even in cases where there is literally no human intervention, what is to be identified as the cause of some occurrence; the cause, though not a literal intervention, is a *difference* to the normal course which accounts for the difference in the outcome.

In these basic cases involving human manipulation the cause is not only an intervention but one which characteristically involves movement of things; for when we bring about changes in things by manipulating them or other things, the first stages of this process consist of movements of our own body or parts of it, and consequently movements of things or parts of the things which we manipulate. Very often these initiating movements are accompanied by experiences characteristically associated with the exertion of pressure or force. The prominent part played in the simple cases by movement is responsible for two related ways of speaking about causes. First, it has bred a whole host of metaphors: causes quite outside the range of the simple cases we are considering are spoken of as "forces" "being active," "operating," "coming to rest," having "power" or "potency," "active force," even when it is clearly realized that what is thus spoken of does not consist of movement or of anything like it. We find, for example, courts using such expressions freely: even the question whether the sale of a gun to a child was the cause of some injury has been discussed in the form of the inquiry as to whether or not the sale was an "active force" that had "come to rest" when the child's mother took the gun from him.[1] Conversely, preoccupation with the basic simple cases, where causes literally are movements, is the undiagnosed source of the difficulties which some theorists have experienced in seeing how a "static condition" or a "negative condition" or an omission could be the cause of anything. Mill in his footnotes argued against just such an objection, but the analogies with a thing which is active or moves have darkened many a discussion of causation.[2] The

---

[1] *Henningsen* v. *Markowitz* (1928), 132 Misc. 547, 230 N.Y.S. 313.

[2] See *Rocca* v. *Stanley Jones & Co.* (1914), 7 B.W.C.C. 101, where a doctor's failure to attend to an injured workman and not the original injury was treated as the cause of the subsequent disability; but as late as 1944 du Parcq L.J. said: "Where . . . injury is left to take the course which nature . . . prescribes it might be that, were the point free from authority, the last state . . . could only be attributed to the original injury": *Rothwell* v. *Caverswall Stone Company*, [1944] 2 All E.R. 350, 356. But sceptical doubts about "negative" causes are still

position here is a curious, though not unfamiliar one when the terminology used in a given type of case is extended to cases which are only partly analogous. On the one hand it is perfectly common and intelligible in ordinary life to speak of static conditions or negative events as causes: there is no convenient substitute for statements that the lack of rain was the cause of the failure of the corn crop, the icy condition of the road was the cause of the accident, the failure of the signalman to pull the lever was the cause of the train smash. On the other hand the theorist, when he attempts to analyse the notion of a cause, is haunted by the sense that since these ways of speaking diverge from the paradigm cases where causes are events or forces, they must be somehow improper. The corrective is to see that in spite of differences between these cases and the simple paradigms, the very real analogies are enough to justify the extension of causal language to them.

In these simple cases, where we speak of a deliberate human intervention or the primary changes initiated by it as the cause of an occurrence, we rely upon general knowledge and commit ourselves to a general proposition of some kind; but this is something very different from causal "laws" or general propositions asserting invariable sequence which Mill regarded as essential to causal connexion. When we assert that A's blow made B's nose bleed or A's exposure of the wax to the flame caused it to melt, the general knowledge used here is the knowledge of the familiar "way" to produce, by manipulating things, certain types of change which do not normally occur without our intervention. If formulated they are broadly framed generalizations, more like recipes[3] in which we assert that doing one thing will "under normal conditions" produce another than statements of "invariable sequence" between a complex set of specified conditions and an event of the given kind. Mill's description of common sense "selecting" the cause from such a set of conditions is a *suggestio falsi* so far as these simple causal statements are concerned; for, though we may gradually come to know more and more of the conditions required for our interventions to be successful, we do not 'select' from them the one we treat as the cause. Our intervention is regarded as the cause from the start before we learn more than a few of the other necessary conditions. We simply continue to call it the cause when we know more.

It is, moreover, a marked feature of these simple causal statements that we do not regard them as asserted unjustifiably or without warrant in a particular case

---

voiced. See comment on *Rothwell*'s case in (1945) 61 *L.Q.R.* 6: "The negligence was negative, for it consisted in not treating the injured man . . . we should have thought it clear that mere failure to act could not be said to cause an incapacity," and comment to the same effect on *Hogan* v. *Bentinck West Collieries Ltd.* in (1948) 64 *L.Q.R.* 162.

In French law there is strict liability under s. 1384 of the civil code for "acts" of a thing which the defendant has in his control. At first there was a tendency to hold that a thing "acted" only when it moved. Later decisions concentrate on whether the thing was in the position or state which one would normally expect. If so, it has not "acted," otherwise it may have. Thus it has been decided that the owner of a stationary vehicle left unlighted at night is liable to a person who suffers injury from driving into it on the ground that, in the absence of rebutting evidence, there is no ground for supposing that the stationary vehicle played a purely "passive" part. It must therefore be presumed to be the "generating" cause of the accident. Civ. 20.3.1933, *Sirey* 1933.1.257; Civ. 19.2.1941, *Sirey* 1941.1.49; Civ. 5.3.1947, *Dalloz* 1947 J.296. There is a full discussion in Mazeaud, *Traité de la responsabilité civile* (1949), ii. 161-80.

[3] For this aspect of causation see D. Gasking, "Causation as Recipes," *Mind* (1955), xciv. 479. [Reprinted above.]

if the maker of them cannot specify any considerable number of the further required conditions. It is perfectly legitimate to say that A's blow caused B's nose to bleed and to feel confidence in the truth of his statement, though we could not formulate or would have very little confidence in a generalization purporting to specify conditions under which blows are invariably followed by bleeding from the nose. Yet even at this simple level where the cause is our own deliberate intervention *propter hoc* is recognized to be different from *post hoc*. It is *possible* that just at the moment A struck, B independently ruptured a blood-vessel; experience may alert us to such possibilities, and science teach us how to recognize them. Yet this would be a remarkable coincidence and there is a presumption, which is normally fulfilled (but rebuttable), that when we deliberately intervene in nature to bring about effects which in fact supervene, no other explanation of their occurrence is to be found. Hence to make this type of causal statement is justified if there is no ground for believing this normally fulfilled presumption not to hold good. It is, however, a feature of this, as of other types of empirical statement, that exceptionally they are not vindicated in the result and have to be withdrawn. But this does not mean that in asserting these causal statements we claim that they are instances of some general proposition asserting invariable sequence. We shall see later that even with causal statements of a more sophisticated kind somewhat similar qualifications must be put on the "invariable sequence" doctrine.

CAUSATION AND EXPLANATION

The use of the word "cause" in ordinary life extends far beyond the relatively simple cases where 'effects' are deliberately produced by human actions: it is also generally used whenever an *explanation* is sought of an occurrence by which we are puzzled because we do not understand why it has occurred. Causal statements made in answer to such requests for an explanation were distinguished at the end of Chapter I from attributive causal statements where perplexities are of a different kind which may exist even though we need no explanation of what has occurred. In this section we shall be concerned only with explanatory causal statements and with one feature of them: the distinction between cause and mere conditions to which common sense adheres in face of the the demonstration that cause and conditions are "equally necessary" if the effect is to follow. In attempting to characterize the ways in which this distinction is drawn in typical contexts, we shall *provisionally* adopt Mill's account of the generalizations involved in singular causal statements and we shall *provisionally* speak as if it were true that what common sense distinguishes as the cause is one of a set of conditions believed to be *invariably* followed by the effect. We do this because the serious qualifications to be made clear if the principal ways of distinguishing the cause from other equally necessary conditions are well understood. The two questions: "How are causes distinguished from mere conditions?" and "What sorts of generalizations are involved in singular causal statements?" are more intimately connected than has been thought.

The line between cause and mere condition[4] is in fact drawn by common sense on principles which vary in a subtle and complex way, both with the type of causal question at issue and the circumstances in which causal questions arise. Any general account of these principles is therefore always in danger of over-simplifying them. Some philosophers have succumbed to this temptation. Collingwood, who notices much that Hume and Mill neglected, treats the question "What is the cause of an event?" as if it was always equivalent to "How can we produce or prevent this?" On his view the cause is always the event or state of things which we can produce or prevent in order to produce or prevent the effect. This is to identify all cases with the fundamental type of case considered above: whereas in fact often only *analogies* with the fundamental type can be found. Such a view would make it improper to speak of knowing, for example, the cause of cancer if we could not use our knowledge to prevent it.[5] Perhaps the only general observation of value is that in distinguishing between causes and conditions two contrasts are of prime importance. These are the contrasts between what is abnormal and what is normal in relation to any given thing or subject-matter, and between a free deliberate human action and all other conditions. The notions in this pair of contrasts lie at the root of most of the metaphors which cluster round the notion of a cause and must be used in any literal discussion of the facts which they obscure. We shall now consider separately how these contrasts serve to distinguish causes from mere conditions in explanatory inquiries.

A. Abnormal and Normal Conditions

(i) In the sciences causes are often sought to explain not *particular* occurrences but *types* of occurrence which usually or normally happen: the processes of continuous growth, the tides, planetary motions, senile decay. In ordinary life, by contrast, the particular causal question is most often inspired by the wish for an explanation of a *particular* contingency of the occurrence of which is puzzling because it is a departure from the normal, ordinary or reasonably expected course of events: some accident, catastrophe, disaster or other deviation from the usual course of events. With this in mind it is possible to see at once why certain types of conditions are classified as mere conditions and would be rejected as the cause. In the case of a building destroyed by fire "mere conditions" will be factors such as the oxygen in the air, the presence of combustible material or the dryness of the building. In a railway accident they will be such factors as the normal speed and load and weight of the train and the routine stopping or acceleration. These factors are, of course, just those which are present alike both in the case where such accidents occur and in the normal cases where they do not; and it is this consideration that leads us to reject them as the cause of the accident, even though it is true that without them the accident would not have occurred. It is plain, of course,

---

[4] Modern philosophical discussions of the distinction drawn by common sense between cause and conditions include C. J. Holloway, *Language and Intelligence,* pp. 68 et seq.; P. Gardiner, *The Nature of Historical Explanation,* pp. 5-12, 99-111; G. J. Warnock, "Every Event has a Cause," in *Logic and Language,* series ii, pp. 95, 103-4; R. G. Collingwood, "On the So Called Idea of Causation," *Proceedings of the Aristotelian Society* (1938), xxxviii. 85.

[5] Collingwood accepted this corollary of his own doctrine (op. cit., p. 90).

that to cite factors which are present both in the case of disaster and of normal functioning would explain nothing: such factors do not "make the difference" between disaster and normal functioning, as the bent rail or the dropping of a lighted cigarette do. Mill's suggestion that the mere conditions are those which the inquirer is already aware of at the outset of the inquiry touches only a subordinate aspect of this more fundamental distinction between what is normal and abnormal for a given subject-matter. Very often but not always Mill's criterion and this more fundamental one coincide: in most cases a person who is told that there has been a railway accident in which lives have been lost, or that a house has been burnt down, and who is moved by this to ask what was the cause of the accident or the fire, would know of or assume the existence of many factors. These are treated as mere conditions because they are present both in the case of the disaster and of normal functioning. Very often some of such mere conditions, like the presence of oxygen in the air, will not only be a normal feature of the thing or place concerned, but will be a pervasive omnipresent feature of the human environment: other mere conditions, such as the weight and speed of the train, will not be universal features of our environment, but normal features of the thing in question. So in many cases the existence of such factors will very often be taken for granted by anyone who inquires into the cause. Yet this is not always so: we are very often quite ignorant of many factors which science may show us as common to the cases both of disaster and normal functioning; yet when we learn of these we still classify them as mere conditions. The dropping of a lighted cigarette remains the cause of a fire even when we learn from science, what we may not have initially known, that the presence of oxygen is among the conditions required for its occurrence.

This, then, is the character of one principal distinction between normal and abnormal conditions: normal conditions (and hence in causal inquiries mere conditions) are those conditions which are present as part of the usual state or mode of operation of the thing under inquiry: some of such usual conditions will also be familiar, pervasive features of the environment: and very many of them will not only be present alike in the case of disaster and of normal functioning, but will be very generally known to be present by those who make causal inquiries. The analogy here with the fundamental case of the deliberate production of effects is plain. What is abnormal in this way "makes the difference" between the accident and things going on as usual. It is easy, therefore, to think of such causes as "intervening" or to use the metaphor of "intruding" into an existing state of affairs. Yet we should be aware of the metaphor and be prepared to explicate it in terms of factors abnormal in this sense.

(ii) What is normal and what is abnormal is, however, relative to the context of any given inquiry in two different ways, and it is important to see precisely what this relativity is. Otherwise we may surrender prematurely to the temptation to say that the distinction between causes and mere conditions, which depends upon it, is arbitrary or subjective. If a fire breaks out in a laboratory or in a factory, where special precautions are taken to exclude oxygen during part of an experiment or manufacturing process, since the success of this depends on safety from fire, there would be no absurdity at all in *such* a case in saying that the presence of oxygen was the cause of the fire. The exclusion of oxygen in such a case, and not its presence, is part of the normal functioning of the laboratory and the factory, and hence a mere condition; so the presence of oxygen in such a case is not a feature common (as the relative dryness of the building is) both to the disaster and normal functioning. It is therefore in such a case treated as "making the difference" and so as the cause of the disaster.

There is, however, a different type of relativity to context: in one and the same case (not in different cases as in the oxygen example) the distinction between cause and conditions may be drawn in different ways. The cause of a great famine in India may be identified by the Indian peasant as the drought, but the World Food authority may identify the Indian government's failure to build up reserves as the cause and the drought as a mere condition. A woman married to a man who suffers from an ulcerated condition of the stomach might identify eating parsnips as the cause of his indigestion: a doctor might identify the ulcerated condition of his stomach as the cause and the meal as a mere occasion. It is cases of this sort that have led writers, notably Collingwood, to insist that the identification of a cause among other "mere" conditions is always dictated by practical interest; and to attribute the relativity of the distinction to the varying means at the disposal of different people to produce results. But though this motive is often present in the identification of the cause it seems clear that it has not the great scope which Collingwood suggests. The willingness of common sense to classify a factor as the cause does not seem to depend directly upon ability to use it or interfere with it as a method of control. The discovery of the cause of cancer would still be the discovery of the cause, even if it were useless for the cure or avoidance of the disease; drought is the cause of failure of the crops and so of famine, lightning the cause of a fire for those who can do nothing about them and even if no one can. Indeed when we do learn to establish techniques for controlling these things we may cease to look upon them as the cause and shift to speaking of the failure to use the established technique (in the case of famine and drought, food reserves and catchment areas) as the cause.

The relevance of controllability is often in fact quite indirect; it is usually a subordinate aspect of the principal criterion for "mere conditions," viz. the normal or usual: for the factors which we cannot control may persist and, however unwelcome, become known and accepted as the normal course of things, as the standing conditions or environment of our lives to which we adjust ourselves more or less well. When things go wrong and we then ask for the cause, we ask this on the assumption that the environment persists unchanged, and something has "made the difference" between what normally happens in it and what has happened in it on this occasion. So the wife of the man with the ulcerated stomach, who looks upon the parsnips as the cause of his indigestion, in asking what has given him indigestion is in fact asking: "What has given this man in his condition indigestion when usually he gets by without it?" The doctor who gives the man's ulcerated condition as the cause approaches the case with a wider outlook and and a different set of assumptions; but they are different not because the disease in question is something that can be controlled or cured, but because he is professionally concerned only with a restricted type of abnormalities, i.e., diseases or deviations from the standard physical condition of human beings. His question (in contrast with the wife's) is: "What gave *this* man indigestion when other men do not get it?"; for him what the man ate (controllable though it is) is a mere occasion—part of the normal conditions of most men's lives. So though *often* what cannot be controlled may be accepted or assumed to be the normal standing condition of some thing or subject-matter, it is *this* assumption, not just the inability to control, that leads to its classification as a mere condition; just as it is the abnormality rather than the controllability of some factors which leads to its classification as the cause. What very often brings "controllability" and cause together is the fact that our motive in looking for the abnormality which "makes the difference" is most often the wish to control it and, through it, its sequel.

(iii) Though what is treated as normal represents in many ways our practical interests and our attitude to nature, it would be wrong to identify as the normal and so always as part of the "mere conditions" of events the ordinary course of nature unaffected by human intervention. This is an over-simplification, because what is taken as normal for the purpose of the distinction between cause and mere conditions is very often an artefact of human habit, custom, or convention. This is so because men have discovered that nature is not only sometimes harmful *if* we intervene, but is also sometimes harmful *unless* we intervene, and have developed customary techniques, procedures and routines to counteract such harm. These have become a second "nature" and so a second "norm." The effect of drought is regularly neutralized by governmental precautions in conserving water or food; disease is neutralized by inoculation; rain by the use of umbrellas. When such man-made normal conditions are established, deviation from them will be regarded as exceptional and so rank as the cause of harm. It is obvious that in such cases what is selected as the cause from the total set of conditions will often be an omission which coincides with what is reprehensible by established standards of behaviour and may be inhibited by punishment. But this does not justify the conclusion which some have drawn that it is so selected merely because it is reprehensible.[6]

(iv) A deviation from such man-made norms will very often be an omission, i.e. a failure to act in some way expected or required by the norm. Much of the difficulty found in admitting that an omission could be the cause of an occurrence is due to preoccupation with those cases where human manipulation or alteration of the environment is the cause. The terminology of "active force" is influential here; yet there are other sources of perplexity. One source is confusion about negative statements: we easily think of omissions as "negative events" and these in turn as "simply nothing." The corrective here is to realize that negative statements like "he did not pull the signal" are ways of describing the world, just as affirmative statements are, but they describe it by *contrast* not by *comparison* as affirmative statements do. "He pulled the signal" *compares* this case with the standard situation which we describe this way: "He did not pull the signal" *contrasts* this case with the standard situation but it describes the world, a real state of affairs, not just "nothing." The most respectable objection to treating omissions as causes may perhaps be best expressed as follows. A gardener whose duty it is to water the flowers fails to do so and in consequence they die. It can be said that it is impossible to treat the gardener's omission here as the cause unless we are prepared to say that the "failure" on the part of everybody else to water the flowers was

---

Or "a useful point at which public pressure can be placed" see F. S. Cohen "Field Theory and Judicial Logic," (1950) 59 *Yale L.J.* 238, 251-6.

equally the cause, and in ordinary life we do not do this. This can however be explained consistently with the analysis we have given of the distinction between cause and mere conditions. The "failure" on the part of persons other than the gardener to water the flowers would, accordingly, be a normal though negative condition and, just because such negative conditions are normal, no mention of them would usually be made. The gardener's failure to water the flowers, however, stands on a different footing. It is not merely a breach of duty on his part, but also a deviation from a system or routine. It is, however, true that in such cases there is a coincidence of a deviation from the usual routine with a reprehensible dereliction from duty.

      (v) It is natural but mistaken to think of the mere conditions of an event as always existing contemporaneously with what is identified as the cause of that event; perhaps this is due to the natural metaphors of a "background" or a "medium" for the "operation" of causes which we use when we refer to mere conditions. But it is vital to appreciate that what are contrasted with the cause as mere conditions always include some events or conditions subsequent in time to the cause. Conditions are *mere* conditions as distinct from causes because they are normal and not because they are contemporaneous with the cause. Thus if X lights a fire in the open, and shortly after, a normal gentle breeze gets up and the fire spreads to Y's property, X's action is the cause of the harm, though without the subsequent breeze no harm would have occurred; the bare fact that the breeze was subsequent to X's action (and also causally independent of it) does not destroy its status as a mere condition or make it a "superseding" cause. To achieve the latter status, a subsequent occurrence must at least have some characteristic by which common sense usually distinguishes causes from mere conditions.

      (vi) We have said that the distinctions so far considered between normal and abnormal conditions depend upon the fact that in ordinary life the request for a causal explanation is most often prompted by the occurrence of something unusual, of accidents, catastrophes, deviations from the normal. We must now consider a different ground, altogether neglected by Mill, for refusing the title of cause to certain conditions though they are as much required as it for the production of the effect. We do not call these either "cause" or "mere conditions" on or in which the cause 'operates': in fact the only way to describe them is by saying that they are merely parts of the process by which the "effect" is always produced, or mere detail of the manner in which it is produced. Take, for example, a case where one man shoots another and kills him. Here we should treat the shooting, not the later deprivation of his blood-cells of oxygen as the explanation and the cause of his death, although it is perfectly true that we could predict the man's death from the knowledge of the latter more certainly than we could from knowledge of the earlier parts of the process. Plainly, in passing over these in the search for the explanation of the man's death, we are passing over a whole set of sufficient conditions, not merely distinguishing one member of a set from other mere conditions, though we do that when we reach the shooting and identify *it,* not its attendant "conditions" as the cause. One (but only one) important motive for rejecting the later conditions as the causal explanation in such common-sense inquiries is the fact that in such cases we are not looking for the cause of "death," but for the cause of death *under circumstances which call for an explanation.* We want to know why Smith died when he did; we do not want to be told what is always the case whenever death occurs. The former is typical of the common-sense interest in causal inquiries ("Why did this happen when normally it would not?"); the second is typical of the experimental sciences ("What are the general conditions of death?"), though of course the applied sciences like medicine approximate to the former type.

So here the title of cause is refused to such later stages of the process, not of course because they are normal conditions, which they are not; but because they are common to all cases of a very general kind. It is the particularity of our interest in a given man's death at a given time that leads us to reject the latest phases of the process as the cause: these do not explain *this* man's death *now*. The basis of this discrimination can be made to appear, if we state in detail precisely what the puzzle is which the inquiry into the cause is to solve. Very little pressure is needed to allow that by "What was the cause of death?" in such cases is meant "What caused this man's death at this time?"

These considerations constitute one reason why common sense, far from rejecting the idea that an omission may be the cause of something, insists on regarding it as such. In circumstances where the cause of the flowers dying is said to be the gardener's failure to water them the only alternative to citing this omission as the cause would be to cite the later physical conditions which led to their death. But to cite these would not satisfy the special interest in the particular case: it would show what *always* happens when flowers die, why *flowers* die: whereas an explanation is wanted not of that, but of the death of *these* flowers when normally *they* would have lived: what made *this* difference was the gardener's omission—an abnormal failure of a normal condition.

There is, however, a second distinct motive for refusing the title of cause to events which are later phases in the processes initiated by abnormal events of interventions. These later phases only come to light *after* we have identified through common experience abnormal occurrences or human interventions of certain broadly described kinds ("shooting," "blows," etc.), which brings about disturbances of or deviations from the normal course of things. Our knowledge of these later phases of the process is therefore a more precise, but *secondary* knowledge (often supplied by science) of what is regarded as mere ancillary detail which accompanies the cause; it is regarded as a mere further specification of the cause itself. Knowledge of these stages of the process between what has been identified already as the cause, and its effect, is thus a mere refinement of our primary knowledge. The initial disturbance of the normal condition of the thing affected is the cause: these are merely details of the way it develops. To cite these later phases of the process as the cause would be pointless in any explanatory inquiry; for we only know of them as the usual or necessary accompaniments of the abnormal occurrence or human intervention, which has been already recognized as "making the difference" between the normal course of events and what has in fact occurred, and so as explaining the latter. The details of the process have in themselves no explanatory force.

B. Voluntary Action

(i) Often when we look for the explanation of some particular occurrence a human action will be found among the set of conditions required to produce it, and will be identified as the cause. Sometimes the action will be a deliberate voluntary action intended to bring about what in fact has occurred: sometimes it will be an action which by the standards of ordinary life is considered not a voluntary one or not wholly voluntary. In common speech, and in much legal usage, a human action is said not to be voluntary or not fully voluntary if some one or more of a quite varied range of circumstances are present: if it is done "unintentionally" (i.e., by mistake or by accident); or "involuntarily," (i.e., where normal muscular control is absent); "unconsciously," or under various types of pressure exerted by other human beings (coercion or duress); or even under the pressure of legal or moral obligation, or as a choice of the lesser of two evils, which is often expressed by saying that the agent "had no choice" or "no real choice." Of course the terms "voluntary" and "not voluntary" are not always used in this way; sometimes an action done under coercion is spoken of as voluntary: we say (though in Latin) *coactus voluit*.[7]

In many cases a human action which (in this relatively narrow but most common sense of voluntary) is not wholly voluntary may be identified as the cause of some occurrence simply on the score of its abnormality in relation to the thing or subject-matter affected, on the principles already discussed: for it is plain that such an action may be as much a disturbance of or interference with the normal course of things, or a deviation from some normal man-made routine, as the most deliberate voluntary intervention. What we call "accidents" are often, though not always, occurrences of an untoward or surprising character which have as their explanation, and so as their cause, a human action which is done unintentionally or involuntarily. Someone may discharge a gun by an involuntary movement or pull the trigger in the mistaken belief that it is not loaded; if another person's death is the upshot these actions of a non-voluntary character are the explanation of the disaster and the cause of it. Such cases, although involving human action, fall under the principles for distinguishing causes from mere conditions already discussed.

Yet a voluntary human action intended to bring about what in fact happens, and in the manner in which it happens, has a special place in causal inquiries; not so much because this, if present among a set of conditions required for the production of the effect, is often treated as the cause (though this is true), but because, when the question is how far back a cause shall be traced through a number of intervening causes, such a voluntary action very often is regarded both as a limit and also as still the cause even though other later abnormal occurrences are recognized as causes. We shall illustrate these two different points in the next two sections. They both concern the extent to which it is true that the cause of a cause is itself regarded as the cause of the "effect."

(ii) If unusual quantities of arsenic are found in a dead man's body, this is up to a point an explanation of his death and so the cause of it: but we usually press for a further and more satisfying explanation and may find that someone

---

[7] This use of 'voluntary' and 'not voluntary' depends, no doubt, on a conception of a human agent as being most free when he is placed in circumstances which give him a fair opportunity to exercise normal mental and physical powers and he does exercise them without pressure from others. As Aristotle (*Nic. Eth.* III. i. 2-19) first pointed out, human actions may be "not voluntary" for many irreducibly different reasons of which he identified two: coercion and mistake (βία, ἄγνοια). This wide notion of what is not voluntary or fully voluntary and its reflection in legal usage is discussed further in Chap. VI.

deliberately put arsenic in the victim's food. This is a fuller explanation in terms of human agency; and of course we speak of the poisoner's action as the cause of the death; though we do not withdraw the title of cause from the presence of arsenic in the body—this is now thought of as an ancillary, the "mere way" in which the poisoner produced the effect. Once we have reached this point, however, we have something which has a special *finality* at the level of common sense: for though we may look for and find an explanation of why the prisoner did what he did in terms of motives like greed or revenge, we do not regard his motive or speak of it as the cause of the *death* into which we are inquiring, even if we do (as is perhaps rare) call the poisoner's motive the "cause" of his action. The causal explanation of the particular occurrence is brought to a stop: when the death has been explained by the deliberate act, the discovery of the motive adds nothing to our understanding of what initially puzzled us. We do not trace the cause *through* the deliberate act.

(iii) Conversely we do very often trace the cause through other causes to reach a deliberate act. It is to be noted that, despite what is commonly said by philosophers, causal relationships are not always "transitive": a cause of a cause is not *always* treated as the cause of the 'effect', even when the cause of the cause is something more naturally thought of as a cause than a man's motive is. Thus the cause of a fire may be lightning, but it would be rare to cite the cause of the lightning (the state of electric charges in the atmosphere) as the cause of the fire: similarly the cause of the motor accident may be the icy condition of the road, but it would be odd to cite the cold as the cause of the accident. By contrast, we do not hesitate to trace the cause back through even very abnormal occurrences if the sequence is deliberately produced by some human agent: if I take advantage of the exceptional cold and plan the car accident accordingly by flooding the road with water my action is the cause of what happened. Like the poisoner's arsenic, the icy condition of the road is now regarded as a mere means by which the effect is produced. The analogy of the simple cases discussed in section I is obviously very close here: the deliberate act "reduces" the intermediate abnormalities to the status of mere "means" and the law recognizes somewhat similar principles in its adage that "intended consequences cannot be too remote." It is, however, true that the causal relationship is sometimes transitive in other cases: notably when there is some other ground for thinking of the intermediate causes as analogous to "means" by which the earlier cause produces its effects. This will be so when it is *well known* that a given event is likely, by leading to the intermediate cause, to lead to the "effect." Thus, when we discover that a short circuit was the cause of the fire and later learn that the cause of the short circuit was the decay of the insulating material, the latter would naturally be cited as an explanation or "fuller explanation" of the fire.[8]

A deliberate human act is therefore most often a barrier and a goal in tracing back causes in such inquiries: it is something *through* which we do not trace the cause of a later event and something *to* which we do trace the cause through

---

[8] There are other principles at work accounting for the transitivity of the causal relation where the cause of a cause is a deliberate act and the upshot is contrived. Such an act excludes the notion of a *coincidence*: which is also excluded if (as in the short-circuit example) the intermediate event is, because of its appreciable likelihood, thought of as analogous to the means by which the first event commonly produces its effects.

intervening causes of other kinds. In these respects a human action which is not voluntary is on a par with other abnormal occurrences: sometimes but not always we trace causes through them, and sometimes but not always we trace effects to them through other causes.

SAMUEL GOROVITZ

30. Causal Judgments and Causal Explanations*

There is no science which will enable a man to bethink himself of that which will suit his purpose.

J. S. MILL

I. CAUSAL JUDGMENTS

Consider the following two instances of the lighting of a match: First, a match is struck in a railroad smoking car, and the match lights. Second, a match, having been pulled from the assembly line in a match factory, is struck in a supposedly evacuated chamber, the purpose being to test the hardness of the match head. But the chamber has not been properly sealed, and the match lights. In the first case, it seems correct to say that the cause of the lighting of the match was the striking of the match. In the second case, however, the cause can reasonably be said to be the presence of oxygen, and not the striking. Rather, we say that the striking is a condition of the lighting, not the cause; whereas in the first case the presence of oxygen is a condition, and the striking is the cause.

Mill opposed such talk, arguing that "The real cause is the whole of these antecedents; and we have, philosophically speaking, no right to give the name of cause to one of them exclusively of the others."[1] Indeed, Mill went on to assert that "Nothing can better show the absence of any scientific ground for the distinction between the cause of a phenomenon and its conditions, than the capricious manner in which we select from among the conditions that which we choose to denominate the cause" (p. 215). Although many writers, and particularly the

Reprinted by permission of the author and the publisher from Samuel Gorovitz, "Causal Judgments and Causal Explanations," the *Journal of Philosophy* vol. 62, no. 23 (December 2, 1965): 695-711. Footnotes included.

*Part of the material contained here appeared initially in Chapter II of my unpublished dissertation, *Deductive Models for Causal Explanation*, Stanford, 1963. A second version was presented in a colloquium at Wayne State University, and a third version, improved largely through the sound criticism of my former colleagues in the Wayne department and especially Professor Edmund Gettier, was delivered to the Western Division of the American Philosophical Association in May, 1964, under the title "Explanations and the Relativistic Nature of Causal Judgment." I am grateful to my present colleagues for help with this latest version, and particularly to Professor Isaac Levi, whose keen insight has resulted in many substantial changes in the article.

[1] J. S. Mill, *A System of Logic* (London: Longmans, 1961), p. 214.

logical empiricists, have voiced no opposition to Mill's view even within the context of discussion of causal judgment and causal explanation, this tradition is by no means unchallenged. Ducasse, for example, addressed himself to Mill's denial of the justifiability of the distinction between causes and conditions and attempted to provide a principle on the basis of which the distinction could be defended. He wrote:

> The *cause* of a phenomenon is a change in its antecedent circumstances which was sufficient to bring it about. A *condition* of a phenomenon, on the other hand, is a change or more frequently a state, of its antecedent circumstances which was *necessary* to its having occurred when it did ... [Mill calls the distinction capricious.] But he is wrong. There is nothing capricious about it. His believing this is, in fact, due to the obsession under which he labors all along, namely, that inquiry into causation is inquiry into laws. The truth is on the contrary that it is directly and primarily an inquiry concerning *single individual events*. If the engine of my car stops, and I ask "Why," I am not asking for a statement of invariable succession or of law, even though one such may, conceivably, be inferable from the answer that it was because the magneto wire became disconnected at that moment. What I want to know is whether the latter occurrence was the single difference between the circumstances of the engine at the moment when it was running, and at the moment when it was not. ... If it is the cause that we seek, we look for a *difference* in those circumstances between the moment when the phenomenon occurred, and the preceding moment. And the field among the entities of which the conditions lie is thereby also denied: It is that of circumstances which *remain constant* over the two moments.[2]

But this will not do. For there are many cases in which the distinction between cause and condition seems to violate the principle proposed by Ducasse. If, for example, A is in the habit of turning on his radio each morning when he gets into his car, and B one night wires the radio switch to a bomb so that the car explodes the next morning when A turns on the radio, we would be required by Ducasse to say that the cause of the explosion was A's turning of the switch. This, however, does violence to our intuitions about causality. Surely, B's planting of the bomb was the cause. It is instructive in this connection to consider what judgments would in all likelihood arise in a court of law. B's defense could hardly be based on a claim that it was A who in fact caused the explosion. Nor would we be willing to grant that, although A's action was the cause of the explosion, nonetheless B is responsible for the explosion. Rather, our judgment that B is responsible is based on our determination that B's action was the cause.

A further objection to Ducasse's principle results from his inability to account for those cases in which we are inclined to cite as the cause of an event the fact that some prior event which was to be expected did not in fact occur. Thus the seizing up of the engine of a Saab automobile, which is both powered and lubricated by a mixture of gasoline and oil, might be attributed to the driver's failure to add oil to the gasoline. Ducasse would be forced to describe this example in some significantly different way. But it would be premature to judge this type of causal assertion to be philosophically suspect in the absence of further attempts to account for it.

---

[2] C. J. Ducasse, *Causation and the Types of Necessity* (Seattle: Univ. of Washington Press, 1924), p. 19.

Like Mill, and those writing in his tradition, Ducasse has failed to make any explicit distinctions among various kinds of talk about causation. But Ducasse has recognized that Mill's analysis cannot account for important characteristics of much of the use of causal language in ordinary discourse.

Collingwood has developed an analysis of causal language which, like that of Ducasse, opposes the tradition of Mill, and aims to provide a principle that supports the distinction between causes and conditions. But Collingwood's analysis differs from Ducasse's in an essential respect—for the notion of "the cause" is on Collingwood's view a notion dependent on a context of inquiry. For Ducasse, the cause of an event is the same for all inquirers into the cause. For Collingwood, it is not. He states his position thus:

> . . . the "selection" of one condition to be dignified by the name of cause is by no means arbitrary. It is made according to a principle. The "condition" which I call the cause (in sense II) of an event in which I take a practical interest is the condition I am able to produce or prevent at will.[3]

He then illustrates the use of his principle with the following case:

> For example, a car skids while cornering at a certain point, strikes the kerb, and turns turtle. From the car-driver's point of view the cause of the accident was cornering too fast, and the lesson is that one must drive more carefully. From the county surveyor's point of view the cause was a defect in the surface or camber of the road, and the lesson is that greater care must be taken to make roads skid-proof. From the motor-manufacturer's point of view the cause was defective design in the car, and the lesson is that one must place the centre of gravity lower (p. 304).

Collingwood does well to distinguish among various senses of 'cause', and his discussion of the uses of the various senses of 'cause' makes it clear that, on his view, whenever we speak of a cause in contexts of the kind we have been considering, we do so on the basis of our judgment of what is in our power to produce or prevent. His principle thus provides a relativistic account of how we distinguish the cause of an event from its conditions.

Collingwood's analysis can account for a vast number of examples. Yet, like Ducasse's, it is subject to counterexamples. Thus, on Collingwood's view, as Hart and Honoré point out, it is "improper to speak of knowing, for example, the cause of cancer if we could not use our knowledge to prevent it."[4] Moreover, the analysis seems to be based on the assumption that there is in each situation just one factor that satisfies Collingwood's criterion. We are left to wonder what would be the proper analysis of Collingwood's example if in fact the driver of the car happened to be the county surveyor. The virtue of Collingwood's analysis lies in his explicit recognition of the fact that there are various kinds of talk about causation, each with its own appropriate analysis, and his recognition of the relation between our desire to control events and our criteria for causal judgment.

Dray, discussing this analysis, writes:

> Collingwood's analysis of the pragmatic test for causes is not exhaustive, however. For many other practical considerations besides

---

[3] R. J. Collingwood, *An Essay on Metaphysics* (New York: Oxford, 1940), p. 302. [Reprinted above.]

[4] H. L. A. Hart and A. M. Honoré, *Causation in the Law* (New York: Oxford, 1959), p. 31. [Reprinted above.]

manipulability could be elicited from our ordinary use of causal language. A causal explanation is often, for instance designed to show what went wrong; it focuses attention not just on what was or could have been done, but on what *should* or *should not* have been done by certain historical agents. Thus, selecting the causal condition [cause] sometimes cannot be divorced from assigning blame.[5]

We shall return later to the question of the connection between moral judgment and causal assertion. Meanwhile, we note that Dray's criticism of Collingwood's analysis applies equally well to Ducasse's analysis. Both have the virtue of reflecting a major factor in the way we select causes, but neither has the generality to provide a fully adequate analysis. What is required is a broader account that takes in those features of the selection process singled out by Dray, Collingwood, and Ducasse, as well as those cited originally by Mill himself.

I shall attempt to provide some groundwork for such an account, by offering a statement of conditions each of which must be satisfied by c if we are to be correct in speaking of c as the cause of some event e. The conditions will be stated in terms of some notions which will themselves be explicated, and others which will be left in serious need of explication. I shall not accept the principle, implicit in Ducasse's analysis and explicitly stated by Ryle, that causes must be happenings or events, as opposed to standing conditions.[6] Further, the analysis will show the notion of the cause of an event to be relativistic, that is, dependent upon the value of a variable which ranges over what I shall call "standards of comparison." After presenting the analysis, I shall attempt to provide some evidence that it is correct, and, in Section II, that it is useful.

Since the analysis which I shall present arises directly out of that offered by Hart and Honoré, it will be of use to recount briefly the essentials of their view. They claim that "Conditions are *mere* conditions as distinct from causes because they are normal" (*op. cit.,* p. 36). Causes, then, are deviations from what is normal or to be expected. Of those factors which are not eligible for selection as causes, Hart and Honoré write:

> These factors are, of course, just those which are present alike both in the case where such accidents [as described in previous examples] occur and in the normal cases where they do not; and it is this consideration that leads us to reject them as the cause of the accident, even though it is true that without them the accident would not have occurred. It is plain, of course, that to cite factors which are present both in the case of the disaster and of normal functioning would explain nothing: such factors do not make the difference between disaster and normal functioning, as the bent rail or the dropping of a lighted cigarette do (p. 32).

With this remark, they reveal the basic intuition about causality that underlies their analysis: if an event c_1 of type A occurs in situation S_1 and is followed by an event of type B, but an event c_2 also of type A occurs in situation S_2 with no following event of type B, then there must be a difference (between c_1 and c_2 or S_1 and S_2) that makes the difference between the occurrence and non-occurrence of an event

---

[5] W. Dray, *Laws and Explanation in History* (New York: Oxford, 1957), p. 99.
[6] Cf., e.g., G. Ryle, *The Concept of Mind* (London: Hutchinson, 1949): "Motives are not happenings, and are not therefore the right type to be causes" (p. 114).

of type *B*. The analysis provided by Hart and Honoré characterizes causal inquiry as inquiry into just what that difference is which makes the difference between the situation in question and the "normal" situation which, though expected, did not occur.

The most obvious weakness of this analysis is that it can account for the way in which we select the cause from among the conditions of an event only in terms of the obscure notion of "normal" functioning. Hart and Honoré recognize that "what is normal and what is abnormal is . . . relative to the context of any given inquiry in two different ways" (p. 33). The first source of relativity is this: what is normal in one situation in which an event of type *E* occurs may be abnormal in another situation in which an event of the same type occurs. Whereas the presence of oxygen is normal in the smoking car, it may well be cited as the cause of the flame in the laboratory, where it is abnormal. Thus, the selection of the cause is relative to the *context of occurrence*. The second source of relativity is this: in one particular case, that which is cited as the cause of an event under one particular description may vary from one person to the next as a function of the interests and purposes of the individual inquirers. Hart and Honoré illustrate this relativity to the *context of inquiry* with the following example, which provides a clue to the explication of the notion of "normal functioning":

> So the wife of the man with the ulcerated stomach, who looks upon the parsnips as the cause of his indigestion, in asking what has given him indigestion, is in fact asking: "What has given this man in his condition indigestion when usually he gets by without it?" The doctor who gives the man's ulcerated stomach as the cause approaches the case with a wider outlook and a different set of assumptions; . . . His question (in contrast with the wife's) is: "What gave *this* man indigestion when other men do not get it?" (p. 34)

Here the wife and doctor select different causes because they are contrasting the actual course of events with different standards of comparison. To the wife, the normal state is exemplified when her husband does not get indigestion. To the doctor, the normal state is exemplified when other men do not get indigestion. And the factor that differentiates the actual state from the wife's standard of comparison is not the same as that which differentiates the actual state from the doctor's standard of comparison.

The "normal-functioning" analysis as developed by Hart and Honoré suffers from their failure to generalize on the insight revealed in the preceding example. Such a generalization will remove from the shoulders of the defender of their analysis the burden of providing general criteria for distinguishing between normal and abnormal states of affairs. Clearly, some such move must be made, since an accident can be described as normal—in the sense that what occurred can be accounted for in terms of simple principles of mechanics; and an accident-free situation can be described as abnormal—in the sense that it has characteristics that differentiate it from most other situations.

The observation that an inquiry into the cause of an event may be considered a request for identification of the factors that differentiate the situation in which that event occurs from some particular standard of comparison eliminates the need to formulate the principle of selection of causes in terms of unexplicated normality.[7] The "normal state of affairs" is just that class of situations (actual or hypothetical) with which the individual or point of view in question contrasts the actual state of affairs.

We are now in a position to state formally the conditions that must be met if c is to be correctly cited as the cause of e.

A. c is the cause of event e under description d with respect to the standard of comparison T *only if* c is a factor that differentiates the situation S in which e occurs from T, where T is a class of situations not including S.

B. A situation class T is differentiated from a situation S in which an event e considered under description d occurs, *if and only if*:

1. c is causally relevant to e under d.
2. (a) e would not have occurred if c had not occurred (i.e., all conditions simultaneous to c but not including c do not constitute a jointly sufficient set for e);[8] or else
    (b) c is a number of a minimal set of conditions such that e would not have occurred unless some member of that set had been fulfilled.
3. No event of kind C occurs in any T situation, where the class C is determined by the description under which c is cited.
4. No event of kind D occurs in any T situation, where the class D is determined by the description d of e.

This completes the formal statement of conditions. Of course, before I could claim to have a thoroughly clear analysis, the question of what constitutes *causal relevance* would have to be answered. And I am certain neither how to answer this question nor even that it can be answered adequately for a deep defense of the views developed here. But I think that the analysis, even as it stands, can shed some light, and I shall point out what I think that light is after considering some specific examples in terms of the analysis, presupposing for the present the adequacy of our preanalytic understanding of the language of the analysis.

The analysis presented above, which I shall call the "differentiating-factor analysis," easily handles the two cases considered initially. We cite the striking of the match as the cause of the lighting in the smoking car, for the striking is the factor that differentiates the actual situation from all of those wherein other matches are not struck, and those situations form the most natural comparison class T. But, in the case of the match struck in the laboratory, the most natural standard of comparison is the class of previous tests in the evacuated chamber, when struck matches failed to light. Hence, with respect to this standard, the striking cannot be called the cause; B3 is violated. Rather, the presence of oxygen is the differentiating

---

[7] Cf., in this regard: "The possession of bodily organs is a known condition, and to give that as the cause of a person's death, would not supply the information sought. Once conceive that a doubt could exist as to his having bodily organs, or that he were to be compared with some being who had them not, and cases may be imagined in which it might be said that his possession of them was the cause of his death" (Mill, *op. cit.*, p. 217 n).

[8] An alternative formulation, due to Dr. Chin-Tai Kim, is "c is a member of a set jointly sufficient for e, and under the circumstances [i.e., in S] no jointly sufficient set for e and not containing c was satisfied."

factor. In similar fashion, the indigestion example is readily handled; the doctor and the wife use different standards of comparison. In the case where it is true of a man who ate parsnips, and as a result got indigestion, that if he had not eaten parsnips he would have eaten garlic and that if he had eaten garlic he would have gotten indigestion, condition B2a is violated.[9] But B2b accounts for such cases.

Of course, if we take as standard of comparison for inquiry into the cause of the lighting in the railroad car the class of all situations in which matches are struck in the absence of oxygen, we will select the presence of oxygen as the differentiating factor and hence the cause. No part of the differentiating-factor analysis rules out the possibility of selecting such a value for T or enforces the selection of the most natural class as that with respect to which the cause is sought. Rather, the standard of comparison—or the scope and diversity of the many standards of comparison—which a man or point of view will select in a given instance depends on the over-all aims of the broader inquiry in which the causal quest plays a role, be that inquiry scientific, historical, legal, or otherwise.

The selection of standards of comparison, though not enforced by the analysis, is nonetheless guided by principles which reveal important features of the selection process and account for large numbers of cases. For example, consider:

> Do not select T as a standard of comparison for inquiry into the cause of an event e occurring in situation S unless
>
> (P_1) It is not obvious prior to e from the context in which e occurs that S is not a T situation.

The adoption of P_1 would eliminate the possibility of citing the presence of oxygen as the cuase of the lighting in the railroad car, since selection of any class of situations in which oxygen is absent will violate P_1. We may consider it obvious that a situation S, in which people may sit, read, converse, or smoke, is not included in any class of situations in which oxygen is absent. Similarly, P_1 would rule out citing the striking as the cause in the laboratory. But, as we shall see, P_1 cannot be accepted as an inviolable condition of acceptability for standards of comparison.

Consider next the case of a man who seeks the cause of the shabby condition of his grounds because he is uncertain whether or not on this occasion it is the groundskeeper's frequent failure to work that is the cause. The inquiry does not stem from the landowner's wish to have the actual situation differentiated from the one he expected, i.e., would have predicted; but rather from his wish to have it differentiated from the situation which, in his judgment, ought to have been actual. if he judges that the shabby condition of his grounds is indeed due to the groundskeeper's failure to work, rather than to the unusual severity of the recent winds, his selection of a standard of comparison is guided by his evaluative judgment that the groundskeeper *ought* to have maintained the grounds in spite of the winds. But if the winds had been of hurricane force, we would wish to say that the landowner's claim that the groundskeeper's failure to work was the cause of the shabby condition of the grounds was flatly false. Yet it is the groundskeeper's failure to work that differentiates the actual state of affairs from the one the landowner uses for comparison, in which the groundskeeper, in spite of personal peril, battles the

---

[9] This example is due to Gettier.

hurricane to maintain the grounds. Here, it seems, the causal judgment is offensive because it is made with respect to a standard of comparison the selection of which presupposes that the groundskeeper is culpable, when in fact he is not.[10] We could rule out the landowner's standard of comparison by adopting

> (P$_2$) If c is an act (or omission) by agent a and if c differentiates S from T, it is appropriate to blame a for doing c.

But neither P$_2$ nor any such principle can be given unqualified acceptance. Consider the case of a man who eats parsnips intentionally, knowing that mild indigestion will result, in order to avoid hurting the feelings of the sensitive aunt who has served the parsnips.[11] Here, it seems plain that the cause of his getting indigestion was his eating of parsnips. Yet P$_2$ would rule out all values of T that could be differentiated from S by the eating of the parsnips, since it would not be appropriate to blame the man for eating the parsnips. Note, as well, that this case also shows the inadequacy of P$_1$. For, at least to the agent, the situation S is, from the very beginning, obviously one in which he will get indigestion, and hence (in light of B4) it will be obvious, for any choice of T, that S is not a T situation. Even making causal judgment relative to the knowledge of the inquirer by having P$_1$ apply only to the inquirer will not do; we would still want to permit the agent to speak of his eating the parsnips as the cause of his getting indigestion.

Thus, satisfaction of the above-listed conditions is clearly not sufficient for causal judgment, and supplmentation by principles that enforce selection of standards of comparison does not seem possible.[12]

Another difficulty demonstrates that the set of conditions I have enumerated cannot be accepted as a sufficient set for causal judgment. Consider the series of events from the eating of parsnips to indigestion. The parsnip is ingested, acids act on it, irritant gas is produced, and the gas acts on the intestinal tract. The analysis as it stands provides no way of distinguishing among these various events, all of which could satisfy the conditions for some one assignment of values to all the parameters. Yet in a given situation, depending on the circumstances, one or another of the events in this sequence might be cited as the cause of the indigestion. Thus, again, the conditions are not sufficient to account for the way in which we make causal judgments. Moreover, as is evident, the conditions presuppose the crucial notion of causal relevance. But, although the analysis is surely no panacea for epistemological maladies, it sheds some light on certain aspects of the function of causal language which have not been sufficiently examined elsewhere.

I should perhaps make it clear at this point that it is my view that no single analysis of causal language can ever be adequate for all the contexts in which such language is used. The word 'cause' functions in many ways in our language, and I

---

[10] Dray illustrates well the evaluative basis of some causal judgments in his discussion, "Some Causal Accounts of the American Civil War," *Daedalus* (Autumn, 1962): 587.

[11] This example is due to Professor Hans Herzberger.

[12] I surely do not pretend to have considered all the principles that might serve to guide selection of standards. I wish merely to illustrate the role that such principles play, and the difficulty of specifying the principles. One such principle which I have not considered is suggested by I. Scheffler: ". . . .require the condition in question to be effectively avoidable within the limits of available technology and accepted moral principles" [*The Anatomy of Inquiry* (New York: Knopf, 1963), p. 24].

suspect that there cannot be for any one of them an adequate analysis in the sense of an account of the meaning of causal language so used that makes no essential use of causal notions. The unavoidability of talking about 'cause' in such terms as, e.g., "sufficient to produce," "results in," "necessary for the occurrence of," etc.—all "causal" terms themselves—arises from the extent to which causal notions are embedded in our language and from the generic nature of the word 'cause' itself. There is, however, no reason to despair of the possibility of providing fruitful analysis of causal language. For to discover relationships among the species is to discover something about the genus. And we can certainly do that.

I wish, then, to make three claims for what the differentiating-factor analysis does, even as sketched out here. First, if we accept the analysis, then we will in some cases reject the claim that something is the cause of some event because it fails to differentiate the actual situation from the appropriate standard, and it will turn out that if it fails to do so simply because it is not causally relevant to the event in question. To be sure, this smacks of damaging circularity. Yet the analysis does some work. For, although in some cases we will judge that something is not the cause simply and unenlighteningly because it is not causally relevant, in other cases it will be for some other reason that we judge something not to be the cause. And the analysis helps to bring to light what sort of reasons those other reasons can be.

Second, it seems to me, the analysis provides a reasonably clear characterization of the notion of differentiation—at least to the extent of reducing it to notions by which we were bothered initially. Since the differentiating function is an essential feature of much causal language, it is of use to see how (in a logical sense) it is performed.

Finally, it seems to me that the analysis importantly clarifies a number of currently disputed issues concerning the logic and structure of causal explanation, to which the following section is addressed.

II. CAUSAL EXPLANATION

To see the importance of the differentiating-factor analysis for the concept of causal explanation, we should begin by considering once again the two cases wherein a match is lit. In the first, ordinary case, it seems correct to answer the question "Why did the match light?" by saying "It was struck," that is, by citing the occurrence of that which it seems correct to speak of as being the cause of the lighting. But in the second, experimental case, it seems that the appropriate answer would be "Oxygen was present." In both cases, it seems that we have explained why an event occurred by citing the cause of that event.

Hempel, as the leading spokesman of the logical empiricists, argues that we commonly explain by "indicating the causes or determining factors" of the event. But his discussion makes it clear that, although he would recognize the naturalness of the explanations offered above, he would go on to say that there is a sense in which they are deficient. For, though Hempel agrees that we explain by citing causes, he makes it plain that, on his view, to cite causes, at least insofar as it is done properly, is to cite conditions and occurrences which, according to general laws, are jointly sufficient for production of the event in question. That is to say,

Hempel, in the tradition of Mill, would deny that we can adequately explain either event considered above merely by citing as the cause the striking of the match or the presence of oxygen. Rather, we must cite all the causes or determining factors which together constitute the set Mill would designate as the "real cause." And when, commonly, we single out one or another of these factors for special mention, it is only because the context makes clear the presence of the remaining factors that our explanation seems complete.[13]

If we are willing to construe an adequate answer to a request for the cause of an event as an explanation of the event and, further, to accept the differentiating-factor analysis as an adequate representation of what, logically, is happening when we cite the cause of the event, to that extent the differentiating-factor analysis provides a basis for opposition to those fundamentalist versions of the covering-law theory of explanation which hold that explanation must provide adequate premises for deduction of the statement that the event in question occurred. For we can, of course, identify in some instances the factor that differentiates the situation in which an event occurred from some standard of comparison without providing an enumeration of all the causally relevant antecedent conditions—and hence without providing enough information to permit deduction of the claim that the event in question occurred. Thus, it seems, an event can be adequately explained when we merely cite the cause of that event (as opposed to the causal conditions)—even when the inquirer lacks information about the existence of those necessary conditions which we do not mention. And thus it is that we can explain the lighting of the match in the one case by citing the striking, in the other by citing the presence of oxygen. For in each case we have cited that factor which differentiates the actual situation from the most natural standard of comparison.

Of course, to take such a line is not to argue, or even to suggest, that laws are not essentially involved in the provision of an explanation. On the contrary, reliance on laws is essential. For the claim that some factor c is the cause of some event e—i.e., that c differentiates the situation in which e occurs from some acceptable standard of comparison—entails the claim (B1) that c is causally relevant to e. And this entails that there is some law connecting c-like events with e-like events (though not necessarily or even usually under the descriptions we use when we cite c as the cause or ask for the cause of e).[14] Thus, if we were to attempt to justify the claim that c satisfies the conditions—and hence can be the cause of e—we might have to provide a law, or evidence that there is one, connecting c-like events with e-like events. Further, our selection of a standard of comparison is guided by the laws we accept. If, when we see people smoking in a railroad car, we are justified in concluding that the presence of oxygen is obvious, our conclusion is justified only insofar as we rely on such empirical generalizations as specify that oxygen is requisite for the maintenance of fire and the conduct of human affairs.

It perhaps may seem at this point as though I offer the differentiating-factor analysis, and the remarks about explanation that are based upon it, as being incompatible with the basic tenets of the covering-law theory of explanation and

---

[13] Hempel's view, refined in subsequent articles over the years, first appears in "The Function of General Laws in History," this Journal, 39, 2 (Jan. 15, 1942): 36-48.

[14] In this regard, see D. Davidson, "Actions, Reasons, and Causes," this Journal, 60, 23 (Nov. 7, 1963): 685-700, especially p. 698.

the concept of causal judgment, in the Mill tradition, with which it is linked. Such a conclusion would be premature. For the analysis, in addition to revealing the sense in which the ideal covering-law explanation is inappropriate, can also reveal the sense in which it is superior.

The scientist, we are often reminded, is concerned, in his efforts to organize and systematize knowledge about the physical world with generality.[15] He wants to know not only why *this* event occurred, but more broadly why in general events of this kind occur. And thus, we are told, he is distinguished from, for example, the historian, whose concern is of a different sort.[16] I suggest that we can discover a basis of truth in this position, and can gain new insight into the place of the covering-law theory in the analysis of explanation, by considering the differentiating-factor analysis in a new way.

If we construe the scientist's search for the explanation of an event as the attempt to discover what differentiates the actual state of affairs not just from some particular standard of comparison, but from all possible standards of comparison, then we find that the answer—far from being "the cause" as opposed to "the conditions"—will be just that set of determining factors which Mill insisted jointly constituted the cause. Put differently, the cause in Mill's sense of an event e which occurs in situation S is just the set of all factors c such that there is a standard of comparison T that can be differentiated from S by c. In both cases of the matches, Mill would include in the cause the striking, the dryness, and the presence of oxygen. If we ignore principles P_1 and P_2, as I shall argue we must, we can easily see the application of the theory to these cases.

Let c_1, c_2, and c_3 refer respectively to the striking, the dryness, and the presence of oxygen. Then, if S is the smoking-car situation and d is 'the lighting of match m', we find that c_1, c_2, and c_3 differentiate S from T_1, T_2, and T_3, respectively the cases wherein other matches are not struck, matches are struck while wet or underwater, and matches are struck in evacuated chambers. Here, T_3 would have been ruled out as an unacceptable standard of comparison for inquiry into the cause of the lighting by P_1, on the grounds that the presence of oxygen is obvious. But P_1 and P_2 are ignored. Thus the analysis provides c_1, c_2, and c_3 and, thereby, enumerates the factors Mill would demand. And extraneous factors are ruled out; e.g., c_4, that the match was wooden, would not be included. There is no T_4 such that c_4 differentiates S from T_4, since c_4 violates requirement B1. In the second instance of match lighting, c_1, c_2, and c_3 are again selected in similar fashion, except that here it is T_1, and hence, c_1, that would have been ruled out by the retention of P_1.

Of course, this is not quite the whole story—the match must not have been immersed, just prior to the striking, in liquid nitrogen; there must not have been a strong blast of cold air aimed at the match head at the time of the striking, and so on. Thus c_1, c_2, and c_3 will not quite do.

But all that this shows is that the perennial problem of specifying genuinely sufficient conditions and of filling out *ceteris paribus* clauses is not solved by

[15] Cf. e.g., Hart and Honoré, *op. cit.*, ch. I *passim*; Hempel, *loc. cit. passim* and especially section 2.2.

[16] Cf., e.g., P. Gardiner, *The Nature of Historical Explanation* (New York: Oxford, 1952), pp. 40-46.

relying on the view that the cause in Mill's sense is a set of differentiating factors. Rather, the problem of finding all possible T's for a given S may be considered equivalent to that of completing Mill's set of antecedent conditions or Hempel's set of determining factors.

We have seen that P_1 must be ignored. To see that P_2 must be ignored, as well, consider the case mentioned previously wherein leaves accumulate on a driveway. If the winds were mild, we might judge c_1, the groundskeeper's failure to work, as the cause. If the winds were of hurricane force, we might judge c_2, the winds, to be the cause. P_2 prevents us from judging c_1 to be the cause if the winds were excessive. Mill would presumably want to include c_1 and c_2 in either case, and P_2 must be waived to permit this.

I have argued thus far that P_1 and P_2 must be ignored if we are to succeed in characterizing Mill's inquiry in terms of differentiating factors. But I do not think the rejection of these principles is ad hoc or arbitrary. For P_1 and P_2 are precisely those principles which introduce into causal judgment typically non-scientific factors. The question of what is obvious in a given context is one the answer to which is dependent upon consideration of what knowledge the inquirer has and what generalizations he accepts as true, and the subjectivity thus introduced into causal judgment by P_1 is eliminated when the principle is ignored. Similarly, P_2, which reveals the way in which causal judgment is dependent upon evaluative factors in the typically ethical sense, introduces considerations that are characteristically out of place in the scientist's deliberations.[17]

Thus we may consider the scientific explanation of an event that occurs in situation S to be the provision of a set of differentiating factors which, independently of evaluative or subjective factors, yields an account of why the situation S in question was the actual situation—not merely as opposed to some particular comparative standard—but as opposed to all possible such standards. And this enables us to see the sense in which explanations of Hempel's sort are deeper, more complete, and better suited to the scientist's concern with generality than are explanations that fall short of providing sufficient conditions for the event in question. But we may also see now why this kind of explanation is superfluous and perhaps even inappropriate in some cases. For, if we have a particular standard of comparison in mind and seek to have the actual situation differentiated from that standard, then we can be satisfied—our puzzlement can be allayed—when we are told what the appropriate differentiating factor is. And if, in such a situation, we are given instead what for Mill would be the cause, the answer may be less clear—even if more complete—than the simple citation of the appropriate single factor.

Philosophers of history have often argued that historians, unlike scientists, are concerned with unique events and, thus, seek a different sort of explanation. The untenability of any such distinction has been amply enough demonstrated; every event is unique, and every event is an instance of a type about which generali-

[17] For a discussion of the place of evaluative factors in scientific deliberations (in a somewhat different context), see the dialogue presented in: R. Rudner, "The Scientist qua Scientist Makes Value Judgments," *Philosophy of Science*, 20, (1953): 1-6; R. C. Jeffrey, "Valuation and Acceptance of Scientific Hypotheses," *Philosophy of Science*, 23 (1956): 237-246; and I. Levi, "Must the Scientist Make Value Judgments?" this Journal, 58, 11 (May 26, 1960): 345-347.

zations may be made or sought.[18] But perhaps a case can be made out all the same for the view that historical explanation differs from scientific explanation. If the historian is at least in part concerned with finding the cause of an event and if we view that concern as a desire for differentiation from a particular standard or class of standards that is limited in some specific way, then the historian can quite legitimately be satisfied with explanations that do not meet Hempel's standards.

If, as I have suggested, principles such as P_1 and P_2 are characteristic of the way in which causal judgments are made and if, further, these principles are ignored in the case of scientific inquiry—in light of the scientist's concern with objectivity and generality—then it comes as no surprise that the notion of cause tends to be replaced in theoretical science by that of jointly sufficient antecedent conditions. Nor should it be a surprise that one who is concerned with causal inquiry need not satisfy the more taxing requirements of inquiry into jointly sufficient antecedent conditions. To say all of this is admittedly to imply that causal inquiry is in some sense nonscientific. But we have seen precisely what that sense is, and there is no reason to suppose that it lacks all utility in virtue of its nonscientific characteristics. Rather, causal inquiry is an important and legitimate sort of inquiry—in history and elsewhere. Indeed, the very features that constitute its nonscientific aspects contribute to its importance; in legal contexts, for example, where the question of responsibility for an event involves causal judgment, the evaluative principle P_2 is what makes the causal judgment appropriate in light of the fact that judgments of responsibility are dependent on the value structure prevalent in the context in which they are made. Of further relevance to the importance of causal judgments in judicial and historical contexts is the fact that omissions, negligent or reckless acts, and intentions can all be differentiating factors, as can reasons, desires, beliefs, and the like. (cf. Davison, op. cit.).

One final point. Dray has argued that "Causes must be important to the inquirer as well as for the effect" (op. cit., p. 98). May Brodbeck, on the other hand, denies the dependence of causal language on such contextual factors, insisting that one must look exclusively to what is "in the facts themselves, or, to be accurate, in the statements asserting them, rather than in the minds or behavior of a particular person or group" for the evidence upon which to base a characterization of, e.g., a causal explanation.[19] I take it that the widespread agreement that contextual factors matter is justified and that, therefore, the question of interest is not whether they matter, but what contextual parameters are involved, and in what way. This I hope to have shown by introducing the notion of a standard of comparison for causal inquiry and by discussing some of the considerations that influence the selection of such standards of comparison.

---

[18] Cf., e.g., Scheffer, op. cit., pp. 78-79.

[19] M. Brodbeck, "Explanation, Prediction, and 'Imperfect' Knowledge," in Minnesota Studies in the Philosophy of Science, vol. III, ed. H. Feigl and G. Maxwell (Minneapolis: Univ. of Minnesota Press, 1962), p. 239.

Suggested Readings for Part Six

Achinstein, Peter. *Law and Explanation.* New York: Oxford University Press, 1971.

Braybrooke, David. "Vincula Vindicata." *Mind* 66 (1957): 222-27. [Earlier critique of Hanson.]

Dray, William. *Laws and Explanation in History.* New York: Oxford University Press, 1957.

Ducasse, C. J. "Cause and Condition." *Journal of Philosophy* 63 (1966): 238-41. [Reply to Gorovitz.]

Fain, Haskell. "Hart and Honoré on Causation in the Law." *Inquiry* 9 (1966): 322-38.

Fain, Haskell. "Some Problems of Causal Explanation." *Mind* 72 (1963): 519-32.

Foot, Philippa. "Hart and Honoré: Causation in the Law." *Philosophical Review* 72 (1963): 505-15.

Hempel, Carl and Oppenheim, P. "Studies in the Logic of Explanation." *Philosophy of Science* 15 (1948). Reprinted in Hempel, *Aspects of Scientific Explanation and Other Essays in the Philosophy of Science.* New York: Free Press, 1965.

Ruddick, William. "Causal Connection." *Synthese* 19 (1968): 46-67.

Scriven, Michael. "Causes, Connections and Conditions in History." In *Philosophical Analysis and History,* edited by W. H. Dray. New York: Harper & Row, 1966.

Shope, Robert K. "Explanation in Terms of 'the cause.' " *Journal of Philosophy* 64 (1967): 312-20. [Response to Gorovitz.]

Wallace, William A. *Causality and Scientific Explanation.* Ann Arbor, Mich.: The Univ. of Michigan Press, 1972, Vols. 1-2. [Detailed historical survey.]

Walsh, W. H. *Metaphysics.* New York: Harcourt, Brace & World, 1963, chapter 7.